THE PULPIT OF
THE AMERICAN REVOLUTION

A Da Capo Press Reprint Series

THE ERA OF THE AMERICAN REVOLUTION

GENERAL EDITOR: LEONARD W. LEVY

Brandeis University

THE PULPIT OF
THE AMERICAN REVOLUTION

Political Sermons of the Period of 1776

Historical Introduction and Notes by

JOHN WINGATE THORNTON

DA CAPO PRESS • NEW YORK • 1970

A Da Capo Press Reprint Edition

This Da Capo Press edition of *The Pulpit of the American Revolution* is an unabridged republication of the first edition published in Boston in 1860.

Library of Congress Catalog Card Number 71-109611

SBN 306-71907-X

Published by Da Capo Press
A Division of Plenum Publishing Corporation
227 West 17th Street, New York, N. Y. 10011
All Rights Reserved

Manufactured in the United States of America

THE PULPIT OF
THE AMERICAN REVOLUTION

Jonathan Mayhew

BORN OCT. 8TH 1720_DIED JULY 19TH 1766.

Eng^d for Thornton's Pulpit of the Revolution".

see p. 46.

THE

PULPIT

OF THE

AMERICAN REVOLUTION:

OR, THE

𝔓𝔬𝔩𝔦𝔱𝔦𝔠𝔞𝔩 𝔖𝔢𝔯𝔪𝔬𝔫𝔰 𝔬𝔣 𝔱𝔥𝔢 𝔓𝔢𝔯𝔦𝔬𝔡 𝔬𝔣 1776.

WITH A

HISTORICAL INTRODUCTION, NOTES, AND ILLUSTRATIONS.

BY

JOHN WINGATE THORNTON, A.M.

BOSTON:

GOULD AND LINCOLN,

59 WASHINGTON STREET.

NEW YORK: SHELDON AND COMPANY.

CINCINNATI: GEORGE S. BLANCHARD.

1860.

ANDOVER:

ELECTROTYPED AND PRINTED

BY W. F. DRAPER.

PREFACE.

THE true alliance between Politics and Religion is the
lesson inculcated in this volume of Sermons, and apparent in
its title, "THE PULPIT OF THE REVOLUTION." It is the voice
of the Fathers of the Republic, enforced by their example.
They invoked God in their civil assemblies, called upon their
chosen teachers of religion for counsel from the Bible, and
recognized its precepts as the law of their public conduct.
The Fathers did not divorce politics and religion, but they
denounced the separation as ungodly. They prepared for the
struggle, and went into battle, not as soldiers of fortune, but,
like Cromwell and the soldiers of the Commonwealth, with the
Word of God in their hearts, and trusting in him. This was
the secret of that moral energy which sustained the Republic
in its material weakness against superior numbers, and discipline, and all the power of England. To these Sermons — the
responses from the Pulpit — the State affixed its *imprimatur*,
and thus they were handed down to future generations with
a two-fold claim to respect.

The Union of the colonies was a condition precedent to
American Nationality. One nationality, and that of a Protestant people, was essential to constitutional liberty in America. If the colonies had become separate independencies at
different times, America would have but repeated the history

of European divisions and wars. The combination and balance
of forces necessary to the grand result seems to have been calculated with the nicety of a formula. France, the champion of
the Papal system of intellectual and political slavery and despotism, and England, the assertor of enlightened freedom, com-
peted for the dominion of America. The red cross of St.
George shielded the brotherhood of English Protestants from
the extermination meditated by Papal France, whose military
cordon reached along our northern and western frontiers, and
thus insured to England the fealty of her Atlantic colonies, till,
" in the fulness of time," France, by the treaty of 1763, relin-
quished Canada. Then the colonies, relieved from the hostile
pressure, became restless under the restraints of dependency,
and England was the only power whose strength and common
relation to them could at once endanger the liberty of all, impel
them to a league of domestic amity, and bind them in fraternal
resistance to a common enemy. But a brief contest would have
left danger of colonial disintegration; and the stupid obstinacy
of George III. was necessary to prolong the war in order to
blend the colonists, by communion under a national flag, in
national feeling, and by general intercourse, common interests, and common sufferings. So God formed the fair Temple
of American Liberty.

In his Election Sermon of 1783, republished in this volume,
President Stiles says, with sublime eloquence, that Jefferson
"POURED THE SOUL OF THE CONTINENT INTO THE MONU-
MENTAL ACT OF INDEPENDENCE." The SOUL of the Revolution is embodied in documents like these, rather than in the
statistics of sieges and battles, which were the fruits of their
inspiration, and, under God, the vindication of their truth.

The second Discourse in this volume is on the Repeal of the

Stamp Act. The colonists, sheltered under the flag of England, permitted her to regulate their *foreign* commerce; but the Stamp Act violated their *domestic* independence; and they showed, by custom, by equity, and by their charters from the king, that Parliament had no jurisdiction *within* their territories, and they refused to submit. England sent her armies to compel submission, and the colonists appealed to Heaven. The Stamp Act[1] involved the principle in dispute for the next eighteen years.

In his Sermon of 1750, Jonathan Mayhew declared the Christian principles of government in the faith of which Washington, ordained of God, won liberty for America, not less for England, and ultimately for the world; so that the engraving of Mayhew and that of the Stamp fitly introduce these Sermons of the Revolution. By the conflict with her children, England herself was rescued from the slough of unlimited power into which she was fast drifting under George III. The reäction roused her from political apathy, and revived the ancient principles of freedom. By defeating England, America saved the liberty of both. Both governments rest upon

---

[1] A stamp duty was a familiar tax in England. It had existed as far back as 4th William and Mary, 1694; and the act of 1765 was simply to "extend"[2] this mode of taxing to the colonies. The engraving upon the title-page was taken from a veritable stamp, issued under that act, and loaned to the publishers by Mr. Samuel Foster Haven, of the American Antiquarian Society, through Mr. Charles Emery Stevens, of Worcester, whose valuable suggestions in the preparation of the work are also gratefully acknowledged. The impression is on a blue, spongy paper, capable of receiving a sharp, distinct outline, in which was imbedded a slip of lead, or soft white metal, as indicated in the engraving. The paper is pasted on parchment, and on the reverse is the royal cipher, "G. R." The word "America" was the only difference between the English and American stamps. They were issued in sheets, like our postage stamps.

[2] Bancroft's U. S., iv. ch. viii; Knight's England, vi. 271.

the right of revolution, and the will of the people is the constitutional basis of each.

On presenting his credentials as American ambassador, June 1, 1785, Mr. Adams, in his address to King George III., said : " I shall esteem myself the happiest of men if I can be instrumental in restoring an entire esteem, confidence, and affection; or, in better words, the old good-nature and the old good-humor between people, who, although separated by ocean, and under different governments, have the same language, a similar religion, and kindred blood."[1] God grant that this benign spirit of generous brotherhood, this blessed unity of which he was the Author, may never be imperilled by malign counsels. Now, after three-quarters of a century, these ties of nature, stronger than treaties, reässert their genial sway; and the heir of the Throne of England — the guest of the Nation — and the President of the Republic stand reverently at the Tomb of WASHINGTON.

[1] See Index, " America and England, Unity of."

BOSTON, NOV. 21, 1860.

CONTENTS.

CONTENTS.

INTRODUCTION.

THIS collection of Sermons presents examples of the politico-
theological phase of the conflict for American Independence, —
a phase not peculiar to that period. Its origin was coëval
with the colonization of New England; and a brief review of
some leading points in our history will afford the best explanation of its rise and development.

There is a natural and just union of religious and civil
counsels, — not that external alliance of the crosier and sword
called " Church and State," — but the philosophical and deeper
union which recognizes GOD as Supreme Ruler, and which is
illustrated in this volume of occasional Discourses and " Election
Sermons," — a title equivalent, in the right intent of the term,
to " political preaching."

There is also a historical connection, which is to be found
rather in the general current of history than in particular
instances. In this we may trace the principle, or vital cord,
which runs through our own separate annals since our fathers
came to the New World, and also marks the progress of liberty
and individual rights in England. " New England has the proud
distinction of tracing her origin to causes purely moral and
intellectual, — a fact which fixes the character of her founders
and planters as elevated and refined, — not the destroyers of

cities, provínces, and empires, but the founders of civilization in America."

The word *clergie* is in itself historical, meaning, in the Norman tongue, *literature*.   In early times, when learning was almost exclusively with the clergy, they, by this monopoly, held almost the whole power of church and state.   We may see an illustration of this union of civil and ecclesiastical functions in the Annals of the See of Bath and Wells, which yielded from its diocesan list to the civil state of England six Lord Chancellors, eight Lord High Treasurers, two Lords Privy Seal, one Master of the Rolls, one Lord President of Wales, one principal Secretary of State ; and to higher Episcopal office, five Archbishops of Canterbury, three Archbishops of York, and, says the annalist of the diocese, "to the Protestant Episcopal Church, the cause of Monarchy, and of Orthodoxy, one MARTYR, William Laud."

But, of all the names in that priestly catalogue, to ARTHUR LAKE belongs the transcendent honor, the highest distinction ; for it was his missionary spirit that originated the movement which led to the colonization of Massachusetts, — an enterprise greatly indebted for its success to the unhappy zeal of his immediate successor in the office of bishop, the "martyr" Laud. As this execrable[1] prelate embodied the principles and spirit of the hierarchy ; as he had a controlling agency in the settlement of New England, by "harrying" the Puritans out of Old England ; and as he has ever been remembered with abhorrence by their descendants, some of whose early Puritan "prejudices," not yet eradicated, may very possibly reach future generations, mention of a characteristic act in his official life may be per-

---

[1] For an opposite view of Archbishop Laud's character, and the *principles* involved in it, read his "Life and Times," by John Lawson Parker. 2 vols. 8vo. London : 1829.

tinent to our inquiry. It was this : Mr. Leighton, a Scotch divine, being convicted of writing a book denouncing the severities of the hierarchy, Bishop Laud pulled off his hat when sentence was pronounced on the offender, and gave God thanks for the victory. This was in the Star Chamber, and in keeping with the general tone of proceedings which prevailed in this court, in the council, and in the government generally, during Laud's time.

Mr. Leighton "was severely whipped ; then, being set in the pillory, his ear was cut off, his nose slit, and his cheek was branded, with a red-hot iron, S. S., as a Sower of Sedition. On that day week — the sores on his back, ears, nose, and face not being cured — he was whipped again at the pillory, in Cheapside, and the remainder of his sentence executed by cutting off his other ear, slitting the other side of his nose, and branding his other cheek."

This man, Laud, who conceived, perpetrated, revelled in, and recorded in his private diary these disgusting details, was by Charles I. promoted step by step in Episcopal office, till, in 1633, three years after the outrage on Leighton, and the next after his brutality on Prynne, — this man was *consecrated* Archbishop of Canterbury, the primate of the Episcopal Church, the representative man of the hierarchy. The New Englanders always spoke of him as " our great enemy."

Early in the next year — 1634 — this primate, " with my Lord Privy Seal," after an examination in council of Governor Cradock[1]

---

[1] Governor Mathewe Cradock, though prominent in early Massachusetts annals, never set foot in New England. The house built on his plantation, in what is Medford, in 1634, is yet standing, — one of the precious memorials of early times. Brooks' History of Medford honors him as " the founder " of the town, and contains a picture of the house. After the removal of the colony from Cape Ann to Salem, in 1626, under Governor Conant, some of the persevering members of " the Dorchester Company," which had originated the enterprise of colonizing Massachusetts, effected, with new associates, a new organization, for *continuing and expanding* the colonization of New England, which was at a later period — March 4, 1628-9 — " confirmed " by charter from Charles I. Of this new "*company*" Cradock was appointed the first governor, and John Endecott was

and other friends of the colonists, and of " all their correspondence" with " the brethren" in New England, called them all " imposturous knaves," promised " the cropping of Mr. Winthrop's ears," the loss of the colonial charter, and a " general governor " over all the colonies, to do his bloody behests. " If Jove vouchsafe to thunder, the charter and the kingdom of the separatists will fall asunder," and so end " King Winthrop, with all his inventions, and his Amsterdam and fantastical ordinances, his preachings, marriages, and other abusive ceremonies, which exemplify his *detestation of the Church of England*, and contempt of his Majesty's authority and *wholesome laws"!* Winthrop's ears were not cropped, and Laud became a — "*martyr*"*!*

From such a gospel the New England Puritans fled; and in the celebrated pulpit at Saint Paul's Cross, in London, its clergy preached often and bitterly against the New England colonies and planters, especially Massachusetts, who, by limiting their franchise to members of their own communion, kept out of political power those enemies[1] who followed them hither, and who would have overturned the Commonwealth, — which some attempted, as in the case of Child, Vassal, the infamous Maverick, and others. When the Colony became a State, with an educated people, the bars were let down, and suffrage was extended.

---

the first, if not the only, governor of the *colony* under *this* charter. — Massachusetts Col. Rec., " The Landing at Cape Ann," and authorities there cited. See note 1, p. xxiii.

[1] In the admirable state paper from Massachusetts Bay to the Parliament, in 1651, they say: " We, . . being men able enough to live in England with our neighbours, and being helpfull to others, and not needing the help of any for outward thinges, about three or four and twenty years since, seeing just cause to feare the persecution of the then bishops and high commission, for not conforming to the ceremonies then pressed upon the consciences of those under their power, we thought it our safest course *to get outside of the world, out of their view, and beyond their reach*, ... coming hither at our proper charges without the help of the State, . . . having expended, first and last, ... divers hundreds of thousands pounds."

It was well said in Stoughton's Election Sermon, preached in 1668, that " God sifted a whole nation that he might send choice grain over into this wilderness." . . . " They were men of great renown in the nation from whence the Laudian persecution exiled them; their learning, their holiness, their gravity, struck all men that knew them with admiration. They were Timothies in their houses, Chrysostoms in their pulpits, Augustines in their disputations." Indeed, this exodus of so many of the choicest of England's educated and Christian sons, consequent upon this fanaticism for *the* church, — not religion, — alarmed the sober-minded. We find an expression of this in the anecdote of the vice-chancellor's strenuous exception to printing the two lines in Herbert's " Temple,"—

> " Religion stands a-tiptoe in our land,
> Ready to pass to the American strand," —

when they requested his *imprimatur* for that poem; and his reluctant assent was given with the " hope that the world would not take Herbert for an inspired prophet." This was in 1633. Towards the close of Queen Elizabeth's reign, the judicious Hooker defined the " clergy as a state" — or order of men — " whereunto the rest of God's people *must* be subject, as touching " — only — " things that appertain to their soul's health." This was a great advance in the right; but the leaven of Puritanism had then been some time fermenting in England, and many of the churchmen now challenged this claim of the priesthood.

A late able writer[1] sums up clearly " the points upon which the Puritan clergy and their lords were at issue. In substance the prelates claimed that every word, ceremony, and article, written in the Book of Common Prayer, and in the Book of Ordination, was as faultless and as binding as the Book of God, and must be acknowl-

---

[1] Hopkins, " Puritanism and Queen Elizabeth," vol. ii. p. 369.

edged as such. The Puritans dared not say it. The prelates claimed to themselves — or, more modestly, to the church which they personified — an infallibility of judgment in *all* things pertaining to religion. The Puritans denied the claim. The prelates claimed obedience; the Puritans, manhood; the prelates, spiritual lordship; the Puritans, Christian liberty." And these preposterous claims of the prelates rested upon acts of Parliament!

The quarrel was *in* the church. Some of these Puritans fled to New England. They came hither protesting against these prelatical assumptions, and were really *a church rather than a state.* Separation from the Church of England was at first viewed by those of Massachusetts with repugnance; but it was facilitated by a quasi adoption of a very mild type of the Genevan or Presbyterian polity, the validity of whose ordination had been repeatedly recognized by the hierarchy, and also declared by Act of Parliament, 13th Elizabeth; the very same authority which created the " Established " Church, and tinkered its " infallibility " to suit the changing times. But soon " they read this clearly," as did Oliver Cromwell, John Milton, and John Cotton, that

" New Presbyter is but Old Priest writ large."

As they were already imbued with the spirit, they gradually adopted the principles of Independency, — absolute democracy, — essentially as held and taught by their Plymouth brethren. This was the legitimate result of the Reformation, and it was distinctly conceded to be such by one of Hooker's ablest scholars, George Cranmer. In a letter to his teacher, he said : " If the positions of the Reformers be true, I cannot see how the main and general conclusions of Brownism "— Independency — " should be false."[1] That great man, Sir James Mackintosh, incidentally renders them a noble tribute, in

[1] In the Appendix to Izaak Walton's Life of Mr. Richard Hooker.

his admirable article on the philosophical genius of Bacon and Locke. Mr. Locke was admitted to Christ Church College in 1651, when Dr. Owen, the Independent, was Dean, — the same who was thought of for the presidency of Harvard College. " Educated," says Sir James, " among the English Dissenters, during the short period of their political ascendency, he early imbibed *the deep piety and ardent spirit of liberty which actuated that body of men;* and he probably imbibed also, in their schools, the disposition to metaphysical inquiries which has everywhere accompanied the Calvinistic theology. Sects, founded on the right of private judgment, naturally tend to purify themselves from intolerance, and in time to learn to respect in others the freedom of thought to the exercise of which they owe their own existence. By the Independent divines, who were his instructors, our philosopher was taught *those principles of religious liberty which they were the first to disclose to the world.*"

Such was the origin of New England ; such the men who founded it. Religion, the church, was the great thought, and civil interests were only incidental. This is not only evident in our history, as already narrated, but it is distinctly avowed and reiterated in the writings of the fathers of New England from the very beginning. Thus Roger Conant, the first Governor of Massachusetts Colony, suggested to the Rev. John White, of Dorchester, that it might be a refuge from the coming storm " *on account of religion.*" [1] Protestantism seemed to be in great danger on the Continent and in England, where the king, court, and many of the hierarchy were more than suspected of sympathy with Popery. Mr. White conferred with Bishop Lake, who favored the suggestion, especially as an opportunity for Christian missions among the Indians, and entered

1 History of New England, Edit. 1848, p. 107, by Hubbard, who, no doubt, had the facts from Governor Conant himself, who lived at Beverly, near Ipswich, Hubbard's residence.

into it with such zeal as to say to Mr. White that "he would go himself but for his age."[1]

This most Christian bishop availed himself of an early and providential opportunity to speak, with apostolic earnestness, on the national neglect and duty in this matter. On the second of July, 1625, he "preached in Westminster, before his Majestie, the Lords, and others of the Upper House of Parliament, at the opening of the Fast,"[2] which had been ordered throughout the kingdom, on petition of the Puritan Parliament. It was on account of the public calamities, civil and religious. He spoke with great plainness. "There is," he said, "a kind of metaphysical locusts and caterpillars, — locusts that come out of the bottomless pit, — I mean popish priests and Jesuits, — and caterpillars of the Commonwealth, projectors and inventors of new tricks" — well known to the king and others who listened to these words — "how to exhaust the purses of the subjects, covering private ends with public pretences; . . . in well-governed states they were wont to be called *Pestes Reipublicæ*, Plagues of the Commonwealth." Near the close of his sermon, the preacher said: "Neither is it enough for us to make much of God's truth for our own good, but also we should propagate it to others. And here let me tell you, that there lieth a great guilt upon Christian states, and England among the rest, that they have not been careful to bring them that sit in darkness and in the shadow of death to the knowledge of Christ and participation of the gos-

1 The anecdote seems to come direct from the lips of Mr. White to Mr. Hugh Peter, who records it in his autobiography, — "Last Legacy to his Daughter," Boston, Ed. 1717, p. 77, — and says, "That good man, my dear firm friend, Mr. White, of Dorchester, and Bishop Lake, occasioned, yea, founded that work;" *i. e.*, Massachusetts Colony. It is a curious fact, that part of Archbishop Laud's library came into the possession of Mr. Peter, who intended to send it to New England. There is an interesting reference to Mr. White and Mr. Peter in Governor Cradock's letter to Governor Endecott. Mass. Records, i. 384.

2 "Svndrie Sermons de tempore, by Arthur Lake, D. of Diuinitie, Lord Bishop of Bath and Welles." London, 1629: folios 200—220.

pel. Much travelling to the Indies, East and West, but wherefor ?
Some go to possess themselves of the lands of the infidels, but
most, by commerce, to grow richer by their goods. But where
is the prince or state that pitieth their souls, and, without any
worldly respects, endeavours the gaining of them unto God ? Some
show we make, but it is a poor one ; for it is but an accessorie to
our worldly desire ; it is not our primary intention ; whereas Christ's
method is, *first seek ye the kingdom of God, and then all other things
shall be added unto you; you shall fare the better for it in your
worldly estate.* If the apostles and apostolic men had affected our
salvation no more, we might have continued to this day such as
sometimes we were, barbarous subjects of the Prince of Darkness."

In exact accordance with these teachings, the king and colonists
declared " the principal ende of this plantation" of Massachusetts
to be, " to win and incite the natives of the country to the knowledge and obedience of the only true God and Saviour of mankind,
and the Christian faith ; " and to complete the moral unity of the
bishop's missionary sermon, and the designs of our fathers, we parallel with his anathema against the Papacy the *first* of their " general considerations for the plantation in New England," which was
in these words : " It will be a service to the church, of great consequence, to carry the gospell into those parts of the world, and to
raise a bulwarke against the kingdom of antichrist, which the Jesuits[1]
labor to rear up in all places of the world."

When the " governor and companie" — that branch of the
Massachusetts government which, under the charter, had its legal
residence in England — were about emigrating to the colony, they
issued a manifesto, April 7, 1630, declaring themselves to be a

---

[1] " The Jesuits," wrote John Cotton, in 1647, " have professed to some of our
merchants and marriners, they look at our plantations (and at some of us by
name) as dangerous supplanters of the Catholick cause " in America, especially in
Canada.

CHURCH, " a weake *colonie* from their brethren in and of the *Church* of England," as " the *Church* of Philippi was a *colony* of the church at Rome." The Rev. John Norton, in the Election Sermon of 1661, said that they came " into this wilderness to live under the *order of the gospel ;* " " that our polity may be a gospel *polity,* and may be compleat according to the Scriptures, answering fully the Word of God: this is the work of our generation, and the very work we engaged for into this wilderness ; this is the scope and end of it, that which is *written upon the forehead of New England,* viz., the compleat walking in the faith of the gospel, according to the *order* of the gospel."

The venerable Higginson, of Salem, in his Election Sermon of 1663, stated the point with great fulness, as follows : " It concerneth New England always to remember that they are originally a plantation religious, not a plantation of trade. The profession of the purity of doctrine, worship, and discipline, is written upon her forehead. Let merchants, and such as are increasing cent. per cent., remember this : that worldly gain was not the end and design of the people of New England, but religion. And if any man among us make religion as twelve, and the world as thirteen, such an one hath not the spirit of a true New England man."

In the Election Sermon of 1677, the Rev. Dr. Increase Mather uttered these words : " It was love to God and to Jesus Christ which brought our fathers into this wilderness. . . . They did not, in their coming hither, propound any great matters to themselves respecting this world ; only that they should have liberty to serve God, and to walk with him in all the wayes of his worship. . . . There never was a generation that did so perfectly shake off the dust of Babylon, *both as to ecclesiastical* and *civil constitution,* as the first generation of Christians that came into this land for the gospel's sake."

The Rev. William Hubbard, the historian, in a Fast-day sermon, preached June 24, 1682, declared that the fathers "came not hither for the world, or for land, or for traffic; but for religion, and for liberty of conscience in the worship of God, which was their only design."

The historical fact was stated by President Stiles, of Yale College, in 1783: "It is certain that civil dominion was but the second motive, religion the primary one, with our ancestors, in coming hither and settling this land. It was not so much their design to establish religion for the benefit of the state, as civil government for the benefit of religion, and as subservient, and even necessary, towards the peaceable enjoyment and unmolested exercise of religion — of that religion for which they fled to these ends of the earth." [1]

The result of all this was, a new community, voluntarily gathered in New England, primarily for religion, organized into many "independent" churches, each of them a petty democracy, electing its officers and ministers, making its own laws, and regulating its own affairs, so far as possible, by the system of polity indicated with more or less distinctness in holy Scripture. Out of this condition of things the state was gradually developed. Here was individualism, — an admirable system for making good full-blooded Puritan *citizens*, but very poor and unmanageable *subjects*. So George III. and George Grenville, "The Gentle Shepherd," found it in 1763 and afterward.

By the change, the clergy could retain no *authority*, but their influence was probably increased. They had "great power in the people's hearts," says Winthrop. Religion predominated over all other interests.

"As near the law of God as they can" be, was the instruction of the General Court to their committee of laity and ministry, ap-

1 This very exact statement of fact explains the *exclusive* policy of the early legislation. It was at that time absolutely necessary to self-preservation against the plottings of the hierarchy, to confine the privilege of franchise to their known friends.

pointed to frame laws for the Commonwealth. Their first[1] written code, under the charter of 1629, was drawn by a minister. Rev. Nathaniel Ward, of Ipswich, Hugh Peter, and Thomas Welde, ministers, were the colonial agents from Massachusetts to the mother country in 1641, to aid " *in furthering the work of the reformation of the churches there*," and in relation to our colonial affairs; but " some reasons were alleged " — though ineffectually — " that officers should not be taken from their churches for civil occasions."

This was coïncident, in time and spirit, with the exclusion of the bishops from Parliament, which, says Hallam, was the latest concession that the king made before his final appeal to arms at the battle of Edgehill, October 23, 1642. Sir Edward Verney, who was there killed, declared his reluctance to fight *for the bishops, whose cause he took it to be.*

The name of Hugh Peter reminds us that New England shared in the English revolution of 1640; sent preachers and soldiers, aid and comfort, to Cromwell; gave an asylum to the tyrannicides, Whalley, Goffe, and Dixwell; reäffirmed the same maxims of liberty in the revolution of 1688, and so stood right on the record for the third revolution of 1776.

Hutchinson says that the Rev. John Cotton was supposed to have been more instrumental in the settlement of their civil as well as ecclesiastical polity than any other man. He too, the representative man of New England, was, as could not be otherwise expected, remembering his life, a sound " Commonwealth's " man. To him, " Pastor of the Church at Boston, in New England," Cromwell wrote,[2] in a letter from London, 2d October, 1651 : . . . " I received yours a few days since. It was welcome to me because

---

1 Rev. Dr. Felt (Ecclesiastical History, vol. i. p. 166) shows that laws had been enacted, under Governor Endecott's administration, prior to the transfer of the " companie " to the colony in 1629.

2 Carlyle's Cromwell, Letter cxxv., and Harris's Lives, iii. 518, where the letter was first published. Cotton's letter is in Hutchinson's Coll. 233.

signed by you, whom I love and honor in the Lord; but more *to see some of the same grounds of our acting stirring in you that are in us, to quiet us in our work, and support us therein."*

Here we cannot but stop for a moment by the way to notice a beautiful and significant incident, of recent date, which must excite delight, if not exultation. It is this: The very Episcopal authorities which silenced the voice of Cotton within the venerable walls of Boston Church, in Lincolnshire, in England, and banished him and his Puritan brethren, after the lapse of two centuries invited us, the descendants of those exiles, to join with them in brotherly union to render distinguished honors to his memory. The "Founder's Chapel" of the noble church, beautifully renovated, was reöpened as "Cotton Chapel," and in the eastern arch was set a large, highly ornamented memorial tablet of brass, bearing an inscription in Latin, from the classical pen of Mr. Everett; in English, as follows:

In perpetual remembrance of
JOHN COTTON,
Who, during the reigns of James and Charles,
Was for many years a grave, skilful, learned, and
laborious Vicar of this Church.
Afterwards, on account of the miserable commotion
amongst sacred affairs
In his own country,
He sought a new settlement in a New World,
And remained even to the end of his life
A pastor and teacher
Of the greatest reputation and of the greatest authority
In the first church of Boston, in New England,
Which receives this venerable name
In honor of Cotton.
Ccxxv years having passed away since his migration,
His descendants and the American citizens of Boston were incited
to this pious work by their English
brethren,
In order that the name of an illustrious man,
The love and honor of both worlds,
Might not any longer be banished from that noble
temple,
In which he diligently, learnedly, and sacredly
Expounded the divine oracles for so many years;
And willingly and gratuitously caused this shrine to be restored
and this tablet to be erected,
In the year of our recovered salvation 1857.

The American flag and the British color floated majestically from St. Botolph's tower.[1]

The Bishop of Lincoln, the Bishop of London (Laud's successor), and other clergy, took part in the proceedings of the day. The Bishop of Lincoln preached, taking for his text the fourth chapter of Ezra, fourth verse: *"Let us build with you, for we seek your God as ye do;"* and this reöpening of St. Botolph's, as if to give more emphasis to the occasion and the words, was his first official act as diocesan of Lincoln.

The significance of this celebration can be best appreciated, perhaps, by conjecturing the amazement of Archbishop Laud, and his victim, the Rev. John Cotton, could they have witnessed the occasion! Each of them will be judged according to his works; and the world has learned wisdom by them.

To resume our point: In 1662, at the earnest solicitation of the General Court and of the ministry, Mr. Simon Bradstreet and Rev. John Norton went to England, as colonial agents, to secure the charter against their ancient foes, who had distinguished their restoration to power by the cruel Act of Uniformity; and twenty-five years later, in a most important crisis, we find Massachusetts again represented by a clergyman, the Rev. Dr. Increase Mather, who procured the provincial charter of 1694. Indeed, the clergy were generally consulted by the civil authorities; and not infrequently the suggestions from the pulpit, on election days and other special occasions,[2] were enacted into laws. The

---

1 Boston, Lincolnshire, England, derives its name from Mr. Botolph, or St. Botolph, who there built a monastery in 654; and in *Botolph's town* the present magnificent church, 245 by 98 feet within its walls, was built in 1309; and its lofty tower, 300 feet in height, is named in honor of St. Botolph. Mr. Pishey Thompson's History of Boston contains an elegant engraving and a minute account of this venerable pile.

2 Among the causes for "fasting and humiliation," or "thanksgiving," as they appeared upon the records, are, " to seek the Lord for his direction " — " to intreat the help of God " — " for humiliation to seek the face of God " —

statute-book, the reflex of the age, shows this influence. *The State was developed out of the Church.*

The annual " ELECTION SERMON " — *a perpetual memorial,* continued down through the generations from century to century — still bears witness that our fathers ever began their civil year and its responsibilities with an appeal to Heaven, and recognized *Christian morality as the only basis of good laws.*

The origin of this anniversary is to be found in the charter of "the governor and COMPANIE of the Massachusetts Bay in New England," which provided that " one governor, one deputy-governor, and eighteen assistants, and all other officers of the said companie," — not of the colony[1] — should be chosen in their

" novelties, oppression, atheism, excess, superfluity, idleness, contempt of authority, and troubles in other parts " of the world " to be remembered " — " for the want of rain, and help of brethren in distress " — " in regard of our wants, and the dangers of our native country " — " for God's great mercy to the churches in Germany and the Palatinate " — " for a bountiful harvest, and for the arrival of persons of special use and quality " — " for success and safe return of the Pequot expedition, success of the conference at Newton, and good news from Germany " — " sad condition of our native country." These occurred before the year 1644. May 29th, of that year, it was " ordered, the printer shall have leave to print the *Election* Sermon, with Mr. Mather's consent, and the *Artillery* Sermon, with Mr. Norton's consent."

1 These were the officers of the " COMPANIE " in England; but the charter also provided for another government in New England — " for the formes and ceremonies of government and magistracie fitt and necessary" in and for the " plantation," or colony. Thus the charter ordained two governments, — one for the " COMPANIE " in England, and resident there, and one in and for the COLONY in New England, — and two such governments existed, Mathewe Cradock being governor of the " companie," and Endecott governor of the colony. The illegal transfer of the government of the " companie" to New England invalidated both governments, and rendered the colonial government, as provided for by the charter, practically impossible. As we have seen, Endecott was the legally elected governor of the " plantation," and he was never legally displaced. On the 20th of October, 1629, Cradock resigning, Winthrop succeeded him as governor of the " companie," but not of the colony, for one year; and as the records show no election after, till May 18, 1631, there was an interregnum of about seven months, till Winthrop became *de facto*, but not *de jure*, governor, — the *charter* distinction between the " companie " and the " plantation " being winked out of sight, and the two made one in fact. " The whole structure of the charter pre-

" general court, or assemblie," on " the last Wednesday in Easter
Terme, yearely, for the yeare ensuing."

About the year 1633, the governor and assistants began to
appoint one to preach on the day of election, and this was the first
of our " Election Sermons." In a few years, the deputies, or representatives, jealous of the power of the magistrates, challenged the
appointment as theirs; and the magistrates, unwilling " to have any
fresh occasion of contestation with the deputies," yielded, though
some judged it " a betraying, or, at least, weakening, the power of
the magistrates, and a countenancing of an unjust usurpation.
For," says Winthrop, " the deputies could do no such act, as an act
of court, without the concurrence of the magistrates; and out of
court they had no power at all, but only for regulating their own
body ; and it was resolved and voted at last court, according to the
elders'" — ministers'— " advice, that all occurrents " — orders —
" out of court belong to the magistrates to take care of, being the
standing council of the Commonwealth." Such were the trifles which
involved the popular character of our institutions. The occasion was
simple ; the principle was momentous. So it was when Hampden
refused to pay twenty shillings, and when our grandfathers resisted
the Stamp Act and tea duty. Governor Winthrop's critical notice
of the discourse by the Rev. Nathaniel Ward, of Ipswich, in June
1641, is, perhaps, the earliest sketch of an " Election Sermon " now
to be found. It appears that " some of the freemen, without the
consent of the magistrates or governor, had chosen Mr. Nathaniel
Ward to preach at this court, pretending that it was a part of their
liberty. The governor (whose right, indeed, it is, — for, till the
court be assembled, the freemen are but private persons) would

supposes the residence of the company in England, and the transaction of all its
business there." The removal was an " usurpation of authority; " but of its
expediency and wisdom there can be no doubt. — Story on the Constitution, 1.
§§ 64, 65. Winthrop was not, *de jure*, governor, as were Conant and Endecott.
See note 1, p. xi.

not strive about it; for, though it did not belong to them, yet, if they would have it, there was reason " — since it could not be helped — " to yield it to them. Yet they had no great reason to choose him, — though otherwise very able, — seeing he had cast off his pastor's place at Ipswich, and was now no minister by the received determination of our churches. In his sermon he delivered many useful things, but in a *moral and political discourse*, grounding his propositions much upon the old Roman and Grecian governments, which sure is an error; for, if religion and the word of God make men wiser than their neighbors, and these men have the advantage of all that have gone before us in experience and observation, it is probable that, by all these helps, *we* may better *frame rules of government for ourselves* than to receive others upon the bare authority of the wisdom, justice, etc., of those heathen commonwealths. Among other things, he advised *the people to keep all their magistrates in an equal rank, and not give more honor or power to one than to another*, which is easier to advise than to prove, seeing it is against the practice of Israel (where some were rulers of thousands, and some but of tens), and of all nations known or recorded. Another advice he gave, that magistrates should not give private advice, and take knowledge of any man's cause before it came to public hearing. *This was debated after in the general court, where some of the deputies moved to have it ordered* " and enacted into a law.

By the charter of William and Mary, October 7th, 1691, the last Wednesday of May was established as election-day, and it remained so till the Revolution. The important part which this institution of the Election Sermon played at that period, and an account of its observance, are minutely and accurately presented by the Rev. William Gordon, of Roxbury, the contemporary historian of the Revolution, and in a manner so pertinent to our purpose that we give it entire.

He says that the " ministers of New England, being mostly Congregationalists, are, from that circumstance, in a professional way, more attached and habituated to the principles of liberty than if they had spiritual superiors to lord it over them, and were in hopes of possessing, in their turn, through the gift of government, the seat of power. They oppose arbitrary rule in civil concerns from the love of freedom, as well as from a desire of guarding against its introduction into religious matters. The patriots, for years back, have availed themselves greatly of their assistance. Two sermons have been preached annually for a length of time, the one on general election-day, the last Wednesday in May, when the new general court have been used to meet, according to charter, and elect counsellors for the ensuing year; the other, some little while after, on the artillery election-day, when the officers are reëlected, or new officers chosen. On these occasions political subjects are deemed very proper; but it is expected that they be treated in a decent, serious, and instructive manner. The general election preacher has been elected alternately by the council and House of Assembly. The sermon is styled the *Election Sermon*, and is printed. Every representative has a copy for himself, and generally one or more for the minister or ministers of his town. As the patriots have prevailed, the preachers of each sermon have been the zealous friends of liberty; and the passages most adapted to promote the spread and love of it have been selected and circulated far and wide by means of newspapers, and read with avidity and a degree of veneration on account of the preacher and his election to the service of the day. Commendations, both public and private, have not been wanting to help on the design. Thus, by their labors in the pulpit, and by furnishing the prints with occasional essays, the ministers have forwarded and strengthened, and that not a little, the opposition to the exercise of that parliamentary claim of right to bind the colonies in all cases whatever."

Protestantism exchanged the altar for the pulpit, the missal for the Bible; the "priest" gave way to the "preacher," and the gospel was "preached." The ministers were now to instruct the people, to reason before them and with them, to appeal to them; and so, by their very position and relation, the people were constituted the judges. *They* were called upon to decide; *they* also reasoned; and in this way — as the conflicts *in* the church respected *polity* rather than *doctrine* — the Puritans, and especially the New Englanders, had, from the very beginning, been educated in the consideration of its elementary principles. In this we discover how it was, as Governor Hutchinson remarked, that "men took sides in New England upon mere speculative points in government, when there was nothing in practice which could give any grounds for forming parties." This was a remarkable feature in the opening of the Revolutionary war. It was recognized by Edmund Burke, in his speech of March 22d, 1775, "on conciliation with the colonies." "Permit me, sir," he said, "to add another circumstance in our colonies, which contributes no mean part towards the growth and effect of this untractable spirit, — *I mean their education.* In no country in the world, perhaps, is the law so general a study. The profession itself is numerous and powerful, and in most provinces it takes the lead. The greater number of the deputies sent to the congress" — at Philadelphia — "were lawyers. But all who read — and most do read — endeavor to obtain some smattering in that science. I have been told by an eminent bookseller, that in no branch of his business, after tracts of popular devotion, were so many books as those on the law exported to the plantations. The colonists have now fallen into the way of printing them for their own use. I hear that they have sold nearly as many of Blackstone's Commentaries in America as in England. General Gage marks out this disposition very particularly in a letter on your table. He states that *all the people in his government are lawyers*, or smatterers in law; and that in Boston they have been enabled, by successful chicane, wholly to evade many parts of your capital penal constitutions. . . . *Abeunt studia in mores.* This study renders men acute, inquisitive, dexterous, prompt in attack, ready in defence, full of resources. In other countries, the people, more simple, and of a less mercurial cast, judge of an ill principle in government only by an actual grievance ; here," — in the colonies — " they anticipate the evil, and judge of the pressure of the grievance by the badness of the principle. They augur misgovernment at a distance, and snuff the approach of tyranny in every tainted breeze."

Mr. Webster studied this phase of our history. He says our fathers " went to war against a preamble ; they fought seven years against a declaration ; " that " we are not to wait till great public mischiefs come, till the government is overthrown, or liberty itself put in extreme jeopardy. We should not be worthy sons of our fathers were we so to regard great questions affecting the general freedom. *Those fathers accomplished the Revolution on a strict question of principle.* The Parliament of Great Britain asserted a right to tax the colonies in all cases whatsoever ; and it was precisely on this question that they made the Revolution turn. The amount of taxation was trifling, but the claim itself was inconsistent with liberty ; and that was, in their eyes, enough. It was against the recital of an act of Parliament, rather than against any suffering under its enactments, that they took up arms. . . . . They poured out their treasures and their blood like water, in a contest in opposition to an assertion, which those less sagacious, and not so well schooled in the principles of civil liberty, would have regarded as barren phraseology, or mere parade of words.

" They saw in the claim of the British Parliament a seminal principle of mischief, the germ of unjust power ; they detected it, dragged it forth from underneath its plausible disguises, struck at it ; nor did it elude either their steady eye or their well-directed blow till they had extirpated and destroyed it to the smallest fibre. On this question of principle, while actual suffering was yet afar off, they raised their flag against a power to which, for purposes of foreign conquest and subjugation, Rome, in the height of her glory, is not to be compared; a 'power which has dotted over the surface of the whole globe with her possessions and military posts; whose morning drum-beat, following the sun and keeping company with the hours, circles the earth daily with one continuous and unbroken strain of the martial airs of England." It is in this habitual study of political ethics, of " the liberty of the gospel," — perhaps the principal feature in New England history, — that we discern the source of that earnestness which consciousness of right begets, and of those appeals to principle which distinguished the colonies, and which they were ever ready to vindicate with life and fortune. It is an interesting fact, in this connection, that the very able and learned defence of the ecclesiastical polity of New England, written by the Rev. John Wise, of Ipswich, one of the victims of the despotism of the infamous Andros, in 1687, was republished in the year 1772, as a sound political document for the times, teaching that " Democracy is Christ's government in Church and in State." Thus the church polity of New England begat like principles in the state. The pew and the pulpit had been educated to self-government. They were accustomed " to CONSIDER." The highest glory of the American Revolution, said John Quincy Adams, was this : *it connected, in one indissoluble bond, the principles of civil government with the principles of Christianity.*

With these antecedents of history and principle, it is apparent that nothing could be more revolting to the heart and head of New England than the idea of a bishopric within her borders; and the rumor of such a project excited general alarm, and deepened the old loathing. Lord Chatham, in his celebrated letter to the king, wrote : " They left their native land in search of freedom, and found it in a desert. Divided as they are into a thousand forms of policy and religion, *there is one point in which they all agree:* they equally detest the pageantry of a king, and the supercilious hypocrisy of a bishop." Mr. Thomas Hollis, of London, wrote to Rev. Doctor Mayhew, of Boston, in the year 1763 : " You are in no real danger at present in respect to the creation of bishops in America, if I am rightly informed, though a matter extremely desired by our clergy and prelates, and even talked of greatly at this time among themselves. You cannot, however, be too much on your guard on this so very important an affair." Secker, the Archbishop of Canterbury, had connived at the sending of a popish bishop to Quebec; and this exposed to full view the dishonesty, the utter recklessness of principle, and the popish sympathies, which then distinguished the government of England.

The pulpit and the press were alive to the danger, and this alarm was but initiatory to the coming contest against civil wrong. They detected the same foe under the mitre and the gown. " If Parliament could tax us, they could establish the Church of England, with all its creeds, articles, tests, ceremonies, and tithes, and prohibit all other churches, as conventicles and schism-shops." [1]

A contemporary print, entitled " An Attempt to land a Bishop in America," gives the pressure of the times. The scene is at the wharf. Exclamations from the colonists, " No lords, spiritual or temporal, in New England !" " Shall they be obliged to maintain bishops who cannot maintain themselves !" salute the bishop's ears. On a banner, surmounted by a liberty-cap, is " Liberty and Freedom of Conscience ; " and " Locke," " Sydney on Government," " Calvin's Works," and " Barclay's Apology," bless his eyes ! The ship is shoved off shore ; on the deck is the bishop's carriage, the wheels off ; the crosier and mitre hang in the rigging ; and the " saint in lawn," with his gown floating in the breeze, has mounted

---

1 John Adams's Works, x. 287, 288.

An Attempt to land a Bishop in America.

the shrouds half way to the mast-head, and ejaculates, " Lord, now Lord, lettest thou thy servant depart in peace!"[1]

The unanimity and efficient service of the Puritan clergy in the war of the Revolution, and the zeal of the Episcopal ministers and "missionaries" in their hostility to it, — in perfect consistency with their spirit and principles, as exhibited by Dr. Mayhew, in 1750, in his discourse on King Charles's " Saintship and Martyrdom," — are stated with almost statistical accuracy in a letter from Rev. Charles Inglis, Rector of Trinity Church, New York, October 31, 1776. The writer was an Oxford D. D., and a missionary " for Propagating the Gospel in Foreign Parts." He was rewarded by a bishopric in Nova Scotia, none being attainable in the other colonies, except in Canada, where the preference of the government was for one *direct* from Rome. He states " that *all* the Society's missionaries, . . . and *all* the other clergy of *our* church, . . . have, to the utmost of their power, opposed the spirit of disaffection; . . . . and, although their joint endeavors could not wholly prevent the rebellion, yet they checked it considerably for some time, and prevented many thousands from plunging into it, who otherwise would certainly have done so. . . . . In their sermons they confined themselves to the doctrines of the gospel" — as *honor the king* — " without touching on politics.[2]

---

1 For the use of this plate, reëngraved from the Political Register of 1769, for Mr. Frothingham's History of the Siege of Boston, grateful acknowledgment is made to that gentleman.

2 " Without touching on politics"! The *honesty* of this Rev. Dr. is transparent. His letter is wholly a boast of the *political* fidelity and services of the Episcopal clergy. The spirit of this " gospel " can be understood by the Rev. Dr. Tucker, Dean of Gloucester's, eulogy on the Roman Catholics, in 1779, which concludes that, " as to the behaviour of the Popish Priests of Canada, would to God that those who call themselves the Protestant ministers of the Gospel of Peace in New England had behaved half as well"! Could the Crown have flooded the country with its clergy of Oxford, or Rome, and " gospel " of absolute obedience, and have silenced the Puritan clergy, who, with apostolic fidelity, " shunned not to declare unto you *all* the counsel of God," every " seditious" or " rebellious" aspiration would have been hushed into the silence of — death.

. . . Although liberty was the ostensible object, . . . it is now past all doubt that an abolition of the Church of England was one of the principal springs of the dissenting leaders' conduct, and hence the *unanimity* of the dissenters. . . . Nor have I been able, after strict inquiry, to hear of any who did not, by preaching, and every effort in their power, promote all the measures of the Congress, however extravagant. . . . I have not a doubt but . . . his Majesty's arms will be successful. . . . In that case, if the steps are taken which reason, prudence, and common sense dictate," — lords spiritual, tithes, etc., — " the church will indubitably increase. . . . The dissenters will ever clamor against anything that will tend to benefit or increase the church " — hierarchy — " here. The present rebellion is certainly one of the most causeless, unprovoked, and unnatural, that ever disgraced any country ; a rebellion with peculiarly aggravated circumstances of guilt and ingratitude." [1]

The religious character and views of the founders of New England also appear in bold relief in the foundation of the venerable seat of learning at Cambridge. "CHRISTO ET ECCLE-SIÆ" heads the ancient seal of Harvard College, and *the church was the colony.* On the long roll of the benefactors of Harvard, the name of HOLLIS [2] must ever stand preëminent in the regard of the whole country. In the year 1766, Thomas Hollis [3] wrote to the Rev. Dr. Mayhew, " More books, *especially on government,* are going for New England. Should those go safe, it is hoped that no principal books on that FIRST subject will be wanting in Har-

---

1 Copied from " Hawkins's Missions" into the Congregational Quarterly, 1860, p. 311.

2 For an account of this distinguished Baptist family, see President Quincy's History of Harvard College, *index.*

3 He caused the reprint and circulation in England of James Otis's " Rights of the British Colonies Asserted and Proved," John Adams's " Dissertation on the Canon and Feudal Law," and Dr. Mayhew's writings. Allibone's " Dictionary of Authors " has an ample notice of him.

vard College, from the days of Moses to these times. Men of New
England, brethren, use them for yourselves, and for others; and
God bless you!" And again : " I confess to bear propensity, affection, towards the people of North America, those of Massachusetts
and Boston in particular, believing them to be a good and brave
people. Long may they continue such! and the spirit of luxury,
now consuming us to the very marrow here at home, kept out
from them! One likeliest means to that end will be, to watch
well over their youth, by bestowing on them a reasonable, manly
education ; and selecting thereto the wisest, ablest, most accomplished of men that art or wealth can obtain ; for nations rise and
fall by individuals, not numbers, as I think all history proveth.
With ideas of this kind have I worked for the *public* library at
Cambridge, in New England."

An eloquent writer, thoroughly imbued with the spirit of those
days, remarks, that " this truly *ingenuous* Englishman, in the range
and direction of his literary beneficence, effectually refuted the
seeming paradox, that a loyal subject of the monarchy in Britain
might be an ardent and intelligent friend of the cause of freedom in America. The books he sent were often political, and
of a republican stamp. And it remains for the perspicacity of our
historians to ascertain what influence his benefactions and correspondence had in kindling that spirit which emancipated these
States from the shackles of colonial subserviency, by forming ' high-
minded men,' who, under Providence, achieved our independence.

" Doubtless at the favored Seminary her sons drank deeply of
the writings of MILTON, HARRINGTON, SYDNEY, LUDLOW, MAR-
VELL, and LOCKE.[1] These were there, by Mr. Hollis's exer-

---

[1] In 1775, Dr. Tucker, Dean of Gloucester, announced as "preparing for the
press, An expostulatory Letter, addressed to the Ministers of the several Denominations of Protestants in North America, occasioned by their preferring and
inculcating principles of Mr. Lock, instead of those of the Gospel, relative to the
original titles of civil governors."

tions, political text-books.   And the eminent men of that day
were —

       'By antient learning to the enlightened love
       Of antient freedom warmed.' "1

President Stiles, of Yale College, said, in 1783: "The colleges
have been of singular advantage in the present day.   When
Britain withdrew all of her wisdom from America, this Revolution
found above two thousand in New England only, who had been
educated in the colonies, intermixed among the people, and communicating knowledge among them."

In Dr. Franklin's library were Locke, Hoadley, Sydney, Montes-
quieu, Priestley, Milton, Price, Gordon's Tacitus; and in a picture
of John Hancock, published in 1780, are introduced portraits of
Hampden, Cromwell, and Sydney.   There are extant American
reprints of these authors, or of portions of their works, issued prior
to and during the Revolution, in a cheap form, for popular circulation, addressing, not passion, but reason, diffusing sound principles,
and begetting right feeling.   There could hardly be found a more
impressive, though silent, proof of the exalted nature of the contest
on the part of the Americans, than a complete collection of their
publications of that period.

Who can limit the influences exerted over the common mind
by these volumes of silent thought, eloquent for the rights of man
and the blessings of liberty, fervid against wrong, the miseries of
oppression and slavery, — teaching that resistance to tyrants is
obedience to God ?   Who can doubt from what fountains he drank
who dedicated "to all the patrons of real, perfect, and unpolluted
liberty, civil and religious, throughout the world," his history of
Whalley, Goffe, and Dixwell, "three of its most illustrious and
heroic, but unfortunate defenders" ?   These books and libraries

---

1 Rev. Dr. William Jenks's Eulogy on Bowdoin, Sept. 2d, 1812.

were the nurseries of "sedition;" they were as secret emissaries propagating in every household, in every breast, at morning, in the noonday rest, by the evening light, in the pulpit, the forum, and the shop, principles, convictions, resolves, which sophistry could not overthrow, nor force extinguish. This was the secret of the strength of our fathers. Let us cherish it as worthy sons of noble sires. One yet among us, whose first inspiration was of the air breathed by the sons of liberty, whose patriot father's laurels are green around his own brow,[1] has given a lively picture of the reverential regard for the clergy at the period of the Revolution.

"The whole space before the meeting-house was filled with a waiting, respectful, and expecting multitude. At the moment of service, the pastor issued from his mansion, with Bible and manuscript sermon under his arm, with his wife leaning on one arm, flanked by his negro man on his side, as his wife was by her negro woman, the little negroes being distributed, according to their sex, by the side of their respective parents. Then followed every other member of the family, according to age and rank, making often, with family visitants, somewhat of a formidable procession. As soon as it appeared, the congregation, as if moved by one spirit, began to move towards the door of the church; and, before the procession reached it, all were in their places. As soon as the pastor entered

---

1 Hon. Josiah Quincy's sketch of Rev. Jonathan French, of Andover, in Sprague's Annals of the American Pulpit, vol. ii. p. 48. It is of singular interest to refer to the following affectionate tribute to the memory of one of the noblest patriots, coupled as it is with a prayer for his only son, whose living presence among us is its answer. The passage is in a letter from the Rev. William Gordon, of Roxbury, dated April 26th, 1775. He says: "My friend Quincy has sacrificed his life for the sake of his country. The ship in which he sailed arrived at Cape Anne within these two days; but he lived not to get on shore, or to hear and triumph at the account of the success of the Lexington engagement. His remains will be honorably interred by his relations. Let him be numbered with the patriotic heroes who fall in the cause of liberty; and let his memory be dear to posterity. *Let his only surviving child, a son of about three years, live to possess his noble virtues, and to transmit his name down to future generations.*"

the church the whole congregation rose, and stood until the pastor was in the pulpit and his family were seated, — until which was done, the whole assembly continued standing.   At the close of the service, the congregation stood until he and his family had left the church, before any one moved towards the door.   Forenoon and afternoon the same course of proceeding was had, expressive of the reverential relation in which the people acknowledged that they stood towards their clergymen." But this was not " obedience ; " for there was no " authority," and no wish for it.   The idea was foreign to New England ; for resistance to it was the proximate cause of her colonization.   It was a nobler, voluntary offering of respect, — the decorum of the times.   Such are the history, principles, education, position, and influence of the clergy, except the few, of foreign sympathy, and alien to the Commonwealth, who, at the opening of the war,

> " Left their country for their country's good ; "

and with what spirit, with what wisdom, with what learning and power they preached the liberty of the gospel, let these pages — their own words — bear witness.   The story of their passive endurance, their personal bravery and manly participation in their country's service in the years of her deepest misery, belongs not here ; they yet wait for justice from the historian.   We have room for only one or two illustrations.   In Danvers, the deacon of the parish was elected captain of the minute-men, and the minister his lieutenant.   The company, after its field exercise, would sometimes repair to the meeting-house to hear a patriotic sermon, or partake of an entertainment at the town-house, where the zealous sons of liberty would exhort them to fight bravely for God and their country.   At Lunenburg, the minute company, after going through several military manœuvres, marched to a public house, where the officers had provided an elegant entertainment for the company, a number of the respectable inhabitants of the town, and patriotic ministers of the towns adjacent. They then marched in military procession to the meeting-house, where the Rev. Mr. Adams delivered an excellent sermon, suitable to the occasion, from Psalm xxvii. 3. Mr. Frothingham, from whose excellent history of the siege of Boston these instances are taken, says that the journals of the period abound in paragraphs of similar interest.

In 1774, when the whole country was in misery, in the travail which preceded the birth of the nation, the First Provincial Congress of Massachusetts acknowledged with profound gratitude the public obligation to the ministry, as friends of civil and religious liberty, and invoked their aid, in the following address :

" REVEREND SIRS : — When we contemplate the friendship and assistance our ancestors, the first settlers of this province (while overwhelmed with distress), received from the pious pastors of the churches of Christ, who, to enjoy the rights of conscience, fled with them into this land, then a savage wilderness, we find ourselves filled with the most grateful sensations. And we cannot but acknowledge the goodness of Heaven in constantly supplying us with preachers of the gospel, whose concern has been the temporal and spiritual happiness of this people.

" In a day like this, when all the friends of civil and religious liberty are exerting themselves to deliver this country from its present calamities, we cannot but place great hopes in an order of men who have ever distinguished themselves in their country's cause ; and do, therefore, recommend to the ministers of the gospel in the several towns and other places in the colony, that they assist us in avoiding that dreadful slavery with which we are now threatened, by advising the people of their several congregations, as they wish their prosperity, to abide by, and strictly adhere to, the resolutions of the Continental Congress," at Philadelphia, in October, 1774, " as the most peaceable and probable method of preventing confusion and bloodshed, and of restoring that harmony between Great Britain and these colonies, on which we wish might be established not only the rights and liberties of America, but the opulence and lasting happiness of the whole British empire.

"*Resolved*, That the foregoing address be presented to all the ministers of the gospel in the province."

Thus it is manifest, in the spirit of our history, in our annals, and by the general voice of the fathers of the republic, that, in a very great degree, —

To the Pulpit, the PURITAN PULPIT, we owe the moral force which won our Independence.

J. W. T.

Boston, October, 1860.

A

DISCOURSE

C O N C E R N I N G

Unlimited Submiſſion

A N D

Non-Reſiſtance

T O   T H E

HIGHER POWERS:

With ſome REFLECTIONS on the RESISTANCE made to

King CHARLES I.

A N D   O N   T H E

Anniversary of his Death:

In which the MYSTERIOUS Doctrine of that Prince's Saintſhip and Martyrdom is UNRIDDLED:

The Subſtance of which was delivered in a S E R M O N preached in the Weſt Meeting-Houſe in *Boſton* the LORD'S-DAY after the 30th of *January*, 1749 | 50.

Publiſhed at the Requeſt of the Hearers.

By JONATHAN MAYHEW, A. M.

Paſtor of the Weſt Church in *Boſton*.

Fear GOD, honour the King.　　　Saint PAUL.
He that ruleth over Men, muſt be juſt, ruling in the Fear of GOD.
　　　　　　　　　　　　　　　　　Prophet SAMUEL.
I have ſaid, ye are Gods— but ye ſhall die like Men, and fall like one of the PRINCES.　　　　　　　　　King DAVID.

Quid memorem infandas cædes? quid facta TYRANNI
Effera? Dii CAPITI ipſius GENERIQUE reſervent—
Necnon Threïcius *longa cum veſte* SACERDOS
Obloquitur——　　　　　　　　　　*Rom. Vat. Prin.*

B O S T O N, Printed and Sold by D. FOWLE in Queen-ſtreet; and by D. GOOKIN over againſt the South Meeting-Houſe. 1750.

EDITOR'S PREFATORY NOTE.

THIS celebrated discourse was delivered on the anniversary of the death of the tyrant Charles I. of England, which, at the suggestion of the courtiers, on the restoration of the monarchy, was, by the "Supreme Governor of the Church," made a national fast, and the tyrant canonized as one of "the noble army of martyrs." After enjoying the nobility of martyrdom for about two centuries, the tyrant's name has, by Act of Parliament, 1859, been quietly expunged from the prayer-book, this holy-day of "The Christian Year" abolished; and thus the "martyr," and whole reams of partisan rhetoric, rhapsodies, and poetry, are left among the other follies of the past. The church could no longer bear the reproach. "Let his memory, O Lord, be ever blessed among us," could no longer be uttered with solemn mockery at the altar.

The anniversary has been observed in a manner worthy of its hero and his admirers. By authority, the minister was compelled on that day to read the Oxford homily "against disobedience and wilful rebellion, or preach a sermon of his own composing upon the same argument"! One example of their impious utterances will suffice. It is the title of one of their sermons: "A true Parallel betwixt the Sufferings of our Saviour and our Sovereign in divers particulars." Another of these reverend blasphemers, preaching before a convocation of the church in 1701, said: "One would imagine that they were resolved to take St. Paul's expression in the most literal sense the words will bear, and crucify to themselves the Lord afresh, and, in the nearest likeness that could be, put him to an open shame. If, with respect to the dignity of the person, to have been born King of the Jews was what ought to have screened our Saviour from violence, here is also one not only born to a crown, but actually possessed of it;

. . . . . . he was not just dressed up for an hour or two in purple robes, and saluted with a 'Hail, king.' . . . . . . In respect only of their being heated to the degree of frenzy and madness, the plea in my text may seem to have some hold of them. 'Father, forgive them, for they know not what they do.' " Such were the usual "church" oracles on this Fast-day. "Among his own partisans," says Godwin, "the death of Charles was treated, and was spoken of, as a sort of *deicide.*" Clarendon gave the key-note: "The most execrable murder ever committed since that of our blessed Saviour"! The servile and degrading tenet of absolute obedience was taught; and why should it not be, since the University of Oxford declared "*submission and obedience, clear, absolute, and without exception, to be the badge and character of the Church of England.*" Hallam says that the high tory principles of the Anglican clergy, of absolute non-resistance, had nearly proved destructive of the whole constitution. "It was the tenet of their homilies, their canons, their most distinguished divines and casuists. . . . We can frame no adequate conception of the jeopardy in which our liberties stood under the Stuarts, especially in this particular period, without attending to this spirit of servility which had been so sedulously excited."

It was ever a darling project with these worthies to establish American bishoprics. The "Society for Propagating the Gospel in Foreign Parts," established in 1701, as it was administered by its clerical managers, seemed to be rather a society for propagating the hierarchy, especially in New England. Archbishop Tenison, its first president, dying in 1715, bequeathed to it £1000 towards maintaining the first bishop who should be settled in America, and Archbishop Secker left another £1000 for the same purpose.

The "Society for the Propagation of the Gospel in Foreign Parts" seemed, to intelligent men in New England, to be a mere disguise for introducing prelacy[1] — "lords spiritual" — into the land, and it was

---

[1] We find a notice of the society, at this day, by an English correspondent of *The Independent*, May 24, 1860, who says that it "enjoys the patronage of the High-Church dignitaries, and has a large income, say $600,000, annually. It has three hundred missionaries, supplemented by schoolmasters, catechists, and Scripture-readers. It is an affecting fact, that this old and strong society for the 'propagation of the gospel' propagates another gospel which is not another, and is inimical to the cross of Christ. Its gospel is prelacy and clerical authority. It insists that men shall be called master, and that rites and

Mr. Mayhew's "desire to contribute a mite towards carrying on a war against this common enemy" that produced the following discourse. By its bold inquisition into the slavish teachings veiled in "the mysterious doctrine of the saintship and martyrdom" of Charles I., and its eloquent exposition of the principles of good government and of Christian manhood in the state, maddening the corrupt, frightening the timid, rousing the apathetic, and bracing the patriot heart, this celebrated sermon may be considered as the MORNING GUN OF THE REVOLUTION, the *punctum temporis* when that period of history began.[1] Of the several English editions, one was published in Barrow's "Pillars of Priestcraft Shaken," 1752, in a copy of which Thomas Hollis, of London, wrote: "This very curious dissertation on government . . . is the first on that subject that has been produced" — in later times — "from the American world." It was the medium of Mr. Hollis's friendship to Mayhew and Harvard College; and so, incidentally, operated wonderfully in favor of the cause of liberty, civil and religious, in America. Its effect on the public mind was decided and permanent. From this moment — the dawn of independence — the spirit of the people was aroused, ever gathering force and intensity, ever narrowing and concentrating in the idea of *resistance*, more and more distinctly as the spirit of arbitrary power expressed itself in acts more and more offensive, until RESISTANCE culminated in bloodshed in 1775, and triumphed in peace in 1783. Robert Treat Paine called Dr. Mayhew "The Father of Civil and Religious Liberty in Massachusetts and America."

The preacher was then in the thirtieth year of his age. The manner

observances, taught and practised by the proper masters of ceremonies, avail everything. The essential spirit of Popery pervades the society, and its secretary, the Rev. Ernest Hawkins, was one of the earliest adherents to the new" — revived — "Oxford apostasy."

[1] The total change of political relation and ideas, of manners and prejudices, — the fading of the old feeling of deference for rank, the last tinge of feudality, — effected in the changes and passages of a century, renders it difficult now to realize the severity of the tests of temper, of courage, manliness, faithfulness, amid which these words were spoken from Dr. Mayhew's pulpit; — words so bold, so decided; allusions so direct and pointed that none could mistake, none could evade; principles so fatal to despotic polity in church or state as to wear the very garb of rebellion. Though now familiar to the public mind, and of the essence of our institutions, they then required a courage of the highest quality, the truest temper.

in which the discourse was received by the Tories and Churchmen may be inferred from the manly and characteristic " advertisement " prefixed to the first edition. It was as follows: " The author of this discourse has been credibly informed, that some persons, both formerly and lately, have wrote either at or about him — or something (he cannot well tell what) in the common newspapers, which he does not often read. He, therefore, takes this opportunity to assure the writers of *that rank*, and in *that form*, once for all, that *they* may slander him as much as they please, without his notice, and, very probably, without his knowledge. But if any person of *common sense* and *common honesty* shall condescend to animadvert, in a *different* way, upon anything which he has published, he may depend upon having all proper regard shown to him. J. M."

The authorship, and of course the nature, of this " slander," is more than hinted at by the elder President Adams, who exclaims, after speaking of Dr. Mayhew as " a whig of the first magnitude, — a clergyman equalled by very few of any denomination in piety, virtue, genius, or learning; whose works will maintain his character as long as New England shall be free, integrity esteemed, or wit, spirit, humor, reason, and knowledge admired;" yet "how was he treated from the press? Did not the *reverend tories* who were pleased to write against him, the *missionaries* of defamation as well as *bigotry and passive obedience*, in their pamphlets and newspapers, bespatter him all over with their filth? Did they not, with equal falsehood and malice, charge him with every evil thing?"

It was Dr. Mayhew who suggested to James Otis the idea of committees of correspondence, a measure of the greatest efficiency in producing concert of action between the colonies — a thing of vital importance. Dr. Mayhew died soon after this, and the letter to Otis is interesting as his last word for the liberty of his country:

" LORD'S-DAY MORNING, June 8th, 1766.

" SIR: — To a good man all time is holy enough; and none is too holy to do good, or to think upon it. Cultivating a good understanding and hearty friendship between these colonies appears to me so necessary a part of prudence and good policy, that no favorable opportunity for that purpose should be omitted. I think such an one now presents.

"Would it not be proper and decorous for our assembly to send circulars to all the rest, on the late repeal of the Stamp Act and the present favorable aspect of affairs? — letters conceived at once in terms of friendship and regard, of loyalty to the king, filial affection towards the parent country, and expressing a desire to cement and perpetuate union among ourselves, by all laudable methods. . . . . Pursuing this course, or never losing sight of it, may be of the greatest importance to the colonies, perhaps the only means of perpetuating their liberties. . . . . You have heard of the *communion of churches;* and I am to set out to-morrow morning for Rutland, to assist at an ecclesiastical council. Not expecting to return this week, while I was thinking of this in my bed, the great use and importance of a *communion of colonies* appeared to me in a strong light; which led me immediately to set down these hints to transmit to you. Not knowing but the General Court may be prorogued or *dissolved* before my return, or my having an opportunity to speak with you, I now give them, that you may make such use of them as you think proper, or none at all."

A very comprehensive notice of Dr. Mayhew's character and writings is among the elder Adams's papers. He says: "This divine had reputation both in Europe and America, by the publication of a volume of seven sermons, in the reign of King George the Second, 1749, and by many other writings, particularly a sermon, in 1750, on the 30th of January, on the subject of passive obedience and non-resistance, in which the saintship and martyrdom of King Charles the First are considered, seasoned with wit and satire superior to any in Swift or Franklin. It was read by everybody; — celebrated by friends, and abused by enemies. During the reigns of King George the First and King George the Second, the reigns of the Stuarts, the two Jameses and the two Charleses, were in general disgrace in England. In America they had always been held in abhorrence. The persecutions and cruelties suffered by their ancestors under those reigns had been transmitted by history and tradition, and Mayhew seemed to be raised up to revive all the animosities against tyranny, in church and state, and at the same time to destroy their bigotry, fanaticism, and inconsistency. David Hume's plausible, elegant, fascinating, and fallacious apology, in which he varnished over the crimes of the Stuarts, had not then appeared. To draw the character of Mayhew would be to transcribe a dozen volumes. This transcendent genius threw all the weight of his great fame into the scale of his country in 1761, and maintained it there with zeal and ardor till his death, in 1766."

Dr. Mayhew was born, of an honorable family, at Martha's Vineyard, on the 8th of October, 1720. On the 17th of June, 1747, three years after his graduation at Harvard College with great reputation, he was ordained pastor of the West Church in Boston, of which the venerable Dr. Lowell is now pastor. The charge on the occasion came from the lips of his father, the Rev. Experience Mayhew, the distinguished missionary.to the Indians. In his sermon on the repeal of the Stamp Act, 1766, there is this passage of autobiography: "Having been initiated in youth in the doctrines of civil liberty, as they were taught by such men as Plato, Demosthenes, Cicero, and other renowned persons, among the ancients; and such as Sydney and Milton, Locke and Hoadley, among the moderns, I liked them; they seemed rational. And having learnt from the holy Scriptures that wise, brave, and virtuous men were always friends to liberty, — that God gave the Israelites a king in his anger, because they had not sense and virtue enough to like a free commonwealth, — and that where 'the Spirit of the Lord is, there is liberty,' — this made me conclude that freedom was a great blessing."

His degree of Doctor of Divinity was presented to him, by the University of Aberdeen, in 1751, the year after his sermon of January 30th.

Critical notices of his numerous publications may be found in Dr. Eliot's admirable sketch of his life and character, one of the best of Dr. Eliot's biographical delineations.

Beloved for his pastoral fidelity and generous deeds, distinguished for his genius and intellectual strength, eminent in both Englands as a scholar and divine, revered as a true lover of liberty and ardent Christian patriot, this noble man died, at Boston, July 19th, 1766, aged forty-five years, mourned by the great and the good.

The likeness of Dr. Mayhew in this volume is copied from a print in the Memoirs of Thomas Hollis, Esq., 1780. The original was a crayon, taken in Boston, probably by Smibert. Mr. Hollis paid Cypriani thirty guineas for the allegorical designs and engraving, which, being in quarto, could not be all reproduced in this smaller picture.

PREFACE.

THE ensuing Discourse is the *last of three upon the same subject,* with some little alterations and additions. It is hoped that but few will think the subject of it an improper one to be discoursed on in the pulpit, under a notion that this is *preaching politics,* instead of Christ. However, to remove all prejudices of this sort, I beg it may be remembered that " all Scripture is profitable for doctrine, for reproof, for correction, for instruction in righteousness." [a][1] Why, then, should not those parts of Scripture which relate to *civil government* be examined and explained from the desk, as well as others? Obedience to the civil magistrate is a Christian duty; and if so, why should not the nature, grounds, and extent of it be considered in a Christian assembly? Besides, if it be said that it is out of character for a Christian minister to meddle with such a subject, this censure will at last fall upon the holy apostles. They write upon it in their epistles to Chris-

[a] 2 Peter iii. 16.

[1] The author's notes are designated by *letters;* the editor's by figures, and signed — ED.

tian churches; and surely it cannot be deemed either criminal or impertinent to attempt an explanation of their doctrine.

It was the near approach of the *thirtieth of January* that turned my thoughts to this subject: on which solemnity the slavish doctrine of passive obedience and non-resistance is often warmly asserted,[1] and the *dissenters from the Established*

[1] For example: On the day of the execution of Lord William Russell, 1683, the University of Oxford declared " *submission and obedience, clear, absolute, and without exception, to be the badge and character of the Church of England.*"

The Rev. John Clerke, in a sermon at Rochester Cathedral, May 29, 1684, said: " Whosoever shall compare the trial of our blessed Saviour Jesus Christ, before Pontius Pilate's first high court of justice, with the arraignment of our late most barbarously murdered king before John Bradshaw's second, shall find them to differ no more than a faithful copy from its original, with conditions exactly parallel, and, I had almost said, alike in sufferings, alike in innocence; . . . *the Breath of our nostrils*, the Anointed of the Lord, . . . the only true Vicegerent of Jesus Christ, that supreme Bishop of our souls."

The Rev. Henry Sacheverell, D. D., preached at the cathedral in London, November 5, 1709, " the subject's obligation to *absolute and unconditional obedience* to the supreme power in *all* things lawful, and the utter illegality of resistance, upon any pretence whatsoever. The Englishman is born with an innate, sullen principle of discontent, which directly interferes with that inward quiet, that sedate serenity of mind, which is alone able to yield true peace and satisfaction, . . . and he will forsake the *true Fountain of living water*, the *Church of England*. . . . He sends his children, in their tender years, to suck in those deadly envenomed principles that are but too *commonly prated up in conventicles*, — those seminaries of *murmuring* and *nurseries of rebellion* ; . . . and actually engage their unstable minds . . . against the king's sacred person, his serene and happy government."

" It may be hoped," said the philosopher Locke, " the ages to come, redeemed from the impositions of these *Egyptian* under-task-masters, will *abhor the memory* of such servile flatterers, who, whilst it seemed to serve their turn, resolved all government into absolute tyranny, and would have all men born to, *what their mean souls fitted them for, slavery.*" Yet in New England, and in our own times, these " Egyptian " monstrosities are eulogized as "*sentiments of the highest sublimity,*" " the badge and character of the Church of England." — Oliver's *Puritan Commonwealth*, 1856, pp. 482-3. Indeed, Lord King says, " As for toleration, or any true notion of religious liberty, or any general freedom of conscience, we owe them not in the least degree to what is called the Church of England. On the contrary, we owe all these to the Independents in the time of the Commonwealth, and to Locke, their most illustrious and enlightened disciple." — ED.

Church represented not only as *schismatics* (with more of triumph than of truth, and of choler than Christianity), but also as persons of seditious, traitorous, and rebellious principles.[1] God be thanked! one may, in any part of the British dominions, speak freely — if a decent regard be paid to those in authority — both of government and religion, and even give some broad hints that he is engaged on the side of liberty, the Bible, and common sense, in opposition to tyranny, priestcraft, and nonsense, without being in danger either of the Bastile or the Inquisition, — though there will always be some interested politicians, contracted bigots, and hypocritical zealots for a party, to take offence at such freedoms. Their censure is praise ; their praise is infamy. A spirit of domination is always to be guarded against, both in church and state, even in times of the greatest security, — such as the

---

1 The author wrote to Benjamin Avery, LL. D., of Grey's Hospital, London: " I have ventured to send you a discourse which I published last winter, about the time that the Episcopal clergy here are often seized with a strange sort of frenzy, which I know not how to describe, unless it be by one or two of its most remarkable symptoms. These are, preaching passive obedience, worshipping King Charles I., and cursing the Dissenters and Puritans for murdering him. You possibly have seen persons in this melancholy condition, as you have so much concern with a *hospital*, but especially if your humanity — as is very likely — has ever led you to *Bedlam*, to relieve the pitiable objects there." Thirteen years afterward, Dr. Mayhew, referring to this passage, wrote: " Some of the Episcopal clergy here used, on the same occasion, to assert the divine, hereditary, and indefeasible right of kings, in direct, manifest opposition to the principles of the *Revolution;* almost deifying Archbishop LAUD, as well as Charles I.; calumniating Nonconformists as schismatics, fanatics, persons of republican, rebellious principles, and imitating, *as far as they were able*, the manner and style of the keenest, severest sermons ever published in England on the same occasion " — January 30th. — ED.

present is among us, at least as to the latter. Those nations who are now groaning under the iron sceptre of tyranny were once free ; so they might probably have remained, by a seasonable precaution against despotic measures. Civil tyranny is usually small in its beginning, like "the drop of a bucket," [a] till at length, like a mighty torrent, or the raging waves of the sea, it bears down all before it, and deluges whole countries and empires. Thus it is as to ecclesiastical tyranny also — the most cruel, intolerable, and impious of any. From small beginnings, "it exalts itself above all that is called God and that is worshipped." [b] People have no security against being unmercifully priest-ridden but by keeping all imperious bishops, and other clergymen who love to "lord it over God's heritage," from getting their foot into the stirrup at all.[1] Let them be once fairly mounted, and their "beasts, the laity," [c] may prance and flounce about to no purpose ; and they will at length be so jaded and hacked by these reverend jockeys, that they will not even have spirits enough to complain that their backs are galled, or, like Balaam's ass, to "rebuke the madness of the prophet." [d]

"The mystery of iniquity began to work" [e] even in the days of some of the apostles. But the kingdom of Antichrist was then, in one respect, like the kingdom of heaven, how-

a Isaiah xi. 15.   c Mr. Leslie.   e 2 Thess. ii. 7.
b 2 Thess. ii. 4.   d 2 Peter ii. 16.

1 Especially in America, toward which they did cast longing eyes. — Ed.

over different in all others; — it was " as a grain of mustard-seed." [a] This grain was sown in Italy, that fruitful field, and, though it were " the least of all seeds," it soon became a mighty tree. It has long since overspread and darkened the greatest part of Christendom, so that we may apply to it what is said of the tree which Nebuchadnezzar saw in his vision : — " The height thereof reacheth unto heaven, and the sight thereof to the end of all the earth ; and the beasts of the field have shadow under it." Tyranny brings ignorance and bru-tality along with it. It degrades men from their just rank into the class of brutes ; it damps their spirits ; it suppresses arts ; it extinguishes every spark of noble ardor and gener-osity in the breasts of those who are enslaved by it ; it makes naturally strong and great minds feeble and little, and tri-umphs over the ruins of virtue and humanity. This is true of tyranny in every shape : there can be nothing great and good where its influence reaches. For which reason it be-comes every friend to truth and human kind, every lover of God and the Christian religion, to bear a part in opposing this hateful monster. It was a desire to contribute a mite towards carrying on a war with this common enemy [1] that

a Matt. xiii. 21.

1 To Dr. George Benson he wrote: " I was, about this time, much provoked by the senseless clamors of some tory-spirited Churchmen ; this being the strange spirit which seems to prevail among the Episcopal clergy here even to this day." — ED.

produced the following Discourse; and if it serve in any measure to keep up a spirit of civil and religious liberty amongst us, my end is answered. There are virtuous and candid men in all sects; all such are to be esteemed. There are also vicious men and bigots in all sects, and all such ought to be despised.

> "To Virtue only and her friends a friend;
> The world beside may murmur or commend:
> Know, all the distant din *that* world can keep
> Rolls o'er my grotto, and but soothes my sleep." — POPE.

JONATHAN MAYHEW.

DISCOURSE I.

UNLIMITED SUBMISSION AND NON-RESISTANCE TO THE HIGHER POWERS.

LET EVERY SOUL BE SUBJECT UNTO THE HIGHER POWERS. FOR THERE IS NO POWER BUT OF GOD: THE POWERS THAT BE ARE ORDAINED OF GOD. WHOSOEVER THEREFORE RESISTETH THE POWER, RESISTETH THE ORDINANCE OF GOD: AND THEY THAT RESIST SHALL RECEIVE TO THEMSELVES DAMNATION. FOR RULERS ARE NOT A TERROR TO GOOD WORKS, BUT TO THE EVIL. WILT THOU THEN NOT BE AFRAID OF THE POWER? DO THAT WHICH IS GOOD, AND THOU SHALT HAVE PRAISE OF THE SAME; FOR HE IS THE MINISTER OF GOD TO THEE FOR GOOD. BUT IF THOU DO THAT WHICH IS EVIL, BE AFRAID; FOR HE BEARETH NOT THE SWORD IN VAIN: FOR HE IS THE MINISTER OF GOD, A REVENGER TO EXECUTE WRATH UPON HIM THAT DOETH EVIL. WHEREFORE YE MUST NEEDS BE SUBJECT, NOT ONLY FOR WRATH, BUT ALSO FOR CONSCIENCE' SAKE. FOR, FOR THIS CAUSE PAY YOU TRIBUTE ALSO: FOR THEY ARE GOD'S MINISTERS, ATTENDING CONTINUALLY UPON THIS VERY THING. RENDER THEREFORE TO ALL THEIR DUES: TRIBUTE TO WHOM TRIBUTE IS DUE; CUSTOM TO WHOM CUSTOM; FEAR TO WHOM FEAR; HONOR TO WHOM HONOR. — Romans xiii. 1—8.

IT is evident that the affairs of civil government may properly fall under a moral and religious consideration, at least so far forth as it relates to the general nature and end of magistracy, and to the grounds and extent of that submission which persons of a private character ought to yield to those who are vested with authority. This must be allowed by all who acknowledge the divine original of Christianity. For, although there be a sense, and a very plain and important sense, in which Christ's kingdom is not of this world,[a] his inspired apostles have, nevertheless, laid down some general principles concerning the office

a John xviii. 36.

of civil rulers, and the duty of subjects, together with the reason and obligation of that duty. And from hence it follows, that it is proper for all who acknowledge the authority of Jesus Christ, and the inspiration of his apostles, to endeavor to understand what is in fact the doctrine which they have delivered concerning this matter. It is the duty of Christian magistrates to inform themselves what it is which their religion teaches concerning the nature and design of their office. And it is equally the duty of all Christian people to inform themselves what it is which their religion teaches concerning that subjection which they owe to the higher powers. It is for these reasons that I have attempted to examine into the Scripture account of this matter, in order to lay it before you with the same freedom which I constantly use with relation to other doctrines and precepts of Christianity; not doubting but you will judge upon everything offered to your consideration with the same spirit of freedom and liberty with which it is spoken.

The passage read is the most full and express of any in the New Testament relating to rulers and subjects; and therefore I thought it proper to ground upon it what I had to propose to you with reference to the authority of the civil magistrate, and the subjection which is due to him. But, before I enter upon an explanation of the several parts of this passage, it will be proper to observe one thing, which may serve as a key to the whole of it.

It is to be observed, then, that there were some persons amongst the Christians of the apostolic age, and particularly those at Rome, to whom St. Paul is here writing, who seditiously disclaimed all subjection to civil authority; refusing to pay taxes, and the duties laid upon their traffic and merchandise; and who scrupled not to speak of their rulers without any due regard to their office and character.

Some of these turbulent Christians were converts from Judaism, and others from Paganism. The Jews in general had, long before this time, taken up a strange conceit, that, being the peculiar and elect people of God, they were therefore exempted from the jurisdiction of any heathen princes or governors. Upon this ground it was that some of them, during the public ministry of our blessed Saviour, came to him with that question, "Is it lawful to give tribute unto Cæsar, or not?"[a] And this notion many of them retained after they were proselyted to the Christian faith. As to the Gentile converts, some of them grossly mistook the nature of that liberty which the gospel promised, and thought that by virtue of their subjection to Christ, the only king and head of his church, they were wholly freed from subjection to any other prince; as though Christ's kingdom had been of this world in such a sense as to interfere with the civil powers of the earth, and to deliver their subjects from that allegiance and duty which they before owed to them. Of these visionary Christians in general, who disowned subjection to the civil powers in being where they respectively lived, there is mention made in several places in the New Testament. The apostle Peter, in particular, characterizes them in this manner: them that "despise government, presumptuous are they; self-willed; they are not afraid to speak evil of dignities."[b] Now, it is with reference to these doting Christians that the apostle speaks in the passage before us. And I shall now give you the sense of it in a paraphrase upon each verse in its order; desiring you to keep in mind the character of the persons for whom it is designed, that so, as I go along, you may see how just and natural this address is, and how well suited to the circumstances of those against whom it is levelled.

a Matt. xxii. 17.   b 2 Pet. ii. 10.

The apostle begins thus: "Let every soul^a be subject
unto the higher powers;^b for there is no power^c but of
God; the powers that be^d are ordained of God;^e"^f *q. d.*,
" Whereas some professed Christians vainly imagine that
they are wholly excused from all manner of duty and subjection to civil authority, refusing to honor their rulers
and to pay taxes; which opinion is not only unreasonable
in itself, but also tends to fix a lasting reproach upon the
Christian name and profession — I now, as an apostle and
ambassador of Christ, exhort every one of you, be he who
he will, to pay all dutiful submission to those who are
vested with any civil office; for there is, properly speaking, no authority but what is derived from God, as it is
only by his permission and providence that any possess
it. Yea, I may add, that all civil magistrates, as such,
although they may be heathens, are appointed and ordained
of God. For it is certainly God's will that so useful an

a " Every soul." This is a Hebraism, which signifies *every man;* so that the
apostle does not exempt the clergy, such as were endowed with the gift of
prophecy or any other miraculous powers which subsisted in the church at that
day. And by his using the Hebrew idiom, it seems that he had the Jewish converts principally in his eye.

b " The higher powers;" more literally, the *over-ruling powers;* which term
extends to all civil rulers in common.

c By " power" the apostle intends, not lawless strength and brutal force, without regulation and proper direction, but just authority; for so the word here
used properly signifies. There may be power where there is no authority. No
man has any authority to do what is wrong and injurious, though he may have
the power to do it.

d " The powers that be." Those persons who are in fact vested with authority;
those who are in possession. And who those are, the apostle leaves Christians to
determine for themselves; but whoever they are, they are to be obeyed.

e " Ordained of God." As it is not without God's providence and permission
that any are clothed with authority; and as it is agreeable to the positive will
and purpose of God that there should be some persons vested with authority for
the good of society; — not that any rulers have their commission from God, the
supreme Lord of the universe. If any assert that kings, or any other rulers, are
ordained of God in the latter sense, it is incumbent upon them to show the commission which they speak of under the broad seal of heaven. And when they do
this, they will, no doubt, be believed.

f Rom. xiii. 1.

institution as that of magistracy should take place in the world for the good of civil society." The apostle proceeds: "Whosoever, therefore, resisteth the power, resisteth the ordinance of God; and they that resist shall receive to themselves damnation."[a] *q. d.*, "Think not, therefore, that ye are guiltless of any crime or sin against God, when ye factiously disobey and resist the civil authority. For magistracy and government being, as I have said, the ordinance and appointment of God, it follows, that to resist magistrates in the execution of their offices, is really to resist the will and ordinance of God himself; and they who thus resist will accordingly be punished by God for this sin, in common with others." The apostle goes on: "For rulers are not a terror to good works, but to the evil.[b] Wilt thou, then, not be afraid of the power? Do that which is good, and thou shalt have praise of the same; for he is the minister of God to thee for good." [c] *q. d.*, "That you may see the truth and justness of what I assert (viz., that magistracy is the ordinance of God, and that you sin against him in opposing it), consider that even pagan rulers are not, by the nature and design of their office, enemies and a terror to the good and virtuous actions of men, but only to the injurious and mischievous to society. Will ye not, then, reverence and honor magistracy, when ye see the good end and intention of it? How can ye be so unreasonable? Only mind to do your duty as members of society, and this will gain you the

[a] Rom. xiii. 2.

[b] "For rulers are not a terror to good works, but to the evil." It cannot be supposed that the apostle designs here, or in any of the succeeding verses, to give the true character of Nero, or any other civil powers then in being, as if they were in fact such persons as he describes, a terror to evil works only, and not to the good. For such a character did not belong to them; and the apostle was no sycophant, or parasite of power, whatever some of his pretended successors have been. He only tells what rulers would be, provided they acted up to their character and office.

[c] Rom. xiii. 3, 4.

applause and favor of all good rulers. For, while you do
thus, they are by their office, as ministers of God, obliged
to encourage and protect you : it is for this very purpose
that they are clothed with power." The apostle subjoins :
" But if thou do that which is evil, be afraid ; for he beareth not the sword in vain. For he is the minister of God,
a revenger, to execute wrath upon him that doeth evil.^a"^b
q. d., " But, upon the other hand, if ye refuse to do your
duty as members of society ; if ye refuse to bear your
part in the support of government; if ye are disorderly,
and do things which merit civil chastisement, — then,
indeed, ye have reason to be afraid. For it is not in
vain that rulers are vested with the power of inflicting
punishment. They are, by their office, not only the ministers of God for good to those that do well, but also his
ministers to revenge, to discountenance, and punish those
that are unruly, and injurious to their neighbors." The
apostle proceeds : " Wherefore ye must needs be subject
not only for wrath, but also for conscience' sake." ^c *q. d.,*
" Since, therefore, magistracy is the ordinance of God, and
since rulers are by their office benefactors to society, by
discouraging what is bad and encouraging what is good,

---

a It is manifest that when the apostle speaks of it as the office of civil rulers to
encourage what is good and to punish what is evil, he speaks only of civil good
and evil. They are to consult the good of society, as such; not to dictate in religious concerns; not to make laws for the government of men's consciences, and
to inflict civil penalties for religious crimes. It is sufficient to overthrow the
doctrine of the authority of the civil magistrate in affairs of a spiritual nature (so
far as it is built upon anything which is here said by St. Paul, or upon anything
else in the New Testament) only to observe that all the magistrates then in the
world were heathen, implacable enemies to Christianity ; so that, to give them
authority in religious matters, would have been, in effect, to give them authority
to extirpate the Christian religion, and to establish the idolatries and superstitions of paganism. And can any one reasonably suppose that the apostle had
any intention to extend the authority of rulers beyond concerns merely civil and
political, to the overthrowing of that religion which he himself was so zealous in
propagating? But it is natural for those whose religion cannot be supported
upon the footing of reason and argument, to have recourse to power and force,
which will serve a bad cause as well as a good one, and, indeed, much better.

b Rom. xiii. 4.   c Rom. xiii. 5.

and so preserving peace and order amongst men, it is evident that ye ought to pay a willing subjection to them; not to obey merely for fear of exposing yourselves to their wrath and displeasure, but also in point of reason, duty, and conscience. Ye are under an indispensable obligation, as Christians, to honor their office, and to submit to them in the execution of it." The apostle goes on : " For, for this cause pay you tribute also; for they are God's ministers, attending continually upon this very thing." [a] *q. d.,* " And here is a plain reason also why ye should pay tribute to them, — for they are God's ministers, exalted above the common level of mankind, — not that they may indulge themselves in softness and luxury, and be entitled to the servile homage of their fellow-men, but that they may execute an office no less laborious than honorable, and attend continually upon the public welfare. This being their business and duty, it is but reasonable that they should be requited for their care and diligence in performing it; and enabled, by taxes levied upon the subject, effectually to prosecute the great end of their institution, the good of society." The apostle sums all up in the following words: " Render, therefore, to all their dues; tribute[b] to whom tribute is due; custom[b] to whom custom; fear to whom fear; honor to whom honor." [c] *q. d.,* " Let it not therefore be said of any of you hereafter, that you contemn government, to the reproach of yourselves and of the Christian religion. Neither your being Jews by nation, nor your becoming the subjects of Christ's kingdom, gives you any dispensation for making disturbances

a Rom. xiii. 6.

b Grotius observes, that the Greek words here used answer to the *tributum* and *vectigal* of the Romans: the former was the money paid for the soil and poll, the latter the dues laid upon some sorts of merchandise. And what the apostle here says deserves to be seriously considered by all Christians concerned in that common practice of carrying on an illicit trade and running of goods.

c Rom. xiii. 7.

in the government under which you live. Approve yourselves, therefore, as peaceable and dutiful subjects. Be
ready to pay to your rulers all that they may, in respect of
their office, justly demand of you. Render tribute and
custom to those of your governors to whom tribute and
custom belong; and cheerfully honor and reverence all
who are vested with civil authority, according to their
deserts."

The apostle's doctrine, in the passage thus explained,
concerning the office of civil rulers, and the duty of subjects, may be summed up in the following observations,[a]
viz.:

That the end of magistracy is the good of civil society,
as such.

That civil rulers, *as such,* are the ordinance and ministers of God; it being by his permission and providence
that any bear rule, and agreeable to his will that there
should be *some persons* vested with authority in society,
for the well-being of it.

That which is here said concerning civil rulers extends
to all of them in common. It relates indifferently to monarchical, republican, and aristocratical government, and to
all other forms which truly answer the sole end of government — the happiness of society; and to all the different
degrees of authority in any particular state; to inferior
officers no less than to the supreme.

That disobedience to civil rulers in the due exercise of
their authority is not merely a political sin, but a heinous
offence against God and religion.

That the true ground and reason [b] of our obligation to be

---

a The several observations here only mentioned were handled at large in two
preceding discourses upon this subject.

b Some suppose the apostle, in this passage, enforces the duty of submission
with two arguments quite distinct from each other; one taken from this consideration, that rulers are the ordinance and the ministers of God (vs. 1, 2, 4), and

subject to the higher powers is, the usefulness of magistracy (when properly exercised) to human society, and its subserviency to the general welfare.

That obedience to civil rulers is here equally required under all forms of government which answer the sole end of all government — the good of society; and to every degree of authority, in any state, whether supreme or subordinate.   From whence it follows —

That if unlimited obedience and non-resistance be here required as a duty under any one form of government, it is also required as a duty under all other forms, and as a duty to subordinate rulers as well as to the supreme.

And, lastly, that those civil rulers to whom the apostle enjoins subjection are the persons *in possession ; the powers that be ;* those who are actually vested with authority.[a]

the other from the benefits that accrue to society from civil government (vs. 3, 4, 6). And, indeed, these may be distinct motives and arguments for submission, as they may be separately viewed and contemplated. But when we consider that rulers are not the ordinance and the ministers of God but only so far forth as they perform God's will by acting up to their office and character, and so by being benefactors to society, this makes these arguments coincide, and run up into one at last; at least so far that the former of them cannot hold good for submission where the latter fails. Put the supposition, that any man bearing the title of a magistrate should exercise his power in such a manner as to have no claim to obedience by virtue of that argument which is founded upon the usefulness of magistracy, and you equally take off the force of the other argument also, which is founded upon his being the ordinance and the minister of God; for he is no longer God's ordinance and minister than he acts up to his office and character by exercising his power for the good of society. This is, in brief, the reason why it is said above, in the singular number, *that the true ground and reason*, etc. The use and propriety of this remark may possibly be more apparent in the progress of the argument concerning resistance.

a This must be understood with this proviso, that they do not grossly abuse their power and trust, but exercise it for the good of those that are governed. Who these persons were — whether Nero, etc., or not — the apostle does not say, but leaves it to be determined by those to whom he writes. God does not interpose in a miraculous way to point out the persons who shall bear rule, and to whom subjection is due. And as to the unalienable, indefeasible right of primogeniture, the Scriptures are entirely silent, or, rather, plainly contradict it, — Saul being the first king among the Israelites, and appointed to the royal dignity during his own father's lifetime; and he was succeeded, or rather superseded, by " David, the last born among many brethren." Now, if God has not invariably

There is one very important and interesting point which remains to be inquired into, namely, the *extent* of that subjection to the higher powers which is here enjoined as a duty upon all Christians. Some have thought it warrantable and glorious to disobey the civil powers in certain circumstances, and in cases of very great and general oppression, when humble remonstrances fail of having any effect; and, when the public welfare cannot be otherwise provided for and secured, to rise unanimously even against the sovereign himself, in order to redress their grievances; to vindicate their natural and legal rights; to break the yoke of tyranny, and free themselves and posterity from inglorious servitude and ruin.[1] It is upon this principle that many royal oppressors have been driven from their thrones into banishment, and many slain by the hands of their subjects. It was upon this principle that Tarquin

determined this matter, it must, of course, be determined by men. And if it be determined by men, it must be determined either in the way of force or of compact; and which of these is the most equitable can be no question.

[1] Milton was of the same mind. " It is not," said he, " neither ought to be, the glory of a Protestant state never to have put their king to death; it is the glory of a Protestant king never to have deserved death. And if the Parliament and military council do what they do without precedent, if it appear their duty, it argues the more wisdom, virtue, and magnanimity, that they know themselves able to be a precedent to others, who perhaps in future ages, if they prove not too degenerate, will look up with honor, and aspire towards these exemplary and matchless deeds of their ancestors, as to the highest top of their civil glory and emulation; which heretofore, in the pursuance of fame and foreign dominion, spent itself vaingloriously abroad; but henceforth may learn a better fortitude, to dare execute highest justice on them that shall by force of arms endeavor the oppressing and bereaving of religion and their liberty at home. That no unbridled potentate or tyrant, but to his sorrow, for the future may presume such high and irrepressible license over mankind, to havoc and turn upside down whole kingdoms of men, as though they were no more in respect of his perverse will than a nation of pismires."— *The Tenure of Kings and Magistrates.* — ED.

was expelled from Rome, and Julius Cæsar, the conqueror of the world and the tyrant of his country, cut off in the senate-house.   It was upon this principle that King Charles I. was beheaded before his own banqueting-house.[1] It was upon this principle that King James II. was made to fly that country which he aimed at enslaving ; and upon this principle was that revolution brought about which has been so fruitful of happy consequences to Great Britain.   But, in opposition to this principle, it has often been asserted [2] that the Scripture in general, and the passage under consideration in particular, makes all resistance to princes a crime, in any case whatever.   If they turn tyrants, and become the common oppressors of those whose welfare they ought to regard with a paternal affection, we must not pretend to right ourselves, unless it be by prayers, and tears, and humble entreaties.   And if these methods fail of procuring redress, we must not have recourse to any other, but all suffer ourselves to be robbed and butchered at the pleasure of the "Lord's anointed," lest we should incur the sin of rebellion and the punishment of damnation ! — for he has God's authority and commission to bear him out in the worst of crimes so far that he may not be withstood or controlled.   Now, whether we are obliged to yield such an absolute submission to our prince, or whether disobedience and resistance may not be justifiable in some cases, notwithstanding anything in the passage before us, is an inquiry in which we all are concerned ; and this is the inquiry which is the main design of the present discourse.

[1] Charles employed Inigo Jones to prepare the plans for a magnificent Whitehall, — now Whitehall Chapel, — from the centre window of which the unhappy tyrant passed to his scaffold. — ED.

[2] By Filmer, Brady, Mackenzie, Sherlock, and generally by the Church of England writers, with few exceptions. — ED.

Now, there does not seem to be any necessity of supposing that an absolute, unlimited obedience, whether active or passive, is here enjoined, merely for this reason — that the precept is delivered in absolute terms, without any exception or limitation expressly mentioned. We are enjoined to be "subject to the higher powers;"[a] and to be "subject for conscience' sake."[b] And because these expressions are absolute and unlimited, or, more properly, general, some have inferred that the subjection required in them must be absolute and unlimited also, — at least so far forth as to make passive obedience and non-resistance a duty in all cases whatever, if not active obedience likewise; — though, by the way, there is here no distinction made betwixt active and passive obedience; and if either of them be required in an unlimited sense, the other must be required in the same sense also, by virtue of the present argument, because the expressions are equally absolute with respect to both. But that unlimited obedience of any sort cannot be argued merely from the indefinite expressions in which obedience is enjoined, appears from hence, that expressions of the same nature frequently occur in Scripture, upon which it is confessed on all hands that no such absolute and unlimited sense ought to be put. For example: " Love not the world, neither the things that are in the world,"[c] "Lay not up for yourselves treasures upon earth,"[d] "Take therefore no thought for the morrow,"[e] are precepts expressed in at least equally absolute and unlimited terms; but it is generally allowed that they are to be understood with certain restrictions and limitations; some degree of love to the world and the things of it being allowable. Nor, indeed, do the *Right Reverend Fathers in God*, and other *dignified clergymen* of the

a Rom. xiii. 1.   c 1 John ii. 15.   e Matt. vi. 34.
b Rom. xiii. 5.   d Matt. vi. 19.

Established Church, seem to be altogether averse to admitting of restrictions in the latter case, how warm soever any of them may be against restrictions and limitations in the case of submission to authority, whether civil or ecclesiastical. It is worth remarking, also, that patience and submission under private injuries are enjoined in much more peremptory and absolute terms than any that are used with regard to submission to the injustice and oppression of civil rulers. Thus: "I say unto you, that ye resist not evil; but whosoever shall smite thee on the right cheek, turn to him the other also. And if any man will sue thee at the law, and take away thy coat, let him have thy cloak also. And whosoever shall compel thee to go a mile with him, go with him twain."[a] Any man may be defied to produce such strong expressions in favor of a passive and tame submission to unjust, tyrannical rulers, as are here used to enforce submission to private injuries. But how few are there that understand those expressions literally! And the reason why they do not, is because (with submission to the Quakers) common sense shows that they were not intended to be so understood.

But, to instance in some Scripture precepts which are more directly to the point in hand: Children are commanded to obey their parents, and servants their masters, in as absolute and unlimited terms as subjects are here commanded to obey their civil rulers. Thus this same apostle: "Children, obey your parents in the Lord; for this is right. Honor thy father and mother, which is the first commandment with promise. Servants, be obedient to them that are your masters according to the flesh, with fear and trembling, with singleness of your heart, as unto Christ."[b] Thus, also, wives are commanded to be obedient

a Matt. v. 39, 40, 41.   b Eph. vi. 1, etc.

to their husbands : " Wives, submit yourselves unto your own husbands, as unto the Lord ; for the husband is head of the wife, even as Christ is the head of the church. Therefore, as the church is subject unto Christ, so let the wives be to their own husbands in everything." ᵃ In all these cases, submission is required in terms at least as absolute and universal as are ever used with respect to rulers and subjects. But who supposes that the apostle ever intended to teach that children, servants, and wives, should, in all cases whatever, obey their parents, masters, and husbands respectively, never making any opposition to their will, even although they should require them to break the commandments of God, or should causelessly make an attempt upon their lives? No one puts such a sense upon these expressions, however absolute and unlimited. Why, then, should it be supposed that the apostle designed to teach universal obedience, whether active or passive, to the higher powers, merely because his precepts are delivered in absolute and unlimited terms? And if this be a good argument in one case, why is it not in others also? If it be said that resistance and disobedience to the higher powers is here said positively to be a sin, so also is the disobedience of children to parents, servants to masters, and wives to husbands, in other places of Scripture. But the question still remains, whether, in all these cases, there be not some exceptions. In the three latter it is allowed there are ; and from hence it follows, that barely the use of absolute expressions is no proof that obedience to civil rulers is in all cases a duty, or resistance in all cases a sin. I should not have thought it worth while to take any notice at all of this argument, had it not been much insisted upon by some of the advocates for passive obedience and non-resistance ; for it is in itself perfectly trifling,

a Eph. v. 22—24.

and rendered considerable only by the stress that has been laid upon it for want of better.

There is, indeed, one passage in the New Testament where it may seem, at first view, that an unlimited submission to civil rulers is enjoined: " Submit yourselves to every ordinance of man for the Lord's sake." [a] To *every ordinance of man.* However, this expression is no stronger than that before taken notice of with relation to the duty of wives: " So let the wives be subject to their own husbands *in everything.*" But the true solution of this difficulty (if it be one) is this : By " every ordinance of man" [b] is not meant every command of the civil magistrate without exception, but every order of magistrates appointed by man, whether superior or inferior ; for so the apostle explains himself in the very next words : " Whether it be to the king as supreme, or to governors, as unto them that are sent," etc.   But although the apostle had not subjoined any such explanation, the reason of the thing itself would have obliged us to limit the expression " every ordinance of man" to such human ordinances and commands as are not inconsistent with the ordinances and commands of God, the Supreme Lawgiver, or with any other higher and antecedent obligations.[1]

It is to be observed, in the next place, that as the duty

a 1 Peter ii. 13.

b Literally, every human institution, or appointment. By which manner of expression the apostle plainly intimates that rulers derive their authority immediately, not from God, but from men.

1 Milton considers this text, in his " Defence of the People of England," much at length. He says : " It being very certain that the doctrine of the gospel is neither contrary to reason nor the law of nations, that man is truly subject to the higher powers who obeys the laws and the magistrates so far as they govern according to law. So that St. Paul does not only command the people, but princes themselves, to be in subjection; who are not above the laws, but bound by them ; . . . but whatever power enables a man, or whatsoever magistrate takes upon him, to act contrary to

of universal obedience and non-resistance to the higher powers cannot be argued from the absolute, unlimited expressions which the apostle here uses, so neither can it be argued from the scope and drift of his reasoning, considered with relation to the persons he was here opposing. As was observed above, there were some professed Christians in the apostolic age who disclaimed all magistracy and civil authority in general, despising government, and speaking evil of dignities; some, under a notion that Jews ought not to be under the jurisdiction of Gentile rulers, and others that they were set free from the temporal powers by Christ. Now, it is with persons of this licentious opinion and character that the apostle is concerned; and all that was directly to his point was to show that they were bound to submit to magistracy in general. This is a circumstance very material to be taken notice of, in order to ascertain the sense of the apostle; for, this being considered, it is sufficient to account for all that he says concerning the duty of subjection and the sin of resistance to the higher powers, without having recourse to the doctrine of unlimited submission and passive obedience in all cases whatever. Were it known that those in opposition to whom the apostle wrote allowed of civil authority in general, and only asserted that there were some cases in which obedience and non-resistance were not a duty, there would then indeed be reason for interpreting this passage as containing the doctrine of unlimited obedience and non-resistance, as it must, in this case, be supposed to have

what St. Paul makes the duty of those that are in authority, neither is that power nor that magistrate ordained of God. And consequently to such a magistrate no subjection is commanded, nor is any due, nor are the people forbidden to resist such authority; for in so doing they do not resist the power nor the magistracy, as they are here excellently well described, but they resist a robber, a tyrant, an enemy."— ED.

been levelled against such as denied that doctrine. But since it is certain that there were persons who vainly imagined that civil government in general was not to be regarded by them, it is most reasonable to suppose that the apostle designed his discourse only against them ; and, agreeably to this supposition, we find that he argues the usefulness of civil magistracy in general, its agreeableness to the will and purpose of God, who is over all, and so deduces from hence the obligation of submission to it. But it will not follow that because civil government is, in general, a good institution, and necessary to the peace and happiness of human society, therefore there are no supposable cases in which resistance to it can be innocent. So that the duty of unlimited obedience, whether active or passive, can be argued neither from the manner of expression here used, nor from the general scope and design of the passage.

And if we attend to the nature of the argument with which the apostle here enforces the duty of submission to the higher powers, we shall find it to be such a one as concludes not in favor of submission to all who bear the title of rulers in common, but only to those who actually perform the duty of rulers by exercising a reasonable and just authority for the good of human society. This is a point which it will be proper to enlarge upon, because the question before us turns very much upon the truth or falsehood of this position. It is obvious, then, in general, that the civil rulers whom the apostle here speaks of, and obedience to whom he presses upon Christians as a duty, are good rulers,[a] such as are, in the exercise of their office

[a] By " good rulers" are not intended such as are good in a moral or religious, but only in a political, sense; those who perform their duty so far as their office extends, and so far as civil society, as such, is concerned in their actions.[1]

[1] Dr. Mayhew may have had in mind the apologies often made for

and power, benefactors to society. Such they are described
to be throughout this passage. Thus, it is said that they
are not a terror to good works, but to the evil; that they
are God's ministers for good; revengers to execute wrath
upon him that doeth evil; and that they attend continually upon this very thing. St. Peter gives the same
account of rulers: They are "for a praise to them that
do well, and the punishment of evil doers."[a] It is manifest
that this character and description of rulers agrees only to
such as are rulers in fact, as well as in name; to such as govern well, and act agreeably to their office. And the apostle's
argument for submission to rulers is wholly built and
grounded upon a presumption that they do in fact answer
this character, and is of no force at all upon supposition
of the contrary. If rulers are a terror to good works, and
not to the evil; if they are not ministers for good to
society, but for evil and distress, by violence and oppression; if they execute wrath upon sober, peaceable persons,
who do their duty as members of society, and suffer rich

---

[a] See notes, pp. 57, 58.

Charles the First and other tyrants — their good lives as private men; but
certainly he did not mean that it is a thing of indifference that bad men
should be rulers. In his Election Sermon of 1754, he says that morals
and religion "ought doubtless to be encouraged by the civil magistrate
by his own pious life and good example." What is the security, or probability, that the weak or the bad, in private life, will be able and good
men in public life, especially if it be, as Hume says, "that men are generally more honest in a private than in a public capacity, and will go greater
lengths to serve a party than when their own private interest is alone concerned"? "Nations rise and fall by individuals, not numbers, as I think
all history proveth," said Hollis. It was the *virtue* of Washington only
that saved the republic, when, in 1782, the suffering army suggested to
their leader the "title of king." Had his been a "*low* ambition," what
then would have been our history? The political motto, "Principles, not
men," is a dangerous doctrine. The monument to Pitt, in the Guildhall,
London, was raised to show "that the means by which Providence raises
a nation to greatness are the *virtues* infused into great men."— ED.

and honorable knaves to escape with impunity; if, instead
of attending continually upon the good work of advancing the public welfare, they attend continually upon the
gratification of their own lust and pride and ambition, to
the destruction of the public welfare; — if this be the case,
it is plain that the apostle's argument for submission does
not reach them; they are not the same, but different
persons from those whom he characterizes, and who must
be obeyed, according to his reasoning.　Let me illustrate
the apostle's argument by the following similitude (it is
no matter how far it is from anything which has, in fact,
happened in the world): Suppose, then, it was allowed,
in general, that the clergy[1] were a useful order of men;
that they ought to be "esteemed very highly in love for
their works' sake,[a] and to be decently supported by those
they serve, "the laborer being worthy of his reward."[b]
Suppose, further, that a number of reverend and right
reverend drones, who worked not; who preached, perhaps, but once a year, and then not the gospel of Jesus
Christ, but the divine right of tithes, the dignity of their
office as ambassadors of Christ, the equity of sinecures
and a plurality of benefices, the excellency of the devotions in that prayer-book which some of them hired chaplains to use for them, or some favorite point of church-
tyranny and anti-Christian usurpation; — suppose such
men as these, spending their lives in effeminacy, luxury, and
idleness, — or, when they were not idle, doing that which is
worse than idleness; — suppose such men should, merely
by the merit of ordination and consecration, and a peculiar,

---

[a] 1 Thess. v. 13.　　　　　　[b] 1 Tim. v. 18.

[1] The Church of England does not recognize as "clergy" any but its
own ministry, unless that of the papal church; but at one time it was less
exclusive, and recognized Presbyterian ordination. — Hopkins's *Puritans
and Queen Elizabeth*, vol. ii. ch. 4. — ED.

odd habit, claim great respect and reverence from those whom they civilly called the beasts of the laity,[a] and demand thousands per annum for that service which they never performed, and for which, if they had performed it, this would be more than a *quantum meruit;* — suppose this should be the case (it is only by way of simile, and surely it will give no offence), would not everybody be astonished at such insolence, injustice, and impiety?[1] And ought not such men to be told plainly that they could not reasonably expect the esteem and reward due to the ministers of the gospel unless they did the duties of their office? Should they not be told that their title and habit claimed no regard, reverence, or pay, separate from the care and work and various duties of their function? — and that, while they neglected the latter, the former served only to render them the more ridiculous and contemptible?[2] The application of this similitude to the case in hand is very easy. If those who bear the title of civil rulers do not perform the duty of civil rulers, but act directly counter to the sole end and design of their office; if they injure and oppress their subjects, instead of defending their rights and doing them good, they have not the least pretence to be honored, obeyed, and rewarded, according

---

[a] Mr. Leslie.

[1] Charles Leslie, whose works were republished at Oxford, in 1832, in seven volumes, lived from 1650 to 1722. He was an eminent controversialist. His expression "*their beasts, the laity,*" twice quoted by Dr. Mayhew, indicates his principles. He resigned his preferments on the flight of James II., and was ever a firm adherent to the Stuarts. He contended for absolute power, despotism — denying all right in the people either to confer or coerce government. — ED.

[2] This was the American view of the Church of England, and they loathed the idea of its establishment in America, — a scheme assiduously prosecuted under pretence of " propagating the gospel in foreign parts," etc. — ED.

to the apostle's argument. For his reasoning, in order to show the duty of subjection to the higher powers, is, as was before observed, built wholly upon the supposition that they do, in fact, perform the duty of rulers.

If it be said that the apostle here uses another argument for submission to the higher powers besides that which is taken from the usefulness of their office to civil society when properly discharged and executed, namely, that their power is from God, that they are ordained of God, and that they are God's ministers; and if it be said that this argument for submission to them will hold good, although they do not exercise their power for the benefit, but for the ruin and destruction of human society, — this objection was obviated, in part, before.[a] Rulers have no authority from God to do mischief. They are not God's ordinance, or God's ministers, in any other sense than as it is by his permission and providence that they are exalted to bear rule; and as magistracy duly exercised, and authority rightly applied, in the enacting and executing good laws, — laws attempered and accommodated to the common welfare of the subjects, — must be supposed to be agreeable to the will of the beneficent Author and supreme Lord of the universe, whose "kingdom ruleth over all,"[b] and whose "tender mercies are over all his works."[c]   It is blasphemy to call tyrants and oppressors God's ministers. They are more properly "the messengers of Satan to buffet us."[d]   No rulers are properly God's ministers but such as are "just, ruling in the fear of God."[e]   When once magistrates act contrary to their office, and the end of their institution, — when they rob and ruin the public, instead of being guardians of its peace and welfare, — they

a See notes, pp. 60, 61.   c Ps. cxlv. 19.   e 2 Sam. xxiii. 3.
b Ps. ciii. 19.   d 2 Cor. xii. 7.

immediately cease to be the ordinance and ministers of God, and no more deserve that glorious character than common pirates and highwaymen.[1] So that, whenever that argument for submission fails which is grounded upon the usefulness of magistracy to civil society, — as it always does when magistrates do hurt to society instead of good, — the other argument, which is taken from their being the ordinance of God, must necessarily fail also; no person of a civil character being God's minister, in the sense of the apostle, any further than he performs God's will by exercising a just and reasonable authority, and ruling for the good of the subject.

This in general. Let us now trace the apostle's reasoning in favor of submission to the higher powers a little more particularly and exactly; for by this it will appear, on one hand, how good and conclusive it is for submission to those rulers who exercise their power in a proper manner, and, on the other, how weak and trifling and inconnected it is if it be supposed to be meant by the apostle to show the obligation and duty of obedience to tyrannical, oppressive rulers, in common with others of a different character.

The apostle enters upon his subject thus: " Let every soul be subject unto the higher powers; for there is no power but of God : the powers that be are ordained of

[1] Parallel with this is Milton's distinction, where he says: " If I inveigh against tyrants, what is this to kings ? whom I am far from associating with tyrants. As much as an honest man differs from a rogue, so much I contend that a king differs from a tyrant. Whence it is clear that a tyrant is so far from being a king, that he is always in direct opposition to a king."—*The Second Defence.* James I., in 1603 and 1609, in his speeches to parliament, said: " A king ceases to be a king, and degenerates into a tyrant, as soon as he leaves off to rule according to his laws." And Locke, of " Civil Government," says: " *Wheresoever the authority ceases, the king ceases too, and becomes like other men who have no authority.*"— ED.

God." [a] Here he urges the duty of obedience from this topic of argument : that civil rulers, as they are supposed to fulfil the pleasure of God, are the ordinance of God. But how is this an argument for obedience to such rulers as do not perform the pleasure of God by doing good, but the pleasure of the devil by doing evil ; and such as are not, therefore, God's ministers, but the devil's ? " Whosoever, therefore, resisteth the power, resisteth the ordinance of God ; and they that resist shall receive to themselves damnation." [b] Here the apostle argues that those who resist a reasonable and just authority, which is agreeable to the will of God, do really resist the will of God himself, and will, therefore, be punished by him. But how does this prove that those who resist a lawless, unreasonable power, which is contrary to the will of God,[1] do therein resist the will and ordinance of God ? Is resisting those who resist God's will the same thing with resisting God ? Or shall those who do so " receive to themselves damnation ? For rulers are not a terror to good works, but to the evil. Wilt thou then not be afraid of the power? Do that which is good, and thou shalt have praise of the same. For he is the minister of God to thee for good." [c] Here the apostle argues, more explicitly than he had before done, for revering and submitting to magistracy, from this consideration, that such as really performed the

---

a Rom. xiii. 1. b Rom. xiii. 2. c Rom. xiii. 3, 4.

1 This lesson was well conned : hear one of Dr. Mayhew's disciples, John Adams, twenty-five years afterward, in 1775, in defence of resistance to the despotism of the British Parliament : " We are not exciting rebellion. Opposition, nay, open, avowed resistance by arms against usurpation and lawless violence, is not rebellion by the law of God or the land. Resistance to lawful authority makes rebellion. Hampden, Russell, Sydney, Somers, Holt, Tillotson, Burnet, Hoadley, etc., were no tyrants nor rebels, although some of them were in arms, and the others undoubtedly excited resistance against the tories."— ED.

duty of magistrates would be enemies only to the evil actions of men, and would befriend and encourage the good, and so be a common blessing to society. But how is this an argument that we must honor and submit to such magistrates as are not enemies to the evil actions of men, but to the good, and such as are not a common blessing, but a common curse to society? "But if thou do that which is evil, be afraid: for he is the minister of God, a revenger, to execute wrath upon him that doth evil." [a] Here the apostle argues, from the nature and end of magistracy, that such as did evil, and such only, had reason to be afraid of the higher powers; it being part of their office to punish evil-doers, no less than to defend and encourage such as do well. But if magistrates are unrighteous, — if they are respecters of persons, — if they are partial in their administration of justice, — then those who do well have as much reason to be afraid as those that do evil: there can be no safety for the good, nor any peculiar ground of terror to the unruly and injurious; so that, in this case, the main end of civil government will be frustrated. And what reason is there for submitting to that government which does by no means answer the design of government? "Wherefore ye must needs be subject not only for wrath, but also for conscience' sake." [b] Here the apostle argues the duty of a cheerful and conscientious submission to civil government from the nature and end of magistracy, as he had before laid it down; i. e., as the design of it was to punish evil-doers, and to support and encourage such as do well; and as it must, if so exercised, be agreeable to the will of God. But how does what he here says prove the duty of a cheerful and conscientious subjection to those who forfeit the character of rulers? — to

[a] Rom. xiii. 4. [b] Rom. xiii. 5.

those who encourage the bad and discourage the good? The argument here used no more proves it to be a sin to resist such rulers than it does to resist the devil, that he may flee from us.[a] For one is as truly the minister of God as the other. "For, for this cause pay you tribute also; for they are God's ministers, attending continually upon this very thing." [b] Here the apostle argues the duty of paying taxes from this consideration, that those who perform the duty of rulers are continually attending upon the public welfare. But how does this argument conclude for paying taxes to such princes as are continually endeavoring to ruin the public; and especially when such payment would facilitate and promote this wicked design? "Render therefore to all their dues; tribute to whom tribute is due; custom to whom custom; fear to whom fear; honor to whom honor."[c] Here the apostle sums up what he has been saying concerning the duty of subjects to rulers; and his argument stands thus: "Since magistrates who execute their office well are common benefactors to society, and may in that respect properly be called the ministers and ordinance of God, and since they are constantly employed in the service of the public, it becomes you to pay them tribute and custom, and to reverence, honor, and submit to them in the execution of their respective offices." This is apparently good reasoning. But does this argument conclude for the duty of paying tribute, custom, reverence, honor, and obedience to such persons as, although they bear the title of rulers, use all their power to hurt and injure the public? — such as are not God's ministers, but Satan's? such as do not take care of and attend upon the public interest, but their own, to the ruin of the public? — that is, in short, to such as have no just claim at all to

<hr>

[a] James iv. 7.   [b] Rom. xiii. 6.   [c] Rom. xiii. 7.

tribute, custom, reverence, honor, and obedience? It is to
be hoped that those who have any regard to the apostle's
character as an inspired writer, or even as a man of common understanding, will not represent him as reasoning in
such a loose, incoherent manner, and drawing conclusions
which have not the least relation to his premises. For
what can be more absurd than an argument thus framed:
"Rulers are, by their office, bound to consult the public
welfare and the good of society; therefore, you are bound
to pay them tribute, to honor, and to submit to them, even
when they destroy the public welfare, and are a common
pest to society by acting in direct contradiction to the
nature and end of their office"?

Thus, upon a careful review of the apostle's reasoning
in this passage, it appears that his arguments to enforce
submission are of such a nature as to conclude only in
favor of submission to such rulers as he himself describes;
i. e., such as rule for the good of society, which is the only
end of their institution. Common tyrants and public
oppressors are not entitled to obedience from their subjects by virtue of anything here laid down by the inspired
apostle.

I now add, further, that the apostle's argument is so
far from proving it to be the duty of people to obey and
submit to such rulers as act in contradiction to the public
good,[a] and so to the design of their office, that it proves
the direct contrary. For, please to observe, that if the
end of all civil government be the good of society; if this
be the thing that is aimed at in constituting civil rulers;
and if the motive and argument for submission to government be taken from the apparent usefulness of civil

---

[a] This does not intend their acting so in a few particular instances, which the
best of rulers may do through mistake, etc., but their acting so habitually, and
in a manner which plainly shows that they aim at making themselves great by the
ruin of their subjects.

authority, — it follows, that when no such good end can
be answered by submission, there remains no argument or
motive to enforce it ; and if, instead of this good end's
being brought about by submission, a contrary end is
brought about, and the ruin and misery of society effected
by it, here is a plain and positive reason against submission in all such cases, should they ever happen.   And
therefore, in such cases, a regard to the public welfare
ought to make us withhold from our rulers that obedience
and submission which it would otherwise be our duty to
render to them.   If it be our duty, for example, to obey
our king merely for this reason, that he rules for the public
welfare (which is the only argument the apostle makes use
of), it follows, by a parity of reason, that when he turns
tyrant, and makes his subjects his prey to devour and
destroy, instead of his charge to defend and cherish, we
are bound to throw off our allegiance to him, and to resist;
and that according to the tenor of the apostle's argument
in this passage.   Not to discontinue our allegiance in this
case would be to join with the sovereign in promoting the
slavery and misery of that society, the welfare of which
we ourselves, as well as our sovereign, are indispensably
obliged to secure and promote, as far as in us lies.   It is
true the apostle puts no case of such a tyrannical prince ;
but, by his grounding his argument for submission wholly
upon the good of civil society, it is plain he implicitly
authorizes, and even requires us to make resistance, whenever this shall be necessary to the public safety and happiness.   Let me make use of this easy and familiar similitude
to illustrate the point in hand : Suppose God requires a
family of children to obey their father and not to resist
him, and enforces his command with this argument, that
the superintendence and care and authority of a just and
kind parent will contribute to the happiness of the whole

family, so that they ought to obey him for their own sakes more than for his; suppose this parent at length runs distracted, and attempts in his mad fit to cut all his children's throats. Now, in this case, is not the reason before assigned why these children should obey their parent while he continued of a sound mind — namely, their common good — a reason equally conclusive for disobeying and resisting him, since he is become delirious and attempts their ruin? It makes no alteration in the argument whether this parent, properly speaking, loses his reason, or does, while he retains his understanding, that which is as fatal in its consequences as anything he could do were he really deprived of it. This similitude needs no formal application.

But it ought to be remembered that if the duty of universal obedience and non-resistance to our king or prince can be argued from this passage, the same unlimited submission, under a republican or any other form of government, and even to all the subordinate powers in any particular state, can be proved by it as well, which is more than those who allege it for the mentioned purpose would be willing should be inferred from it; so that this passage does not answer their purpose, but really overthrows and confutes it. This matter deserves to be more particularly considered. The advocates for unlimited submission and passive obedience do, if I mistake not, always speak with reference to kingly and monarchical government as distinguished from all other forms, and with reference to submitting to the will of the king in distinction from all subordinate officers acting beyond their commission and the authority which they have received from the crown. It is not pretended that any persons besides kings have a divine right to do what they please, so that no one may resist them without incurring the guilt of factiousness and rebellion. If any other powers oppress the people, it is generally allowed that the people may get redress by resistance, if other methods prove ineffectual. And if any officers in a kingly government go beyond the limits of that power which they have derived from the crown (the supposed original source of all power and authority in the state), and attempt illegally to take away the properties and lives of their fellow-subjects, they may be forcibly resisted, at least till application can be made to the crown. But as to the sovereign himself, he may not be resisted in any case, nor any of his officers, while they confine themselves within the bounds which he has prescribed to them. This is, I think, a true sketch of the principles of those who defend the doctrine of passive obedience and non-resistance. Now, there is nothing in Scripture which supports this scheme of political principles. As to the passage under consideration, the apostle here speaks of civil rulers in general, — of all persons in common vested with authority for the good of society, without any particular reference to one form of government more than to another, or to the supreme power in any particular state more than to subordinate powers. The apostle does not concern himself with the different forms of government.[a] This he

a The essence of government (I mean good government, and this is the only government which the apostle treats of in this passage) consists in the making and executing of good laws — laws attempered to the common felicity of the governed. And if this be, in fact, done, it is evidently in itself a thing of no consequence at all what the particular form of government is; — whether the legislative and executive power be lodged in one and the same person, or in different persons; whether in one person, whom we call an absolute monarch; whether in a few, so as to constitute an aristocracy; whether in many, so as to constitute a republic; or whether in three coördinate branches, in such manner as to make the government partake something of each of these forms, and to be, at the same time, essentially different from them all. If the end be attained, it is enough. But no form of government seems so unlikely to accomplish this end as absolute monarchy. Nor is there any one that has so little pretence to a divine original, unless it be in this sense, that God first introduced it into, and thereby overturned, the commonwealth of Israel, as a curse upon that people for

supposes left entirely to human prudence and discretion. Now, the consequence of this is, that unlimited and passive obedience is no more enjoined in this passage under monarchical government, or to the supreme power in any state, than under all other species of government which answer the end of government, or to all the subordinate degrees of civil authority, from the highest to the lowest. Those, therefore, who would from this passage infer the guilt of resisting kings in all cases whatever, though acting ever so contrary to the design of their office, must, if they will be consistent, go much further, and infer from it the guilt of resistance under all other forms of government, and of resisting any petty officer in the state, though acting beyond his commission in the most arbitrary, illegal manner possible. The argument holds equally strong in both cases. All civil rulers, as such, are the ordinance and ministers of God, and they are all, by the nature of their office, and in their respective spheres and stations, bound to consult the public welfare. With the same reason, therefore, that any deny unlimited and passive obedience to be here enjoined under a republic or aristocracy, or any other established form of civil government, or to subordinate powers acting in an illegal and oppressive manner; with the same reason others may deny that such obedience is enjoined to a king or monarch, or any civil power whatever. For the apostle says nothing that is *peculiar to kings ;* what he says extends equally to all other persons whatever vested with any civil office. They are all, in exactly the same sense, the ordinance of God and the ministers of God, and obedience is equally enjoined to be paid to them all. For, as the apostle expresses it, there is

their folly and wickedness, particularly in desiring such a government. (See 1 Sam. ch. viii.) Just so God before sent quails amongst them, as a plague and a curse, and not as a blessing. Numb. ch. xi.

no power but of God ; and we are required to render to all their *dues*, and not *more* than their dues.   And what these dues are, and to whom they are to be rendered, the apostle saith not, but leaves to the reason and consciences of men to determine.

Thus it appears that the common argument grounded upon this passage in favor of universal and passive obedience really overthrows itself, by proving too much, if it proves anything at all, — namely, that no civil officer is, in any case whatever, to be resisted, though acting in express contradiction to the design of his office, — which no man in his senses ever did or can assert.

If we calmly consider the nature of the thing itself, nothing can well be imagined more directly contrary to common sense than to suppose that millions of people should be subjected to the arbitrary, precarious pleasure of one single man, — who has naturally no superiority over them in point of authority, — so that their estates, and everything that is valuable in life, and even their lives also, shall be absolutely at his disposal, if he happens to be wanton and capricious enough to demand them.   What unprejudiced man can think that God made *all* to be thus subservient to the lawless pleasure and frenzy of *one*,[1] so

---

[1] This will suggest to many readers Milton's noble passage : " Our liberty is not Cæsar's; it is a blessing we have received from God himself; it is what we are born to; to lay down this at Cæsar's feet, which we derive not from him, which we are not beholden to him for, were an unworthy action, and a degrading of our very nature.   If one should consider attentively the countenance of a man, and inquire after whose image so noble a creature were framed, would not any one that heard him presently make answer, that he was made after the image of God himself?   Being, therefore, peculiarly God's own, and consequently things that are to be given to him, we are entirely free by nature, and cannot without the greatest sacrilege imaginable be reduced into a condition of slavery to any man, especially to a wicked, unjust, cruel tyrant."—Defence of the People of England. — ED.

that it shall always be a sin to resist him? Nothing but
the most plain and express revelation from heaven could
make a sober, impartial man believe such a monstrous,
unaccountable doctrine; and, indeed, the thing itself appears so shocking, so out of all proportion, that it may be
questioned whether all the miracles that ever were wrought
could make it credible that this doctrine really came from
God. At present there is not the least syllable in Scripture
which gives any countenance to it. The hereditary, indefeasible, divine right of kings, and the doctrine of non-
resistance, which is built upon the supposition of such a
right, are altogether as fabulous and chimerical as tran-
substantiation, or any of the most absurd reveries of ancient or modern visionaries. These notions are fetched
neither from divine revelation nor human reason; and, if
they are derived from neither of those sources, it is not
much matter from whence they come or whither they go.
Only it is a pity that such doctrines should be propagated
in society, to raise factions and rebellions,[1] as we see they
have, in fact, been, both in the last and in the present
reign.

But, then, if unlimited submission and passive obedience
to the higher powers, in all possible cases, be not a duty,
it will be asked, "How far are we obliged to submit? If
we may innocently disobey and resist in some cases, why
not in all? Where shall we stop? What is the measure
of our duty? This doctrine tends to the total dissolution

---

[1] As, for instance, those of the high-church, divine-right party, in 1714,
1715, which occasioned the Riot Act, the law of the land to this day.
"Down with the Roundheads! God bless Dr. Sacheverell!" was their cry
when they destroyed the meeting-houses of the dissenters; and their violences were unprecedented. They sought to replace the Stuarts, as at
Preston, Nov. 13, 1715, and at Culloden Moor, April 16, 1746. These will
call to mind Campbell's celebrated poem, "Lochiel's Warning," and
Scott's romance, "Waverley."— ED.

of civil government, and to introduce such scenes of wild anarchy and confusion as are more fatal to society than the worst of tyranny."

After this manner some men object; and, indeed, this is the most plausible thing that can be said in favor of such an absolute submission as they plead for. But the worst, or, rather, the best of it is, that there is very little strength or solidity in it; for similar difficulties may be raised with respect to almost every duty of natural and revealed religion. To instance only in two, both of which are near akin, and indeed exactly parallel to the case before us: It is unquestionably the duty of children to submit to their parents, and of servants to their masters; but no one asserts that it is their duty to obey and submit to them in all supposable cases, or universally a sin to resist them. Now, does this tend to subvert the just authority of parents and masters, or to introduce confusion and anarchy into private families? No. How, then, does the same principle tend to unhinge the government of that larger family the body politic? We know, in general, that children and servants are obliged to obey their parents and masters respectively; we know also, with equal certainty, that they are not obliged to submit to them in all things without exception, but may, in some cases, reasonably, and therefore innocently, resist them. These principles are acknowledged upon all hands, whatever difficulty there may be in fixing the exact limits of submission. Now, there is at least as much difficulty in stating the measure of duty in these two cases as in the case of rulers and subjects; so that this is really no objection — at least, no reasonable one — against resistance to the higher powers. Or, if it is one, it will hold equally against resistance in the other cases mentioned. It is indeed true, that turbulent, vicious-minded men may take occasion, from this principle that their rulers may in some cases be lawfully resisted, to raise factions and disturbances in the state, and to make resistance where resistance is needless, and therefore sinful. But is it not equally true that children and servants, of turbulent, vicious minds, may take occasion, from this principle that parents and masters may in some cases be lawfully resisted, to resist when resistance is unnecessary, and therefore criminal? Is the principle, in either case, false in itself merely because it may be abused, and applied to legitimate disobedience and resistance in those instances to which it ought not to be applied? According to this way of arguing, there will be no true principles in the world; for there are none but what may be wrested and perverted to serve bad purposes, either through the weakness or wickedness of men.[a]

a We may very safely assert these two things in general, without undermining government: One is, that no civil rulers are to be obeyed when they enjoin things that are inconsistent with the commands of God. All such disobedience is lawful and glorious; particularly if persons refuse to comply with any *legal establishment of religion*, because it is a gross perversion and corruption — as to doctrine, worship, and discipline — of a pure and divine religion, brought from heaven to earth by the Son of God, — the only King and Head of the Christian church, — and propagated through the world by his inspired apostles. All commands running counter to the declared will of the Supreme Legislator of heaven and earth are null and void, and therefore disobedience to them is a duty, not a crime. (See note a, p. 58.) Another thing that may be asserted with equal truth and safety is, that no government is to be submitted to at the expense of that which is the sole end of all government — the common good and safety of society. Because, to submit in this case, if it should ever happen, would evidently be to set up the means as more valuable and above the end, than which there cannot be a greater solecism and contradiction. The only reason of the institution of civil government, and the only rational ground of submission to it, is the common safety and utility. If, therefore, in any case, the common safety and utility would not be promoted by submission to government, but the contrary, there is no ground or motive for obedience and submission, but for the contrary.

Whoever considers the nature of civil government, must indeed be sensible that a great degree of implicit confidence must unavoidably be placed in those that bear rule : this is implied in the very notion of authority's being originally a trust committed by the people to those who are vested with it, — as all just and righteous authority is. All besides is mere lawless force and usurpation; neither God nor nature having given any man a right of dominion over any society independently of that society's approbation and consent to be governed by him.

A people, really oppressed in a great degree by their sovereign, cannot well be insensible when they are so oppressed; and such a people — if I may allude to an ancient fable — have, like the hesperian fruit, a dragon for their

Now, as all men are fallible, it cannot be supposed that the public affairs of any state should be always administered in the best manner possible, even by persons of the greatest wisdom and integrity. Nor is it sufficient to legitimate disobedience to the higher powers that they are not so administered, or that they are in some instances very ill-managed; for, upon this principle, it is scarcely supposable that any government at all could be supported, or subsist. Such a principle manifestly tends to the dissolution of government, and to throw all things into confusion and anarchy. But it is equally evident, upon the other hand, that those in authority may abuse their trust and power to such a degree, that neither the law of reason nor of religion requires that any obedience or submission should be paid to them; but, on the contrary, that they should be totally discarded, and the authority which they were before vested with transferred to others, who may exercise it more to those good purposes for which it is given. Nor is this principle, that resistance to the higher powers is in some extraordinary cases justifiable, so liable to abuse as many persons seem to apprehend it. For, although there will be always some petulant, querulous men in every state, — men of factious, turbulent, and carping dispositions, glad to lay hold of any trifle to justify and legitimate their caballing against their rulers, and other seditious practices, — yet there are, comparatively speaking, but few men of this contemptible character. It does not appear but that mankind in general have a disposition to be as submissive and passive and tame under government as they ought to be. Witness a great, if not the greatest, part of the known world, who are now groaning, but not murmuring, under the heavy yoke of tyranny ! While those who govern do it with any tolerable degree of moderation and justice, and in any good measure act up to their office and character by being public benefactors, the people will generally be easy and peaceable, and be rather inclined to flatter and adore than to insult and resist them. Nor was there ever any *general* complaint against any administration, which lasted long, but what there was good reason for. Till people find themselves greatly abused and oppressed by their governors, they are not apt to complain; and whenever they do, in fact, find themselves thus abused and oppressed, they must be stupid *not* to complain. To say that subjects in general are not proper judges when their governors oppress them and play the tyrant, and when they defend their rights, administer justice impartially, and promote the public welfare, is as great treason as ever man uttered. 'T is treason, not against one *single* man, but the state — against the whole body politic; 't is treason against mankind, 't is treason against common sense, 't is treason against God. And this impious principle lays the foundation for justifying all the tyranny and oppression that ever any prince was guilty of. The people know for what end they set up and maintain their governors, and they are the proper judges when they execute their trust as they ought to do it; — when their prince exercises an equitable and paternal authority over them; when from a prince and common father he exalts himself into a tyrant ; when from subjects and children he degrades them into the class of slaves, plunders them, makes them his prey, and unnaturally sports himself with their lives and fortunes.

protector and guardian.   Nor would they have any reason
to mourn if some Hercules should appear to dispatch him.
For a nation thus abused to arise unanimously and resist
their prince, even to the dethroning him, is not criminal,
but a reasonable way of vindicating their liberties and
just rights : it is making use of the means, and the only
means, which God has put into their power for mutual and
self defence.   And it would be highly criminal in them not
to make use of this means.   It would be stupid tameness
and unaccountable folly for whole nations to suffer *one*
unreasonable, ambitious, and cruel man to wanton and
riot in their misery.   And in such a case, it would, of the
two, be more rational to suppose that they that did not
resist, than that they who did, would receive to themselves damnation.

And this naturally brings us to make some reflections
upon the resistance which was made, about a century since,
to that unhappy prince King Charles I., and upon the anniversary of his death.   This is a point which I should not
have concerned myself about, were it not that some men
continue to speak of it, even to this day,[1] with a great
deal of warmth and zeal, and in such a manner as to undermine all the principles of liberty, whether civil or religious, and to introduce the most abject slavery both in
church and state — so that it is become a matter of universal concern.   What I have to offer upon this subject will
be comprised in a short answer to the following queries,
viz. :

[1] " The Episcopalians in New England, as well as the parent kingdom,
regarded this anniversary as a sacred day, and observed it as a FAST.
They took occasion not only to dwell on the great injustice done to the
king in person, and the outrage, as they called it, committed against the
crown, but to exalt and glorify Episcopacy and monarchy, and to abuse
both Republicans and Puritans." — Dr. Bradford's Life of Mayhew, 103,
117.   See note to the Preface. — ED.

For what reason the resistance to King Charles the First was made.

By whom it was made.

Whether this resistance was rebellion,[a] or not.

How the anniversary of King Charles's death came at first to be solemnized as a day of fasting and humiliation. And, lastly,

Why those of the Episcopal clergy who are very high in the principles of ecclesiastical authority continue to speak of this unhappy man as a great saint and a martyr.

For what reason, then, was the resistance to King Charles made? The general answer to this inquiry is, that it was on account of the tyranny and oppression of his reign. Not a great while after his accession to the throne, he married a French Catholic,[1] and with her seemed to have wedded the politics, if not the religion of France, also. For afterwards, during a reign, or, rather, a tyranny of many years, he governed in a perfectly wild and arbitrary manner, paying no regard to the constitution and the laws of the kingdom, by which the power of the crown was limited, or to the solemn oath which he had taken at his coronation. It would be endless, as well as needless, to give a particular account of all the illegal and despotic measures which he took in his administration, — partly from his own natural lust of power, and partly from the influence of wicked counsellors and ministers. He committed many illustrious members of both Houses of Parliament to the Tower for opposing his arbitrary schemes. He levied many taxes upon the people without consent of Parliament, and then imprisoned great numbers

[a] N. B. — I speak of rebellion, treason, saintship, martyrdom, etc., throughout this discourse, only in the scriptural and theological sense. I know not how the *law* defines them — the study of *that* not being my employment.

[1] Henrietta Maria, daughter of Henry IV. of France. — ED.

of the principal merchants and gentry for not paying them. He erected, or at least revived, several arbitrary courts, in which the most unheard-of barbarities were committed with his knowledge and approbation. He supported that more than fiend, Archbishop Laud, and the clergy of his stamp, in all their church-tyranny[1] and hellish cruelties. He authorized a book in favor of sports upon the Lord's day; and several clergymen were persecuted by him and the mentioned *pious* bishop for not reading it to the people after divine service.[2] When the Parliament complained to him of the arbitrary proceedings of his corrupt ministers, he told that august body, in a rough, domineering, unprincely manner, that he wondered any one should be so foolish and insolent as to think that he would part with the meanest of his servants upon their account. He refused to call any Parliament at all for the space of twelve years together, during all which time he governed in an absolute, lawless, and despotic manner. He took all opportunities to encourage the Papists, and to promote them to the highest offices of honor and trust. He (probably) abetted the horrid massacre in Ireland, in which two hundred thousand Protestants were butchered by the Roman Catholics. He sent a large sum of money, which he had raised by his arbitrary taxes, into Germany, to raise foreign troops,[3] in order to force more arbitrary taxes upon

---

1 The intimate connection of this with New England history is touched upon in the Introduction to this volume. — ED.

2 " One Dr. Dawson read it,"— in church, as commanded, — " and presently after read the Ten Commandments; then said: ' Dearly beloved, you have heard now the commandments of God and man: obey which you please.' "— Knight's History of England, iii. 415. — ED.

3 " Foreign troops." In 1627 Charles sent funds to Germany for mercenary German troops, to repel any insurrection consequent on the collection of the excise without grant by the Parliament. In 1628 the Commons "remonstrated" against this " bringing in of strangers for aid, as pernicious to most

his subjects. He not only, by a long series of actions, but also in plain terms, asserted an absolute, uncontrollable power, — saying, even, in one of his speeches to Parliament, that, as it was blasphemy to dispute what God might do, so it was sedition in subjects to dispute what the king might do! Towards the end of his tyranny he came to the House of Commons, with an armed force,[a] and demanded five of its principal members to be delivered up to him ; and this was a prelude to that unnatural war which he soon after levied against his own dutiful subjects, whom he was bound, by all the laws of honor, humanity, piety, and, I might add, of interest also, to defend and cherish with a paternal affection. I have only time to hint at these facts[1] in a general way, all which, and many

---

[a] Historians are not agreed what number of soldiers attended him in this monstrous invasion of the privileges of Parliament. Some say three hundred, some four hundred; and the author of " The History of the Kings of Scotland " says five hundred.

states, but to England fatal," and " we are bold to declare to your Majesty and the whole world, that we hold it far beneath the heart of any Englishman to think that this victorious nation should now stand in need of German soldiers to defend their now king and kingdom." The king's insolent reply was, "*I owe the account of my actions to God alone!*" and so prorogued the Parliament. In the year before he had said to them, at the opening of the session, " I mean not to spend much time in words. . . . I need but point out to you what to do. I will use but few persuasions. . . . Take not this as a threatening, for I scorn to threaten any but my equals." When George II. brought German troops into England in 1756, " That state alone," exclaimed Pitt, " is a sovereign state which stands by its own strength, not by the help of another country." George III. bought with British money " the hireling sword of German boors and vassals" to reduce the American colonies, and this was one of the wrongs set forth in the Declaration of July 4, 1776: " transporting large armies of foreign mercenaries."— ED.

[1] This summary, by Dr. Mayhew, in 1750, of the crimes of Charles I. which led to the Revolution of 1640, bears to Mr. Jefferson's " declaration" of the complaints against George III. — the " causes" which led to the Revolution of 1775 — a resemblance so remarkable, both in form and spirit,

more of the same tenor, may be proved by good authorities. So that the figurative language which St. John uses concerning the just and beneficent deeds of our blessed Saviour may be applied to the unrighteous and execrable deeds of this prince, viz.: " And there are also many other things which" King Charles " did, the which, if they should be written every one, I suppose that even the world itself could not contain the books that should be written." [a] Now, it was on account of King Charles's thus assuming a power above the laws, in direct contradiction to his coronation oath, and governing, the greatest part of his time, in the most arbitrary, oppressive manner — it was upon this account that resistance was made to him, which at length issued in the loss of his crown, and of that head which was unworthy to wear it.

But by whom was this resistance made? Not by a private junto, not by a small seditious party, not by a few desperadoes, who to mend their fortunes would embroil the state ; but by the Lords and Commons of England. It was they that almost unanimously opposed the king's measures for overturning the constitution, and changing that free and happy government into a wretched, absolute monarchy. It was they that, when the king was about levying forces against his subjects in order to make himself absolute, commissioned officers, and raised an army to defend themselves and the public ; and it was they that maintained the war against him all along, till he was made a prisoner. This is indisputable ; though it was not, properly speaking, the Parliament, but the army, which put

a John xxi. 25.

that a careful parallel of the two would not discredit a tradition, were there one, that Dr. Mayhew's was the model for that of a quarter of a century later. It is certain that Dr. Mayhew's sermon was circulated and read everywhere. — ED.

him to death afterwards. And it ought to be freely acknowledged that most of their proceeding, in order to get this matter effected,[1] and particularly the court by which the king was at last tried and condemned, was little better than a mere mockery of justice.

The next question which naturally arises is, whether this resistance which was made to the king by the Parliament was properly rebellion or not? The answer to which is

[1] "It is much to be doubted whether his trial and execution have not, as much as any other circumstance, served to raise the character of the English nation in the opinion of Europe in general."— CHARLES JAMES FOX.

"Having share in the government, sirs, that is nothing pertaining to the people. A subject and a sovereign are clean different things."— KING CHARLES I. on the scaffold.

"Now Charles, to a degree which can scarcely be exceeded, conspired against the liberty of his country. To assert his own authority without limitation was the object of all his desires and all his actions, so far as the public was concerned. . . . . For that purpose he commenced war against the English Parliament, and continued it by every expedient in his power for four years. . . . He could never be reconciled; he could never be disarmed; he could never be convinced. His was a war to the death, and there had the utmost aggravation that can belong to a war against the liberty of a nation. . . . . It is not easy to imagine a greater criminal than the individual against whom the sentence was awarded."— WILLIAM GODWIN.

"They were men sufficiently provided with daring; men, we are bound to see, who sat there as in the presence of the Maker of all men, as executing the judgment of Heaven above, and had not the fear of any man or thing on the earth below. . . . I reckon it perhaps the most daring action any body of men to be met with in history ever, with clear consciousness, deliberately set themselves to do."— THOMAS CARLYLE.

"God has endued you with greatness of mind to be the first of mankind, who, after having conquered their own king, and having had him delivered into their hands, have not scrupled to condemn him judicially, and, pursuant to that sentence of condemnation, to put him to death."— JOHN MILTON.

"Illustrious and heroic defenders of real, perfect, and unpolluted liberty, civil and religious, throughout the world."— EZRA STILES. — ED.

plain, — that it was not, but a most righteous and glorious stand, made in defence of the natural and legal rights of the people, against the unnatural and illegal encroachments of arbitrary power. Nor was this a rash and too sudden opposition. The nation had been patient under the oppressions of the crown, even to long-suffering, for a course of many years, and there was no rational hope of redress in any other way. Resistance was absolutely necessary,[1] in order to preserve the nation from slavery, misery, and ruin. And who so proper to make this resistance as the Lords and Commons, — the whole representative body of the people, — guardians of the public welfare; and each of which was, in point of legislation, vested with an equal, coördinate power with that of the crown?[a] Here

---

[a] The English constitution is originally and essentially free. The character which Julius Cæsar and Tacitus both give of the ancient Britains so long ago is, that they were extremely jealous of their liberties, as well as a people of a martial spirit. Nor have there been wanting frequent instances and proofs of the same glorious spirit, in both respects, remaining in their posterity ever since, in the struggles they have made for liberty, both against foreign and domestic tyrants. Their kings hold their title to the throne solely by grant of Parliament; — i. e., in other words, by the voluntary consent of the people; — and, agreeably hereto, the prerogative and rights of the crown are stated, defined, and limited by law; and that as truly and strictly as the rights of any inferior officer in the state, or, indeed, of any private subject. And it is only in this respect that it can be said that " the king can do no wrong." Being restrained by the law, he cannot, while he confines himself within those just limits which the law prescribes to him as the measure of his authority, injure and oppress the subject. The king, in his coronation oath, swears to exercise only such a power as the constitution gives him; and the subject, in the oath of allegiance, swears only to obey him in the exercise of such a power. The king is as much bound by his oath not to infringe the legal rights of the people as the people are bound to yield subjection to him. From whence it follows, that as soon as the prince sets himself up above law, he loses the king in the tyrant. He does, to all intents and purposes,

[1] Lord Camden relates that somebody asked the great Mr. Selden, whom Grotius called the glory of England, in what law-book, in what records or archives of the state, might be found the law for resisting tyranny. " I don't know," said Selden, " whether it would be worth your while to look deeply into books on this matter; but I will tell you what is most certain, that it has always been the CUSTOM of England, and the *custom* of England is the law of the land." — ED.

were two branches of the legislature against one; two, which had law and equity and the constitution on their side, against one which was impiously attempting to overturn law and equity and the constitution, and to exercise a wanton, licentious sovereignty over the properties, consciences, and lives of all the people; — such a sovereignty as some inconsiderately ascribe to the Supreme Governor of the world. I say, inconsiderately, because God himself does not govern in an absolutely arbitrary and despotic manner. The power of this almighty King — I speak it not without caution and reverence — the power of this almighty King is limited by law; not indeed by acts of Parliament, but by the eternal laws of truth, wisdom, and equity, and the everlasting tables of right reason, — tables that cannot be repealed, or thrown down and broken like those of Moses. But King Charles set himself up above all these,[1] as much as he did above the written laws of the realm, and made mere humor and caprice, which are no rule at all, the only rule and measure of his administration. And now is it not perfectly ridiculous to call resistance to such a tyrant by the name of *rebellion?* — the grand rebel-

unking himself by acting out of and beyond that sphere which the constitution allows him to move in; and in such cases he has no more right to be obeyed than any inferior officer who acts beyond his commission. The subject's obligation to allegiance then ceases, of course; and to resist him is no more rebellion than to resist any foreign invader. There is an essential difference betwixt government and tyranny, at least under such a constitution as the English. The former consists in ruling according to law and equity; the latter, in ruling contrary to law and equity. So, also, there is an essential difference betwixt resisting a tyrant, and rebellion. The former is a just and reasonable self-defence; the latter consists in resisting a prince whose administration is just and legal; and this is what denominates it a crime. Now, it is evident that King Charles's government was illegal, and very oppressive, through the greatest part of his reign; and, therefore, to resist him was no more rebellion than to oppose any foreign invader, or any other domestic oppressor.

[1] Very distinctly he did so. He began his reasons for dissolving the Parliament (March 10, 1628) with this: " *Howsoever, princes are not bound to give account of their actions but to God alone.*" — Rushworth, i., Appendix. — ED.

lion? Even that ——— Parliament which brought King Charles II. to the throne, and which run loyally mad, severely reproved one of their own members for condemning the proceedings of that Parliament which first took up arms against the former king. And upon the same principles that the proceeding of this Parliament may be censured as wicked and rebellious, the proceedings of those who, since, opposed King James II., and brought the Prince of Orange to the throne, may be censured as wicked and rebellious also. The cases are parallel. But, whatever some men may think, it is to be hoped that, for their own sakes, they will not dare to speak against the Revolution, upon the justice and legality of which depends,[1] in part, his present majesty's right to the throne.

If it be said that although the Parliament which first opposed King Charles's measures, and at length took up arms against him, were not guilty of rebellion, yet certainly those persons were who condemned and put him to death, — even this, perhaps, is not true; for he had, in fact, unkinged himself long before, and had forfeited his title to the allegiance of the people. So that those who put him to death were, at most, only guilty of murder, — which indeed is bad enough, if they were really guilty of *that*, — which is, at least, disputable.[2] Cromwell, and those who were principally concerned in the (nominal) king's death, might possibly have been very wicked and designing men. Nor shall I say anything in vindication of the reigning hypocrisy of those times, or of Cromwell's[3]

---

[1] This point was used, and with great power, during the next thirty years. We shall find it frequently made in the sermons in this collection. — ED.

[2] See note 1, p. 62. — ED.

[3] Carlyle says: "It is beautiful . . . to see how the memory of Cromwell . . . has been steadily growing clearer and clearer in the

mal-administration during the interregnum ; for it is truth, and not a party, that I am speaking for. But still, it may be said that Cromwell and his adherents were not, properly speaking, guilty of rebellion, because he whom they beheaded was not, properly speaking, their king, but a lawless tyrant ; much less are the whole body of the nation at that time to be charged with rebellion on that account : for it was no national act ; it was not done by a free Parliament. And much less still is the nation at present to be charged with the great sin of rebellion for what their ancestors did, or, rather, did not, a century ago.

But how came the anniversary of King Charles's death to be solomnized [1] as a day of fasting and humiliation ?

popular English mind; onwards to this day, the progress does not stop." He declares Cromwell the " English hero; " " the soul and life of Puritanism; " " the most English of Englishmen; " " a great man, denizen of all centuries, or he could not have been, as he was, the pattern one of the seventeenth." — Letters and Speeches of Cromwell. — Ed.

[1] The diary of Evelyn, recently published, contains interesting notices of this "Fast." " January 30th, 1661, was the first solemn fast and day of humiliation to deplore the sins which so long had provoked God against this afflicted church and people, ordered by Parliament to be annually celebrated to expiate the guilt of the execrable murder of the late king. " This day (O the stupendous and inscrutable judgments of God!) were the carcasses of those arch-rebels, Cromwell, Bradshaw (the judge who condemned his Majesty), and Ireton (son-in-law to the usurper), dragged out of their superb tombs in Westminster, among the kings, to Tyburn, and hanged on the gallows there from nine in the morning till six at night, and then buried under that fatal and ignominious monument, in a deep pit; thousands of people who had seen them in all their pride being spectators. Look back at October 22, 1658,"— Oliver's funeral, — " and be astonished, and fear God and honor the king; but meddle not with them who are given to change." But times change, and we change with them. Not thirty years had passed before the " martyr's " family was banished from the throne and nation. "And now," says Evelyn, " the clergy began to change their note, both in pulpit and discourse, on their old passive obedience, so as people begin to talk of the bishops being cast out of the House;" and on the 30th of January, 1689, he writes : " The anniversary of

The true answer in brief to which inquiry is, that this fast was instituted by way of court and compliment to King Charles II. upon the restoration. All were desirous of making their court to him, of ingratiating themselves, and of making him forget what had been done in opposition to his father, so as not to revenge it. To effect this they ran into the most extravagant professions of affection and loyalty to him, insomuch that he himself said that it was a mad and hair-brained royalty which they professed. And, amongst other strange things which his first Parliament did, they ordered the thirtieth of January — the day on which his father was beheaded — to be kept as a day of solemn humiliation, to deprecate the judgments of Heaven for the rebellion which the nation had been guilty of, in that which was no national thing, and which was not rebellion in them that did it. Thus they soothed and flattered their new king at the expense of their liberties, and were ready to yield up freely to Charles II. all that enormous power which they had justly resisted Charles I. for usurping to himself.

The last query mentioned was, Why those of the Episcopal clergy who are very high in the principles of ecclesiastical authority continue to speak of this unhappy man as a great saint and a martyr. This we know is what they constantly do, especially upon the thirtieth of January — a day sacred to the extolling of him, and to the reproaching of those who are not of the Established Church. " Out of the same mouth," on this day, " proceedeth blessing and cursing ; "[a] therewith bless they their God, even Charles, and therewith curse they the dissenters. And their " tongue can no man tame ; it is an unruly evil, full of

[a] James iii. 8, 9, 10.

King Charles the First's *martyrdom;* but in all the public offices and pulpit prayers the collects and litany for the king and queen were curtailed and mutilated." — ED.

deadly poison." King Charles is upon this solemnity frequently compared to our Lord Jesus Christ, both in respect of the holiness of his life and the greatness and injustice of his sufferings; and it is a wonder they do not add something concerning the merits of his death also: but "blessed saint" and "royal martyr" are as humble titles as any that are thought worthy of him.

Now this may, at first view, well appear to be a very strange phenomenon; for King Charles was really a man black with guilt, and "laden with iniquity,"[a] as appears by his crimes before mentioned. He lived a tyrant; and it was the oppression and violence of his reign that brought him to his untimely and violent end at last. Now, what of saintship or martyrdom is there in all this? What of saintship is there in encouraging people to profane the Lord's day? What of saintship in falsehood and perjury? What of saintship in repeated robberies and depredations? What of saintship in throwing real saints and glorious patriots into jails? What of saintship in overturning an excellent civil constitution, and proudly grasping at an illegal and monstrous power? What of saintship in the murder of thousands of innocent people, and involving a nation in all the calamities of civil war? And what of martyrdom is there in a man's bringing an immature and violent death upon himself by "being wicked overmuch"?[b] Is there any such thing as grace without goodness; as being a follower of Christ without following him; as being his disciple without learning of him to be just and beneficent; or as saintship without sanctity?[c] If not, I fear it will be hard to prove this

---

[a] Isa. i. 4.   [b] Eccles. vii. 17.

[c] Is it any wonder that even persons who do not walk after their own lust should scoff at such saints as this, both in the first and in the last days, even from everlasting to everlasting? (2 Pet. iii. 3, 4.) But perhaps it will be said that these things are mysteries, which, although very true in themselves, lay understandings cannot comprehend; or, indeed, any other persons amongst us besides

man a saint. And verily one would be apt to suspect that that church must be but poorly stocked with saints and martyrs which is forced to adopt such enormous sinners into her calendar in order to swell the number.

But, to unravel this mystery of (nonsense as well as of) iniquity, which has already worked for a long time amongst us,[a] or, at least, to give the most probable solution of it, it is to be remembered that King Charles, — this burlesque upon saintship and martyrdom, — though so great an oppressor, was a true friend to the church, — so true a friend to her that he was very well affected towards the Roman Catholics, and would probably have been very willing to unite Lambeth and Rome. This appears by his marrying a true daughter of that true "mother of harlots,"[b] which he did with a dispensation from the Pope, that supreme bishop, to whom, when he wrote, he gave the title of Most Holy Father. His queen was extremely bigoted to all the follies and superstitions, and to the hierarchy, of Rome, and had a prodigious ascendency over him all his life. It was in part owing to this that he (probably) abetted the massacre of the Protestants in Ireland, — that he assisted in extirpating the French Protes-

---

those who, being *inwardly moved by the Holy Ghost*, have taken a trip across the Atlantic to obtain episcopal ordination and the indelible character.[1] However, if these consecrated gentlemen do not quite despair of us, it is hoped that, in the abundance of their charity, they will endeavor to elucidate these dark points, and at the same time explain the creed of another of their eminent saints, which we are told that unless we believe faithfully, *i. e.*, believingly, we cannot be saved; — which creed, or rather riddle, notwithstanding all the labors of the pious and metaphysical Dr. Waterland, remains somewhat enigmatical still.

a 2 Thess. ii. 7.   b Rev. xvii. 5.

1 Among these were Rev. Samuel Johnson, D. D., first President of King's College, and Rev. Timothy Cutler, D. D., President of Yale College; Rev. Samuel A. Peters, LL. D., author of the remarkable " History of Connecticut;" the Rev. East Apthorp, missionary " in foreign parts," at Cambridge, Massachusetts; and, of later date, the Rev. Jacob Bailey, A. M., happily commemorated as " The Frontier Missionary " by the Rev. William S. Bartlett, A. M. — ED.

51994

tants [1] at Rochelle, — that he all along encouraged Papists and popishly affected clergymen, in preference to all other persons, — and that he upheld that monster of wickedness, Archbishop Laud, and the bishops of his stamp, in all their church tyranny and diabolical cruelties. In return to his kindness and indulgence in which respects they caused many of the pulpits throughout the nation to ring with the divine, absolute, indefeasible right of kings — with the praises of Charles and his reign, and with the damnable sin of resisting the "Lord's anointed," let him do what he would ; so that not Christ, but Charles, was commonly preached to the people. In plain English, there seems to have been an impious bargain struck up betwixt the sceptre and the surplice for enslaving both the bodies and souls of men. The king appeared to be willing that the clergy should do what they would, — set up a monstrous hierarchy like that of Rome, a monstrous Inquisition like that of Spain or Portugal, or anything else which their own pride and the devil's malice could prompt them to, — provided always that the clergy would be *tools* to the crown ; that they would make the people believe that kings had God's authority for breaking God's law, — that they had a commission from Heaven to seize the estates and lives of their subjects at pleasure, — and that it was a damnable sin to resist them, even when they did such

[1] Many of the French Protestants found refuge in New England. They settled the town of Oxford, in Massachusetts, in 1686. Some of them settled in Boston, and their church in School Street must have been familiar to Dr. Mayhew, who would have peculiar sympathy with them as refugees. Many of their names are familiar to us: FANEUIL Hall, in Boston; BOWDOIN College, in Maine; LEGARE, of the bar; DEHON, of the clergy; SIGOURNEY (by marriage), among the poets. Interesting particulars in Drake's History of Boston, Rev. Dr. Holmes's Memoir of the French Protestants who settled at Oxford, Massachusetts, A. D. 1686, and in Mr. Joseph Willard's tract on Naturalization in the American Colonies. — ED.

things as deserved more than damnation. This appears to be the true key for explaining the mysterious doctrine of King Charles's saintship and martyrdom. He was a saint, not because he was in his life a good man, but a good Churchman; not because he was a lover of holiness, but the hierarchy; not because he was a friend to Christ, but the craft. And he was a martyr in his death, not because he bravely suffered death in the cause of truth and righteousness, but because he died an enemy to liberty and the rights of conscience; *i. e.*, not because he died an enemy to sin, but dissenters. For these reasons it is that all bigoted clergymen and friends to church power paint this man as a saint in his life, though he was such a mighty, such a *royal sinner;* and as a martyr in his death, though he fell a sacrifice only to his own ambition, avarice, and unbounded lust of power. And, from prostituting their praise upon King Charles, and offering him that incense which is not his due, it is natural for them to make a transition to the dissenters, — as they commonly do, — and to load them with that reproach which they do not deserve, — they being generally professed enemies both to civil and ecclesiastical tyranny. We are commonly charged, upon the thirtieth of January, with the guilt of putting the king to death, under a notion that it was our ancestors that did it; and so we are represented in the blackest colors, not only as schismatics, but also as traitors and rebels, and all that is bad. And these lofty gentlemen usually rail upon this head in such a manner as plainly shows that they are either grossly ignorant of the history of those times which they speak of, or — which is worse — that they are guilty of the most shameful prevarication, slander, and falsehood. But every petty priest with a roll and a gown thinks he must do something in imitation of his betters in lawn, and show himself a true son of the church: and thus, through a foolish ambition to appear considerable, they only render themselves contemptible.[1]

But, suppose our forefathers did kill their mock saint and martyr a century ago, what is that to us now? If I mistake not, these gentlemen generally preach down the doctrine of the imputation of Adam's sin to his posterity as absurd and unreasonable, notwithstanding they have solemnly subscribed what is equivalent to it in their own articles of religion ; and therefore one would hardly expect that they would lay the guilt of the king's death upon us, although our forefathers had been the only authors of it : but this conduct is much more surprising when it does not appear that *our* ancestors had any more hand in it than *their own*. However, bigotry is sufficient to account for this and many other phenomena which cannot be accounted for in any other way.

Although the observation of this anniversary seems to have been at least superstitious in its original; and although it is often abused to very bad purposes by the established clergy, as they serve themselves of it to per-

[1] Dr. Bradford, the biographer of Dr. Mayhew, says: "It should be recollected that the governors in Massachusetts were then appointed by the king, and were Episcopalians, sent over from England. Their particular patronage and favor were bestowed on the few Episcopal clergy; which served to render them overbearing, and unwilling to allow the Congregational clergy to be ministers of the gospel. So haughty and censorious were most of them, that one was led to say of them, ' They know not what they are of.'   Great efforts were then making to settle Episcopal clergy in New England, who were most anxious to increase the members of the English Episcopal church, and to interfere with the other clergy. These Episcopal ministers were supported by the English hierarchy; and the civil administration of the British government particularly favored and encouraged this plan, for the purpose of supporting the political measures and views of the ministers, then strongly leaning to tory doctrines. It was considered important to increase and extend Episcopacy in the colonies, with a view to secure obedience to all political measures and plans. ' No bishops, no kings,' was the opinion and party-cry of many." — ED.

petuate strife, a party spirit, and divisions in the Christian church; yet it is to be hoped that one good end will be answered by it, quite contrary to their intention : It is to be hoped that it will prove a standing memento that Britons will not be slaves, and a warning to all corrupt counsellors and ministers not to go too far in advising to arbitrary, despotic measures.

To conclude : Let us all learn to be free and to be loyal; let us not profess ourselves vassals to the lawless pleasure of any man on earth; but let us remember, at the same time, government is sacred, and not to be trifled with. It is our happiness to live under a prince who is satisfied with ruling according to law, as every other good prince will. We enjoy under his administration all the liberty that is proper and expedient for us. It becomes us, therefore, to be contented and dutiful subjects. Let us prize our freedom, but not " use our liberty for a cloak of maliciousness." [a] There are men who strike at liberty under the term licentiousness ; there are others who aim at popularity under the disguise of patriotism. Be aware of both. Extremes are dangerous. There is at present amongst us, perhaps, more danger of the latter than of the former; for which reason I would exhort you to pay all due regard to the government over us, to the king, and all in authority, and to " lead a quiet and peaceable life." [b] And, while I am speaking of loyalty to our earthly prince, suffer me just to put you in mind to be loyal also to the Supreme Ruler of the universe, " by whom kings reign and princes decree justice; " [c] — to which King, eternal, immortal, invisible, even to " the only wise God," [d] be all honor and praise, dominion and thanksgiving, through Jesus Christ our Lord. AMEN.

[a] 1 Peter ii. 16.   [b] 1 Tim. ii. 2.   [c] Prov. viii. 15.   [d] 1 Tim. i. 17.

A

DISCOURSE

On "the good News from
a far Country."

Deliver'd *July* 24*th*.

A Day of Thanks-giving to Almighty God,
throughout the Province of the *Maſſachuſetts-
Bay* in *New-England*, on Occaſion of the
Repeal of the STAMP-ACT ; appointed
by his Excellency, the Governor of ſaid
Province, at the Deſire of it's Houſe of Re-
presentatives, with the Advice of his
Majesty's Council.

By Charles Chauncy, D.D.
A Paſtor of the firſt Church in *Boſton*.

B O S T O N: N. E.

Printed by Kneeland and Adams, in Milk-ſtreet,
for Thomas Leverett, in Corn-hill.

MDCCLXVI.

EDITOR'S PREFATORY NOTE.

THE origin of the Stamp Act can be best understood by a glance at the previous political relations of the colonies to the mother land.

England, "a shop-keeping nation," [1] gained her riches by the commercial monopoly under the "Navigation Acts,"— a system invented by Sir George Downing, the one whose name stands second on Harvard College catalogue. These acts were modified as the changes of commerce required, and the "Stamp Act," but one of the series, was intended to retain the old monopoly of American trade, which was greatly endangered by the conquest of Canada. This was its origin and motive.

The dispute resolved itself into this naked question, whether "the king in Parliament [2] had full power to bind the colonies and people of America in all cases whatsoever," or in none.

The colonists argued that, by the feudal system, the king, lord paramount of lands in America, as in England, as such, had disposed of them on certain conditions. James I., in 1621, informed Parliament that "America was not annexed to the realm, and that it was not fitting that Parliament should make laws for those countries;" and Charles I. told them "that the colonies were without the realm and jurisdiction of Parlia-

---

[1] This phrase is from a tract, 1766, by Tucker, Dean of Gloucester. At that date he advocated "a separation, parting with the colonies entirely, and then making leagues of friendship with them, as with so many independent states;" but, said he, "it was too enlarged an idea for a mind wholly occupied within the narrow circle of trade," and a "stranger to the revolutions of states and empires, thoroughly to comprehend, much less to digest."

[2] The answers of the Massachusetts Council, January 25th, and House of Representatives, January 26th, to Governor Hutchinson's speech, January 6th, 1775, are rich in historical illustrations of this point, presented with great force of reason, and are decisive.

ment." The colonists showed that the American charters were *compacts* between the king and his subjects who " transported themselves *out of* this kingdom of England *into* America," by which they owed allegiance to him personally as sovereign, but were to make their own laws and taxes: for instance, a revenue was raised in Virginia by a law " *enacted by the King's most excellent Majesty, by and with the consent of the General Assembly of the Colony of Virginia.*" They denied the authority of the legislature of Great Britain over them, but acknowledged his Majesty as a part of the several colonial legislatures.

But the colonies, while jealous of their internal self-control, had permitted the British Parliament to " regulate" their *foreign* trade, and, upon precedent, the latter now claimed *authority* to bind the colonies " in all cases whatsoever." Relying upon the royal compact in their charters, the spirit of the British constitution, and " their rights as Englishmen," the Americans denied the jurisdiction of their " brethren" in England.

" Nil Desperandum, Christo Duce," was the motto on the flag of New England in 1745, when her Puritan sons conquered Louisburg, the stronghold of Papal France in the New World, and thus gave peace to Europe. This enterprise, in its spirit, was little less a crusade than was that to redeem Palestine from the thraldom of the Mussulman, and the sepulchre of Jesus from the infidels. One of the chaplains carried upon his shoulder a hatchet to destroy the images in the Romish churches. " O," exclaimed a good old deacon, to Pepperell, " O that I could be with you and dear Parson Moody in that church, to destroy the images there set up, and hear the true gospel of our Lord and Saviour there preached! My wife, who is ill and confined to her bed, yet is so spirited in the affair . . . . . that she is very willing all her sons should wait on you, though it is outwardly greatly to our damage. One of them has already enlisted, and I know not but there will be more." [1] " Christo Duce!" The extinction of French dominion was quickly completed by the conquest of Canada in 1759–60, and at the same moment ceased the colonial need of the red-cross flag of St. George, whose nationality had been their protection against the aggressions of the French. The French being driven from Canada, New England could stand alone. This was the point " in the course of human events" when the sovereignty of England over the colonies was ended, though their formal " Declaration of American Independence," and of the dissolution of " the political

[1] Life of Pepperell, by Usher Parsons, M. D.   3d ed., 1856, p. 52.

bands" with the mother country, was not issued till several years later. The conquest of Canada was the emancipation of the colonies, as the opponents of the war predicted. British parliaments, though backed by British guns, and all the canons of the English church, were powerless against "the laws of nature and nature's God;" and the Stamp Act was merely a touchstone for certain "self-evident truths"— not mere "sounding and glittering generalities"— enunciated on the Fourth of July, 1776. This attempt at despotism resulted in the *alienation* of the colonists from their brethren in England, the Union, the War of the Revolution, and the birth of a Nation. By it England lost her American dominion, won defeat and dishonor, and added to the national debt one hundred and four million pounds sterling, on which she is now paying interest, — the work of George III. and his servile ministers, his "domestics," as they were called. But America saved not only her own liberty, but the liberty of England; the policy of George III. and his government, which the colonies defeated, if attempted at this day, would not only sever every colony, but overthrow the throne itself. In January, 1766, Mr. Pitt himself declared the American controversy to be "a great common cause," and that "America, if she fell, would fall like a strong man. She would embrace the pillars of the state, and pull down the constitution along with her." Hear Lord Camden, also: "I will say, not only as a statesman, politician, and philosopher, but as a common lawyer, you have no right to tax America. The natural rights of man and the immutable laws of nature are all with that people." And General Burgoyne declared in Parliament, in 1781, that he "was now convinced the principle of the American war was wrong, . . . only one part of a system levelled against the constitution and the general rights of mankind." It was equally for the sake of England as of America that Mr. Pitt and the high-minded men of that day "rejoiced" in our resistance to tyranny. "Passive obedience" then became an obsolete gospel.

One of the most efficient causes of the Revolution in the minds and hearts of the people — an accomplished fact before the war commenced — was the controversy begun in 1763 by the Rev. Dr. Mayhew in his attack on the conduct of the "Society for Propagating the Gospel in Foreign Parts." The most insidious scheme for reducing the colonies to slavery was that of this society, which was known to be only an association for propagating "lords spiritual" in America,[1] who should inculcate, in the

---

[1] Mr. Arthur Lee, of Virginia, wrote from London, Sept. 22, 1771: "The com-

name of religion, the Church of England principles of "submission and obedience, clear, absolute, and without exception." Dr. Mayhew exposed this pious fraud. The Bishop of Landaff, in his sermon of 1766, before this society, ingenuously declared, that when Episcopacy should be established in America, "*then this society will be brought to the happy issue intended*"!

This excited general alarm. The hierarchy could be established only by Parliament; and if, they reasoned, Parliament can authorize bishops, tithes, ceremonies, and tests in America, they can tax us; and what can they not do? The question was, really, Does the British Parliament, three thousand miles off, in which we have neither voice nor vote, own us, three million people, souls and bodies? The people considered the matter, and gradually got ready to fight about it, seeing no more "divine right" of parliaments than of kings, which last had been "unriddled" by Dr. Mayhew in 1750.

The plot was to annul the charters, reduce the popular assemblies to a manageable size, and increase the royal appointments; revise all the colonial acts, in order to set aside those which provided for the support of the ministers. "But, if the temper of the people makes it necessary, let a new bill for the purpose of supporting them pass the House, and the Council refuse their concurrence; if that will be improper, then the governor to negative it. If that cannot be done in good policy, then the bill to go home,"— that is, to England, — "and let the king disallow it. Let bishops be introduced, and provision be made for the support of the Episcopal clergy. Let the Congregational and Presbyterian clergy who will receive ordination be supported, and the leading ministers among them be bought off by large salaries. Let the liturgy be revised and altered. Let Episcopacy be accommodated as much as possible to the cast of the people. Let places of power, trust, and honor be conferred only upon Episcopalians, or those that will conform. When Episcopacy is once established, *increase its resemblance to the English hierarchy at pleasure*"![1]

missary of Virginia is now here, with a view of prosecuting the scheme of an American Episcopate. He is an artful, though not an able man. You will consider, sir, in your wisdom, whether any measures on your side may contribute to counteract this dangerous innovation. Regarding it as threatening the subversion of both our civil and religious liberties, it shall meet with all the opposition in my power." To the Speaker of the House of Representatives, Massachusetts.

[1] Dr. Stiles, in Gordon's History of the American Revolution, i. 102, 103. ed. 1794.

The wealth of England had been created by the "commercial servitude"[1] of her American colonies; and not only this monopoly of the colonial trade, but the commerce itself, was endangered by the aggressions of France, which had surrounded the English colonies by a chain of forts and settlements which reached from the mouth of the St. Lawrence to the mouth of the Mississippi. To save her commerce, her wealth, and her revenue, England drove "the haughty and insolent Gallic" out of Canada; not without ruinous drafts of men and money, especially from the northern colonies, which thereby contracted enormous debts and oppressive taxes. But England represented her own debt as a bill incurred for the benefit of the colonies, and so "the Commons of Great Britain in Parliament, . . . for the purpose of raising a further REVENUE within his Majesty's dominions of America," assumed "to *give and grant*" to his Majesty "a stamp duty" of pounds, shillings, and pence, upon all sorts of documents used by merchants, lawyers, in courts and custom-houses, or in any of the transactions of daily life. No farmer or tradesman could hang an "almanac" in the chimney-corner without paying the "stamp duty of twopence" or "fourpence" *if* this hated act was enforced. But, long before the "first day of November, one thousand seven hundred and sixty-five," — the day when it was to take effect, — there burst forth in the colonies such a universal storm of wrath, that it was suddenly manifest that the Church of England gospel of implicit obedience did not prevail in America.

"Your Majesty's Commons in Britian," said Mr. Burke, "undertake *absolutely to dispose of the property of their fellow-subjects in America, without their consent*, . . . for they are not represented in Parliament; and indeed we think it impracticable; it is not reconcilable to any ideas of liberty. . . . I only say, that a great people, who have their property, without any reserve, in all cases, disposed of by another people at an immense distance from them, will not think themselves in the enjoyment of freedom. It will be hard to show to those who are in such a state which of the usual parts of the definition or description of a free people are applicable to them. . . . Tell me what one character of liberty the Americans have, and what one brand of slavery they are free from, if they are bound in their property and industry by all the restraints you can imagine on commerce, and at the same time are made pack-horses of every tax you choose to impose, without the least share in granting them? When they bear the burdens of unlimited monopoly, will you bring them

---

1 Burke.

to bear the burdens of unlimited revenue too? The Englishman in America will feel that this is slavery; that it is legal slavery, will be no compensation either to his feelings or understanding. . . . The feelings of the colonies were formerly the feelings of Great Britian; theirs were formerly the feelings of Mr. Hampden when called upon for the payment of twenty shillings. Would twenty shillings have ruined Mr. Hampden's fortune? No; but the payment of half twenty shillings, on the principle upon which it was demanded, would have made him a SLAVE."

Among the "Navigation Acts" was one of 6th George II., "An Act for the better securing and encouraging the Trade of his Majesty's Colonies in America," which was commonly called the "Molasses Act." The articles of molasses and sugar, it was demonstrated by Mr. Otis, entered into every branch of our commerce, fisheries, manufactures, and agriculture. The duty of sixpence on molasses was full one-half of its value, and its enforcement would have ruined commerce. Mr. Otis roundly declared that if the King of Great Britain in person were encamped on Boston Common, at the head of twenty thousand men, with all his navy on our coast, he would not be able to execute these laws; for "taxation without representation was tyranny." This was in 1762, when the tyrannical *writs of assistance*[1] were applied for, to search for and seize smuggled goods, and under which the sanctuary of no home, no dwelling, no treasure would be sacred from the pollution and violence of any catchpole ready for the odious service, backed by the forms of law.

John Adams said: "Wits may laugh at our fondness for molasses, and we ought all to join in the laugh with as much good humor as General Lincoln did. General Washington, however, always asserted and proved that Virginians loved molasses as well as New England men did. I know not why we should blush to confess that *molasses was an essential ingredient in American independence.* Many great events have proceeded from much smaller causes."

These acts were repealed while America was in open resistance. *"See what firmness and resolution will do,"* said the Sons of Liberty, when a copy of the act of repeal was received in Boston. With this act of repeal was another, simply declaratory of the authority of Parliament to bind the

---

[1] Just as the above is going to press, there is brought to light, by Mr. David Roberts, an original volume of the Salem custom-house records, May 22, 1761—1775, which fills an important gap in the documentary history of the writs of assistance. — Hist. Collect. Essex Inst., August, 1860. 169.

colonies "in all cases whatsoever." "But," said JUNIUS, "it is truly astonishing that . . . they should have conceived that a *compliance which acknowledged the rod to be in the hands of the Americans, could ever induce them to surrender it.*" Mr. Grenville desired Mr. Knox's opinion of the effects which the repeal would produce in America. The answer was, "*Addresses of thanks and measures of rebellion.*"

The contemporary accounts from every part of the colonies show that never before had there been such rejoicings in America. It is a source of supreme satisfaction to reflect that Dr. Mayhew lived to share in this triumph of liberty.

We naturally feel a certain curiosity as to the places which are associated with great names and memorable scenes. Fortunately we have a lively description of the *Council Chamber* as it was when James Otis so eloquently opposed the *writs of assistance*, written by one who then heard the great patriot lawyer, and was familiar with its aspect, adornment, and fittings. "Whenever," said the venerable Adams, "you shall find a painter, male or female, I pray you to suggest a scene and subject: The scene is the *Council Chamber* of the *Old Town House in Boston;* the date is the month of February, 1761. That Council Chamber was as respectable an apartment, and more so too, in proportion, than the House of Lords or House of Commons in Great Britain, or that in Philadelphia in which the Declaration of Independence was signed in 1776. In this chamber, near the fire, were seated five judges, with Lieutenant-Governor Hutchinson at their head as Chief Justice, all in their new, fresh robes of scarlet English cloth, in their broad bands, and immense judicial wigs. In this chamber was seated, at a long table, all the barristers of Boston and its neighboring county of Middlesex, in their gowns, bands, and tye-wigs. They were not seated on ivory chairs, but their dress was more solemn and more pompous than that of the Roman senate when the Gauls broke in upon them. In a corner of the room must be placed wit, sense, imagination, genius, pathos, reason, prudence, eloquence, learning, science, and immense reading, hung by the shoulders on two crutches, covered with a cloth great-coat, in the person of Mr. Pratt, who had been solicited on both sides, but would engage on neither, being about to leave Boston forever, as Chief Justice of New York. Two portraits, at more than full length, of King Charles the Second and King James the Second, in splendid golden frames, were hung up on the most conspicuous side of the apartment. If my young eyes or old memory have not deceived me, these were the finest pictures I have seen. The colors of their long flowing robes and their royal ermines were the most glowing, the figures the most noble and graceful, the features the most distinct and characteristic: far superior to those of the King and Queen of France in the Senate Chamber of Congress. I believe they were Vandyke's. Sure I am there was no painter in England capable of them at that time. They had been sent over, without frames, in Governor Pownall's time; but, as he was no admirer of Charleses or Jameses, they were stowed away in a garret among rubbish till Governor Bernard came, had them cleaned, superbly framed, and placed in council for the admiration and imitation of all men, no doubt with the concurrence of Hutchinson and all the junto." . . .

"Now for the actors and performers. Mr. Gridley argued with his characteristic learning, ingenuity, and dignity, and said everything that could be said in favor of Cockle's petition; all depending, however, on the — 'If the Parliament of Great Britain is the sovereign legislator of all the British empire.' Mr. Thatcher followed him, on the other side, and argued with the softness of manners, the ingenuity, the cool reasoning which were peculiar to his amiable character. But Otis was a flame of fire. With a promptitude of classical allusions, a depth of research, a rapid summary of historical events and dates, a profusion of legal authorities, a prophetic glare of his eyes into futurity, and a rapid torrent of impetuous eloquence, he hurried away all before him. American Independence was then and there born. The seeds of patriots and heroes, to defend the *Non Sine Diis Animosus Infans*, to defend the vigorous youth, were then and there sown. Every man of an immense crowded audience appeared to me to go away, as I did, ready to take arms against writs of assistance. Then and there was the first scene of the first act of opposition to the arbitrary claims of Great Britain. Then and there the child Independence was born. In fifteen years — that is, in 1776 — he grew up to manhood, and declared himself free."

Dr. Chauncy, the preacher, was one of the greatest divines in New England, and no one except President Edwards and Dr. Jonathan Mayhew had been so much known among the *literati* of Europe. He was zealous for liberty, and, on the death of Dr. Mayhew, continued the war against its most specious enemy with great power and learning. He was born January 1, 1705, graduated at Harvard College in 1721, and was pastor of the first church in Boston from 1727 till his death in 1787.

This sermon — an admirable historical picture, drawn by a master, himself a leader of the hosts — abounds in facts, discusses the great principles involved with energy and power, and with the calmness and precision of the statesman.

The following witty lines, from the London "Craftsman" newspaper of March 29th, 1766, give a lively and just idea of the effect of the Stamp Act on British industry, temper, and politics.

CHAPTER IV. OF THE BOOK OF AMERICA.

1. *The men of the cities assemble.* 3. *Their discourse to each other.* 11. *They petition the Grand Sanhedrim.* 14. *The lamentation of George the Treasurer.* 19. *Newspapers.* 22. *And hireling Scribes.* 25. *These Scribes write against taking off the tribute.* 26. *The subject of their letters.* 32. *They prevail not.* 34. *But are answered.* 38. *The tribute taken off.* 39. *Great rejoicings thereat.* 41. *The song of the people.*

1 ¶ AFTER these things the men of London, and the men of Birmingham, and the men of the great cities and strong towns; even all who made cloth, and worked in iron and in steel, and in sundry metals, communed together.

2 And they met in the gates of their cities, and of their towns;

3 ¶ And they said unto each other, Behold now the children of America are waxed strong; and they have not only opposed the men who were sent by *George* the *Treasurer* to collect the tribute on the marks which are called *stamps;*

4 But they make unto themselves the wares wherewith we were wont to furnish them;

5 And they will buy no more of us unless this tribute is taken off:

6 And, moreover, they cannot pay unto us the monies which they owe; and the loss is great unto us, and the burthen thereof exceeding grievous:

7 Neither can we give bread unto those who labored for us; and behold! they, and their wives, and their little ones, have not bread to eat.

8 What then shall we do? and wherewithal shall we be comforted?

9 Shall we not petition our Lord the King, and his Princes, and the wise men of the nation, even the *Grand Sanhedrim* of the nation?

10 For we know that they are good and gracious, and will hearken to the voice of the people, who open their mouths and cry unto them for bread.

11 ¶ Then the men of London, and the men of the great cities, sat them down and wrote petitions.

12 And they sent men from amongst them, that were goodly men to look at; and they stood before the *Grand Sanhedrim:*

13 And they presented their petitions, and they were read, and days were appointed to consider them.

14 ¶ Now it came to pass, that while these things were doing, that *George* the *late Treasurer,* and those who had joined in laying the tribute on the *stamps,* were wroth, and their countenances fell;

15 And they said in themselves, If this tribute is taken off, then *William* the *late Scribe,* and those who are now in authority, and who have taken our places, will be had in remembrance of men.

16 And we also shall be had in remembrance, but it will be with *evil remembrance indeed.*

17 For behold the people will say, It is *we* that have *cursed* the land; and it is *they* who have *blessed* it.

18 Therefore we must bestir ourselves like men, to oppose the taking off the tribute, let whatsoever hap besides.

19 ¶ And in those days there were papers sold daily among the men of Britain, which declared those which were joined in marriage, those which were gathered unto their fathers, and those who had found favour in the eyes of the King and his rulers, and were exalted above their brethren,

20 And also of whatsoever was done in the land.

21 And these papers were called *newspapers;* and all men read them.

22 ¶ And there were certain also Scribes who let themselves out unto hire.

23 And one of the chief of these was a *Levite,* and his name was *Anti Sejanus.*

24 And these Scribes were hired to poison the minds of the people, and to cause them to set their faces against the men of *America* their brethren.

25 ¶ Then came *Anti Sejanus,* and *Pacificus,* and *Pro Patria,* and sundry other *children of Belial,* and they wrote letters which were put into the newspapers.

26 ¶ And they said in those letters, Men and brethren! Behold, the men of *America* are rich, and they are grown insolent, being full of bread;

27 And they are not mindful of the days of old when they were poor, but they would withdraw themselves from under the wings of their mother *Britain.*

28 And they would establish themselves as a people, and suffer us to have no power over them.

29 Behold, they have opposed the *edict,* and they are become as *rebels.*

30 Wherefore then go we not forth with a strong hand, and force them unto obedience to us? ·

31 And if they are still murmuring, and shall still oppose our authority, why do we not send fire and sword into their land, and cut them off from the face of the earth?

32 ¶ And these *children of Belial* who dipped their pens for hire, and would scatter plagues in wantonness, and say, *This is sport;*

33 Even these men wrote still more. Yet they prevailed not.

34 ¶ For they were answered, So the men of *America* are our brethren; they are the children of our forefathers; and shall we seek their blood? If they are mistaken shall we not pity them, and keep them obedient unto us through love?

35 For behold, it is a wise saying of old, That *many flies may be caught with a little honey; but with much vinegar ye can catch not one.*

36 Neither are they inclined to be a people of themselves, but wish yet to be under our wing.

37 And the counsel of these men prevailed; for the counsel of the hireling Scribes was defeated; even as was the counsel of *Achitophel* in the days of *David,* King of *Israel.*

38 ¶ For behold, the *Grand Sanhedrim* took off the tribute from the people; and *George* THE GRACIOUS King of Britain assented thereto.

39 ¶ Then were great rejoicings made throughout the land; and fires were lighted up in the streets, and the people eat, drank, and were merry.

40 And they sang a new song, saying,

41 ¶ Long live the King; let his name be glorious, and may his rule over us be happy.

42 And may the princes and the rulers of the land, and the wise men of the Lord the King, and all those who joined to take off this tribute, be blessed.

43 For they have listened unto the cries of the people, and have given ear unto the voice of calamity; they have procured the payment of the debts of the merchants of this land, ease to the children of *America,* and labor and bread to the poor.

44 And the women shall sing their praises; and the little children shall lisp out, *Bless the King and his Sanhedrim.*

45 For we were desolate and distressed; our hammers and our shuttles were useless; for we got no work; neither had we bread to eat for ourselves, nor our little ones.

46 But now can we work, rejoice, and be exceeding glad.
47 And there was peace in the land.
48 But to *Anti Sejanus* and the rest of the hirelings there was shame, and the scorn of all good men fell upon them, and their employers, so that their names were had in abomination.

BY HIS EXCELLENCY

FRANCIS BERNARD, ESQ.,

Captain-General and Governor-in-Chief in and over His Majesty's Province of Massachusetts Bay in New England, and Vice-Admiral of the same.

A PROCLAMATION

FOR A DAY OF PUBLIC THANKSGIVING.

Whereas the House of Representatives of this Province having in the last session taken into their consideration the kind interposition of Providence in disposing our most gracious Sovereign and both Houses of Parliament to hearken to the united supplications of his dutiful and loyal Subjects in *America*, and to remove the great difficulties which the Colonies in general, and this Province in particular, labored under, occasioned by the Stamp Act, did resolve that the Governor be desired to appoint a Day of General Thanksgiving to be observed throughout this Province, that the good People thereof may have an opportunity in a public manner to express their Gratitude to Almighty GOD for his great Goodness in thus delivering them from their Anxiety and Distress and restoring the Province to its former Peace and Tranquillity: which Resolution was concurred in by the Council, and has since been laid before me:

In pursuance of such Desire, so signified unto me, I have thought fit to appoint, and I do, by and with the advice of his Majesty's Council, appoint Thursday, the twenty-fourth day of this instant July, to be a Day of Prayer and Thanksgiving; that the ministers of GOD's holy word may thereupon assemble to return Thanks to Almighty GOD for his Mercies aforesaid, and to desire that he would be pleased to give his People Grace to make a right improvement of them, by observing and promoting a dutiful Submission to the Sovereign Power to which they are subordinate, and a brotherly Love and Affection to that People from whom they are derived, and to whom they are nearly related by civil Policy and mutual interests.

And I command and enjoin all Magistrates and Civil Officers to see that said Day be observed as a Day set apart for Religious Worship, and that no servile Labor be permitted therein.

GIVEN *at the Council Chamber in* BOSTON, the fourth day of July, 1766, in the Sixth year of the Reign of our Sovereign Lord GEORGE the Third, by the Grace of GOD, of GREAT BRITAIN, FRANCE, and IRELAND, KING, Defender of the Faith, etc.

FRA. BERNARD.

By His Excellency's Command.
JOHN COTTON, *Dept. Sec'y.*

God save the King.

DISCOURSE II.

A THANKSGIVING SERMON.

AS COLD WATERS TO A THIRSTY SOUL, SO IS GOOD NEWS FROM A FAR
COUNTRY. — Proverbs xxv. 25.

WE are so formed by the God of nature, doubtless for
wise and good ends, that the uneasy sensation to which
we give the name of *thirst* is an inseparable attendant on
the want of some proper liquid; and as this want is increased, such proportionably will be the increase of uneasiness; and the uneasiness may gradually heighten, till
it throws one into a state that is truly tormenting. The
application of cooling drink is fitted, by an established law
of heaven, not only to remove away this uneasiness, but
to give pleasure in the doing of it, by its manner of acting
upon the organs of taste. There is scarce a keener perception of pleasure than that which is felt by one that is
athirst upon being satisfied with agreeable drink. Hence
the desire of spiritual good things, in those who have had
excited in them a serious sense of God and religion, is
represented, in the sacred books, by the "cravings of a
thirsty man after drink." Hence the devout David, when
he would express the longing of his soul to "appear before God in his sanctuary," resembles it to the "panting
of a hart after the water-brooks." In like manner, "cold
water to a thirsty soul" is the image under which the wise
man would signify, in my text, the gratefulness of "good

news." 'T is refreshing to the soul, as cold waters to the tongue when parched with thirst. Especially is good news adapted to affect the heart with pleasure when it comes "from a far country," and is big with important blessings, not to a few individuals only, but to communities, and numbers of them scattered over a largely extended continent.

Such is the "good news" lately brought us[1] from the other side the great waters. No news handed to us from Great Britain ever gave us a quicker sense, or higher degree, of pleasure. It rapidly spread through the colonies, and, as it passed along, opened in all hearts the springs of

---

[1] The Massachusetts *Gazette Extraordinary*, Thursday, April 3, 1766, contains an account of the earliest rumor in Boston of the repeal, and of the public enthusiasm: — "Upon a Report from Philadelphia of the Repeal of the *Stamp Act*, on Tuesday last, a great Number of Persons assembled under Liberty Tree," — near the corner of Essex and Washington streets, — "where two Field Pieces were carried, a Royal Salute fired, and three Huzzas given on such a joyful Piece of Intelligence. A considerable Number of the Inhabitants of this Town assembled at Faneuil-Hall on Tuesday last, when they made choice of the Hon. James Otis, Esq., as Moderator of the Meeting. The Moderator then acquainted the Assembly that the Probability of very soon receiving authentic Accounts of the absolute Repeal of the Stamp Act had occasioned the present Meeting; and as this would be an Event in which the Inhabitants of this Metropolis, as well as North America, would have the greatest Occasion of Joy, it was thought expedient by many that this Meeting should come into Measures for fixing the Time when those Rejoicings should be made, and the Manner in which they should be conducted; — whereupon it was

"*Voted*, That the Selectmen be desired, when they shall hear the certain News of the Repeal of the STAMP ACT, to fix upon a Time for general Rejoicings; and that they give the Inhabitants seasonable Notice in such Manner as they shall think best." The expressions of joy were as extravagant throughout England as they were in the colonies. "There were upwards of twenty men, booted and spurred, in the lobby of the Hon. House of Commons, ready to be dispatched express, by the merchants, to the different parts of Great Britain and Ireland, upon this important affair."— ED.

joy. The emotion of a soul just famished with thirst upon taking down a full draught of cold water is but a faint emblem of the superior gladness with which we were universally filled upon this great occasion. That was the language of our mouths, signifying the pleasurable state of our minds, "As cold waters to a thirsty soul, so is this good news from a far country."

What I have in view is, to take occasion, from these words, to call your attention to some of the important articles contained in the good news we have heard, which so powerfully fit it to excite a pungent sense of pleasure in the breasts of all that inhabit these American lands. The way will then be prepared to point out to you the wisest and best use we can make of these glad tidings "from a far country."

The first article in this "good news," obviously presenting itself to consideration, is the kind and righteous regard the supreme authority[1] in England, to which we inviolably owe submission, has paid to the "commercial good" of the nation at home, and its dependent provinces and islands. One of the expressly assigned reasons for the repeal of the Stamp Act is declared in these words: "Whereas the continuance of said act may be productive of consequences greatly detrimental to the commercial interests of these kingdoms, may it therefore please "— The English colonies and islands are certainly included in

[1] This doctrine was expressed by Mr. James Otis, early in 1764, that we "ought to yield obedience to an Act of Parliament, though erroneous, till repealed." And by the Council and House of Representatives, Nov. 3d, 1764: "We acknowledge it to be our duty to yield obedience to it while it continues unrepealed." But want of representation, and, next, that the colonies were not within the realm, soon led to a denial of the authority of Parliament, for a submission to a tax of a farthing would have abandoned the great principle. It was not the amount of the tax, but the *right* to tax, that was in issue. "In for a penny, in for a pound." — ED.

the words "these kingdoms,"[1] for they are as truly parts
of them as either Scotland, Ireland, or even England
itself. It was therefore with a professed view to the commercial good, not only of the nation at home, but of the
plantations also abroad, that the authority of the British
King and Parliament interposed to render null and void
that act, which, had it been continued in force, might in
its consequences have tended to the hurt of this grand interest, inseparably connected with the welfare of both.
From what more noble source could a repeal of this act
have proceeded? Not merely the repeal, but that benevolent, righteous regard to the public good which gave it
birth, is an important ingredient in the news that has
made us glad. And wherein could this "good news"
have been better adapted to soften our hearts, soothe our
passions, and excite in us the sensations of unmingled joy?
What that is conducive to our real happiness may we not
expect from a King and Parliament whose regard to "the
commercial interest"[2] of the British kingdoms has over-

---

[1] That "the colonies were *without the realm* and jurisdiction of Parliament," was demonstrated in the learned and able answers of the Council
and House of Representatives to Governor Hutchinson's speech of January 6, 1773: "Your Excellency tells us, 'you know of no line that can be
drawn between the supreme authority of Parliament and the total independence of the colonies.' If there be no such line, the consequence is,
either that the colonies are the vassals of the Parliament, or that they are
totally independent." In his gratitude, Dr. Chauncy took quite too generous a view of the "repeal." The interests of the colonies were always
subordinate. The Navigation Act, 12th Chas. II. ch. 19, and the colonial
policy of England, as of all nations, considered only the interests of the
realm. — ED.

[2] Mr. Burke, in his speech on "American taxation," years afterward,
1774, said the laws were repealed "because they raised a flame in America, for reasons *political*, not commercial: as Lord Hillsborough's letter
well expresses it, to regain 'the confidence and affection of the colonies,
on which the glory and safety of the British empire depend.'" — ED.

powered all opposition from resentment, the display of sovereign pleasure, or whatever other cause, and influenced them to give up even a crown revenue for the sake of a greater national good! With what confidence may we rely upon such a supreme legislature for the redress of all grievances, especially in the article of trade, and the devising every wise and fit method to put and keep it in a flourishing state! Should anything, in time to come, unhappily be brought into event detrimental in its operation to the commerce between the mother country and these colonies, through misrepresentations from "lovers of themselves more than lovers" of their king and country, may we not encourage ourselves to hope that the like generous public spirit that has relieved us now will again interpose itself on our behalf? Happy are we in being under the government of a King and Parliament who can repeal as well as enact a law, upon a view of it as tending to the public happiness. How preferable is our condition to theirs who have nothing to expect but from the arbitrary will of those to whom they are slaves[1] rather than subjects!

Another thing, giving us singular pleasure, contained in this "good news," is, the total removal of a grievous burden we must have sunk under had it been continued. Had the real state of the colonies been as well known at home as it is here, it is not easily supposable any there would have thought the tax imposed on us by the Stamp Act was suitably adjusted to our circumstances and abilities. There is scarce a man[2] in any of e colonies, cer-

---

[1] "If we are not represented, we are slaves." — Letter to Massachusetts agent, June 13, 1764. — ED.

[2] Mr. Burke, in 1763, showing the difficulties of American representation in Parliament, said: "Some of the most considerable provinces of America — such, for instance, as Connecticut and Massachusetts Bay — have not

tainly there is not in the New England ones, that would be deemed worthy of the name of a rich man in Great Britain. There may be here and there a rare instance of one that may have acquired twenty, thirty, forty, or fifty thousand pounds sterling, — and this is the most that can be made of what they may be thought worth, — but for the rest, they are, generally speaking, in a low condition, or, at best, not greatly rising above it; though in different degrees, variously placing them in the enjoyment of the necessities and comforts of life. And such it might naturally be expected would be the true state of the colonists; as the lands they possess in this new country could not have been subdued and fitted for profitable use but by labor too expensive to allow of their being, at present, much increased in wealth. This labor, indeed, may properly be considered as a natural tax, which, though it has made way for an astonishing increase of subjects to the British empire, greatly adding to its dignity and strength, has yet been the occasion of keeping us poor and low. It ought also to be remembered the occasions, in a new country, for the grant or purchase of property, with the obligations arising therefrom, and in instances of comparatively small value, are unavoidably more numerous than in those that have been long settled. The occasions, also, for recourse to the law are in like manner vastly multiplied; for which reason the same tax by stamped paper would take vastly more, in proportion, from the people

in each of them two men who can afford, at a distance from their estates, to spend a thousand pounds a year. How can these provinces be represented at Westminster?" Governor Pownall, at Boston, Sept. 6th, 1757, wrote to Admiral Holbourn: "I am here at the head and lead of what is called a rich, flourishing, powerful, enterprising country. 'T is all puff, 't is all false; they are ruined and undone in their circumstances. The first act I passed was an Act for the Relief of Bankrupts." — ED.

here than in England. And what would have rendered this duty the more hard and severe is, that it must have been paid in addition to the government tax here,[1] which

[1] Massachusetts, of about two hundred and forty thousand inhabitants, expended in the war eight hundred and eighteen thousand pounds sterling, for four hundred and ninety thousand pounds of which she had no compensation. Connecticut, with only one hundred and forty-six thousand inhabitants, expended, exclusive of Parliament grants, upwards of four hundred thousand pounds sterling. Dr. Belknap's pertinent inquiry, in view of the parliamentary pretence for their revenue acts "to defray the expenses of protecting, defending, and securing" the colonies, was, "If we had not done our part toward the protection and defence of our country, why were our expenditures reimbursed by Parliament," even in part? Dr. Trumbull says that Massachusetts annually sent into the field five thousand five hundred men, and one year seven thousand. Connecticut had about three thousand men in the field, and for some time six thousand, and for some years these two colonies alone furnished ten thousand men in actual service. Pennsylvania disbursed about five hundred thousand pounds, and was reimbursed only about sixty thousand pounds. New Hampshire, New York, and especially Rhode Island in her naval enterprise, displayed like zeal. Probably twenty thousand of these men were lost, — "the most firm and hardy young men, the flower of their country." Many others were maimed and enervated. The population and settlement of the country was retarded, husbandry and commerce were injured. "At the same time, the war was unfriendly to literature, destructive of domestic happiness, and injurious to piety and the social virtues."

In 1762 Mr. Otis said: "This province" — Massachusetts — "has, since the year 1754, levied for his Majesty's service, as soldiers and seamen, near thirty thousand men, besides what have been otherwise employed. One year in particular it was said that every fifth man was engaged, in one shape or another. We have raised sums for the support of this war that the last generation could have hardly formed any idea of. We are now deeply in debt."

Mr. Burke, in 1775, cited from their records "the repeated acknowledgment of Parliament that the colonies not only gave, but gave to satiety. This nation has formally acknowledged two things: first, that the colonies had gone beyond their abilities — Parliament having thought it necessary to reimburse them; secondly, that they had acted legally and laudably in their grants of money and their maintenance of troops, since the compensation is expressly given as a reward and encouragement." Indeed, the

was, I have good reason to think, more heavy on us in the late war, and is so still, on account of the great debt then contracted, at least in this province, in proportion to our numbers and abilities, than that which, in every way, was laid on the people either of Scotland, Ireland, or England.[a] This, if mentioned cursorily, was never, that I remember, enlarged upon and set in a striking light in any of the papers written in the late times, as it might easily have been done, and to good purpose. Besides all which, it is

[a] I have been assured, by a gentleman of reputation and fortune in this town, that in the late time of war he sent one of his rate-bills to a correspondent of note in London for his judgment upon it, and had this answer in return from his friend: "That he did not believe there was a man in all England who paid so much, in proportion, towards the support of the government." It will render the above account the more easily credible if I inform the reader that I have lately and purposely conversed with one of the assessors of this town, who has been annually chosen by them into this office for a great number of years, for which reason he may be thought a person of integrity, and one that may be depended on, and he declares to me that the assessment upon this town, particularly in one of the years when the tax on account of the war was great, was as follows: On personal estate, thirteen shillings and fourpence on the pound; that is to say, if a man's income from money at interest, or in any other way, was sixty pounds per annum, he was assessed sixty times thirteen shillings and fourpence, and in this proportion, whether the sum was more or less. On real estate the assessment was at the rate of six years' income; that is to say, if a man's house or land was valued at two hundred pounds per annum income, this two hundred pounds was multiplied by six, amounting to twelve hundred pounds, and the interest of this twelve hundred pounds — that is, seventy-two pounds — was the sum he was obliged to pay. Besides this, the rate upon every man's poll, and the polls of all the males in his house upwards of sixteen years of age, was about nineteen shillings lawful money, which is only one quarter part short of sterling. Over and above all this, they paid their part of an excise that was laid upon tea, coffee, rum, and wine, amounting to a very considerable sum.

How it was in the other provinces, or in the other towns of this, I know not; but it may be relied on as fact, that this was the tax levied upon the town of Boston; and it has been great ever since, though not so enormously so as at that time. Every one may now judge whether we had not abundant reason for mournful complaint when, in addition to the vast sums — considering our numbers and abilities — we were obliged to pay, we were loaded with the stamp duty, which would in a few years have taken away all our money, and rendered us absolutely incapable either of supporting the government here or of carrying on any sort of commerce, unless by an exchange of commodities.

"Albany Plan of Union," a scheme by which America could protect herself against France, had been sent "home" for government approbation; but it was not sanctioned. — ED.

undoubtedly true that the circulating money in all the colonies would not have been sufficient to have paid the stamp duty only for two years;[1] and an effectual bar was put in the way of the introduction of more[2] by the restraints that were laid upon our trade in those instances wherein it might in some measure have been procured.

It was this grievance that occasioned the bitter complaint all over these lands: "We are denied straw, and yet the full tale of bricks is required of us!" Or, as it was otherwise uttered, We must soon be obliged "to borrow money for the king's tribute, and that upon our lands. Yet now our flesh is as the flesh of our brethren, our children as their children: and lo! we must bring into bondage our sons and our daughters to be servants." We should have been stupid had not a spirit been excited in us to apply, in all reasonable ways, for the removal

---

[1] Dr. Franklin testified, in 1766: "In my opinion there is not gold and silver enough in the colonies to pay the stamp duty for one year." — ED.

[2] "Most of our silver and gold, . . . great part of the revenue of these kingdoms, . . . great part of the wealth we see," says an English statistical writer of 1755, we "have from the northern colonies." This *silver and gold* was obtained by the colonial trade with the West Indies, and other markets, where fish, rice, and other colonial products and British manufactures were sold or bartered. This coin, or bullion, was remitted to English merchants, monopolists, who always held a balance against the colonists. "The northern provinces import from Great Britain ten times more than they send in return to us."— BURKE. This left very little "circulating money" in their hands, and much of their trade had to be done by barter. The act of April 5, 1764, for raising a revenue in America, exacted the duties in specie, and at the same time the "regulations" for restricting their trade with the West Indies, enforced by armed vessels and custom officers, cruising on our coasts, suddenly destroyed this best portion of their commerce, and the flow of gold and silver through New England hands as quickly ceased. This spread a universal consternation throughout the colonies, and they likened the threatened slavery under George III. and the Parliament to the Hebrew bondage to Pharaoh. — ED.

of so insupportable a burden. And such a union in spirit was never before seen in the colonies, nor was there ever such universal joy, as upon the news of our deliverance from that which might have proved a yoke the most grievous that was ever laid upon our necks. It affected in all hearts the lively perceptions of pleasure, filling our mouths with laughter. No man appeared without a smile in his countenance. No one met his friend but he bid him joy. That was our united song of praise, " Thou hast turned for us our mourning into dancing; thou hast put off our sackcloth, and girded us with gladness. Our glory [our tongue] shall sing praise to thee, and not be silent : O Lord our God! we will give thanks to thee forever."

Another thing in this "news," making it "good," is, the hopeful prospect it gives us of being ¡ continued in the enjoyment of certain liberties and privileges, valued by us next to life itself. Such are those of being "tried by our equals," and of " making grants for the support of government of that which is our own, either in person or by representatives we have chosen for the purpose." Whether the colonists were invested with a right to these liberties and privileges which ought not to be wrested from them, or whether they were not, 't is the truth of fact that they really thought they were; all of them, as natural heirs to it by being born subjects to the British crown, and some of them by additional charter-grants, the legality of which, instead of being contested, have all along, from the days of our fathers, been assented to and allowed of by the supreme authority at home. And they imagined, whether justly or not I dispute not, that their right to the full and free enjoyment of these privileges was their righteous due, in consequence of what they and their forefathers had done and suffered in subduing and defending these American lands, not only for their own support, but to add extent, strength, and glory to the British crown. And as it had been early and deeply impressed on their minds that their charter privileges were rights that had been dearly paid for by a vast expense of blood, treasure, and labor,[1] without which this continent must have still remained in a wilderness state and the property of savages only, it could not but strongly put in motion their passion of grief when they were laid under a parliamentary restraint as to the exercise of that liberty they esteemed their greatest glory. It was eminently this that filled their minds with jealousy, and at length a settled fear, lest they should gradually be brought into a state of the most abject slavery. This it was that gave rise to the cry, which became general throughout the colonies, " We shall be made to serve as bond-servants ; our lives will be bitter with hard bondage." Nor were the Jews more pleased with the royal provision in their day, which, under God, delivered them from their bondage in Egypt, than were the colonists with the repeal of that act which had so greatly alarmed their fears and troubled their hearts. It was to them as "life from the dead." They "rejoiced and were glad." And it gave strength and vigor to their joy, while they looked upon this repeal not merely as taking off the grievous restraint that had been laid upon their liberties and privileges, but as containing in it an intention of continued indulgence[2]

---

[1] These various considerations were set forth at length in *statements* of the services and expenses of the colonies, which were sent to England to furnish the colonial agents with arguments why the colonies should not be taxed. — Ed.

[2] The colonists claimed the repeal as matter of right, and not of favor. The English merchants urged it as a commercial necessity, and the politicians dared not do less. Hutchinson says : " The act which accompanied it, with the title of ' Securing the Dependency of the Colonies,' caused no alloy of the joy, and was considered as mere naked form."— Ed.

in the free exercise of them. 'T is in this view of it that they exult as those who are " glad in heart," esteeming themselves happy beyond almost any people now living on the face of the earth. May they ever be this happy people, and ever have " God for their Lord "!

This news is yet further welcome to us, as it has made way for the return of our love, in all its genuine exercises, towards those on the other side of the Atlantic who, in common with ourselves, profess subjection to the same most gracious sovereign. The affectionate regard of the American inhabitants for their mother country [1] was never exceeded by any colonists in any part or age of the world. We esteemed ourselves parts of one whole, members of the same collective body. What affected the people of England, affected us. We partook of their joys and sorrows — " rejoicing when they rejoiced, and weeping when they wept." Adverse things in the conduct of Providence towards them alarmed our fears and gave us pain, while prosperous events dilated our hearts, and in proportion to their number and greatness. This tender sympathy with our brethren at home, it is acknowledged, began to languish from the commencement of a late parliamentary act. There arose hereupon a general suspicion whether they esteemed us brethren and treated us with that kindness we might justly expect from them. This jealousy, working in our breasts, cooled the fervor of our love ; and had that act been continued in force, it might have gradually brought on an alienation of heart that would have been greatly detrimental to them, as it would also have been to ourselves. But the repeal, of which we have had authentic accounts, has opened the channels

---

[1] This sentiment was ever appealed to in all our difficulties. Burke and Pitt made frequent use of it. — ED.

for a full flow of our former affection towards our brethren in Great Britain. Unhappy jealousies, uncomfortable surmisings and heart-burnings, are now removed ; and we perceive the motion of an affection for the country from whence our forefathers came, which would influence us to the most vigorous exertions, as we might be called, to promote their welfare, looking upon it, in a sense, our own. We again feel with them and for them, and are happy or unhappy as they are either in prosperous or adverse circumstances. We can, and do, with all sincerity, " pray for the peace of Great Britain, and that they may prosper that love her ; " adopting those words of the devout Psalmist, " Peace be within thy walls, and prosperity within thy palaces. For our brethren's sake we will say, peace be within thee."

In fine, this news is refreshing to us " as cold waters to a thirsty soul," as it has effected an alteration in the state of things among us unspeakably to our advantage. There is no way in which we can so strikingly be made sensible of this as by contrasting the state we were lately in, and the much worse one we should soon have been in had the Stamp Act been enforced, with that happy one we are put into by its repeal.

Upon its being made certain to the colonies that the Stamp Act had passed both Houses of Parliament, and received the king's fiat, a general spirit of uneasiness at once took place, which, gradually increasing, soon discovered itself, by the wiser sons of liberty,[1] in laudable en-

---

1 This name, " SONS OF LIBERTY," was used by Colonel Isaac Barré, in his off-hand reply to Charles Townshend, Wednesday, February 6, 1765, when George Grenville proposed the Stamp Act in Parliament. Jared Ingersoll heard Colonel Barré, and sent a sketch of his remarks to Governor Fitch, of Connecticut, who published it in the New London papers; and, says Bancroft, " May had not shed its blossoms before the words of

deavors to obtain relief; though by others, in murmurings
and complaints, in anger and clamor, in bitterness, wrath,
and strife ; and by some evil-minded persons, taking occasion herefor from the general ferment[1] of men's minds, in
those violent outrages upon the property of others, which,
by being represented in an undue light, may have reflected
dishonor upon a country which has an abhorrence of such
injurious conduct. The colonies were never before in a

Barré were as household words in every New England town. Midsum-
mer saw it distributed through Canada, in French; and the continent
rung from end to end with the cheering name SONS OF LIBERTY." Mr.
Ingersoll, in a note to his pamphlet (New Haven, 1766), p. 16, says : "*I
believe I may claim the honor of having been the author of this title (Sons of
Liberty)*, however little personal good I may have got by it, having been
the *only* person, by what I can discover, who transmitted Mr. Barré's
speech to America."

Boston voted that pictures of Colonel Barré and General Conway "be
placed in Faneuil Hall, as a standing monument to all posterity of the
virtue and justice of our benefactors, and a lasting proof of our gratitude." But the pictures are not there; and Mr. Drake (History of Boston,
p. 705) aptly suggests that the city "would lose none of its honor by replacing them." The town of Barre, in Massachusetts, perpetuates the
memory of this statesman, and of the public indignation toward Hutchinson, whose name it had borne from 1774 to 1777. Towns in Vermont,
New York, and Wilkesbarre in Pennsylvania, also bear the honored name.
— ED.

[1] In August, 1765, when Lieut. Governor Hutchinson's house, Andrew
Oliver's, William Storey's, and the stamp-office in Kilby Street, were ran-
sacked or demolished. A minute account of places and names, and details in these riots, fill several interesting pages in Drake's History of
Boston, chap. lxix.; Bancroft's United States, chap. xvi., 1765.

President Adams said, "None were indicted for pulling down the
stamp-office, because this was thought an honorable and glorious action,
not a riot." And in 1775 he said: "I will take upon me to say, there is
not another province on this continent, nor in his Majesty's dominions,
where the people, under the same indignities, would not have gone to
greater lengths."

"I pardon something to the spirit of liberty," said Burke.

The Bishop of St. Asaph said: "I consider these violences as the natural effects of such measures as ours on the minds of freemen."— ED.

state of such discontent, anxiety, and perplexing solicitude; some despairing of a redress, some hoping for it, and all fearing what would be the event. And, had it been the determination of the King and Parliament to have carried the Stamp Act into effect by ships of war and an embarkation of troops, their condition, however unhappy before, would have been inconceivably more so. They must either have submitted to what they thought an insupportable burden, and have parted with their property without any will of their own, or have stood upon their defence; in either of which cases their situation must have been deplorably sad. So far as I am able to judge from that firmness of mind and resolution of spirit which appeared among all sorts of persons, as grounded upon this principle, deeply rooted in their minds, that they had a constitutional right[a] to grant their own moneys and to be tried by their peers, 't is more than probable they would not have submitted[2] unless they had been obliged to it by

---

[a] The colonists may reasonably be excused for their mistake (if it was one) in thinking that they were vested with this constitutional right, as it was the opinion of Lord Camden, declared in the House of Lords, and of Mr. Pitt, signified in the House of Commons, that the Stamp Act was *unconstitutional*. This is said upon the authority of the public prints.[1]

[1] Lord Camden said: "The British Parliament have no right to tax the Americans. . . . . Taxation and representation are coëval with and essential to this constitution." Mr. Pitt said: "The Commons of America, represented in their several assemblies, have ever been in possession of the exercise of this, their constitutional right, of giving and granting their own money. They would have been slaves if they had not enjoyed it."— ED.

[2] An examination of the newspapers and legislative proceedings of the period admits of no doubt of this. From the passage of the Stamp Act till certain news of its repeal, April, 1766, the newspaper, "The Boston Post Boy," displayed for its heading, in large letters, these words: "The united voice of all His Majesty's *free* and *loyal* subjects in AMERICA, — LIBERTY and PROPERTY, and *no* STAMPS."

Dr. Gordon says the Stamp Act was treated with the most indignant

superior power.   Not that they had a thought in their hearts, as may have been represented, of being an independent people.[1]   They esteemed it both their happiness and their glory to be, in common with the inhabitants of

contempt, by being printed and cried about the streets under the title of *The folly of* ENGLAND *and ruin of* AMERICA.

It was now — May, 1765 — that Patrick Henry, in bringing forward his resolutions against the act, exclaimed, " Cæsar had his Brutus; Charles the First had his Cromwell; and George the Third "—" Treason! " cried the Speaker; " Treason! " cried many of the members — " may profit by their example," was the conclusion of the sentence. " If this be treason," said Henry, " make the most of it! "

President John Adams, referring to this sermon in 1815, said: " It has been a question, whether, if the ministry had persevered in support of the Stamp Act, and sent a military force of ships and troops to force its execution, the people of the colonies would then have resisted. Dr. Chauncy and Dr. Mayhew, in sermons which they preached and printed after the repeal of the Stamp Act, have left to posterity their opinions upon this question. If my more extensive familiarity with the sentiments and feelings of the people in the Eastern, Western, and Southern counties of Massachusetts may apologize for my presumption, I subscribe without a doubt to the opinions of Chauncy and Mayhew. What would have been the consequence of resistance in arms? " (See note to page 136.) Dr. Franklin, before the House of Commons in 1766, said: " Suppose a military force sent into America, they will find nobody in arms; what are they then to do? They cannot force a man to take stamps who chooses to do without them. They will not find a rebellion, *but they can make one.* " — ED.

[1] Not one of the *English* colonies, or provinces, would *now* submit for a moment to the control which the American colonies would *then* have cheerfully accepted. The royal governors are accepted as pageants on which to hang the local governments, which are essentially independent, but enjoy a nationality by this nominal connection with the crown; and it may be doubted if any of them have that *degree* of loyalty which once animated the " rebellious " colonies of 1776. Happily time has destroyed the animosities engendered by a vicious policy, and there is now that nobler unity (for we be brethren) which is cultivated by commerce and the amenities of literature and science. In this view, the cordial reception, at this time, of England's royal representative in our chief cities, and by our National Executive, is an event of great interest. See p. 143 and note. — ED.

England, Scotland, and Ireland, the subjects of King George the Third, whom they heartily love and honor, and in defence of whose person and crown they would cheerfully expend their treasure, and lose even their blood. But it was a sentiment they had imbibed, that they should be wanting neither in loyalty to their king, or a due regard to the British Parliament, if they should defend those rights which they imagined were inalienable, upon the foot of justice, by any power on earth.[a] And had they, upon this principle, whether ill or well founded, stood upon their defence, what must have been the effect? There would have been opened on this American continent a most doleful scene of outrage, violence, desolation, slaughter, and, in a word, all those terrible evils that may be expected as the attendants on a state of civil war. No language can describe the distresses, in all their various kinds and degrees, which would have made us miserable. God only knows how long they might have continued, and whether they would have ended in anything short of our total ruin. Nor would the mother country, whatever

---

[a] The great Mr. Pitt would not have said, in a certain august assembly, speaking of the Americans, "I rejoice that they have resisted," if, in his judgment, they might not, in consistency with their duty to government, have made a stand against the Stamp Act. 'T is certainly true there may be such exercise of power, and in instances of such a nature, as to render non-submission warrantable upon the foot of reason and righteousness; otherwise it will be difficult, if possible, to justify the Revolution, and that establishment in consequence of it upon which his present Majesty sits upon the British throne. That non-submission would have been justifiable, had it been determined that the Stamp Act should be enforced, I presume not to say: though none, I believe, who are the friends of liberty, will deny that it would have been justifiable should it be first supposed that this act essentially broke in upon our constitutional rights as Englishmen. Whether it did or not, is a question it would be impertinent in me to meddle with. It is the truth of the fact that the colonists generally and really thought it did, and that it might be opposed without their incurring the guilt of disloyalty or rebellion; and they were led into this way of thinking upon what they imagined were the principles which, in their operation, gave King William and Queen Mary, of blessed memory, the crown of England.[1]

[1] See Dr. Mayhew's Sermon of 1750, p. 39. — ED.

some might imagine, have been untouched with what was doing in the colonies. Those millions that were due from this continent to Great Britain could not have been paid; a stop, a total stop, would have been put to the importation of those manufactures which are the support of thousands at home, often repeated. And would the British merchants and manufacturers have sat easy in such a state of things? There would, it may be, have been as much clamor, wrath, and strife in the very bowels of the nation as in these distant lands; nor could our destruction have been unconnected with consequences at home infinitely to be dreaded.[1]

But the longed-for repeal has scattered our fears, removed our difficulties, enlivened our hearts, and laid the foundation for future prosperity, equal to the adverse state we should have been in had the act been continued and enforced.

[1] Dr. Chauncy's speculations upon the probable consequences of the enforcement of the Stamp Act, both in the colonies and " at home," as the colonists affectionately called England, the mother country, are singularly coincident with Edmund Burke's " Observations "— published three years later, 1769 — on Grenville's " Present State of the Nation." He said: " We might, I think, without much difficulty, have *destroyed* our colonies; . . . . but *four millions* of debt due to our merchants, the total cessation of a trade worth *four millions* more, a large foreign traffic, much home manufacture, a very capital immediate revenue arising from colony imports, — indeed the produce of every one of our revenues greatly depending on this trade, — all these were very weighty, accumulated considerations; at least well to be weighed before that sword was drawn which, even by its victories, must produce all the evil effects of the greatest national defeat." Really it was a question of life or death, not only to the colonies, but to the commerce of England, — whose dealings with European nations had increased very little since 1700, — which had risen from colony intercourse; " a new world of commerce, in a manner created," says Burke, " grown up to this magnitude and importance within the memory of man; nothing in history is parallel to it." The repeal of the Stamp Act was a commercial necessity; to enforce it would have been like killing the goose that laid the golden egg.— ED.

We may now be easy in our minds — contented with our condition. We may be at peace and quiet among ourselves, every one minding his own business. All ground of complaint that we are "sold for bond-men and bond-women" is removed away, and, instead of being slaves to those who treat us with rigor, we are indulged the full exercise of those liberties which have been transmitted to us as the richest inheritance from our forefathers. We have now greater reason than ever to love, honor, and obey our gracious king, and pay all becoming reverence and respect to his two Houses of Parliament; and may with entire confidence rely on their wisdom, lenity, kindness, and power to promote our welfare. We have now, in a word, nothing to "make us afraid," but may "sit every man under his vine and under his fig-tree," in the full enjoyment of the many good things we are favored with in the providence of God.

Upon such a change in the state of our circumstances, we should be lost to all sense of duty and gratitude, and act as though we had no understanding, if our hearts did not expand with joy. And, in truth, the danger is lest we should exceed in the expressions of it. It may be said of these colonies, as of the Jewish people upon the repeal of the decree of Ahasuerus, which devoted them to destruction, they "had light and gladness, joy and honor; and in every province, and in every city, whithersoever the king's commandment and his decree came, they had joy and gladness, a feast day, and a good day;" saying within themselves, "the Lord hath done great things for us, whereof we are glad." May the remembrance of this memorable repeal be preserved and handed down to future generations, in every province, in every city, and in every family, so as never to be forgotten.

We now proceed — the way being thus prepared for it

— to point out the proper use we should make of this "good news from a far country," which is grateful to us "as cold waters to a thirsty soul."

We have already had our rejoicings, in the civil sense, upon the "glad tidings" from our mother country; and 't is to our honor that they were carried on so universally within the bounds of a decent, warrantable regularity. There was never, among us, such a collection of all sorts of people upon any public occasion. Nor were the methods in which they signified their joy ever so beautifully varied and multiplied; and yet, none had reason to complain of disorderly conduct. The show was seasonably ended, and we had afterwards a perfectly quiet night.[1] There has indeed been no public disturbance since the outrage at Lieut. Governor Hutchinson's house. That was so detested by town and country, and such a spirit at once so generally stirred up, particularly among the people, to oppose such villanous conduct, as has preserved us ever since in a state of as great freedom from mobbish actions as has been known in the country. Our friends at home, it should seem, have entertained fears lest upon the lenity and condescension of the King and Parliament we

---

[1] The repeal was celebrated throughout the colonies by all possible expressions of joy, — by ringing of bells, firing of guns, processions, bonfires, illuminations, thanksgivings. Prisoners for debt were released; Pitt, Camden, and Barré were eulogized; and in Boston "Liberty Tree itself was decorated with lanterns till its boughs could hold no more. . . . . Never was there a more rapid transition of a people from gloom to joy." — BANCROFT. The Sons of Liberty triumphed.

"It has at once," said Mayhew, in his Thanksgiving Sermon, May 23, "in a good measure restored things to order, and composed our minds. Commerce lifts up her head, adorned with golden tresses, pearls, and precious stones; almost every person you meet wears the smile of contentment and joy; and even our slaves rejoice, as though they had received their manumission." See Drake's History of Boston, ch. lxxi., for an account of the celebration in Boston. — ED.

should prove ourselves a factious, turbulent people; and our enemies hope we shall. But 't is not easy to conceive on what the fears of the one or the hopes of the other should be grounded, unless they have received injurious representations of the spirit that lately prevailed in this as well as the other colonies, which was not a spirit to raise needless disturbances, or to commit outrages upon the persons or property of any, though some of those sons of wickedness which are to be found in all places[a] might take occasion, from the stand that was made for liberty, to commit violence with a high hand. There has not been, since the repeal, the appearance of a spirit tending to public disorder, nor is there any danger such a spirit should be encouraged or discovered, unless the people should be needlessly and unreasonably irritated by those who, to serve themselves, might be willing we should gratify such as are our enemies, and make those so who have been our good friends. But, to leave this digression:

[a] It has been said, and in the public prints, that there have been mobbish, riotous doings in London, and other parts of England, at one time and another, and that great men at such times — men far superior to any among us in dignity and power — suffered in their persons by insulting, threatening words and actions, and in their property by the injurious violence that destroyed their substance. Would it be just to characterize London, much more England itself, from the conduct of these disturbers of its peace? It would as reasonably, as certainly, be esteemed a vile reproach, should they on this account be represented as, in general, a turbulent, seditious people, disposed to throw off their subjection to government, and bring things into a state of anarchy and confusion. If this has been the representation that has been made of the colonists, on account of what any may have suffered in their persons or effects by the ungoverned, disorderly behavior of some mobbishly disposed persons, it is really nothing better than a base slander, and no more applicable to them than to the people of England. The colonists in general, the inhabitants of this province in particular, are as great enemies to all irregular, turbulent proceedings, and as good friends to government, and as peaceable, loyal subjects, as any that call King George the Third their rightful and lawful sovereign.[1]

[1] The sacking of Lord Mansfield's house, the destruction of his library and manuscripts in 1780, and of Dr. Priestley's mansion, books, manuscripts, and philosophical apparatus, in 1791, greatly exceeded the outrages in Boston. — ED.

Though our civil joy has been expressed in a decent, orderly way, it would be but a poor, pitiful thing should we rest here, and not make our religious, grateful acknowledgments to the Supreme Ruler[1] of the world, to whose superintending providence it is principally to be ascribed that we have had "given us so great deliverance." Whatever were the means or instruments in order to this, that glorious Being, whose throne is in the heavens, and whose kingdom ruleth over all, had the chief hand herein. He

[1] If there be in our early historical literature any one feature more strongly marked than the rest, it is this universal recognition of God in all our affairs; and Washington was not more true to himself than to the spirit of his country, which, of all men, he best understood, when, in his inaugural address as President of the United States, April 30, 1789, he said:

"It would be peculiarly improper to omit, in this first official act, my fervent supplications to that Almighty Being who rules over the universe, who presides in the councils of nations, and whose providential aids can supply every human defect, that his benediction may consecrate to the liberties and happiness of the people of the United States a government instituted by themselves for these essential purposes, and may enable every instrument employed in its administration to execute with success the functions allotted to his charge. In tendering this homage to the Great Author of every public and private good, I assure myself that it expresses your sentiments not less than my own, nor those of my fellow-citizens at large less than either. No people can be bound to acknowledge and adore the Invisible Hand which conducts the affairs of man more than the people of the United States. Every step by which they have been advanced to the character of an independent nation seems to have been distinguished by some token of providential agency; and in the important revolution just accomplished in the system of their united government, the tranquil deliberations and voluntary consent of so many distinct communities, from which the event has resulted, cannot be compared with the means by which most governments have been established, without some return of pious gratitude, along with a humble anticipation of the blessings which the past seems to presage. These reflections, arising out of the present crisis, have forced themselves too strongly on my mind to be suppressed. You will join with me, I trust, in thinking that there are none under the influence of which the proceedings of a new and free government can more auspiciously commence."— Ed.

sat at the helm, and so governed all things relative to it as to bring it to this happy issue. It was under his all-wise, overruling influence that a spirit was raised in all the colonies nobly to assert their freedom as men and English-born subjects — a spirit which, in the course of its operation, was highly serviceable, not by any irregularities it might be the occasion of (in this imperfect state they will, more or less, mix themselves with everything great and good), but by its manly efforts, setting forth the reasons they had for complaint in a fair, just, and strongly convincing light, hereby awakening the attention of Great Britain, opening the eyes of the merchants and manufacturers there, and engaging them, for their own interest as well as that of America, to exert themselves in all reasonable ways to help us. It was under the same all-governing influence that the late ministry, full of projections[1] tending to the hurt of these colonies, was so seasonably changed into the present patriotic one,[2] which is happily disposed, in all the methods of wisdom, to promote our welfare. It was under the same influence still that so many friends of eminent character were raised up and spirited to appear advocates on our behalf, and plead our cause with irresist-ible force. It was under this same influence, also, that the heart of our king and the British Parliament were so turned in favor to us as to reverse that decree which, had it been established, would have thrown this whole continent, if not the nation itself, into a state of the utmost confusion. In short, it was ultimately owing to

---

[1] Ecclesiastical and civil. — ED.

[2] "The Rockingham Administration" (July 10, 1765—July 30, 1766), in October, had had "letters from all parts of America that a conflagra-tion blazed out at once in North America — a universal disobedience and open resistance to the Stamp Act;" and *because* it "raised a flame in America," says Burke, "for reasons *political*, not commercial," it was repealed. Thus the Grenville policy was abandoned for the time. — ED.

this influence of the God of Heaven that the thoughts, the
views, the purposes, the speeches, the writings, and the
whole conduct of all who were engaged in this great
affair were so overruled to bring into effect the desired
happy event.[1]

And shall we not make all due acknowledgments to
the great Sovereign of the world on this joyful occasion?
Let us, my brethren, take care that our hearts be suitably
touched with a sense of the bonds we are under to the
Lord of the universe; and let us express the joy and gratitude of our hearts by greatly praising him for the greatness of his goodness in thus scattering our fears, removing
away our burdens, and continuing us in the enjoyment of
our most highly valued liberties and privileges. And let
us not only praise him with our lips, rendering thanks to
his holy name, but let us honor him by a well-ordered
conversation. "Behold, to obey is better than sacrifice;"
and "to love the Lord our God with all our heart, and
mind, and strength, and to love our neighbor as ourselves,"

---

[1] "I remember, sir," said Mr. Burke, in 1774, "with a melancholy
pleasure, the situation of the honorable gentleman" — General Conway —
"who made the motion for the repeal; in that crisis, when the whole
trading interest of this empire, crammed into your lobbies, with a trembling and anxious expectation, waited almost to a winter's return of
light their fate from your resolution. When, at length, you had determined in their favor, and your doors, thrown open, showed them the
figure of their deliverer in the well-earned triumphs of his important
victory, from the whole of that grave multitude there arose an involuntary
burst of gratitude and transport. They jumped upon him, like children
on a long-absent father. They clung about him, as captives about their
redeemer. All England, all America joined to his applause. . . . . .
I stood near him; and his face — to use the expression of the Scriptures
of the first martyr — 'his face was as if it had been the face of an angel.'
I do not know how others feel; but if I had stood in that situation, I
never would have exchanged it for all that kings, in their profusion,
could bestow."— ED.

is better than whole burnt-offerings and sacrifices." Actions speak much louder than words. In vain shall we pretend that we are joyful in God, or thankful to him, if it is not our endeavor, as we have been taught by the grace of God, which has appeared to us by Jesus Christ, to " deny all ungodliness and worldly lusts, and to live soberly, righteously, and godly in the world;" doing all things whatsoever it has pleased God to command us.

And as he has particularly enjoined it on us to be " subject to the higher powers, ordained by him to be his ministers for good," we cannot, upon this occasion, more properly express our gratitude to him than by approving ourselves dutiful and loyal to the gracious king whom he has placed over us. Not that we can be justly taxed with the want of love or subjection to the British throne. We may have been abused by false and injurious representations upon this head ; but King George the Third has no subjects — not within the realm of England itself — that are more strongly attached to his person and family, that bear a more sincere and ardent affection towards him, or that would exert themselves with more life and spirit in defence of his crown and dignity. But it may, notwithstanding, at this time,[1] be seasonable to stir up your minds by

---

[1] In his examination before the House of Commons, in 1766, Dr. Franklin answered to the question, " What was the temper of America towards Great Britain *before the year* 1763 ? "— " The best in the world. They submitted willingly to the government of the crown, and paid, in all their courts, obedience to acts of Parliament. Numerous as the people are in the several old provinces, they cost you nothing in forts, citadels, garrisons, or armies, to keep them in subjection. They were governed by this country at the expense of only a little pen, ink, and paper. They were led by a thread. They had not only a respect, but an affection for Great Britain, — for its laws, its customs, and manners, — and even a fondness for its fashions, that greatly increased the commerce. Natives of Britain were always treated with particular regard; to be an *Old England* man

putting you in remembrance of your duty to "pray for kings, and all that are in subordinate authority under them," and to "honor and obey them in the Lord." And if we should take occasion, from the great lenity and condescending goodness of those who are supreme in authority over us, not to " despise government," not to " speak evil of dignities," not to go into any method of unseemly, disorderly conduct, but to " lead quiet and peaceable lives in all godliness and honesty," — every man moving in his own proper sphere, and taking due care to "render unto Cæsar the things that are Cæsar's, and to God the things that are God's," — we should honor ourselves, answer the expectations of those who have dealt thus favorably with us, and, what is more, we should express a becoming regard to the governing pleasure of Almighty God.

It would also be a suitable return of gratitude to God if we entertained in our minds, and were ready to express in all proper ways, a just sense of the obligations we are under to those patrons of liberty and righteousness who were the instruments employed by him, and whose wise and powerful endeavors, under his blessing, were effectual to promote at once the interest of the nation at home, and of these distant colonies. Their names will, I hope, be ever dear to us, and handed down as such to the latest posterity. That illustrious name in special, PITT,[1] will, I trust,

was of itself a character of some respect, and gave a kind of rank among us."

Q. "And what is their temper now? "

A. " O, very much altered." — See note 1, p. 134. — ED.

[1] No name was more venerated in America than that of *William Pitt.* He was born in London, in 1708, grandson of Thomas Pitt, Governor of Madras, and made his first speech in Parliament in 1736. In December, 1756, when "our armies were beaten, our navy inactive, our trade exposed to the enemy, our credit — as if we expected to become bankrupts — sunk to the lowest pitch, so that there was nothing to be found but despondency at

be never mentioned but with honor, as the saviour, under God, and the two kings who made him their prime minister, both of the nation and these colonies, not only from the power of France, but from that which is much worse, a state of slavery, under the appellation of Englishmen. May his memory be blessed! May his great services for his king, the nation, and these colonies, be had in everlasting remembrance!

home and contempt abroad " (Address of City of London), the great Whig statesman graciously accepted the seals of government, and his administration was the most glorious period of English history since the days. of the Commonwealth and of the Revolution of 1688. America rejoiced, and her blood and her treasure flowed freely. She saw the French navy annihilated, and the British flag wave at Louisburg, Niagara, Ticonderoga, Crown Point, Quebec, and all Canada. "Mr. Pitt left the thirteen British colonies in North America in perfect security and happiness, every inhabitant there glowing with the warmest affection to the parent country. At home all was animation and industry. Riches and glory flowed in from every quarter." — Almon. George II. died, in extreme age, October 25, 1760; succeeded by his grandson, George III., with not a drop of English blood in his veins; a very Stuart in principle. He was a youth of twenty-two years, and the crown was placed on his head by the primate Secker, who aspired to be his counsellor as well as his spiritual director. Secker was the very one who suffered at the hands of Dr. Mayhew in the controversy about the society for propagating the hierarchy "in foreign parts;" "and," said the pious Dean Swift, "whoever has a true value for church and state, should avoid" Whigism. Pitt resigned the seals of Secretary of State on the 5th of October, 1761. He opposed with his might the proceedings against America. The peculiarly impressive circumstances of his death, May 11th, 1778, hastened, if not caused, by his zeal and energy in our behalf, are familiar to all by the celebrated picture of the "Death of Chatham," — the piece which established the fame of the eminent Bostonian, Copley, whose son, Lord Lyndhurst, yet lives, one of the most venerable and eloquent members of the House of Peers. Pittsburg in Pennsylvania, Pittsfield in Massachusetts, and many other towns, perpetuate the memory of the national gratitude, which was expressed by legislative addresses, by monuments, and by every mode of public and private regard. He died poor — " stained by no vice, sullied by no meanness." — ED.

To conclude: Let us be ambitious to make it evident, by the manner of our conduct, that we are good subjects and good Christians. So shall we in the best way express the grateful sense we have of our obligations to that glorious Being, to the wisdom and goodness of whose presidency over all human affairs it is principally owing that the great object of our fear and anxious concern has been so happily removed. And may it ever be our care to behave towards him so as that he may appear on our behalf in every time of danger and difficulty, guard us against evil, and continue to us all our enjoyments, both civil and religious. And may they be transmitted from us to our children, and to children's children, as long as the sun and the moon shall endure. AMEN.

A

S E R M O N

Preached at Cambridge,

in the

Audience of his HONOR

THOMAS HUTCHINSON, Esq;

Lieutenant-Governor and Commander in Chief;

The Honorable

His Majesty's COUNCIL,

and the honorable

HOUSE of REPRESENTATIVES,

Of the Province of the

Maſſachuſetts-Bay in *New-England*,

May 30th, 1770.

Being the Anniversary for the Election of His
Majesty's Council for the said Province.

By SAMUEL COOKE, A. M.

Paſtor of the Second Church in Cambridge.

B O S T O N :

Printed by EDES and GILL, Printers to the
honorable HOUSE of REPRESENTATIVES.

MDCCLXX.

IN THE HOUSE OF REPRESENTATIVES, May 30, 1770.

Resolved, That Mr. Gardner of Cambridge, Mr. Remington, and Mr. Gardner of Stow, be a Committee to return the thanks of this House to the Rev. Mr. Samuel Cooke for his Sermon preached yesterday before the General Court, being the day of the election of Councillors; and to desire of him a copy thereof for the press.

Attest,

SAMUEL ADAMS, Clerk.

EDITOR'S PREFATORY NOTE.

THE happiness of America, on the repeal of the Stamp Act, was as transient as the existence of the ministry which effected it; and the outburst of joy, of which Dr. Chauncy's sermon was but a single note, by the contrast, presents in deeper gloom the succeeding woe. Excessive jealousy of ministerial control — a desire of personal "influence" — was a source of misery to George III., and of calamity to the nation. He settled questions of state on personal, not on national grounds. Thus, in the midst of the American war, he declared respecting Mr. Pitt, whose administration had been the glory of the reign of his grandfather, George II., "*No advantage to my country,* nor personal danger to myself, can make me address myself to Lord Chatham, or to any other branch of opposition. Honestly, I would rather lose the crown I now wear than bear the ignominy of possessing it under their shackles." His letters to Lord North show that the war was *his* war; and he said to Mr. Adams, on his presentation as first minister plenipotentiary from the United States, " I have done nothing in the late contest but what *I thought myself* bound to do."

He never could forget his mother's early precept: " George, be king! " and so capricious was he, that " the question at last was," said Burke, " not who could do the public business best, but who would undertake to do it at all." During the first nine years of his reign there were six successive administrations. The Rockingham Administration, which repealed the Stamp Act, March 18th, 1766, lasted only one year and twenty days. When Chatham, the great friend of America, consented to form a new ministry, he had to frame it of such discordant materials, that during his absence, by reason of ill health, " as if it were to insult him," says Mr. Knight, " as well as to betray him, and even long before the close of the

first session of his administration, when everything was publicly transacted, and with great parade, in his name, they made an act declaring it
highly just and expedient to raise a revenue in America." " He made an
administration so checkered and speckled; he put together a piece of
joinery so crossly indented and whimsically dovetailed; a cabinet so variously inlaid; such a piece of diversified mosaic; such a tessellated pave-
ment without cement, — here a bit of black stone, and there a bit of white;
patriots and courtiers, king's friends and republicans, Whigs and Tories,
treacherous friends and open enemies, — that it was indeed a very curious
show, but utterly unsafe to touch, and unsure to stand on. . . . When
his face was hid but for a moment, his whole system was on a wide sea,
without chart or compass." [1]

The Act of June 29th, 1767, imposing duties to be paid by the colonists
on paper, glass, painters' colors, and teas, and authorizing the appointment of an indefinite number of irresponsible officers, with unlimited
salaries, to be paid by the colonies, again put America in an uproar.
During the period to March, 1770, every proceeding of the British government, in Council or in Parliament, served only to exasperate the Americans, and to strengthen them in a common bond of resistance. On the
11th of February, 1768, the House of Representatives of Massachusetts
issued a circular letter to the speakers of the legislative assemblies of the
other colonies, in which they expressed " a disposition freely to communicate their mind to sister colonies, upon a common concern, in the same
manner as they would be glad to receive the sentiments of any other
House of Assembly on the continent." They say in the letter that " the
House have humbly represented to the ministry their own sentiments;
. . . that it is an essential, unalterable right in nature, engrafted into
the British constitution as a fundamental law, and ever held sacred and
irrevocable by the subjects within the realm, that what a man has honestly acquired is absolutely his own, which he may freely give, but cannot
be taken from him without his consent; that the American subjects may,
therefore, exclusive of any consideration of charter rights, with a decent
firmness adapted to the character of free men and subjects, assert this
natural and constitutional right. It is, moreover, their humble opinion,
which they express with the greatest deference to the wisdom of the Parliament, that the acts made there, imposing duties on the people of this
province with the sole and express purpose of raising a revenue, are
infringements of their natural and constitutional rights; because, as they

[1] Burke.

are not represented in the British Parliament, his Majesty's Commons in Britain, by those acts, grant their property without their consent. . . .

" They have also submitted to consideration, whether any people can be said to enjoy any degree of freedom, if the crown, in addition to its undoubted authority of constituting a governor, should appoint him such a stipend as it may judge proper, without the consent of the people, and at their expense; and whether, while the judges of the land, and other civil officers, hold not their commissions during good behavior, their having salaries appointed for them by the crown, independent of the people, hath not a tendency to subvert the principles of equity, and endanger the happiness and security of the subject.

" They take notice of the hardships of the act for preventing mutiny and desertion," — passed at the same session with the repealed Stamp Act, — " which requires the Governor and Council to provide for the king's marching troops, and the people to pay the expenses; and also the commission of the gentlemen appointed commissioners of the customs, to reside in America, which authorizes them to make as many appointments as they think fit, and to pay the appointees what sum they please, for whose mal-conduct they are not accountable; from whence it may happen that officers of the crown may be multiplied to such a degree as to become dangerous to the liberty of the people." [1]

Lord Hillsborough thought this circular " unfair," and, on the 22d of April, wrote to Governor Bernard " to require the House of Representatives in his Majesty's name to rescind . . . that rash and hasty proceeding." In June, Governor Bernard delivered this message, and the House absolutely declined the proposal; for " we should stand self-condemned as unworthy the name of British subjects, descended from British ancestors, intimately allied and connected in interest and inclination with our fellow-subjects, the Commons of Great Britain. . . . We take it to be the native, inherent, and indefeasible right of the subject, jointly or severally, to petition the king for the redress of grievances; . . . and if the votes of the House are to be controlled by the direction of a minister, we have left us but a vain resemblance of liberty. We have now only

---

[1] Mr. Knight, " Popular History of England," vol. vi. 310, quotes an authority, that " In 1758 America had been called 'the hospital of England;' the places in the gift of the crown being filled ' with broken members of Parliament, of bad, if any, principles; valets de chambre, electioneering scoundrels, and even livery servants.' "

to inform you that this House has voted *not to rescind,* and that on a division on the question there were ninety-two nays and seventeen yeas; " and we shall petition the king to remove Mr. Bernard from the government of this province. The governor dissolved the Legislature the next day, according to the royal instructions. Several other colonial assemblies were dissolved for the same reason.

Four thousand British troops were sent to Boston this year — 1768 — to aid in the collection of the duties; but the custom-house officers fled to the castle for safety, and the collector's boat was dragged through the town and burnt on the common. Now were breathed into life resolves, petitions, protests, state-papers, political treatises, that, for vigor of thought and strength and elegance of expression, for profound inquiry into governmental principles and learning, accurate and cogent reasoning, and the noblest love of liberty, must forever remain unsurpassed, and which drove the British government to the last, if not the only argument of despotism — force. These — among the richest legacies ever left by " Sons of Liberty" to their children — demonstrate the intensity of the struggle, their high and holy principles, the fervor of soul, the indomitable will, with which, consecrated by an unceasing recognition of GOD over all, the great stake, LIBERTY, was won. It is only by a diligent and sympathizing study of these writings, and of the lineage and lives of their great authors, that the spirit of the Revolution can be understood.

As the Legislature was dissolved, a " convention " was held, at Boston, September 22d, where the public will expressed itself, without the legal forms of authority, but decisively. Non-importation agreements were entered into, and a commercial policy of " masterly inactivity" prevailed, very annoying to the "friends of government," and not comforting to the "swarms" of hungry vampires of the customs. This "insolence" disturbed Parliament, and Governor Bernard was directed to transmit to England the names of the principal offenders, who were to be dragged thither for trial.

On election-day, May 31, 1769, the House sent a message to the governor, "that an armament by sea and land, investing this metropolis, and a military guard, with cannon pointed at the very door of the State House,"— yet standing at the head of State Street, — " where this Assembly is held, is inconsistent with that dignity, as well as that freedom, with which we have a right to deliberate, consult, and determine," and " we have a right to expect that your Excellency will, as his Majesty's representative, give the necessary and effectual orders for the removal of the above-mentioned forces by sea and land out of this port and the gates of this city, during the session of said Assembly." The governor's answer was: "I have no authority over his Majesty's ships in this port, or his troops in this town; nor can I give any orders for the removal of the same."

On the 15th of July, in answer to two petulant messages from Governor Bernard, whether they would provide, according to act of Parliament, for the king's troops, the House " evinced to the whole world and to all posterity" their idea "of the indefatigable pains of his Excellency, and a few interested persons, to procure and keep up a standing force here, by sea and land, in a time of profound peace, under the mere pretence of the necessity of such a force to aid the civil authority. . . . The whole continent has, for some years past, been distressed with what are called acts for imposing taxes on the colonists, for the express purpose of raising a revenue; and that without their consent, in person or by representative. . . . . In strictness, all those acts may be rather called acts for raising a tribute in America, for the further purposes of dissipation among placemen and pensioners. . . . But of all the new regulations, the Stamp Act not excepted, this under consideration is the most excessively unreasonable. For, in effect, the yet free representatives of the free assemblies of North America are called upon to repay, of their own and their constituents' money, such sum or sums as persons, over whom they can have no check or control, may be pleased to expend! . . . therefore, ... *we shall never make provision for the purposes* in your several messages above mentioned."

Governor Bernard was rewarded, March 20th, by a royal bauble, — a baronetcy, — and, having prorogued the General Court, July 15th, to January 10th, at Boston, he sailed, August 1st, for England, leaving the government in the hands of Lieutenant-Governor Hutchinson, who was no less obsequious to the crown, and faithless and ungrateful to his native land.

The unanimity of the colonies gained strength; for the cause of one was the cause of all. On the fifth of March, 1770, there was a collision of the soldiers and citizens, — " the horrid massacre,"— the anniversary of which was made very serviceable to the patriot cause. Hutchinson, alarmed by the intense public excitement, convened the Council;[1] at the same time

---

[1] The elder Adams, in his account of this scene, has left to us a picture of the Council Chamber, which remained as it was when Otis there argued against the

the people thronged to Faneuil Hall, and, through a committee, declared to the Governor and Council that "nothing can rationally be expected to restore the peace of the town, and prevent blood and carnage, but the immediate removal of the troops." Governor Hutchinson said: "Nothing shall ever induce me to order the troops out of town;" but Mr. Secretary Oliver whispered: "You must either comply or determine to leave the province." This would have been an end to "his Honor's" advancement. The troops were removed to the castle.

In compliance with the mandate of the minister, Governor Hutchinson further prorogued the General Court, to meet at Cambridge, March 15th, instead of at its ancient seat at Boston. They remonstrated, and Hutchinson answered: "I must consider myself, as a servant of the king, to be governed"—solely—"by what appears to be his Majesty's pleasure." Many messages and speeches were exchanged; and on May 30th the House, before electing the Council, entered on its journal a protest against its session at Cambridge being drawn into precedent.

Boston, in the instructions to her representatives in this court, denounces the doctrines of the ministry as "political solecisms, which may take root and spring up under the meridian of modern Rome; but we trust in GOD they will not flourish in the soil and climate of British America. . . . . . We, therefore, enjoin you, at all hazards, to deport yourselves (as we rely your own hearts will stimulate) like the faithful representatives of a free-born, awakened, and determined people, who, being impregnated with the spirit of liberty in conception, and nurtured in principles of freedom from their infancy, are resolved to breathe the same celestial ether till summoned to resign the heavenly flame by that omnipotent God who gave it."

---

writs of assistance: "The same glorious portraits of King Charles the Second and King James the Second, to which might be added little, miserable likenesses of Governor Winthrop, Governor Bradstreet, Governor Endecott, and Governor Belcher, hung up in obscure corners of the room." The latter are now in the Senate Chamber. "Lieutenant-Governor Hutchinson, Commander-in-chief in the absence of the governor, is at the head of the council table. Lieutenant-Colonel Dalrymple, Commander-in-chief of his Majesty's military forces, taking rank of all his Majesty's counsellors, must be seated by the side of the Lieutenant-Governor and Commander-in-chief of the province. Eight and twenty counsellors must be painted, all seated at the council board. Let me see!—what costume? What was the fashion of that day? Large white wigs, English scarlet cloth cloaks; some of them with gold-laced hats, not on their heads indeed, in so august a presence, but on a table before them."—See pp. 113–14.

Such were some of the leading events after Dr. Chauncy's sermon in 1766, and such the condition and spirit of the times when Dr. Cook preached the "Election Sermon" of 1770, — a discourse that must have "come home to men's business and bosoms."

The preacher, a graduate of Harvard College in the class of 1735, then in the sixty-second year of his age, was "a man of science, of a social disposition, distinguished by his good sense and prudence, and a faithful servant of the Lord Jesus." [1] He died June 4, 1783, aged 74.

The spirit and formula of legislative action on "election-day," in the revolutionary period, appear in the following contemporary account:

"BOSTON, May 31, 1770. Wednesday being the Anniversary of the Day appointed by the Royal Charter for the Election of Councillors for this Province, the Great and General Court or Assembly met at Harvard College, in Cambridge, at Nine o'clock in the Morning; when the usual Oaths were administered to the Gentlemen, who were returned to serve as Members of the Honorable House of Representatives, who also subscribed to the Declaration: — The House then made Choice of Mr. SAMUEL ADAMS for their Clerk ; after which they chose the Hon. THOMAS CUSHING, Esq., their Speaker.

"About Ten o'clock His Honor the Lieutenant-Governor, being escorted by the Troop of Guards from his Seat at Milton, arrived at Harvard College, and being in the Chair, a Committee of the House presented the Speaker elect to His Honor, who afterwards sent a Message in Writing, agreeable to the Royal Explanatory Charter, that he approved of their Choice. The House then chose a Committee to remonstrate to His Honor the Calling of the Assembly at that Place.

"At Eleven o'clock His Honor the Lieutenant-Governor, accompanied by the Honorable His Majesty's Council, the Honorable House of Representatives, and a Number of other Gentlemen, preceded by the first Company in Cambridge of the Regiment of Militia, commanded by the Honorable Brigadier Brattle, went in Procession to the Meeting-House, where a Sermon suitable to the Occasion was preached by the Rev'd Mr. SAMUEL COOKE, of Cambridge, from these words: 2 Sam. xxiii. 3, 4. *The God of Israel said, the Rock of Israel spake to me, He that ruleth over man must be just, ruling in the fear of God,* etc. After Divine Service the Procession returned to Harvard-Hall, where an Entertainment was provided.

"Previous to the choice of Councillors, — in the afternoon, — Letters

1 Allen.

were read from the Hon. BENJAMIN LINCOLN, Esq.; the Hon. JOHN HILL, Esq.; the Hon. GAMALIEL BRADFORD, Esq.; resigning their Seats at the Council Board, on account of their Age and Bodily Indisposition.

"The following gentlemen were elected Councillors for the ensuing year, viz.:

For the late Colony of MASSACHUSETTS BAY.

The HONORABLE

SAMUEL DANFORTH, Esq.;	JAMES PITTS, Esq.;
ISAAC ROYALL, Esq.;	SAMUEL DEXTER, Esq.;
JOHN ERVING, Esq.;	† JOSEPH GERRISH, Esq.;
† WILLIAM BRATTLE, Esq.;	† THOMAS SANDERS, Esq.;
† JAMES BOWDOIN, Esq.;	† JOHN HANCOCK, Esq.;
THOMAS HUBBARD, Esq.;	† ARTEMAS WARD, Esq.;
HARRISON GRAY, Esq.;	† BENJA. GREENLEAF, Esq.;
JAMES RUSSELL, Esq.;	† JOSHUA HENSHAW, Esq.;
ROYALL TYLER, Esq.;	† STEPHEN HALL, Esq.

For the late Colony of PLYMOUTH.

† JAMES OTIS, Esq.;	† JERATHMEEL BOWERS, Esq.;
WILLIAM SEVER, Esq.;	† WALTER SPOONER, Esq.

For the late Province of MAINE.

NATHANIEL SPARHAWK, Esq.;   JEREMIAH POWELL, Esq.;
JOHN BRADBURY, Esq.

For SAGADAHOCK.

† JAMES GOWEN, Esq.

AT LARGE.

† JAMES HUMPHREY, Esq.;   † GEORGE LEONARD, JR., Esq.

[Those marked † were not of the Council last year.]

"The list of Councillors chosen Yesterday being this day, agreeable to the Direction of the Royal Charter, presented to the Lieutenant Governor, His Honor was pleased to consent to the Election of the Gentlemen before-mentioned, except the Hon. JOHN HANCOCK, Esq., and JERATH-MEEL BOWERS, Esq. JOSEPH GERRISH, Esq., declined going to the Board."— *The Massachusetts Gazette*, Monday, June 4, 1770.

DISCOURSE III.

AN ELECTION SERMON.

HE THAT RULETH OVER MEN MUST BE JUST, RULING IN THE FEAR OF GOD. AND HE SHALL BE AS THE LIGHT OF THE MORNING WHEN THE SUN RISETH, EVEN A MORNING WITHOUT CLOUDS: AS THE TENDER GRASS SPRINGING OUT OF THE EARTH BY CLEAR SHINING AFTER RAIN. — 2 Sam. xxiii. 3, 4.

THE solemn introduction to the words now read, respectable hearers, is manifestly designed to engage your attention and regard, as given by inspiration from God, and as containing the last, the dying words of one of the greatest and best of earthly rulers, who, by ruling in the fear of God, had served his generation according to the divine will. Transporting reflection! when his flesh and his heart failed, and his glory was consigned to dust.

From this and many other passages in the sacred oracles, it is evident that the Supreme Ruler, though he has directed to no particular mode of civil government, yet allows and approves of the establishment of it among men.

The ends of civil government, in divine revelation, are clearly pointed out, the character of rulers described, and the duty of subjects asserted and explained; and in this view civil government may be considered as an ordinance of God, and, when justly exercised, greatly subservient to the glorious purposes of divine providence and grace: but the particular form is left to the choice and determination of mankind.

In a pure state of nature, government is in a great measure unnecessary. Private property in that state is inconsiderable. Men need no arbiter to determine their rights; they covet only a bare support; their stock is but the subsistence of a day; the uncultivated deserts are their habitations, and they carry their all with them in their frequent removes. They are each one a law to himself, which, in general, is of force sufficient for their security in that course of life.

It is far otherwise when mankind are formed into collective bodies, or a social state of life. Here, their frequent mutual intercourse, in a degree, necessarily leads them to different apprehensions respecting their several rights, even where their intentions are upright. Temptations to injustice and violence increase, and the occasions of them multiply in proportion to the increase and opulence of the society. The laws of nature, though enforced by divine revelation, which bind the conscience of the upright, prove insufficient to restrain the sons of violence, who have not the fear of God before their eyes.

A society cannot long subsist in such a state; their safety, their social being, depends upon the establishment of determinate rules or laws, with proper penalties to enforce them, to which individuals shall be subjected. The laws, however wisely adapted, cannot operate to the public security unless they are properly executed. The execution of them remaining in the hands of the whole community, leaves individuals to determine their own rights, and, in effect, in the same circumstances as in a state of nature. The remedy in this case is solely in the hands of the community.

A society emerging from a state of nature, in respect to authority, are all upon a level; no individual can justly challenge a right to make or execute the laws by which it is to be governed, but only by the choice or general consent of the community. The people, the collective body only, have a right, under God, to determine who shall exercise this trust for the common interest, and to fix the bounds of their authority; and, consequently, unless we admit the most evident inconsistence, those in authority, in the whole of their public conduct, are accountable to the society which gave them their political existence. This is evidently the natural origin and state of all civil government, the sole end and design of which is, not to ennoble a few and enslave the multitude, but the public benefit, the good of the people; that they may be protected in their persons, and secured in the enjoyment of all their rights, and be enabled to lead quiet and peaceable lives in all godliness and honesty. While this manifest design of civil government, under whatever form, is kept in full view, the reciprocal obligations of rulers and subjects are obvious, and the extent of prerogative and liberty will be indisputable.

In a civil state, that form is most eligible which is best adapted to promote the ends of government — the benefit of the community. Reason and experience teach that a mixed government is most conducive to this end. In the present imperfect state, the whole power cannot with safety be entrusted with a single person; nor with many, acting jointly in the same public capacity. Various branches of power, concentring in the community from which they originally derive their authority, are a mutual check to each other in their several departments, and jointly secure the common interest. This may indeed, in some instances, retard the operations of government, but will add dignity to its deliberate counsels and weight to its dictates.

This, after many dangerous conflicts with arbitrary

power, is now the happy constitution of our parent state. We rejoice in the gladness of our nation. May no weapon formed against it prosper; may it be preserved inviolate till time shall be no more. This, under God, has caused Great Britain to exalt her head above the nations, restored the dignity of royal authority, and rendered our kings truly benefactors. The prince upon the British throne can have no real interest distinct from his subjects; his crown is his inheritance, his kingdom his patrimony, which he must be disposed to improve for his own and his family's interest; his highest glory is to rule over a free people and reign in the hearts of his subjects. The Peers, who are lords of Parliament, are his hereditary council. The Commons, elected by the people, are considered as the grand inquest of the kingdom, and, while incorrupt, are a check upon the highest offices in the state. A constitution thus happily formed and supported, as a late writer has observed, cannot easily be subverted but by the prevalence of venality in the representatives of the people. How far septennial parliaments[1] conduce to this, time may further show; or whether this is not an infraction upon the national constitution, is not for me to determine. But the best constitution, separately considered, is only as a

---

[1] The Septennial Bill of George I., extending the duration of Parliaments to seven years, was passed to defeat the intrigues of the Popish faction, whose "conspiracy against the House of Hanover continued," Sir James Mackintosh says, "till the last years of the reign of George II., ... and whose hostility to the Protestant succession was not extinguished till the appearance of their leaders at the court of George III. proclaimed to the world their hope that Jacobite principles might reascend the throne of England with a monarch of the House of Brunswick." It was the effrontery of their propaganda in New England that roused Dr. Mayhew in 1750. See his Sermon on the "Martyrdom" of Charles I., p. 102. — Ed.

line which marks out the enclosure, or as a fitly organized body without spirit or animal life.[1]

The advantages of civil government, even under the British form, greatly depend upon the character and conduct of those to whom the administration is committed. When the righteous are in authority, the people rejoice; but when the wicked beareth rule, the people mourn. The Most High, therefore, who is just in all his ways, good to all, and whose commands strike dread, has strictly enjoined faithfulness upon all those who are advanced to any place of public trust. Rulers of this character coöperate with God in his gracious dispensations of providence, and under him are diffusive blessings to the people, and are compared to the light of morning, when the sun riseth, even a morning without clouds.

By the ruler in the text is intended not only the king as supreme, but also every one in subordinate place of power and trust, whether they act in legislative or executive capacity, or both. In whatever station men act for the public, they are included in this general term, and must direct their conduct by the same upright principle. Justice, as here expressed, is not to be taken in a limited sense, but as a general term, including every quality necessary to be exercised for the public good by those who

---

[1] Pope's explanation of his two celebrated lines, —

> " For forms of government let fools contest:
> Whate'er is best administered is best," —

was, " that no form of government, however excellent in itself, can be sufficient to make a people happy unless it be administered with integrity. On the contrary, the best sort of government, when the form of it is preserved and the administration corrupt, is most dangerous." When the political institutions of our fathers cease to be animated by their spirit and virtues, the forms only will remain, monuments of their wisdom, and not less of our folly.— ED.

accept the charge of it.   Justice must be tempered with
wisdom, prudence, and clemency, otherwise it will degenerate into rigor and oppression.

This solemn charge given to rulers is not an arbitrary
injunction imposed by God, but is founded in the most
obvious laws of nature and reason.   Rulers are appointed
for this very end — to be ministers of God for good.   The
people have a right to expect this from them, and to require
it, not as an act of grace, but as their unquestionable due.
It is the express or implicit condition upon which they were
chosen and continued in public office, that they attend
continually upon this very thing.   Their time, their abilities, their authority — by their acceptance of the public
trust — are consecrated to the community, and cannot, in
justice, be withheld; they are obliged to seek the welfare
of the people, and exert all their powers to promote the
common interest.   This continual solicitude for the common good, however depressing it may appear, is what
rulers of every degree have taken upon themselves; and,
in justice to the people, in faithfulness to God, they must
either sustain it with fidelity, or resign their office.

The first attention of the faithful ruler will be to the subjects of government in their specific nature.   He will not
forget that he ruleth over men, — men who are of the
same species with himself, and by nature equal, — men
who are the offspring of God, and alike formed after his
glorious image, — men of like passions and feelings with
himself, and, as men, in the sight of their common Creator
of equal importance, — men who have raised him to power,
and support him in the exercise of it, — men who are
reasonable beings, and can be subjected to no human
restrictions which are not founded in reason, and of the
fitness of which they may be convinced, — men who are
moral agents, and under the absolute control of the High

Possessor of heaven and earth, and cannot, without the greatest impropriety and disloyalty to the King of kings, yield unlimited subjection[1] to any inferior power, — men whom the Son of God hath condescended to ransom, and dignified their nature by becoming the son of man, — men who have the most evident right, in every decent way, to represent to rulers their grievances, and seek redress. The people forfeit the rank they hold in God's creation when they silently yield this important point, and sordidly, like Issachar, crouch under every burden wantonly laid upon them. And rulers greatly tarnish their dignity when they attempt to treat their subjects otherwise than as their fellow-men, — men[2] who have reposed the highest confidence in their fidelity, and to whom they are accountable for their public conduct, — and, in a word, men among whom they must, without distinction, stand before the dread tribunal of Heaven. Just rulers, therefore, in making and executing the laws of society, will consider who they are to oblige, and accommodate them to the state and condition of men.

Fidelity to the public requires that the laws be as plain and explicit as possible, that the less knowing may understand, and not be ensnared by them, while the artful evade their force. Mysteries of law and government may be made a cloak of unrighteousness. The benefits of the constitution and of the laws must extend to every branch and each individual in society, of whatever degree, that

---

[1] "Three millions of people, so dead to all the feelings of liberty as voluntarily to submit to be slaves, would have been fit instruments to make slaves of the rest" of the nation. — Pitt. "We have counted the cost of this contest, and find nothing so dreadful as voluntary slavery."— Dec. of Congress, July 6, 1775. — ED.

[2] Perhaps the preacher here caught the eye of a Hutchinson or an Oliver. — ED.

every man may enjoy his property, and pursue his honest course of life with security. The just ruler, sensible he is in trust for the public, with an impartial hand will supply the various offices in society; his eye will be upon the faithful; merit only in the candidate will attract his attention. He will not, without sufficient reason, multiply lucrative offices in the community, which naturally tends to introduce idleness and oppression. Justice requires that the emoluments of every office, constituted for the common interest, be proportioned to their dignity and the service performed for the public; parsimony, in this case, enervates the force of government, and frustrates the most patriotic measures. A people, therefore, for their own security, must be supposed willing to pay tribute to whom it is due, and freely support the dignity of those under whose protection they confide.[1] On the other hand, the people may apprehend that they have just reason to complain of oppression and wrong, and to be jealous of their liberties, when subordinate public offices are made the surest step to wealth and ease.[2] This not only increases the expenses of government, but is naturally productive of dissipation and luxury, of the severest animosities among candidates for public posts, and of venality and corruption — the most fatal to a free state.

[1] The preacher alludes to the standing controversy with the crown about *fixed salaries* to the crown appointees, which the colony persistently refused, but voted such sums from year to year as seemed expedient, thus holding the officers to a certain dependence on the people. Beside, if they were freemen, their property was their own, and not the king's; and they quoted John Hampden's case. "If the votes of the House are to be controlled by the direction of a minister, we have left us but a faint semblance of liberty."— ED.

[2] The reference is to the custom house and revenue officers, whose numbers and whose salaries were limited only by the "commissioners," who were as irresponsible to the people as is a slave-trader to his victim. — ED.

Rulers are appointed guardians of the constitution in their respective stations, and must confine themselves within the limits by which their authority is circumscribed. A free state will no longer continue so than while the constitution is maintained entire in all its branches and connections. If the several members of the legislative power become entirely independent of each other, it produceth a schism in the body politic; and the effect is the same when the executive is in no degree under the control of the legislative power,[1]— the balance is destroyed, and the execution of the laws left to arbitrary will. The several branches of civil power, as joint pillars, each bearing its due proportion, are the support, and the only proper support, of a political structure regularly formed. A constitution which cannot support its own weight must fall; it must be supposed essentially defective in its form or administration.

Military aid[2] has ever been deemed dangerous to a free civil state, and often has been used as an effectual engine to subvert it. Those who, in the camp and in the field of battle, are our glory and defence, from the experience of other nations, will be thought, in time of peace, a very improper safeguard to a constitution which has liberty, British liberty, for its basis. When a people are in subjection to those who are detached from their fellow-citizens, under distinct laws and rules, supported in idleness and luxury, armed with the terrors of death, under the most absolute command, ready and obliged to execute the

[1] The royal governors declared themselves absolutely bound by their ministerial instructions. — ED.

[2] The partisans of despotism — Bernard, Hutchinson, Oliver, and others — had induced the crown to send troops, foreign troops, to enforce foreign laws, to dragoon the " subjects " into obedience, in violation of the charter and of the English constitution. — ED.

most daring orders — what must, what has been the consequence ?

Inter arma silent leges.

Justice also requires of rulers, in their legislative capacity, that they attend to the operation of their own acts,
and repeal[1] whatever laws, upon an impartial review, they
find to be inconsistent with the laws of God, the rights of
men, and the general benefit of society. This the community hath a right to expect. And they must have mistaken apprehensions of true dignity who imagine they can
acquire or support it by persisting in wrong measures, and
thereby counteracting the sole end of government. It
belongs to the all-seeing God alone absolutely to be of one
mind. It is the glory of man, in whatever station, to perceive and correct his mistakes. Arrogant pretences to
infallibility, in matters of state or religion, represent human
nature in the most contemptible light. We have a view
of our nature in its most abject state when we read the
senseless laws of the Medes and Persians, or hear the im-
potent thunders of the Vatican. Stability in promoting
the public good, which justice demands, leads to a change
of measures when the interest of the community requires
it, which must often be the case in this mutable, imperfect
state.

The just ruler will not fear to have his public conduct
critically inspected, but will choose to recommend himself
to the approbation of every man. As he expects to be
obeyed for conscience' sake, he will require nothing inconsistent with its dictates, and be desirous that the most
scrupulous mind may acquiesce in the justice of his rule.
As in his whole administration, so in this, he will be ambitious to imitate the Supreme Ruler, who appeals to his

---

[1] As they had done in the case of the Stamp Act, for instance. — ED.

people — "Are not my ways equal?" Knowing, therefore, that his conduct will bear the light,[1] and his public character be established by being fully known, he will rather encourage than discountenance a decent freedom of speech, not only in public assemblies, but among the people. This liberty is essential to a free constitution, and the ruler's surest guide. As in nature we best judge of causes by their effects, so rulers hereby will receive the surest information of the fitness of their laws[2] and the exactness of their execution, the success of their measures, and whether they are chargeable with any mistakes from partial evidence or human frailty, and whether all acting under them, in any subordinate place, express the fidelity becoming their office. This decent liberty the just ruler will consider not as his grant, but a right inherent in the people, without which their obedience is rendered merely passive; and though, possibly, under a just administration, it may degenerate into licentiousness, which in its extreme is subversive of all government, yet the history of past ages and of our nation shows that the greatest dangers have arisen from lawless power. The body of a people are disposed to lead quiet and peaceable lives, and it is their highest interest to support the government under which their quietness is ensured. They retain a reverence for their superiors, and seldom foresee or suspect danger till they feel their burdens.

[1] The colony obtained copies of official correspondence with the British ministry, exposing the secrets and plots against their liberties. Six of Governor Bernard's and one of General Gage's letters had been sent by Mr. Bollan, the colonial agent, to the Council, in April, 1769. The disclosures enraged the people, and made the writers odious. — ED.

[2] In his letter to England, Oct. 20, 1769, Hutchinson wrote: " I have been tolerably treated since the Governor's "— Bernard — " departure, no other charge being made against me in our scandalous newspapers *except my bad principles in matters of government.*" — ED.

Rulers of every degree are in a measure above the fear of man, but are, equally with others, under the restraints of the divine law. The Almighty has not divested himself of his own absolute authority by permitting subordinate government among men. He allows none to rule otherwise than under him and in his fear, and without a true fear of God justice will be found to be but an empty name. Though reason may in some degree investigate the relation and fitness of things, yet I think it evident that moral obligations are founded wholly in a belief of God and his superintending providence. This belief, deeply impressed on the mind, brings the most convincing evidence that men are moral agents, obliged to act according to the natural and evident relation of things, and the rank they bear in God's creation; that the divine will, however made known to them, is the law by which all their actions must be regulated, and their state finally determined.

Rulers may in a degree be influenced to act for the public good from education, from a desire of applause, from the natural benevolence of their temper; but these motives are feeble and inconstant without the superior aids of religion. They are men of like passions with others, and the true fear of God only is sufficient to control the lusts of men, and especially the lust of dominion, to suppress pride, the bane of every desirable quality in the human soul, the never-failing source of wanton and capricious power. "So did not I," said the renowned governor of Judah, "because of the fear of God." He had nothing to fear from the people. His commission he received from the luxurious Persian court, where the voice of distress was not heard, where no sad countenance might appear; but he feared his God. This moved him to hear the cries of his people, and without delay redress their wrongs. He knew this was pleasing to his God, and, while he acted in his fear, trusted he would think upon him for good. This fear doth not intend simply a dread of the Almighty as the Supreme Ruler and Judge of men, but especially a filial reverence, founded in esteem and superlative love implanted in the heart. This will naturally produce a conformity to God in his moral perfections, an inclination to do his will, and a delight in those acts of beneficence which the Maker of all things displays throughout his extended creation. This fear of God is the beginning and also the perfection of human wisdom; and, though dominion is not absolutely founded in grace, yet a true principle of religion must be considered as a necessary qualification in a ruler.

The religion of Jesus teacheth the true fear of God, and marvellously discloseth the plan of divine government. In his gospel, as through a glass, we see heaven opened, the mysteries of providence and grace unveiled, Jesus sitting on the right hand of God, to whom all power is committed, and coming to judge the world in righteousness. Here is discovered, to the admiration of angels, the joy of saints, and the terror of the wicked, the government of the man Christ Jesus, founded in justice and mercy, which in his glorious administration meet together in perfect harmony. The sceptre of his kingdom is a right sceptre; he loveth righteousness and hateth wickedness. And though his throne is on high, — prepared in the heavens, — yet he makes known to the sons of men his mighty acts and the glorious majesty of his kingdom. By him kings reign and princes decree justice, even all the nobles and judges of the earth. His eyes are upon the ways of men. His voice, which is full of majesty, to earthly potentates is, Be wise now, O ye kings; be instructed, ye judges of the earth; serve the Lord with fear, and rejoice in your exalted stations with submissive awe; embrace the Son, lest he be angry, and ye perish from the way.

The Christian temper, wrought in the heart by the divine Spirit, restores the human mind to its primitive rectitude, animates every faculty of the soul, directs every action to its proper end, extends its views beyond the narrow limits of time, and raises its desires to immortal glory. This makes the face of every saint to shine, but renders the ruler, in his elevated station, gloriously resplendent. This commands reverence to his person, attention to his counsels, respect to the laws, and authority to all his directions, and renders an obedient people easy and happy under his rule; — which leads to the consideration of the last thing suggested in the text, viz.: The glorious effects of a just administration of government.

"And he shall be as the light of the morning when the sun riseth, even a morning without clouds; as the tender grass springing out of the earth, by clear shining after rain." This includes both the distinguishing honor and respect acquired by rulers of this character, and the unspeakable felicity of a people thus favored of the Lord. Justice and judgment are the habitation of the throne of the Most High, and he delighteth to honor those who rule over men in his fear. He has dignified them with a title of divinity, and called them, in a peculiar sense, the children of the Highest. And we are not to wonder that, in the darker ages of the world, from worshipping the host of heaven the ignorant multitude were led to pay divine honors to their beneficent rulers, whom they esteemed as demi-gods.

The light of divine revelation has dispelled these mists of superstition and impiety, and opened to the pious ruler's view the sure prospect of unfading glory in the life to come; and in the present state he is not without his reward. To find that his conduct meets with public approbation, that he is acceptable to the multitude of his brethren, greatly corroborates his internal evidence of integrity and impartiality, and especially of his ability for public action, and — which is the height of his ambition in this state of probation — enlarges his opportunity of doing good. The shouts of applause — not from sordid parasites, but the grateful, the artless multitude — the pious ruler receives as the voice of nature — the voice of God. This is his support under the weight of government, and fixes his dependence upon the aid of the Almighty, in whose fear he rules. How excellent in the sight of God and man are rulers of this character!

Truly the light is good, and a pleasant thing it is to behold the sun. Thus desirable, thus benign, are wise and faithful rulers to a people. The beautiful allusion in the text naturally illustrates this. The sun, as the centre of the solar system, connects the planetary worlds, and retains them in their respective orbits. They all yield to the greater force of his attractive power, and thus with the greatest regularity observe the laws impressed upon the material creation. The ruler of the day, as on a throne, shining in his strength, nearly preserves his station, and under the prime Agent directs all their motions, imparting light and heat to his several attendants and the various beings which the Creator has placed upon them. His refulgent rays dispel the gloomy shades, and cause the cheerful light to arise out of thick darkness, and all nature to rejoice. The planets, with their lesser attendants, in conformity to their common head, mutually reflect with feebler beams their borrowed light for the common benefit;

and all, in proportion to their distance and gravity, bear their part to support the balance of the grand machine.

By this apposite metaphor the divine Spirit has represented the character and extensive beneficence of the faithful ruler, who, with a godlike ardor, employs his authority and influence to advance the common interest. The righteous Lord, whose countenance beholdeth the upright, will support and succeed rulers of this character, and it is an evidence of his favor to a people when such are appointed to rule over them. The natural effect of this is quietness and peace, as showers upon the tender grass, and clear shining after rain. In this case a loyal people must be happy, and fully sensible that they are so, while they find their persons in safety, their liberties preserved, their property defended, and their confidence in their rulers entire. The necessary expenses[1] of the government will be borne by the community with pleasure while justice holds the balance and righteousness flows down their streets.

Such a civil state, according to the natural course of things, must flourish in peace at home, and be respectable abroad; private virtues will be encouraged, and vice driven into darkness; industry in the most effectual manner promoted, arts and sciences patronized, the true fear of God cultivated, and his worship maintained. This — this is their only invaluable treasure. This is the glory, safety, and best interest of rulers — the sure protection and durable felicity of a people. This, through the Redeemer, renders the Almighty propitious, and nigh unto a people in all they call upon him for. Happy must the people be that is in such a case; yea, happy is the people whose God is the Lord.

[1] See p. 164, note 1. — ED.

But the affairs of this important day demand our more immediate attention.

With sincere gratitude to our Almighty Preserver, we see the return of this anniversary, and the leaders of this people assembled — though not, according to the general desire, in the city [1] of our solemnities — to ask counsel of God, and, as we trust, in the integrity of their hearts, and by the skilfulness of their hands, to lead us in ways of righteousness and peace. The season indeed is dark ; but God is our sun and shield. When we consider the days of old, and the years of ancient time, the scene brightens, our hopes revive.[2] Our fathers trusted in God ; he was their help and their shield.

These ever-memorable worthies, nearly a century and a half since, by the prevalence of spiritual and civil tyranny, were driven from their delightful native land to seek a quiet retreat in these uncultivated ends of the earth ; and, however doubtful it might appear to them, or others, whether the lands they were going to possess were prop-

[1] At the Town-House, in Boston, from which usual place of legislation the arbitrary interference of the king excluded us. This show of despotism, rather than the inconvenience, is the real objection to sitting at Cambridge. — ED.

[2] Here is a clear and beautiful reference to the principles and history of New England, and of " the glorious Revolution " of 1689 — a reminiscence very profitable for Governor Hutchinson to reflect on, and very suggestive to the Board of Councillors and House of Representatives who hear it, and to all people who may read it. *Samuel Adams*, Clerk, and now " the most active member of the House," will see that it is published and circulated. It suggests precedents for curing the present ills in our body politic, if gentler remedies, such as petitions and remonstrances, prove to be insufficient. Dr. Mayhew, twenty years before this, considered in his pulpit " the *extent* of that subjection to the higher powers which is enjoined as a duty upon all Christians. Some," he said, " have thought it warrantable and glorious to disobey the civil powers in certain cases, and in cases of very great and general oppression," etc. See the passage on pages 62, 63. — ED.

erly under the English jurisdiction, yet our ancestors were desirous of retaining a relation to their native country, and to be considered as subjects of the same prince. They left their native land with the strongest assurances that they and their posterity should enjoy the privileges of free, natural-born English subjects, which they supposed fully comprehended in their charter. The powers of government therein confirmed to them they considered as including English liberty in its full extent; and however defective their charter might be in form, — a thing common in that day, — yet the spirit and evident intention of it appears to be then understood. The reserve therein made, of passing no laws contrary to those of the parent state, was then considered as a conclusive evidence of their full power, under that restriction only, to enact whatever laws they should judge conducive to their benefit.

Our fathers supposed their purchase of the aboriginals gave them a just title to the lands; that the produce of them, by their labor, was their property, which they had an exclusive right to dispose of; that a legislative power, respecting their internal polity, was ratified to them; and that nothing short of this, considering their local circumstances, could entitle them or their posterity to the rights and liberties of free, natural-born English subjects. And it does not appear but that this was the general sentiment of the nation and Parliament.[1] They did not then view their American adventurers in the light ancient Rome did

---

[1] This was a complimentary and politic view, no doubt; but to Massachusetts the price of her liberty had been eternal vigilance. Indifference to the colonies, the changes of government, the contests between liberty and despotism in England, each in turn were opportunities to our fathers for defeating the ceaseless intrigues of our enemies. The history of our charters, treated as a speciality, would be a proud monument to the prudence, judgment, foresight, tact — the statesmanship — of the fathers of New England. — Ed.

her distant colonies, as tributaries unjustly subjected to arbitrary rule by the dread or force of her victorious arms, but as sons, arrived to mature age, entitled to distinct property, yet connected by mutual ties of affection and interest, and united under the common supreme head.

The New England charter was not considered as an act of grace, but a compact between the sovereign and the first patentees. Our fathers plead their right to the privilege of it in their address [1] to King Charles the Second, wherein they say " it was granted to them, their heirs, assigns, and associates forever ; not only the absolute use and propriety of the tract of land therein mentioned, but also full and absolute power of governing all the people

---

[1] After the restoration of monarchy, in 1660, and the "Charles the Martyr" clergy and courtiers were reinstated, — not by the aid of the Independents, — the old Laudian hate of New England became rampant, and we find abundant letters from their emissaries to Clarendon, to the Bishop of London, the Archbishop of Canterbury, and the like, with a plenty of reports, of "articles of high misdemeanor," writs of quo warranto, discourses of petty intrigue, and other spawn of such creatures as Andros, Randolph, and Maverick. The Revolution of 1689, simultaneous in Old England and New England, blasted their hopes. The four commissioners, Nichols, Cartwright, Carr, and Maverick, — any two or three of them to be a quorum, — were commissioned by Charles II., in 1664, to travel through New England to look out for "the reputation and credit of Christian religion, (!) as an evidence and manifestation of our fatherly affection towards all our subjects . . . in New England, . . . their liberties and privileges." (!) "All complaints and appeals, in all causes and matters, as well military as criminal and civil," to be "determined . . . according to their good and sound discretions." Thus, by one dash of his pen, "Charles R." proposed to overthrow every institution of government in New England; and his commissioners — one of them the most active and malicious, and a debased and brutal man, as his name then stood on the criminal records of Massachusetts — are simply, "from time to time, as they shall find expedient, to certify us, or our privy council, of their actings and proceedings touching the premises." This was one of the occasions of the address to King Charles, October 25, 1664. — Hutchinson's Massachusetts, Appendix, xv. xvi. — ED.

of this place by men chosen from among themselves, and according to such laws as they shall from time to time see meet to make and establish, not being repugnant to the laws of England; they paying only the fifth part of the ore of gold and silver that shall be found here, for and in respect of all duties, demands, exactions, and services whatsoever." And, from an apprehension that the powers given by the crown to the four commissioners sent here were in effect subversive of their rights and government, they add: "We are carefully studious of all due subjection to your Majesty, and that not only for wrath, but for conscience' sake." "But it is a great unhappiness to be reduced to so hard a case as to have no other testimony of our subjection and loyalty offered us but this; viz., to destroy our own being, which nature teacheth us to preserve, or to yield up our liberties, which are far dearer to us than our lives; and which, had we any fears of being deprived of, we had never wandered from our fathers' houses into these ends of the earth, nor laid out our labors and estates therein."

But all their humble addresses were to no purpose. As an honorable historian observes: "At this time Great Britain, and Scotland especially, was suffering under a prince inimical to civil liberty; and New England, without a miraculous interposition, must expect to share the same judgments." And, indeed, of this bitter cup, the dregs were reserved for this people, in that and the succeeding happily short but inglorious reign. Our charter was dissolved,[1] and despotic power took place. Sir Ed-

---

[1] On the 18th of June, 1684. James II. was proclaimed in Boston, 1686, April 12th; and, May 15th, Dudley received a commission, as President, with a Council, to govern Massachusetts, which was superseded by the arrival of Andros, December 19, 1686, as Governor of New England. He *reigned* till 10th of April, 1689, when he was seized by the "sovereign"

mund Andros, — a name never to be forgotten, — in imitation of his royal master, in wanton triumph trampled upon all our laws and rights; and his government was only tolerable as it was a deliverance from the shocking terrors of the more infamous Kirk.[1] Sir Edmund at first made high professions of regard to the public good. But it has been observed "that Nero concealed his tyrannical disposition more years than Sir Edmund and his creatures did months."

But the triumphing of the wicked is often short.[2] The glorious revolution, under the Prince of Orange, displayed

people, and late in the year was "sent in safe custody" to England. Andros was a fit instrument for James II., who commended the atrocities of a Jeffries, and would sell his crown and his people to France. — ED.

[1] He was colonel of the troops which assisted Judge Jeffries in his butcheries in the west of England, which the "Catholic" James II. delighted to relate to his foreign ambassadors. "Kirke would give his officers a grand dinner; on the removal of the cloth the health of the king and queen was drunk, and at this signal the executioners hanged, under the very eyes of the guests, and to the sound of military instruments, the latest prisoners, whose dying agonies merely excited hideous mirth." He thus put to death nearly six hundred persons. "When closely pressed to become a Papist, he answered that he was preëngaged; having promised the Emperor of Morocco, if he ever did change his religion, that he would turn Mohammedan." Randolph, the correspondent of Sancroft, Archbishop of Canterbury, in a letter from Boston, in 1686, writes to his "Grace" that the colonists "have been struck with a panicke feare upon the apprehension of Col. Kurck's coming hither to be their governor," and entertains "his Grace" with petty scandal and unscrupulous plottings about "the affaires of our church" in Massachusetts. This was in reply to the prelate's inquiries, who was anxious to "propagate the gospel in foreign parts."— Carrel's Counter-Revolution in England, ed. 1857. 197, 213; Hutchinson's Collections, 549, 552. — ED.

[2] Governor Hutchinson cannot have listened to this sermon, and its implied parallel of the times of Andros with his own official period, without discomfort, and perhaps regret. His own pen had recorded, in his History of Massachusetts, the infamy of the men of these times, and he himself was plainly on the high road to promotion or to — perdition. — ED.

a brighter scene to Great Britain and her colonies; and though no part of its extended empire did bear a greater part in the joy of that memorable event than this province, yet it was then apprehended we were not the greatest sharers in the happy effects of it. I trust we are not insensible of the blessings we then received, nor unthankful for our deliverance from the depths of woe.

We submitted to the form of government established under our present charter,[1] trusting, under God, in the wisdom and paternal tenderness of our gracious sovereign, that in all appointments reserved to the crown a sacred regard would be maintained to the rights of British subjects, and that the royal ear would always be open to every reasonable request and complaint. It is far from my intention to determine whether there has been just reason for uneasiness or complaint on this account. But, with all submission, I presume the present occasion will permit me to say that the importance of his Majesty's Council to this people appears in a more conspicuous light since the endeavors which have been used to render this invaluable branch of our constitution wholly dependent upon the chair. Should this ever be the case, — which God forbid! — liberty here will case. This day of the gladness of our hearts will be turned into the deepest sorrow.

The authority and influence of his Majesty's Council, in various respects, while happily free from restraints, is

[1] The "province" charter of October 7, 1691, was submitted to not without reluctance. By it the governor had the sole appointment of military officers, of officers of the courts of justice with the consent of the Council, and a negative on all others chosen by the General Court; so that, as the governor held his commission from the crown, they were, in effect, royal appointments, though not salaried by the crown. Under the former charter *all* were chosen by the General Court, and so accountable to the people. See note 1, p. 164. — ED.

momentous; our well-being greatly depends upon their wisdom and integrity.[1] The concern of electing to this important trust wise and faithful men belongeth to our honored fathers now in General Assembly convened. Men of this character, we trust, are to be found; and upon such, and only such, we presume will the eye of the electors be this day. It is with pleasure that we see this choice in the hands of a very respectable part of the community, and nearly interested in the effects of it. But our reliance, fathers, under God, is upon your acting in his fear. God standeth in the assembly of the mighty, and perfectly discerns the motives by which you act. May his fear rule in your hearts, and unerring counsel be your guide. You

---

[1] It was usual to elect the lieutenant-governor, provincial secretary, attorney-general, and one or more judges of the Supreme Court, to the Council. They were a sort of privy council. But, in 1766, their seats were filled by the opponents to the Stamp Act, and after this the governor found in each successive year fewer friends in council. The lieutenant-governor, — Hutchinson, — in his History of Massachusetts, published in the next year, — 1767, — treating of the Council, declared the government of Massachusetts, and of other provinces, defective, for want of a branch with " that glorious independence which makes the House of Lords the bulwark of the British constitution." Still he thought " the colonies not ripe for hereditary honors"! In a series of letters, in November and December, 1768, Governor Bernard urges that the king should appoint a royal council, instead of that elected by the people, and suggests an act of Parliament authorizing the king — Governor Bernard being his representative — to supersede *all* commissions to improper persons; and Mr. Oliver, in February, 1769, in letters to England, objects to the Council " as altogether"— too — " dependent on their constituents . . . . to answer the idea of the House of Lords in the British Legislature."

After 1766, the Council and the House harmonized in their measures, and the unhappy governors, left solitary and alone, sought relief by plotting for the overthrow of " this invaluable branch of our constitution." The schemes of these traitors to liberty — names indelible on the darkest roll of political baseness — were adopted by the British ministry four years later, in 1774; but the colonists " trusted in God and kept their powder dry."— ED.

have received a sure token of respect by your being raised to this high trust; but true honor is acquired only by acting in character. Honor yourselves, gentlemen, — honor the council-board, your country, your king, and your God, by the choice you this day make. You will attentively consider the true design of all true government, and, without partiality, give your voice for those you judge most capable and disposed to promote the public interest. Then you will have the satisfaction of having faithfully discharged your trust, and be sure of the approbation of the Most High.

The chief command in this province is now devolved upon one[1] of distinguished abilities, who knows our state, and naturally must care for us, — one who, in early life, has received from his country the highest tokens of honor and trust in its power to bestow; and we have a right to expect that the higher degrees of them conferred by our gracious sovereign will operate through the course of his administration to the welfare of this people. His Honor is not insensible that, as his power is independent of the people, their safety must depend, under Providence, upon his wisdom, justice, and paternal tenderness in the exercise of it. It is our ardent wish and prayer that his administration may procure ease and quietness to himself

[1] Thomas Hutchinson, distinguished as the historian of the province, and excellent in private life, but whose ambition quickened his conscience only in his duty to the king, and made him an enemy to his country. Born September 9, 1711, of an ancient and honorable family, he graduated at Harvard College in 1727, at the early age of sixteen; was of the Council from 1749 to 1766; lieutenant-governor from 1758 to 1771; in 1760 appointed Chief Justice, and was now at the head of the government, after the departure of Governor Bernard. Faithful to the British ministry in all its measures, some of which he suggested, he left his native country June 1st, 1774, and died in England in June, 1780. Eliot and Allen have ample notices of him. — ED.

and the province; and, having served his generation according to the Divine will, he may rise to superior honors in the kingdom of God.

When the elections of this important day are determined, what further remains to be undertaken for the securing our liberties, promoting peace and good order, and, above all, the advancement of religion, the true fear of God through the land, will demand the highest attention of the General Assembly. We trust the Fountain of light, who giveth wisdom freely, will not scatter darkness in your paths, and that the day is far distant when there shall be cause justly to complain, The foundations are destroyed — what can the righteous do? Our present distresses, civil fathers, loudly call upon us all, and you in special, to stir up ourselves in the fear of God. Arise! — this matter belongeth unto you; we also will be with you. Be of good courage, and do it.

Whether any other laws are necessary for this purpose, or whether there is a failure in the execution of the laws in being, I presume not to say. But, with all due respect, I may be permitted to affirm that no human authority can enforce the practice of religion with equal success to your example. Your example, fathers, not only in your public administrations, but also in private life, will be the most forcible law — the most effectual means to teach us the fear of the Lord, and to depart from evil. Then, and not till then, shall we be free indeed; being delivered from the dominion of sin, we become the true sons of God.

The extent of the secular power in matters of religion is undetermined; but all agree that the example of those in authority has the greatest influence upon the manners of the people. We are far from pleading for any established[1]

[1] " Civil rulers ought undoubtedly to be nursing fathers to the church,

mode of worship, but an operative fear of God, the honor of the Redeemer, the everlasting King, according to his gospel. We, whose peculiar charge it is to instruct the people, preach to little purpose while those in an advanced state, by their practice, say the fear of God is not before their eyes; yet will we not cease to seek the Lord till he come and rain down righteousness upon us.

I trust on this occasion I may without offence plead the cause of our African slaves, and humbly propose the pursuit of some effectual measures at least to prevent the future importation of them. Difficulties insuperable, I apprehend, prevent an adequate remedy for what is past. Let the time past more than suffice wherein we, the patrons of liberty, have dishonored the Christian name, and degraded human nature nearly to a level with the beasts that perish. Ethiopia has long stretched out her hands to us. Let not sordid gain, acquired by the merchandise of slaves and-the souls of men, harden our hearts against her piteous moans.[1] When God ariseth, and when he visiteth,

by reproof, exhortation, and their own good and liberal example, as well as to protect and defend her against injustice and oppression; *but the very notion of taxing all to support any religious denomination,*" etc. — Address of the Baptists to the Congress at Cambridge, Nov. 22, 1776.

By the amendment of the constitution, in 1833, the absolute separation of church and state was completed. On this subject see " Life and Times of Isaac Backus," by Rev. Dr. Hovey, 1858. — ED.

[1] The suggestion of the preacher was heeded. "A Bill to prevent the Importation of Slaves from Africa into this Province" was passed in the House, but an amendment was proposed by the Council, and it seems to have gone no further. In 1767 and 1774, Massachusetts passed laws against slavery, which were vetoed by express instructions from England. The inhabitants of Boston, at a town meeting, held May 26, 1766, for instructing their representatives, — Otis, Cushing, Adams, and Hancock, — charged them "to be very watchful . . . for the total abolishing of slavery from among us; . . . to move for a law to prohibit the importation and purchasing slaves for the future." In the first draft of the Declaration of Independence was this paragraph: "He " — the king —

what shall we answer? May it be the glory of this province, of this respectable General Assembly, and, we could wish, of this session, to lead in the cause of the oppressed. This will avert the impending vengeance of Heaven, procure you the blessing of multitudes of your fellow-men ready to perish, be highly approved by our common Father, who is no respecter of persons, and, we trust, an example which would excite the highest attention of our sister colonies. May we all, both rulers and people, in this day of doubtful expectation, know and practise the things of our peace, and serve the Lord our God without disquiet in the inheritance which he granted unto our fathers. These adventurous worthies, animated by sublimer prospects, dearly purchased this land with their treasure ; they and their posterity have defended it with unknown cost,ᵃ in continual jeopardy of their lives, and with their blood.

Through the good hands of our God upon us, we have for a few years past been delivered from the merciless sword of the wilderness,[1] and enjoyed peace in our borders; and there is in the close of our short summer the appearance of plenty in our dwellings; but, from the length of

---

ᵃ " Be it far from me, O Lord," said the ancient hero, " that I should do this. Is not this the blood of the men that went in jeopardy of their lives? " Therefore he would not drink it. Will not the like sentiments rise in a generous mind thrust into our possessions?

" has waged cruel war against human nature itself, violating its most sacred rights of life and liberty in the persons of a distant people who never offended him, captivating and carrying them into slavery in another hemisphere, or to incur miserable death in their transportation thither. This piratical warfare, the opprobrium of *infidel* powers, is the warfare of the CHRISTIAN King of Great Britain. Determined to keep open a market where MEN should be bought and sold, he has prostituted his negative for suppressing every legislative attempt to prohibit or restrain this execrable commerce." — ED.

[1] Not much troubled by French and Indians since the conquest of Canada, in 1759–60. — ED.

our winters, our plenty is consumed, and the one half of our necessary labor is spent in dispersing to our flocks and herds the ingatherings of the foregoing season ; and it is known to every person of common observation that few, very few, except in the mercantile way, from one generation to another, acquire more than a necessary subsistence, and sufficient to discharge the expenses of government and the support of the gospel, yet content and disposed to lead peaceable lives. From misinformations only, we would conclude, recent disquiets have arisen. They need not be mentioned — they are too well known; their voice is gone out through all the earth, and their sound to the end of the world. The enemies of Great Britain hold us in derision while her cities and colonies are thus perplexed.[1] America now pleads her right to her possessions, which she cannot resign while she apprehends she has truth and justice on her side.

Americans esteem it their greatest infelicity that, through necessity, they are thus led to plead with their parent state, — the land of their forefathers' nativity, — whose interest has always been dear to them,[a] and whose wealth they have increased by their removal more than their own. They have assisted in fighting her battles, and greatly enlarged her empire, and, God helping, will yet extend it through the boundless desert, until it reach from sea to sea. They glory in the British constitution, and are abhorrent, to a man, of the most distant thought of withdrawing their allegiance from their gracious sovereign

a Their losses and private expenses, in watches, guards, and garrisons for their defence, and from continual alarms, in all their former wars, have greatly exceeded the public charges.

1 " The enemies of Great Britain " scorned the complaints of the colonies against the arbitrary measures of the ministry as unavailing, and laughed at their supposed helplessness against wrong. — ED.

and becoming an independent state. And though, with unwearied toil, the colonists can now subsist upon the labors of their own hands, which they must be driven to when deprived of the means of purchase, yet they are fully sensible of the mutual benefits of an equitable commerce with the parent country, and cheerfully submit to regulations of trade productive of the common interest. These their claims the Americans consider not as novel, or wantonly made, but founded in nature, in compact, in their right as men and British subjects; the same which their forefathers, the first occupants, made and asserted as the terms of their removal, with their effects, into this wilderness,[a] and with which the glory and interest of their king and all his dominions are connected. May these alarming disputes be brought to a just and speedy issue, and peace and harmony be restored!

But while, in imitation of our pious forefathers, we are aiming at the security of our liberties, we should all be concerned to express by our conduct their piety and virtue, and in a day of darkness and general distress carefully avoid everything offensive to God or injurious to men. It belongs not only to rulers, but subjects also, to set the Lord always before their face, and act in his fear. While under government we claim a right to be treated as men, we must act in character by yielding that subjection which becometh us as men. Let every attempt to secure our liberties be conducted with a manly fortitude, but with that respectful decency which reason approves,

a It is apprehended a greater sacrifice of private interest to the public good, both of Great Britain and the colonies, hath at no time been made than that of the patriotic merchants of this and all the considerable colonies, by their non-importation agreement. And whatever the effects may be, their names will be remembered with gratitude to the latest generations, by all true friends to Britain and her colonies.

and which alone gives weight to the most salutary measures.   Let nothing divert us from the paths of truth and
peace, which are the ways of God, and then we may be
sure that he will be with us, as he was with our fathers,
and never leave nor forsake us.

Our fathers — where are they?   They looked for another
and better country, that is, an heavenly.   They were but
as sojourners here, and have long since resigned these
their transitory abodes, and are securely seated in man-
sions of glory.   They hear not the voice of the oppressor.
We also are all strangers on earth, and must soon, without
distinction, lie down in the dust, and rise not till these
heavens and earth are no more.   May we all realize the
appearance of the Son of God to judge the world in
righteousness, and improve the various talents committed
to our trust, that we may then lift up our heads with joy,
and, through grace, receive an inheritance which cannot
be taken away, even life everlasting!   AMEN.

A

DISCOURSE

PREACHED

December 15th, 1774,

BEING THE DAY RECOMMENDED

By the Provincial Congrefs;

And *Afterwards at the* BOSTON LECTURE.

BY

WILLIAM GORDON

PASTOR OF THE THIRD CHURCH IN ROXBURY

" And the King confulted with the old men that ftood before
" his father, while he yet lived, and faid, how do ye advife,
" that I may anfwer this people ? And they fpake unto him,
" faying, if thou wilt be a fervant unto this people this day,
" and wilt ferve them, and anfwer them, and fpeak good
" words to them, *then* they will be thy fervants for ever."
1 Kings. 12. 6, 7.
" I ardently wifh that the common enemies to both countries
" may fee to their difappointment, that thefe difputes be-
" tween the Mother country, and the colonies have termina-
" ted like the quarrels of lovers, and increafed the affection
" which they ought to bear to each other."

Governor *Gage's* Letter to the Hon. *Peyton Randolph*, Efq;

THE SECOND EDITION.

B O S T O N: Printed for, and Sold by T H O M A S
L E V E R E T T, in *Corn-Hill.* 1775.

NOTE.

The Boston Thursday Lecture, at which Mr. Gordon repeated this sermon, was founded by the Rev. John Cotton, in 1633, and yet retains a lingering existence, as an opportunity for ministerial gatherings. It was the occasion for presenting, and sometimes discussing, questions of general, social, or political interest; and a collection of the Thursday lectures, or sermons, for the first hundred and fifty years, would be a faithful epitome of the current and progress of public opinion during that period. It would hardly be an exaggeration to say that much of the early colonial legislation was merely *declaratory* of what had fallen from oracular lips in the Thursday pulpit. So general was the interest in the occasion, that it was established by authority as the "market day." The institution illustrates the politico-theological history of New England as stated in the Introduction to this volume. "The Shade of the Past" is the title of Rev. N. L. Frothingham's sermon on "The close of the Second Century since the establishment of the Thursday Lecture." Rev. R. C. Waterston preached, December 14, 1843, "A Discourse in the First Church on the Occasion of Resuming the Thursday Lecture." — ED.

EDITOR'S PREFATORY NOTE.

THE reasons which led to the repeal of the Stamp Act prevailed also against the act of 1767, which was repealed in March, 1770, *excepting as to the duty on tea.* The British ministry, with Governor Hutchinson and his fellow-conspirators, found that British bayonets were powerless against non-importation agreements, and that British merchants would not willingly lose their American commerce. Yet Lord North, with singular fatuity, while making this second surrender to the spirit of the "rebel" colonies, said: "A total repeal cannot be thought of *till America is prostrate at our feet*"! — an anomalous position, offering terms of capitulation, and in the same breath demanding unconditional submission!

Mr. Pownall, who had a thorough knowledge of the colonies, moved for a total repeal. "If it be asked," he said, "whether it will remove the apprehensions excited by your resolutions and address of the last year for bringing to trial in England persons accused of treason in America, I answer, no. If it be asked, if this commercial concession would quiet the minds of the Americans as to the political doubts and fears which have struck them to the heart throughout the continent, I answer, no. So long as they are left in doubt whether the Habeas Corpus Act, whether the Bill of Rights, whether the Common Law as now existing in England, have any operation and effect in America, they cannot be satisfied. At this hour they know not whether the civil constitutions be not suspended and superseded by the establishment of a military force. The Americans think they have, in return to all their applications, experienced a temper and discipline that is unfriendly; that the enjoyment and exercise of the common rights of freemen have been refused to them. Never, with these views, will they solicit the favor of this House; never more will they wish to bring before Parliament the grievances under which they conceive themselves to labor. Deeply as they feel, they suffer and endure with a determined and alarming silence. For their liberty they are under no apprehensions. It was first planted under the genius of the constitution; it has grown up into a verdant and flourishing tree; and should any severe strokes be aimed at the branches, and fate reduce it to the bare stock, it would only take deeper root, and spring out again more hardy and durable than before. They trust to Providence, and wait with firmness and fortitude the issue."

The House of Representatives, relying on the Massachusetts charter as a *compact*, in a message to Lieutenant-Governor Hutchinson, July 31, 1770, deny that " even his Majesty in Council has any constitutional authority to decide any controversies whatever that arise in this province, excepting only such matters as are reserved in the charter; " and they " are clearly of opinion that your Honor is under no obligation to hold the General Court at Cambridge, let your instructions be conceived in terms ever so peremptory, inasmuch as it is inconsistent and injurious to the province." They quote Mr. Locke on civil government, in the matter of *prerogative*, that the people have " reserved that ultimate determination to themselves which belongs to all mankind where there lies no appeal on earth, viz., to judge whether they have just cause to make their appeal to Heaven." They add: " We would by no means be understood to suggest that this people have occasion *at present* to proceed to such extremity." On June 19th, 1771, they again " protest against all such doctrines, principles, and practices as tend to establish either ministerial or even royal instructions as laws within the province." Hutchinson replied that the charter was a mere grant of " privileges " from the crown, which might be cancelled at any time, and that he must act in conformity to his " instructions " or not at all. In a message to the governor, on July 5th, they say: " We know of no commissioners of his Majesty's customs, nor of any revenue his Majesty has a right to establish in North America; we know and feel a tribute levied and extorted from those who, if they have property, have a right to the absolute disposal of it."

The apparent lull in public feeling in 1770–72 alarmed the patriot leaders; but it was the calm before a storm. The sight of foreign soldiery and hostile fleets to enforce an odious despotism from another land, daily demonstrated that non-resistance was slavery. The capture and destruction of one of the British armed revenue vessels which lined our coasts — the *Gaspee*, at Providence, R. I., on the night of June 10th, 1772 — was the first overt act of resistance, and the people said Amen!

It would be difficult, perhaps, to assign to any one specially the idea of committees of correspondence as the most efficient means of unity and of concert of action. As already stated,[1] Dr. Mayhew had, in 1766, suggested the thought to Mr. Otis. Gordon says that Mr. Samuel Adams visited Mr. James Warren, at Plymouth, to confer with him on the best plan for counteracting the misrepresentations of Governor Hutchinson that the discontented were a mere faction, and Mr. Warren proposed the committees of correspondence. Mr. Adams was pleased with it, and the machinery was put in operation at the first favorable opportunity. As the government and defence of a free people depend upon its own voluntary support, and Governor Hutchinson refused a salary from the province, and accepted it of the crown, the General Court did " most solemnly protest that the innovation is an important change of the constitution, and exposes the province to a despotic administration of government."

The Boston " Committee of Correspondence," appointed at this juncture " to state the rights of the colonists . . . as men, as Christians, and as subjects; to communicate and publish the same to the several towns in this province, and to the world," made their report, at a town meeting in Faneuil Hall, on the 20th of November, 1772. They quote freely from " Locke on Government," of which there was a Boston edition published soon after. They declare that, "in case of intolerable oppression, civil or religious, men have a right to leave the society they belong to and enter into another." That in religion there should be mutual toleration of all professions " whose doctrines are not subversive of society," — a principle which excludes the Papists, for they teach " that princes excommunicated may be deposed, and those they call *heretics* may be destroyed without mercy; besides their recognizing the Pope in so absolute a manner, in subversion of government, by introducing, as far as possible, into the states under whose protection they enjoy life, liberty, and property, that solecism in politics, *Imperium in imperio*, leading directly to the worst anarchy and confusion, civil discord, war, and bloodshed. . . . That the right to freedom being *the gift* of GOD ALMIGHTY, it is not in the power of man to alienate this gift and voluntarily become a slave." " The colonists," they say, " have been branded with the odious names of traitors and rebels only for complaining of their grievances. *How long such treatment will or ought to be borne, is submitted.*" They enumerate, among their grievances, the revenue acts, the presence of standing armies and of hosts of officers for their enforcement; the rendering

1 See page 44.

the governor, judges,[1] and other officers, independent of the people by
salaries from the crown, "which will, if accomplished, complete our
slavery;" the instructions to the governor whereby he "is made merely
a ministerial engine;" the surrender of the provincial fortress, Castle
William, to the troops, beyond the provincial control; the suspension of
the New York Legislature "until they should quarter the British troops;"
"the various attempts which have been made, and are now made, to
establish an American Episcopate," though "no power on earth can
justly give either temporal or spiritual jurisdiction within this province
except the great and general court."

The report, with "a letter of correspondence," was printed and sent to
"the selectmen of every town in the province." It was like the match to a
well-laid train, and there burst forth from every quarter responses of such
spirit and severity against "these mighty grievances and intolerable
wrongs," the change in the state of affairs was "so sudden and unexpected," as to greatly alarm and perplex the governor, now helpless and
friendless, and his subsequent controversies with the House only tended
to strengthen the colonial cause. Virginia approved of all this; the system
of correspondence was extended to the colonies, and laid the foundation
of that union which resulted in the general congress at Philadelphia, in
September, 1774.

The report of the proceedings of the Boston town-meetings was reprinted
in London in 1773, with a preface, written by Dr. Franklin, to expose the
misrepresentations of Lord Dartmouth and the ministry, that the discontented were only a faction, and to show that the true causes of discontent
might be well understood. This greatly irritated the ministry. The
discovery and publication, in 1773, of the confidential letters of Oliver,
Hutchinson, and other "government" men, exasperated the people against
the authors. Then followed the destruction of the tea in Boston harbor,
and similar conduct in Philadelphia and New York; and the sequence
was, the Boston Port Bill, which recited "That the opposition to the
authority of Parliament had always originated in the colony of Massachusetts, and that the colony itself had ever been instigated to such
conduct by the seditious proceedings of the town of Boston." It destroyed the commerce of the port. Many were distressed for the necessaries of life; but the act operated as a bond of sympathy between the

---

1 "No tyranny so secure, none so intolerable, none so dangerous, none so
remediless, as that of executive courts."—*Josiah Quincy, Jr.*, 1772.

colonies, and excited a feeling of brotherhood and union against England. General Gage arrived at Boston May 13, 1774, as commander-in-chief of the king's forces, and as Governor of Massachusetts. " The Episcopal clergy" and others addressed Governor Hutchinson, just before he sailed for England, June 1st, " *expressing their approbation of his public conduct,* and their affectionate wishes for his prosperity," though he was execrated by all others. On his arrival there he found that the ministry had adopted the policy advised in his letters of 1768-9, and annulled the charter, as to the executive and judicial powers, and thus he saw the ruin of his country, — if it could be effected, — the work of his own ingratitude and selfish ambition. And, as if intended for a beacon, and an exemplar to the other colonies of the animus and real principles of their enemies, another act established in Canada the Papal Church and a civil despotism in harmony with the history and genius of that hierarchy.

In one of their letters, the patriots say, " that a people long inured to hardships lose by degrees the very notions of liberty; they look upon themselves as creatures, *at mercy,* and that all impositions laid on by superior hands are legal and obligatory; so debased that they even rejoice at being subject to the caprice and arbitrary power of a tyrant, and kiss their chains. But, thank Heaven! this is not yet verified in *America.* We have yet some share of public virtue remaining. We are not afraid of poverty, but disdain slavery. The fate of nations is so precarious, and revolutions in states so often take place at an unexpected moment, when the hand of power has secured every avenue of retreat, and the mind of the subject so debased to its purpose, that it becomes every well-wisher to his country, while it has any remains of freedom, to keep an eagle eye upon every innovation and stretch of power in those that have the rule over us. . . . *Let us disappoint the men who are raising themselves on the ruin of this country.*"

The rapid course of events in 1774 electrified the Sons of Liberty. The arrogance of the ministry, and the severity and abruptness of their acts in Parliament, were met by a spirit of stern defiance, and there swept along the Atlantic shores of the American colonies such a chorus for liberty as was never heard before in national tragedy. The Provincial Congress, — representatives of freemen, — assembled now, not by virtue of paltry parchments from blasphemous " sacred Majesty," but by charter from the ALMIGHTY, to whom they make solemn appeal, " assumes every power of a legal government; for"— says General Gage — " their edicts are implicitly obeyed throughout the continent." They " resolve," and the treasury is supplied; to their call for "immediate defence," *minute-men*, armed hosts, come with alacrity from peaceful life, the artisan from his shop,[1] the farmer from his plough, the fisherman from his shallop, the lawyer from his brief, the merchant from his ledger, and the chaplain from his parish — from field and flood they proffer all for liberty, and matron and maid, with eager hands and hearts, help them to their holy duty.

Dr. Joseph Warren wrote to Josiah Quincy in November, 1774: "It is the united voice of America to preserve their freedom, or lose their lives in defence of it. Their resolutions are not the effects of inconsiderate rashness, but the sound result of sober inquiry and deliberation. I am convinced that the true spirit of liberty was never so universally diffused throughout all ranks and orders of people, in any country on the face of the earth, as it now is through all North America." Of the state documents of the General Congress at Philadelphia, Chatham, in the House of Lords, said: "For myself, I must declare and avow, that in all my reading and observation, — I have read Thucydides, and have studied and admired the master states of the world, — that for solidity of reasoning, force of sagacity, and wisdom of conclusion, under such complication of circumstances, no nation or body of men can stand in preference to the General Congress at Philadelphia."

The Provincial Congress, assembled at the meeting-house in Concord, October 13, 1774, in a message to Governor Gage, signed by John Hancock, President, said, "that the sole end of government is protection and security of the people. Whenever, therefore, that power which was originally instituted to effect these important and valuable purposes is

---

1 The Blacksmiths' Convention of Worcester County, Massachusetts, November 8, 1774, illustrates the fervid determination of the people. They resolved that, "deeply impressed with a sense of our duty to our country, paternal affection for our children and unborn millions, as also for our personal rights and liberties, we solemnly covenant . . . that we will not . . . do or perform any blacksmith's work, or business of any kind, ... for any person or persons . . . . commonly known by the name of tories, . . . mandamus counsellors, . . . for every person who addressed Governor Hutchinson at his departure from this province; . . . all of whom should be held in contempt, and those who are connected with them ought to separate from them, laborers to shun their vineyards, merchants, husbandmen, and others, to withhold their commerce and supplies." This, signed by forty-three of the best men, with strong arms and great hearts, ROSS WYMAN, of Shrewsbury, President, and TIMOTHY BIGELOW, of Worcester, Clerk, was widely distributed in handbills, and published in the newspapers.

Lincoln's History of Worcester, chapters vi.—ix., admirably illustrates the spirit of the Revolution.

employed to harass, distress, or enslave the people, in this case it becomes a curse rather than a blessing; . . . . and we request that you immediately desist from the fortress now constructing at the south entrance into the town of Boston, and restore the pass to its natural state." To which the governor answered: "The fortress, unless annoyed, will annoy nobody; . . . and I warn you of the rock you are upon, and require you to desist from such illegal and unconstitutional proceedings."

Letters of the famous tory churchman, Peters, of Connecticut, were laid on the President's table. One, dated September 28, said: "Six regiments are coming over from England, and sundry men-of-war. So soon as they come, HANGING WORK will go on. DESTRUCTION will attend first the seaport towns. . . . . The lintel sprinkled on the sidepost will preserve the faithful," *i. e.*, the Episcopalians. On the first of October he wrote to Rev. Dr. Auchmuty, of New York: "The" — Episcopal — "churches in Connecticut must fall a sacrifice, very soon, to the rage of the Puritan mobility, if the old serpent, that dragon, is not bound. . . . Spiritual iniquity rides in high places, with halberts, pistols, and swords. See the proclamation I sent you by my nephew, on their pious Sabbath day, the fourth of last month, when the preachers and magistrates left the pulpit, etc., for the gun and drum, and set off for Boston, cursing the king and Lord North, General Gage, the bishops and their cursed curates, and the Church of England."

The occasion of the discourse appears in the following "Resolve recommending to the people of this province"— Massachusetts — "to observe a day of public THANKSGIVING throughout the same," passed by the First Provincial Congress, held in the meeting-house, at Cambridge, October 22, 1774:

"From a consideration of the continuance of the gospel among us, and the smiles of Divine Providence upon us with regard to the seasons of the year, and the general health which has been enjoyed; and in particular, from a consideration of the union which so remarkably prevails, not only in this province, but throughout the continent, at this alarming crisis, it is resolved, as the sense of this Congress, that it is highly proper that a day of public thanksgiving should be observed throughout this province; and it is accordingly recommended to the several religious assemblies in the province, that Thursday, the fifteenth day of December next, be observed as a day of thanksgiving, to render thanks to Almighty God for all the blessings we enjoy. And, at the same time, we think it incumbent on this people to humble themselves before God, on account of their sins, for which he hath been pleased, in his righteous judgment, to suffer so great a calamity to befall us as the present controversy between Great Britain and the colonies; as also to implore the Divine blessing upon us, that, by the assistance of his grace, we may be enabled to reform whatever is amiss among us; that so God may be pleased to continue to us the blessings we enjoy, and remove the tokens of his displeasure, by causing harmony and union to be restored between Great Britain and these colonies, that we may again rejoice in the smiles of our sovereign, and in possession of those privileges which have been transmitted to us, and have the hopeful prospect that they shall be handed down entire to posterity under the Protestant succession in the illustrious House of Hanover.   JOHN HANCOCK, PRESIDENT."

The preacher, Mr. Gordon, born at Hitchin, in England, pastor of an Independent church at Ipswich, removed to America in 1770, and was ordained pastor of the Jamaica Plain Church, in Roxbury, July 6, 1772. "His soul was engaged in" the American cause. He was chaplain to the Provincial Congress; and several sermons on public occasions during the struggle show his zeal and prudence as a Son of Liberty. He improved his excellent opportunities for fulness and fidelity in his "History of the Rise, Progress, and Establishment of the Independence of the United States of America: including an account of the late war, and of the thirteen colonies from their origin to that period," first published in 1788, — a candid and impartial work, of which there have been several editions. He returned to England in 1786, and died at Ipswich, October 19, 1807, aged 77. — Allibone, Allen.

This sermon excited the indignation or "the king's friends," one of whom, "a friend to peace and good order," published "observations" upon it as "daring and treasonable, . . . absurd and impertinent, . . . a firebrand of sedition, . . . audacious and wicked;" so awful to "every honest man, every virtuous citizen," that "to let it pass disregarded would argue an inattention to the welfare of the public wholly inexcusable." "Where could this reverend politician, . . clerical disclaimer, . . Christian sower of sedition, . . notable empiric, . . warfaring priest, . . ordained leader, . . this church-militant general, . . have learnt to preach up doctrines of sedition, rebellion, carnage, and blood? Not, I am sure, from the merciful divulger of his religion, for he only taught the precepts of peace and forgiveness. . . . I most heartily wish, for the peace of America, that he and many others of his profession would confine themselves to gospel truths."

DISCOURSE IV.

A THANKSGIVING SERMON.

IT IS OF THE LORD'S MERCIES THAT WE ARE NOT CONSUMED, BECAUSE HIS COMPASSIONS FAIL NOT. — Lam. iii. 22.

THE pulpit is devoted, in general, to more important purposes than the fate of kingdoms, or the civil rights of human nature, being intended to recover men from the slavery of sin and Satan, to point out their escape from future misery through faith in a crucified Jesus, and to assist them in their preparations for an eternal blessedness. But still there are special times and seasons when it may treat of politics. And, surely, if it is allowable for some who occupy it, by preaching up the doctrines of non-resistance and passive obedience,[1] to vilify the principles and to sap the foundations of that glorious revolution that exalted the House of Hanover to the British throne, it ought to be no transgression in others, nor to be construed into a want of loyalty, to speak consistently with those approved tenets that have made George the Third the first of European sovereigns, who otherwise,

---

[1] The publications of the period abound in such finger-points to these "missionaries," who were considered as simply ecclesiastical corps of sappers and miners, busy among the people, disguised as teachers of religion, disseminating doctrines subversive of liberty, and who were secretly in heart as zealous for the British ministry as were their more honorable brethren, the chaplains of the mercenary armies, who took the hazards of open war. Perhaps the sacrifices of the former were the greater. — ED.

with all his personal virtues, might have lived an obscure Elector.

Having, then, the past morning of this provincial thanksgiving, accommodated the text to the case of individuals, I shall now dedicate it, according to its original intention, to the service of the public, the situation of whose affairs is both distressing and alarming.

The capital of the colony is barbarously treated, pretendedly for a crime, but actually for the noble stand she has made in favor of liberty against the partisans of slavery. She has distinguished herself by her animated opposition to arbitrary and unconstitutional proceedings, and therefore has been marked out, by ministerial vengeance,[1]

---

[1] Official insolence and ignorance never received a quicker or more dignified rebuke than in the united and decisive voice of the colonies for Boston and against the ministry. In the debates on the Boston bills, Col. Barré said to the ministry: "You point all your revenge at Boston alone; but I think you will very soon have the rest of the colonies on your back." Salem nobly resented and refused the proffered bribe of the diverted commerce of Boston to her port. The newspapers published numerous acknowledgments of such substantial tokens of "aid and comfort" as this: "On Tuesday morning last came to town," — Boston, — "from Marblehead, eight cart-loads of salt fish; a generous donation from our sympathizing brethren of that small town."

The people of Massachusetts refusing any supplies for the British troops, Gen. Gage sent a vessel to Baltimore for a load of flour, for blankets, etc., but "the committee of correspondence of that place refused to furnish any of the articles until they heard from the General Congress, where they had sent an express to receive directions how they should act on the occasion;" yet that same committee were then freely contributing to the necessities of the Boston patriots. Poor Gage's supplies from England and elsewhere were intercepted and captured by "Yankee" privateers, and he was often reduced to predatory incursions.

A letter from Alexandria, Virginia, of July 6th, 1774, said: "All Virginia and Maryland are contributing for the relief of Boston, — of those who, by the late cruel act of Parliament, are deprived of their daily labor and bread, — to prevent the inhabitants sinking under the oppression, or migrating, to keep up that manly spirit that has made them dear

to be made an example of, whereby to terrify other American cities into a tame submission. She is an example, and, thanks to Heaven! an example of patience and forti-

---

to every American." Enclosed was a list of the cargo of "Schooner Nassau," — corn, flour, wheat, etc., — "consigned to the Hon. John Hancock and James Bowdoin, Esqrs., Mr. Samuel Adams, Isaac Smith, Esq., and the Gentlemen Committee" of Boston, for distribution. The "Gazette," which published this letter, says: "Every part of this extensive continent, so far as we have yet heard, appears to be deeply interested in the fate of this unhappy town. Many and great are the donations we have already received, and many more we have good reason to expect." The same paper contains "Resolutions unanimously entered into by the Inhabitants of South Carolina, at a General Meeting held at Charlestown," in July, 1774, which declare "that not only the dictates of humanity, but the soundest principles of true policy and self-preservation, make it necessary for the inhabitants of all the colonies in America to assist and support the people of Boston."

Now was to be realized the splendid thought of the Rev. Dr. Mayhew's "Lord's-day Morning" meditations [1] — "a communion of the colonies." "Letters of friendship and regard — a desire to cement and perpetuate union among ourselves" — flew like winged messengers of love from colony to colony, and from heart to heart; and on the seventh of October, 1774, George III. saw, not Boston and Massachusetts crushed beneath his German foot, not the fratricidal discord of base men in sordid haste to fatten upon the ruin of sister colonies despoiled by despotism, — for so low was his avowed policy, and so brutal the hope of his *kingly* breast; but, thank God! there was too little of Oxford "obedience," and too few of its minions in America, for such thrift; — he saw not that, but a Continental Congress in session at Philadelphia, composed of "the representatives of his Majesty's faithful subjects in all the colonies from Nova Scotia to Georgia"— a new power in the world. Their committee — Thomas Lynch, of South Carolina, Samuel Adams, of Massachusetts, and Edmund Pendleton, of Virginia — prepared a letter to Gen. Gage, representing "that the town of Boston and province of Massachusetts Bay are considered by all America as suffering in the common cause for their noble and spirited opposition to oppressive acts of Parliament, calculated to deprive us of our most sacred rights and privileges," and remonstrating against his hostile military preparations in that town. His Majesty called them "rebels," and they soon declared and proved themselves to be neither subjects nor rebels, but a free people. — Ed.

1 See his letter on pages 44, 45.

tude, to the no small mortification of her enemies, whose own base feelings led them to imagine that she would immediately become an abject supplicant for royal favor, though at the expense of natural and chartered rights. May some future historian, the friend of mankind and citizen of the world, have to record in his faithful and ever-living page that she never truckled, though British sailors and soldiers, contrary to their natural affection for the cause of liberty, were basely employed to intimidate her, but perseveringly held out through the fiery trial till a revolution of men and measures brought on her deliverance!

But it is not the capital alone that suffers. The late venal Parliament, in compliance with the directions of administration, have, under the false color of regulating the government of the colony, mutilated its charter, and conveyed dangerous powers to individuals for the enforcing and maintaining those encroachments that they have ventured, in defiance of common equity, to make upon the rights of a free people; and had not the calmness and prudence of others supplied their lack of wisdom, the country might by this time have become an Aceldama.[a]

a I take this opportunity of making my public acknowledgments to his Excellency the governor for not having precipitated the country into a civil war — an event which, as appears by his letter,[1] he ardently wishes may never exist. Should the continent be exercised with so great an evil, I promise myself, from the known humanity — the constant attendant of true bravery — the known humanity of the British officers and troops, that they will not add barbarity to the unavoidable calamities of war. But should any hellish policy order its being done, the colonies, 't is to be supposed, will dread all less than slavery to those cruel masters that can issue such savage edicts.

1 General Gage, in his reply of October 20th, 1774, to the letter of the Continental Congress just cited, wrote: "I ardently wish that the common enemies to both countries may see, to their disappointment, that these disputes between the mother country and the colonies have terminated like the quarrels of lovers, and increased the affection which they ought to bear to each other." — ED.

Upon the principles which the British Legislature have adopted, in their late extraordinary proceedings, I see not how we can be certain of any one privilege, nor what hinders our being really in a state of slavery to an aggregate of masters, whose tyranny may be worse than that of a single despot; nor that a man can with propriety say his soul is his own, and not the spring to move his bodily machine in the performance of whatever drudgery his lords may appoint; nor that the public have a permanent and valuable constitution. If the British Legislature is the constitution, or superior to the constitution, Magna Charta, the Bill of Rights, and the Protestant Succession, these boasts of Britons are toys to please the vulgar, and not solid securities.

The operation of the late unconstitutional acts of the British Parliament would not only deprive the colony of invaluable privileges, but introduce a train of evils little expected by the generality, and give the British ministry such an ascendency in all public affairs as would be to the last dangerous.[a]

[a] In support of this paragraph I shall quote the following passages from the protest of the Lords against the regulating act, viz.:

" The new constitution of judicature provided by this bill is improper and incongruous with the plan of the administration of justice in Great Britain.

" The Governor and Council, thus instituted with powers with which the British constitution has not trusted his Majesty and his privy-council, have the means of returning such a jury in each particular cause as may best suit with the gratification of their passions and interests. The lives, liberties, and properties of the subject are put into their hands without control, and the invaluable right of trial by jury is turned into a snare for the people, who have hitherto looked upon it as their main security against the licentiousness of power.

" We see in this bill the same scheme of strengthening the authority of the officers and ministers of state, at the expense of the rights and liberties of the subject, which was indicated by the inauspicious act for shutting up the harbor of Boston.

" By that act, which is immediately connected with this bill, the example was set of a large, important city (containing vast multitudes of people, many of whom must be innocent, and all of whom are unheard), by an arbitrary sentence, deprived of the advantage of that port upon which all their means of livelihood did immediately depend.

" This proscription is not made determinable on the payment of a fine for an

The spirited behavior of the country, under these innovations, has charmed and affrighted numbers, and, should

offence, or a compensation for an injury, but is to continue until the ministers of
the crown shall think fit to advise the king in council to revoke it.

"The legal condition of the subject (standing unattainted by conviction for
treason or felony) ought never to depend upon the arbitrary will of any person
whatsoever."

I would add, also, the clause in the regulating act respecting town meetings [1]
leaves it in the power of a governor to prevent them all at pleasure, those only
excepted for the choice of town officers in March, and for the choice of representatives. Neither the most trifling nor the most important business can be
legally transacted, so as to be binding upon the inhabitants, even in the most
distant towns of the government, without leave first had and obtained of the
governor, in writing, expressing such special business, though it should happen
that if not done within less time than necessary for the obtaining of that leave
it cannot be done at all. The townsmen can neither lay out a new road nor
raise moneys for mending an old one, nor can they settle a minister, without
obtaining the express written leave of the governor. Yea, they are forbid so
much as to talk; for they are not to treat of any other matter at their March
meeting except the election of their officers, nor at any other meeting except the
business expressed in the leave given by the governor, or, in his absence, by the
lieutenant-governor. If this is not to establish slavery by legislative authority,
I beg to know what is. The arbitrary mandates of the grand monarch, enjoining his slaves silence when state affairs are disagreeable to the public, will scarce
be thought by many so great an attack upon the rights of mankind, as an attempt to perpetuate something of the like nature by a permanent law. Should
the favorite of a governor have embezzled the town's money, how shall a meeting be obtained to vote and order a prosecution against him? Should a candidate be reported as a warm friend to the liberties of the people, how shall leave
be had for his being settled, though unanimously approved of and admired?
Should an oppressed town be desirous of stating its grievances and praying a
redress, how shall the inhabitants do it in a corporate capacity, should the commander-in-chief be prejudiced against them? Should the electors be inclined to
instruct their representatives upon matters of the highest concern to them, how
shall they do it without violating the law, when the ruler's interest prevents his
giving them leave? A thousand other events are made to depend upon the arbitrary will of a governor by the clause before us. And why are all the towns
of the colony to be reduced to such a slavish dependence? Because, as the British legislative asserts, "a great abuse has been made of calling town meetings,
and the inhabitants have, contrary to the design of their institution, been misled
to treat upon matters of the most general concern, and to pass many dangerous
and unwarrantable resolves." Oh, abominable! — that a people should be deprived of their precious and long-enjoyed liberties, not for any wilfully perverse
known crime, but because of their being foolishly misled. Why did not the wise
ministry ease themselves of the opposition given them by the city of London, by

[1] The towns were so many commonwealths, petty democracies, and the
British ministers could not have adopted any device which would more
keenly touch the people than this interference with their wonted assemblies. — ED.

it be continued with prudence, unremitted zeal, and true fortitude, will produce monuments of praise, more lasting than brass, even though it should not prove successful, which is scarce supposable.

The distresses that the late acts have already occasioned are many and great, and too well known to require an enumeration; and yet, could we be secure of a speedy relief in the permanent redress of our grievances, we should soon forget them. But we have our fears lest they should be only the beginning of sorrows, and are in doubt whether we may not be called to experience the horrors of a civil war, unless we will disgrace our descent, meanly submit to the loss of our privileges, and leave to posterity — the many millions that shall people this continent in less than a century — bonds and fetters.

The important day is now arrived that must determine whether we shall remain free, or, alas! be brought into bondage, after having long enjoyed the sweets of liberty. The event will probably be such as is our own conduct. Will we conform to the once exploded but again courtly doctrines of passive obedience and non-resistance, rather than hazard life and property — we may have the honor of burning under the heats of summer and freezing under the colds of winter in providing for the luxurious entertainment of lazy, proud, worthless pensioners and placemen.[a]

a like regulation of their charter, upon the ground of the citizens having been misled? Why do they not, upon the same ground, prevent all corporation and county meetings in Great Britain, that so they may not be pestered with any future petitions or remonstrances? But, should the operation of the regulating act be secured, who can tell how long it will be ere the British legislative will assign the solid reason of having been misled to treat upon matters of the most general concern, and to pass many dangerous and unwarrantable resolves for suspending all the American assemblies, or, at least, for reducing the members of each to the more convenient number of the Yorkers?

I decline, as wholly unnecessary, all remarks upon the miscalled act for the impartial administration of justice, etc.

a There are some honorable exceptions to this general intimation, but they are

Will we make our appeal to Heaven against the intended oppression — venture all upon the noble principles that brought the House of Hanover into the possession of the British diadem, and not fear to bleed freely in the cause, not of a particular people, but of mankind in general — we shall be likely to transmit to future generations, though the country should be wasted by the sword, the most essential part of the fair patrimony received from our brave and hardy progenitors — the right of possessing and of disposing of, at our own option, the honest fruits of our industry. However, it is alarming to think that, through the mistaken policy of Great Britain, and the absurd notion of persisting in wrong measures for the honor of government, we may be obliged to pass through those difficulties, and to behold those scenes, and engage in those services that are shocking to humanity, and would be intolerable but for the hope of preserving and perpetuating our liberties. Our trade ruined, our plantations

so few that they can save themselves only, and not the list, from deserved reproach.

In the year 1697 the pensions amounted only to seven thousand and seventy-seven pounds sterling, but in the year 1705 they amounted to eighteen thousand one hundred and eleven pounds. Since then they have increased to a most enormous sum. A late publication informs us that about ten years back there was a million of debt contracted on the sixpence per pound tax laid on pensions. The interest of a million at four per cent. being forty thousand pounds per annum, the pensions, to have answered for it, must have amounted to one million six hundred thousand pounds per annum; if at three per cent., to one million two hundred thousand. There might, possibly, have been a deficiency in this fund; but it cannot be thought that the financier would have proposed it had it been very considerably deficient.

I heartily wish that some who have leisure, and can procure the necessary materials, would inform the public, as near as possible, what sums are exhausted by places and pensions. As to the numerous expenditures in the secret services of rewards, bribery and corruption, jobs and contracts, they must remain among the *arcana imperii*. But, were a virtuous, patriotic administration to close all those unnecessary drains whereby the wealth of Great Britain is carried off, they would, in a few years of peace, greatly reduce the national debt, and have no temptation to gull the people under a pretence of easing them by American taxes, when they design only to provide for their numerous dependents, and to increase the power of the crown, alias the ministry.

trodden down, our cattle slain or taken away, our property plundered, our dwellings in flames, our families insulted and abused, our friends and relatives wallowing and our own garments rolled in blood, are calamities that we are not accustomed to, and that we cannot realize but with the utmost pain; and yet we must expect more or less of these should we be compelled to betake ourselves to the sword in behalf of our rights. It is not a little grievous to be alarmed with the apprehension of such severe trials, unless we will in our conduct resemble those simple ones that, for the sake of indulging themselves in present ease and plenty, barter away their whole interest in future happiness.[a]

But, though the situation of our public affairs is both distressing and alarming, it is by far better than we have deserved from the Sovereign of the universe; it would have been much worse had we been dealt with according to our demerits. "It is of the Lord's mercies that we are not consumed; because his compassions fail not." Some may, at first hearing, object against this, as being too strong an expression, and may think, considering the morals of the people when compared with the inhabitants of other places, that it is misapplied. I am ready to allow that the morals of this people, taken collectively, are superior to those of other places, — Connecticut excepted, where, I suppose, they are nearly the same, — whether in the New or the Old World, all things considered; and I cannot but view

[a] It may be objected that the points in dispute are too trifling to justify the hazard of such severe trials. It will be answered that it is the *principles* the continent is opposing in its attempts to prevent the establishment of precedents. The real dispute is, whether the long-enjoyed constitution of these American colonies, when they are not consenting to it, shall be liable to every alteration that a legislative three thousand miles off shall think convenient and profitable to themselves, and whether a House of Commons at that distance, to which they neither do nor can send a single representative, shall dispose of their property at pleasure. *Obsta principiis.*

as a strong proof hereof the order that prevails through the country now that the execution of the laws, because of the peculiarity of the times, is suspended.[1] And yet, after all, I must hold to the text; and, that we may be fully convinced, and be duly affected with the truth of it, shall make some remarks upon this people considered as the subjects of God's moral government.

I. In the first place, I remark, that the prevalency of any vices and immoralities among this people must be peculiarly provoking.

Circumstances aggravate or alleviate the crimes of societies no less than of single persons; and far more and other is expected from some than from many others in a very different situation and condition.

---

[1] The ministry sought not only " to beggar the colonies into submission" by ruinous restraints on trade, but to reduce them to anarchy by paralyzing their governments, whose life was supposed to emanate from the crown, and then necessity would compel submission; but the result astonished all. New governments sprang directly from the people, and the people obeyed. " Obedience is what makes government," said Burke, commenting on this phenomenon, " and not the names by which it is called; not the name of governor, as formerly, or committee, as at present. . . . We wholly abrogated the ancient government of Massachusetts. We were confident that the first feeling, if not the very prospect of anarchy, would instantly enforce a complete submission. The experiment was tried. A new, strange, unexpected face of things appeared. Anarchy is found tolerable. A vast province has now subsisted, and subsisted in a considerable degree of health and vigor, for nearly a twelvemonth, without governor, without public council, without judges, without executive magistrates. . . . In effect, we suffer as much at home by this loosening of all ties, and this concussion of all established opinions, as we do abroad. For, in order to prove that the Americans have no right to their liberties, we are every day endeavoring to subvert the maxims which preserve the whole spirit of our own. To prove that the Americans ought not to be free, we are obliged to depreciate the value of freedom itself; and we never seem to gain a paltry advantage over them in debate without attacking some of those principles, or deriding some of those feelings, for which our ancestors have shed their blood." — ED.

Now, it should be remembered that this is but a young people, not a hundred and fifty years old; for they were not a people for the few first years of their settlement in this wilderness — no more than a small company, who must have soon perished by the hands of the native Indians had not God interposed. Their youth is an aggravation to the crimes committed by them. For a young person to be given to vice, though he has a corrupted nature the same as others, is highly offensive: we look for a decent, modest, and orderly behavior in him.

In like manner a young state should be pure in its morals; should be addicted to no particular vices; should observe the utmost regularity of behavior, and should not even think of, much less practise, the crimes too generally to be met with in countries of long standing, when attained to their height in power and affluence. There is an utter unfitness in the former's attempting to imitate the latter. Can we say that this rising young state is clear as to this matter; that it has not copied the corrupt manners of its aged parent; and that it hath not its particular vices that are a reproach to it? However willing we may be, through self-love and native fondness, to apologize for it, we cannot conscientiously pronounce it not guilty while we know how notorious intemperance, uncleanness, luxury, and irreligion are among us.

But another thing that makes the vices and immoralities of this people peculiarly provoking is, their descent and education. The sins of a youth descended from pious parents, who has had good examples set him, and who has been carefully educated, are worse than those of a common youth that has not enjoyed such advantages.

Now, the ancestors of this people were eminently godly; it was the strength of their zeal for true, unadulterated religion, and the ardor of their love to God and Christ, that prevailed upon them to venture over the great deep, and to seek an abode in this then inhospitable and dangerous country, and that reconciled them to the numberless difficulties that they had long to encounter without ever attaining to the various comforts that we enjoy. They were concerned to perpetuate the same spirit of piety which they were actuated by; paid great attention to the rising generation, and wisely provided for the good instruction of succeeding ones. Wherein can we charge them with want either of wisdom or faithfulness to posterity? Do we not still reap the fruits of their contrivance and foresight, though not in so ample a manner as might be, through our own faultiness? Judge ye, what could have been done more through their instrumentality for this part of the Lord's vineyard than what has been done? Wherefore, then, hath it brought forth so many wild and bad grapes, when it should have yielded the choicest fruit? Is not this people strangely degenerated, so as to possess but a faint resemblance of that godliness for which their forefathers were eminent? And could these last appear for a while again in this colony, with the common passions and sentiments of human nature, would they not stand amazed at the sinfulness of the present generation, and be ready to disown them for their posterity? Is it not another generation of professors, very different both as to sentiments and practice from that which, by their emigrations for conscience' sake, first planted the gospel in New England? Would not the like zeal for the leading doctrines of Christianity, and the like strictness in morals that prevailed in the first settlers, be severely censured and be stigmatized by some reproachful epithet, as in their day, by the generality among us, though through the spirit of the times the persecution might not be more than that of the tongue? They that will divest themselves of prejudice, and judge impartially, will be obliged, I apprehend, to acknowledge that this people do not answer to the honorableness of their descent, any more than to the care that was taken by their predecessors for their being well educated in the principles and practices of religion; the full benefit of which care though they may not enjoy, through the censurable faultiness of some in neglecting their duty, yet is so far enjoyed as that people in general, including all ranks, are not better instructed and educated anywhere, it is probable, than in this country. But certainly the more honorable their religious descent, and the better their education, the more provoking must their vices and immoralities be; and nothing can be more worthy of their particular consideration, especially in these threatening times, than those words in Amos iii. 2, wherein the Lord addresses the children of Israel, saying: "You only have I known of all the families of the earth; therefore I will punish you for all your iniquities." I might add more particulars to this first remark, but choose to make them distinct ones of themselves.

II. I therefore proceed to mention, in the second place, that the obligations this people are under to holiness are special, from the many appearances of God in their favor, and his having so multiplied and exalted them.

How oft has the Supreme Governor of the universe wonderfully, next to miraculously, interposed for their deliverance when in the utmost danger! Their enemies expected to swallow them up, and were upon the point of doing it, when Providence hath critically interposed, so that they have escaped like a bird out of a snare that has been thrown over it. When their eagerness to coöperate with the parent state, in reducing the power of the common enemy, led them into a bold and dangerous enterprise, in which, if they had miscarried, they would have been subject to an almost irreparable damage, and which must have miscarried, according to the usual course of human and military affairs, had not special events, carrying in them the evident marks of providential appointment,[1] though in the account of the unbeliever purely casual, — I say, which must have miscarried had not special events turned up, — it pleased God to order the existence of them, and, by crowning the expedition with success, not only to avert the train of evils that must otherwise have followed, but to give this people, then indeed in their infancy, a NAME[2] among the warlike veteran states of Europe, and to show the world what a few raw provincials could do, under the smiles and care of Heaven, against fortifications and batteries really strong, and defended by regulars, though not by Britons. May they never lose that name, nor blast the laurels gained at Louisburg by any future cowardly conduct, when it is not conquest, but liberty and property, that are at stake!

God hath not only appeared for this people, but hath greatly multiplied and exalted them. They were at first a few men in number, yea, very few, and strangers in the land. They came from a well-cultivated kingdom to a savage people and a wild country, enough to discourage the stoutest. However, they ventured to take up their

---

[1] The French ship Vigilant, of sixty-four guns, and six hundred men, when within two hours' sail of Louisburg, Cape Breton, May 19th, was led off in pursuit of smaller craft, and captured. Her arrival would have been fatal to the enterprise. The New England men, being in want of balls, were supplied by those sent by the French guns, which they put into their own cannon, and fired back again. — Prince's Thanksgiving Sermon, 1745; Parsons's Life of Sir Wm. Pepperell, Bart. — ED.

[2] Perhaps the capture of Louisburg, in 1745, as a proof of the military prowess of New England, may be taken as the point of time when the colonies became conscious of their strength, and when England became jealous of their dependence. — ED.

abode in it, and, through the original blessing of Heaven
upon them, which, perhaps, never displayed itself and
wrought more effectually, except in the instance of the
Jews, they are become a considerable nation,[1] possess a
tolerable share of wealth, and would enjoy much public
happiness were the painful disputes between them and the
parent country comfortably terminated. The face of the
colony is not less changed for the better since first settled
than what is set forth in the language of Isaiah's prophecy:
"The wilderness and the solitary place shall be glad; the
desert shall rejoice and blossom as the rose. It shall blossom abundantly, and rejoice even with joy and singing;
the glory of Lebanon shall be given unto it; the excellency of Carmel and Sharon. They shall see the glory of
the Lord, and the excellency of our God."[a] These enumerated are special obligations on this people to holiness. But
does their holiness correspond with them? Are the fruits
yielded by them suited to such benefits? Are they that
manner of people that might have been expected, and that
they engaged to be when under difficulties, and in great
perplexity through threatening appearances? — or have
they not, like the Jews of old, after singing the divine
praises, forgot the works of God and the wonders he hath
showed them? And hath not the cast of their after-con-
duct evidenced that, in renewing their engagements with

a Isaiah xxxv. 1, 2.

1 An estimate, made in 1775, by the American Congress:

State.	People.	State.	People.
Massachusetts,	400,000	Pennsylvania,	350,000
New Hampshire,	150,000	Maryland,	320,000
Rhode Island,	59,678	Virginia,	650,000
Connecticut,	192,000	North Carolina,	300,000
New York,	250,000	South Carolina,	225,000
New Jersey,	130,000	Total,	3,026,678

Ed.

him in the day of their affliction, " they did flatter him with
their mouth, and lied unto him with their tongues; and
that their heart was not right with him ; " for " they have
not been steadfast in his covenant," have not walked agreeable to the design and purport of God's covenant of grace,
with which they have in much mercy been made acquainted.

III. I shall now remark, in the third and last place, that
though the appearances of religion among this people are
great and many, yet it is to be feared that real religion is
scarce, that the power of godliness is rare, and that while
there is much outward show of respect to the Deity, there
is but little inward heart conformity to him.

Individuals are justly entitled to the benefit of an exception, notwithstanding which it may be applied with too
much truth to the community as a body, " This people
draweth nigh unto me with their mouth, and honoreth
me with their lips, but their heart is far from me." [a] What
is religion, with the generality, more than being baptized,
attending public worship statedly on the Lord's day, own-
ing the covenant, coming to the Lord's table, and then
being orderly in the outward deportment? If, besides all
now mentioned, there is a strict attendance upon private
prayer, and the further addition of family, though the
prayers shall consist of nothing more than the repeating
of a certain set of words that the tongue has been habituated to, the goodness of such religion must not be questioned, though not proceeding from a work of regenera-
tion, not produced originally by any special influences of
the Holy Spirit, not accompanied with any saving illuminations from above, with any spiritual view of the divine
glories, any true hatred to sin, any sense of the beauty of
holiness, any soul-sanctifying love to God and the Lord

[a] Matthew xv. 8.

Jesus. Is there not a great though unhappy affinity between the case of this people, religiously considered, and
that of the Laodicean church, as described by the Alpha
and Omega in Revelation iii. 15—18?

The above remarks upon this people, considered as the
subjects of God's moral government, being duly weighed,
shall we not be brought to own with humility and gratitude that it is of the Lord's mercies that we are not consumed, because his compassions fail not? As yet we are
not consumed.

Though, when we look down from the adjoining hills,
and behold the capital, we cannot but lament, saying,
"How is the gold become dim! how is the most fine gold
changed! how does her port mourn, because her shipping
come not to her as formerly; all her wharves are desolate; how is she possessed and surrounded by an armed
force, as though in the hands of an enemy!—yet, blessed
be God, she doth not sit solitary; she is full of people;
she is honorable among the nations; she is as a princess
among the provinces, seeing that she hath not meanly
become tributary. She weepeth sore in the night, and
her tears are on her cheeks; but, like beauty in distress,
she is the more engaging. She hath many lovers to comfort her, and her friends have not dealt treacherously with
her, so far from having become her enemies. Her inhabitants are suffering, but not starving. Her priests and her
elders have not given up the ghost while seeking meat
to relieve their soul. The tongue of the sucking child
cleaveth not to the roof of his mouth for thirst. The
young children ask not bread without any man's offering
to break it unto them. We see not her dwellings and
public buildings, both civil and sacred, in flames, and the
whole becoming, by a speedy destruction, a horrid heap
of ruins."

Though, when we survey the country, we bemoan the attempts that have been made upon the ancient foundations of its civil government, which, if successful, will in all probability, after a time, undermine and destroy its religious liberties; yet we are thankful that no dwelling has been destroyed, — that none of any party have as yet perished by the shocks they have occasioned in the state, — that the sword hath not been commissioned by Heaven to destroy, and the way to an accommodation been rendered still more inaccessible through the shedding of blood. We adore the goodness of God, which has kept us from being consumed by the ravages of war. It is of the Lord's mercies that we are not consumed, because his compassions fail not. And much more so that, in the distressing and alarming situation of our public affairs, there have been so many favorable circumstances to preserve us from fainting, to hearten us up, and to encourage our hopes in expecting that we shall at length, in the exercise of prudence, fortitude, and piety, get well through our difficulties.

Here allow me to run through a brief summary of these favorable circumstances, composed of the following particulars: The rising and growing consistency of sentiments in the friends of liberty, which hath led one assembly and another on this continent to attempt preventing the further introduction of slaves [1] among them, though herein

---

[1] One of the articles of the "American Association," formed by the Congress at Philadelphia, in September, pledged entire abstinence from the slave trade, and from any trade with those concerned in it. The prevailing sentiment was expressed by Mr. Jefferson in the original draft of the Declaration of Independence: "Determined to keep open a market where MEN should be bought and sold, he" — George III. — "has prostituted his negative for suppressing every legislative attempt to prohibit or restrain this execrable commerce." On the ministerial plan to excite a slave insurrection, Mr. Burke said, 1774: "An offer of freedom from Eng-

they have been counteracted by governors, and which the American Congress has with so much wisdom and justice adopted; the increasing acquaintance with the rights of conscience in matters of religion, as belonging equally alike to men of all parties and denominations, while they conduct as good members of civil society, without endeavoring to injure their neighbors of different or opposite sentiments; the blundering policy of the British ministry in giving so cruel a cast to the Boston Port Bill, taking away by it private property, and subjecting its restitution to the pleasure of the sovereign; in following that so hastily with other acts, equally unjust and more extensively pernicious, affecting the whole colony, and built upon principles and claims that rendered every dwelling, plantation, and right through the continent precarious, dependent on the will of the Parliament, or, rather, of the junto or individual that hath the power of managing it; in declaring openly, while supporting the bills, that their design was not against a single town or colony, but against all America; in presuming that the other towns and colonies, upon receiving the dreadful news, would turn pale and tremble, conceal their spirit of resentment and opposition in sneaking professions of tame submission, and abandon the distressed, though their own ruin must have followed upon it, however slowly; and, upon such presumption, neglecting to divide in time the different colonies by flattering promises suited to their several situations, and by secret purchases, ere they could form a general union; the reëstablishment of arbitrary power and

land would come rather oddly, shipped to them " — the slaves — " in an African vessel, which is *refused an entry into the ports of Virginia or Carolina with a cargo of three Angola negroes.* It would be curious to see the Guinea captain attempting at the same instant to publish his proclamation of liberty and to advertise his sale of slaves."— ED.

a despotic government in a most extensive and purposely enlarged country,[1] contrary to the royal declaration given a few years before, qualified somewhat to the inhabitants by that formal security of their religious liberty which was noways wanting, but, as is generally, I fear justly taught, with the base, diabolical design of procuring their assistance, if required, in quelling the spirit of freedom among the natural and loyal subjects of Great Britain;[a]

[a] I have no objection to the Canadians being fully secured in the enjoyment of their religion, however erroneous and anti-Christian it may appear to me as a Protestant, but to the British legislative's not having given a universal establishment to the rights of conscience among them. The rights of conscience are too sacred for any civil power on earth to interdict, wherein they produce not overt acts against the necessary and essential rights of civil society. I say necessary and essential, to guard against the reasonings of interested, designing priests of every denomination, who are for forming unnatural alliances between church and state, the sword of the Spirit and the sword of the magistrate. Arguments drawn from the ancient Jewish theocracy are of no avail till the existence of a Christian theocracy is proved, in direct opposition to the words of our great Leader, who has said, "My kingdom is not of this world."

Should the necessity of our affairs convene another congress, hope, among other things, it will be agreed upon, as the proper solid basis for the firmest and most extensive union, that every colony should retain, while the majority of it are so pleased, whatever is its prevailing form of religion, and admit of a universal toleration to all other persuasions, whether professors of Christianity or not.

'T was a special pleasure to me, on my first arrival in America [in 1770], among the friendly Philadelphians, to observe how Papists, Episcopalians, Moravians, Lutherans, Calvinists, Methodists, and Quakers, could pass each other peaceably and in good temper on the Sabbath, after having broke up their respective assemblies, which I could not but take notice of in an early letter to my native country.

It may be said that, notwithstanding this apparent regard for the rights of conscience, I am really unfriendly to them unless I will admit of an American episcopate. Though some may be prejudiced against it from the fibbing, rancorous, and abusive opposition that certain D.D.'s are continually making to measures for preserving the civil rights of this continent (whose conduct I can easily account for, and who have doubtless received intelligence, as well as myself, that the design of sending a bishop to America, as soon as circumstances will permit, is certainly kept in view, and that ——— is intended for the see; and men

[1] This was one of the "causes" set forth in the Declaration of Independence: "For abolishing the free system of English laws in a neighboring province, establishing therein an arbitrary government, and enlarging its boundaries, so as to render it at once an example and *fit instrument* for introducing the same absolute rule into these colonies."—ED.

the speedy arrival of the Port Bill in the common way of
conveyance, whereby some difficulties were avoided and
some advantages enjoyed, while administration was not so
merciful as to attempt giving us the earliest intelligence

whose ambitious hopes of a deanery, arch-deaconship, or crosier, are likely to
be disappointed by the public manœuvres in favor of liberty, will be out of
humor, and should be patiently borne with, though they vent their spleen against
liberty itself), yet the rights of Episcopalians are not thereby forfeited, and
whenever the majority of them, laity included (and not a few of the leading
clergy, who are for more homage than the present equality admits), are desirous
of an American episcopate, and will see to its being with security that the bishop
and every other dignitary shall be confined purely to spiritual matters, shall
have no more rule in civil concerns than the parochial priest, shall be maintained
by no kind of tax, but by voluntary contributions, or from legacies given a
full year before the death of a testator when coming out of a real estate, and
shall be deprived of all power to injure or interrupt other denominations, let
them be gratified. It will have a good effect, and will prevent our young men's
making a trip to England for orders, which generally proves dangerous to their
love of freedom. But it will be long enough ere some who have been arduously
laboring to establish a Protestant American episcopate will, with all their conscientious attachment to and zeal for it, agree to its existence in this New World
upon such equitable conditions, as may be inferred from the little attention paid
to what Lord Sterling mentioned to them at or in the neighborhood of Amboy.

As to the civil establishment given to the Canadians by the Quebec Bill,[1] the
slavery of it has been admirably exposed in the address of the Congress; and yet,
was it a fact that the body of the French inhabitants preferred it to every other
form, I am of Lord Littleton's opinion, that they should have it while they requested it. We have reason, however, to believe that the mode of trial by juries
was desired by the bulk of the people, and that it was taken away to gratify the
petty noblesse of the country, who were for enjoying, as when under France, the
power of oppressing their inferiors. But, surely, care ought to have been taken,
by provisos in the act, that Britons should not have been shut out from settling
in a country for the conquest of which they did and do contribute, without giving up their liberties and commencing slaves; and that a British gentleman,
were he pleased to make the tour of Canada, might not be exposed to an imprisonment by a *lettre de cachet* from a governor in consequence of secret instructions from home, should he have unhappily fallen under the high displeasure of
a British ministry.

[1] The debates in the House of Commons, in the year 1744, on the Bill
for the Government of Quebec, were not given to the public till 1839, when
they were edited and published by Mr. Wright from manuscript notes
of Sir Henry Cavendish, Bart., M. P. They justify the worst apprehensions of our fathers, and demonstrate the servile and unmanly spirit of
the thirteenth Parliament of Great Britain — May 1768 to June 1774 —
perhaps the worst in British history. The splendor of the great names in
it — friends to law and liberty — only sets forth in stronger light the wickedness of the government and its tools. — ED.

of what had been done; its arrival at Boston, New York, and Virginia nearly at the same time; the firmness that the Bostonians showed upon the occasion; the indignation with which it was received, as the news flew through the continent; the spirited behavior[1] of the noble Virginian Assembly,[a] whereby they hastened their own dissolution; the accounts from different places and colonies forwarded to the capital for her encouragement under her distress, and to assure her of assistance and support, and that they considered hers in the true light of a common cause — not in consequence of, but ere they had received her applications for advice and direction, with the state of her situation; the forwardness which showed itself everywhere to contribute to her relief, and to adopt measures that might in the issue recover and secure the liberties of this and the other colonies; the surprising agreement

[a] Many political ministerial writers have, with a malicious cunning, attributed to Massachusetts more merit in opposing the attempts against American rights than it is entitled to. The Episcopal colony[2] of Virginia bravely led in the movements at the time of the Stamp Act, and was the first that, by their assembly, declared against the Boston Port Bill in the strongest terms of an honest indignation.

[1] They resolved to keep June 1st — the day when the Port Bill was to take effect — in fasting, humiliation, and prayer. On this the governor dissolved them; but, before separating, they proposed an annual congress of the colonies, and declared that an attack on one colony was an attack on all, and demanded "the united wisdom of the whole." See page 193. — Ed.

[2] At this time Virginia could hardly be considered as in fact an Episcopal colony. Baptist missionary communities from New England had undermined the Established Church, so that fully two-thirds of the people were dissenters. Patrick Henry became illustrious as their advocate, and Mr. Jefferson received his first clear conceptions of a free civil constitution from the practical exhibition of religious liberty and equality in a Baptist church in his neighborhood. The power of "lords spiritual and temporal" had been already overturned in Virginia by the verdict in the famous tobacco case, making the colonial law supreme. — Curtis's Progress of Baptist Principles, pp. 49–52, 354–57. 1857. — Ed.

in opinion that has prevailed in persons at a great distance from each other while consulting for the general good, whereby they have been led to transmit by letters nearly the same proposals to each other as though the inspiration of the Most High gave them the like understanding; the fixing upon a general congress, and choosing delegates, although in several places governmental chicanery was used to prevent it; the tender, compassionate feelings that every delegate, of whatsoever denomination, without party distinctions, discovered for the Bostonians, under the free and affecting prayer of a worthy Episcopalian,[a] when, at the opening of the congress, they had been alarmed with the false rumor that Boston had been attacked by the military and navy; the amazing consequences that this false alarm did, and continues to produce. It proved the means of showing that the colonists were not to be intimidated, though martial appearances were to terminate in actual hostilities; that they would be volunteers in the cause of liberty; and that they meant not to avoid fighting, whenever it became necessary. It put many thousands upon boldly taking themselves to arms, and marching forward, as they apprehended, to the assistance of their oppressed fellow-subjects. It kindled a martial spirit, that has spread through various

[a] The Rev. Mr. Duché.[1]

[1] The Rev. Jacob Duché, an Episcopal clergyman of Philadelphia, of brilliant talents, distinguished by making the prayer at the opening of the first congress at Philadelphia. He was invited to officiate, on motion of Mr. Samuel Adams. Mr. John Adams wrote to his wife: "Mr. Duché unexpectedly struck out into an extemporary prayer, which filled the bosom of every man present." He was opposed to independence, and wrote to Washington proposing his resignation of the command of the army. Washington transmitted the letter to Congress, and Mr. Duché found it well to leave for England, in 1776. He died in January, 1798, aged about sixty. — Allen's Biog. Dict. — ED.

colonies, and put the inhabitants upon perfecting themselves in the military exercise, that so they may be early prepared for the worst. To that it has been owing, in a great measure, that the continent has put on such a warlike appearance ; that companies have been formed, and are continually training, as far down as to and even in Virginia, if not further;[a] and that they will be better prepared than was ever before the case to repel all invasions that may be made upon their natural and constitutional rights, even though supported by a British army. Should British officers and troops wrongly imagine that their commissions and oaths oblige them to act, though in opposition to those very principles of the constitution that supports them and empowers the king to give them their commissions, instead of recollecting that all obligations entered into must necessarily be attended with this proviso, that they are not contrary to and subversive of the constitution, and that it is a reverence for and love to the constitution that distinguishes the soldier from the mercenary, — still, they would have no inclination to fight with fellow-subjects whose only fault was an excessive love of freedom, and a fixed determination not to submit to what they really believed were designed attacks upon their most precious liberties. In such circumstances, may we not hope that the former would rather wish to escape with honor than to disgrace themselves with conquest, and that the men of might will not find their hands? But should it be otherwise, and their native bravery be sacrificed in support of a bad cause, yet it might be too hard a task for them to subdue their brethren when fighting, *pro aris et focis*, for all that is dear, and who almost universally excel in the art of striking a mark, by which

[a] We are informed of the like in South Carolina.

the waste of ammunition will be greatly prevented.[a] The want of field artillery[1] will not be much nor long felt under a commander that has skill to avoid being attacked, and to choose his ground for attacking, in a country with which he is perfectly acquainted, and where every inhabitant, even the children, are standing spies upon all the motions of an adversary. But, as I earnestly beg of Heaven that the redress of our grievances may be obtained without fighting, I shall not dwell longer upon this point, and proceed to mention those other favorable circumstances, of a pacific kind, that remain to be specified, — such as the generous donations made for the poor of Boston;[2] the union of the colonies; the prevailing harmony and una-

---

[a] Mr. Knoch, then lieutenant in the first regiment of Orange-Nassau, in a treatise on " The Insufficiency of Fire-arms for Attack or Defence, demonstrated from Facts," etc., written in about 1759, proves " that, at a medium taken from any number of battles fought somewhat before that period, not more than one man could have been killed or wounded by eighty shot discharged."[3]

[1] Four cannon constituted the whole train of artillery of the British colonies in North America at the opening of the war, April 19, 1775; two of which, belonging to the province of Massachusetts, were taken by the enemy. The other two were the property of citizens of Boston. They were constantly in service through the war. In 1788, by order of Congress, they were delivered to the Governor of Massachusetts, John Hancock. On one was inscribed, " The Hancock, — sacred to Liberty; " and on the other, " The Adams."— Holmes's Annals, ii. 369.— ED.

[2] The Continental Congress resolved, September 17, 1774, that all the colonies ought to *continue* their contributions for " the distresses of our brethren at Boston, so long as their occasions may require; " and, October 8th, that " all America ought to support Massachusetts in their opposition to the late acts of Parliament." — ED.

[3] " This reverend gentleman has found a method of doing without much ammunition; for certain it is that there is at present no appearance of great quantities, and much less prospect of procuring more in future. How marvellous is sacerdotal invention, when set to work! . . . What American has experience enough to cope with " — General Gage — " a commander-in-chief, bred an officer, and highly distinguished? . . . . Where could he possibly have acquired his knowledge? . . . Not in a review before a governor; . . . not by turn-out every now and then,

nimity among the individuals composing the grand congress; their approbation of the opposition given by this colony to the acts for altering their ancient form of government; their association respecting trade, and the like; [a] the readiness of the people to conform to it; and the intrepid conduct of the southern inhabitants in preventing the introduction of any more teas among them. These are favorable circumstances, beyond what the most sanguine friends of liberty expected; that appear to be of the Lord's doing, and are marvellous in our eyes; that, if foretold, would have been deemed morally impossible by those who are still inimical to them, though evidencing a wonderful interposition of Providence; and that may justly encourage us, as well as keep us from fainting, especially when taken in connection with that spirit of prayer and humiliation which has discovered itself in different places on occasion of the times. Would to God there was more of this! Did it abound universally, we should have greater ground of encouragement by much; for the fervent prayers of the humble, penitent, and returning avail with God, through the mediation of the Lord Jesus. However, from what there is, and the other favorable circumstances, we are warranted to expect that at length, in the exercise of prudence, fortitude, and piety, we shall get well through our difficulties.

a The resolve of an embodied people, in a contest for liberty, when the voice of the majority has been fairly obtained, to interrupt, and, where necessary, forcibly to prevent a trade that would ruin the common cause, and cannot be carried on without subjecting them to slavery, notwithstanding the great injury it may occasion to individuals, I apprehend, will, on the same principles that justify a proscribing a traffic that would hazard the introduction of the pestilence, admit of as much stronger a vindication as slavery is the greater plague.

with *a few facetious parsons* and new-fangled minute-men, to make a ridiculous parade of arms for the amusement and scoff of every woman and child in the village."— Tory " Observations," quoted before on p. 195.— Ed.

We must prudently fall in with the measures recommended by the congress, that so we may not be reported to other colonies as disregarders of them, whereby first a jealousy may be produced, and then a disunion effected. We must promote unanimity among ourselves, peace and good order, that we may not be represented as desirous of confusion in hopes of making an advantage of it. We should let the laws of honor and honesty have their full weight with us, that we may fall under no reproach for abusing the present suspension of human laws. We should diligently provide for the worst, and be upon our guard, that we may not be suddenly stripped of those appurtenances,[1] the loss of which will be severely felt should we be called upon, by a dire necessity, to make our appeal to Heaven.

I have been ready at times to infer, from the military spirit that hath spread through the continent, that though we are to be saved, it is not to be without the sword, or, at least, the strong appearance of it, unless Infinite Wisdom (which we shall heartily rejoice to find is the case) should be in this way preparing the colonies for coöperating with the parent state, after that matters in dispute have been settled to satisfaction, in some important struggle with a common enemy; and therein, by giving her effectual assistance, for wiping away the reproaches that interested calumny and malice have thrown upon them, and for confirming an eternal friendship. But is it the awful determination of Heaven that we shall not retain our liberties without fighting, let no one despair. The continent, after

---

[1] General Gage's seizure of the province powder, at Charlestown, September 1st, was the "first indication of hostile intention;" and in his attempt to destroy the magazines at Concord, in April, the British troops shed the first blood in the war of independence. — Frothingham's Siege of Boston, 13—17, 51—64. — ED.

having discovered consummate wisdom, can never conduct so absurdly as to leave a single colony alone in the dispute. Their own security will constrain them to support whichsoever is attacked. They will rather assist at a distance than have a war upon or within their own borders, and will be sensible that whoever fights on the side of American liberty hazards his life in their battles. Should it be allowed, for argument's sake, that some one province or other, through selfishness or timidity, should basely slink from the common danger, yet would the rest have greater probability of succeeding than had the Dutch when they began to emerge from slavery and to acquire their liberties.[a] Let us be but brave, and we may promise our-

---

[a] "The whole country of the seven United Provinces is not as large as one-half of Pennsylvania, and when they began their contest with Philip the Second for their liberty, contained about as many inhabitants as are now in the province of Massachusetts Bay.[1] Philip's empire then comprehended, in Europe, all Spain and Portugal, the two Sicilies, and such provinces of the Low Countries as adhered to him; many islands of importance in the Mediterranean; the Milanese and many other valuable territories in Italy, and elsewhere; in Africa and Asia, all the dominions belonging to Spain and Portugal; in America, the immense countries subject to those two kingdoms, with all their treasures and yet unexhausted mines; and the Spanish West Indies. His armies were numerous and veteran, excellently officered, and commanded by the most renowned generals. So great was their force, that, during the wars in the Low Countries, his commander-in-chief, the Prince of Parma, marched twice into France, and obliged that great general and glorious king, Henry the Fourth, to raise at one time the siege of Paris, and at another that of Roan. So considerable was the naval power of Philip, that, in the midst of the same wars, he fitted out his dreadful armada to invade England. Yet seven little provinces, or counties, as we should call them (says that eminent Pennsylvanian), inspired by one general resolution 'to die free rather than live slaves,' not only baffled, but brought down into the dust, that enormous power that had contended for universal empire, and for half a century was the terror of the world. Such an amazing change indeed took place, that those provinces afterward actually protected Spain against the power of France."

[1] The history of the name of "Massachusetts Bay," as it appears on the title-page, leads back to the beginning of the colony. "Massachusets, alias Mattachusets, alias Massatusets bay," as it is called in the charter 4th Charles I., originally designating only what is now Boston harbor, was, by force of the royal charters, applied to the colony and to the province, and by custom to the sea within the headlands of Cape Ann and Cape Cod.

selves success. Do we join piety to our prudence and fortitude; do we confess and repent of our sins, justify God
in his so trying us, accept of our punishment at his hands
without murmuring or complaining; do we humble ourselves, amend our ways and doings, give up ourselves to
God, become a holy people, and make the Most High our
confidence, — we may hope that he will be on our side;
and "if the Lord is for us, what can men do unto us?"
Have we the God of hosts for our ally, we might bid
adieu to fear, though the world was united against us.

Let us, then, be pious, brave, and prudent, and we shall
— some of us, at least — have room for thanksgivings, not
merely for promising appearances, but for actual deliverance out of present difficulties, though it should not be
till we have been conversant with the din of arms and the
horrors of war. But should the country be wasted for a
few years, and a number of its inhabitants be destroyed,
ere the wished-for salvation is granted, how soon, after
having secured its liberties, will it regain its former prosperity; yea, become far more glorious, wealthy, and populous than ever, through the thousands and ten thousands
that will flock to it, with riches, arts, and sciences, acquired by them in foreign countries! And how will the
surviving inhabitants and their posterity, together with
refugees who have fled from oppression and hardships,
whether civil or sacred, to our American sanctuary, daily

It was the Indian name of the hill at Squantum, on the southern shore
of Boston harbor.

"Thence Massachusetts took her honored name."[1]

The affix of "Bay" was discontinued in the constitution of 1780. This
was the origin of the popular names, "The Bay People," "The Bay
State," "The Old Bay State."

[1] From the beautiful poem, by Wm. P. Lunt, D.D., at the laying of the corner-
stone of the "Sailors' Snug Harbor" at Quincy. — ED.

give thanks to the Sovereign of the universe that this general asylum was not consumed! How oft will they, with raptures, think upon that noble exertion of courage that prevented it, celebrate the praises of those that led and suffered in the common cause, and with glowing hearts bless that God who owned the goodness of it, and at length crowned it with success! Hallelujah. The Lord God omnipotent reigneth.

The way to escape an attack is to be in readiness to receive it. While administration consists of those that have avowed their dislike to the principles of this continent, and the known friends of America are excluded, there should be no dependence upon the fair speeches or actual promises of any, but the colonies should pursue the means of safety as vigorously as ever, that they may not be surprised. 'T is the most constant maxim of war, that a man ought never to be more upon his guard than while he is in treaty ; for want of attending to it, King Edward the Fourth was suddenly attacked, defeated, and made prisoner, by the Earl of Warwick, in 1470.

Government corrupted by Vice, and recovered by Righteousness.

A

S E R M O N

P R E A C H E D

BEFORE THE HONORABLE

C O N G R E S S

Of the Colony

Of the *Massachusetts-Bay*

IN N E W - E N G L A N D,

Assembled at *WATERTOWN*,

On Wednesday the 31st Day of *May*, 1775.

Being the Anniversary fixed by CHARTER

For the Election of COUNSELLORS.

By SAMUEL LANGDON, D. D.

Prefident of Harvard College in CAMBRIDGE.

As a roaring Lion and a ranging Bear, fo is a
wicked Ruler over the poor People. *Prov.* 28. 15.

W A T E R T O W N:

Printed and Sold by BENJAMIN EDES,
MDCCLXXV.

In Provincial Congress, Watertown, May 31, p. m., 1775.

Ordered, That Mr. Gill, Dr. Whiting, Mr. Pitts, Mr. Jewet, and Col. Lincoln be a Committee to return the thanks of this Congress to the Rev. Dr. Langdon for his excellent Sermon delivered to the Congress in the forenoon; and to request a copy of it for the press.

A true extract from the Minutes.

SAMUEL FREEMAN, Secretary.

EDITOR'S PREFATORY NOTE.

THE last few months in Massachusetts developed a temper in the people, and a persistent policy on the part of Governor Gage, which, manifestly to both parties, must before long end in collision. On the 1st of September, 1774, Governor Gage issued precepts for "the Great and General Court" to be convened at Salem, October 5th; on the 28th of September he issued his " proclamation," that, " from the many tumults and disorders which had since taken place, the extraordinary resolves which had been passed in many of the counties, the instructions given by the town of Boston, and some other towns, to their representatives, and the present disordered and unhappy state of the province," he then thought it highly inexpedient that it should be so convened. But ninety of the representatives did meet at Salem on the 5th, and on the next day, Thursday, organized a convention — John Hancock, Chairman, and Benjamin Lincoln, Clerk. On Friday they "resolved themselves into a Provincial Congress," which, after several sessions, was dissolved, December 10th, — having first " recommended " the election of delegates to another congress, February 1st ensuing, to " consult, deliberate, and resolve upon such further measures as, under God, shall be effectual to save this people from impending ruin, and to secure those inestimable liberties derived to us from our ancestors, and which it is our duty to preserve for posterity." The third Provincial Congress assembled at Watertown, May 31, 1775; and before that body President Langdon delivered this Sermon, it being the day fixed by charter for the election of councillors, — " election-day," — and this was the usual " Election Sermon."

The first blood of the war of the Revolution was shed at Lexington, on the 19th of April, 1775. The fire of British guns gleamed over the colonies, and beneath its flash every heart throbbed, and every soul felt that the die was cast. Yet it was not Englishmen who were in fratricidal war with their American brethren, but England, palsied by the church "gospel" of unlimited submission, and corrupted by her German king. Even then, though shocked, there yet lingered in the American breast the old yearning towards "home," the mother-land, and the fond pride of British nationality, which might have been rekindled, and the dissolution of the political bands deferred; but German obstinacy smothered the flame, and resistance — "rebellion" — became a revolution. Happily, time heals the wounds and dissipates the asperities of political separation; and in the indissoluble unity of the nations in blood, in language, and in faith, there remains a nobler brotherhood, dear to every manly heart and Christian hope.

The resistance and union of the colonies were the very opposite of the results expected by the ministry. Severity defeated its ends. Colonial non-importation, non-exportation, and non-consumption agreements were met by government prohibition of the fisheries and commerce, though it involved a sacrifice of British interests; for it was shown that New England only could successfully prosecute the fisheries, and the table of the House of Commons was loaded with statistics of their enormous value and importance to trade. The sword was two-edged; but with George III. *personal* feelings were superior to national interests.

The Provincial Congress voted, May 5th, that General Gage "ought to be considered and guarded against as an unnatural and inveterate enemy to the country." One hundred thousand pounds lawful money were voted; and thirteen thousand six hundred men, from Massachusetts alone, enlisted, as a superior force was the "only means left to stem the rapid progress of a tyrannical ministry." Force must be met by force; and the colonial militia — men with souls in them, ardent for their own firesides and rights — were ready for the king's mercenary troops. "In the name of the great Jehovah and the Continental Congress" was authority enough. Proclamations from royal governors were as the idle wind. Gage was master of Boston only. The trembling tories detained the wives and children of the patriots in Boston, for the security of the town, though in violation of General Gage's faith for their removal. The inhabitants of the seaports, exposed to the enemy by sea, fled from their homes to the interior, and were in want and suffering. "How much better," said the preacher, oppressed by the sight of all this misery, "for the inhabitants to have resolved, at all hazards, to defend themselves by their arms against such an enemy!" The day at Lexington and Concord, and other principal events, are referred to in the Sermon.

Such, in brief, was the face of affairs on this 31st of May, when the Provincial Congress was convened at Watertown. The old formula of proceedings was observed as far as possible. It was —

"*Ordered*, That Mr. Brown, Doct. Taylor, and Colonel Sayer be [a] committee to wait on the commanding officer of the militia of this town, to thank him for his polite offer to escort the Congress to the meeting-house, and to inform him that, as this Congress are now sitting, the Congress think it needless to withdraw for that purpose: but will, with the reverend gentlemen of the clergy, attend them to Mrs. Coolidge's, if they please to escort them thither, when the Congress adjourns."

By a special vote, Dr. Langdon's Sermon was sent to each minister in the colony, and to each member of the Congress.

The preacher, SAMUEL LANGDON, D. D., born in Boston, in the year 1722, graduated at Harvard College, 1740, and chaplain of a regiment in the *crusade* against Louisburg, 1745, was pastor of a church in Portsmouth, N. H., from 1747 till 1774, when, by reason of his eminent talents, learning, and piety, and of his bold and zealous patriotism, he was appointed to the presidency of Harvard College.

He was moderator of the annual convention of the ministers, held, by special invitation of the Provincial Congress, at Watertown, June 1st, following election-day, when he signed the following letter:

"To the Hon. JOSEPH WARREN, Esq., President of the Provincial Congress of the Colony of the Massachusetts Bay, etc.

" SIR : — We, the pastors of the Congregational churches of the Colony of the Massachusetts Bay, in our present annual convention,"— at Watertown, June 1, 1775, — " gratefully beg leave to express the sense we have of the regard shown by the Honorable Provincial Congress to us, and the encouragement they have been pleased to afford to our assembling as a body this day. Deeply impressed with sympathy for the distresses of our much-injured and oppressed country, we are not a little relieved in beholding the representatives of this people, chosen by their free and unbiassed suffrages, now met to concert measures for their relief and defence, in whose wisdom and integrity, under the smiles of Divine Providence, we cannot but express our entire confidence.

" As it has been found necessary to raise an army for the common safety, and our brave countrymen have so willingly offered themselves to this hazardous service, we are not insensible of the vast burden that their necessary maintenance must"— devolve — " upon the people. We therefore cannot forbear, upon this occasion, to offer our services [1] to the public, and to signify our readiness, with the consent of our several congregations, to officiate, by rotation, as chaplains to the army.

" We devoutly commend the Congress, and our brethren in arms, to the guidance and protection of that Providence which, from the first settlement of this country, has so remarkably appeared for the preservation of its civil and religious rights.

"SAMUEL LANGDON, MODERATOR."

After an able administration, in a period of peculiar embarrassment, he resigned the presidency of the college, and became pastor of the church at Hampton Falls.

In the New Hampshire State Convention of 1788 he was prominent in securing the adoption of the Federal Constitution. He died, November 29th, 1797, beloved and revered for his private and public life.[2]

1 See Address to the Clergy, p. xxxvii.
2 Rev. Rufus W. Clark's sketch in Sprague's Annals of the American Pulpit, i. 455—459.

DISCOURSE V.

AN ELECTION SERMON.

AND I WILL RESTORE THY JUDGES AS AT THE FIRST, AND THY COUNSELLORS AS AT THE BEGINNING; AFTERWARD THOU SHALT BE CALLED THE CITY OF RIGHTEOUSNESS, THE FAITHFUL CITY. — Isaiah i. 26.

SHALL we rejoice, my fathers and brethren, or shall we weep together, on the return of this anniversary, which from the first settlement of this colony has been sacred to liberty, to perpetuate that invaluable privilege of choosing from among ourselves wise men, fearing God and hating covetousness, to be honorable counsellors, to constitute one essential branch of that happy government which was established on the faith of royal charters?

On this day the people have from year to year assembled, from all our towns, in a vast congregation, with gladness and festivity, with every ensign of joy displayed in our metropolis, which now, alas! is made a garrison of mercenary troops, the stronghold of despotism. But how shall I now address you from this desk, remote from the capital, and remind you of the important business which distinguished this day in our calendar, without spreading a gloom over this assembly by exhibiting the melancholy change made in the face of our public affairs?

We have lived to see the time when British liberty is just ready to expire, — when that constitution of government which has so long been the glory and strength of the English nation is deeply undermined and ready to tumble into ruins, — when America is threatened with cruel oppression, and the arm of power is stretched out against New England, and especially against this colony, to compel us to submit to the arbitrary acts of legislators who are not our representatives, and who will not themselves bear the least part of the burdens which, without mercy, they are laying upon us. The most formal and solemn grants of kings to our ancestors are deemed by our oppressors as of little value; and they have mutilated the charter of this colony, in the most essential parts, upon false representations, and new-invented maxims of policy, without the least regard to any legal process. We are no longer permitted to fix our eyes on the faithful of the land, and trust in the wisdom of their counsels and the equity of their judgment; but men in whom we can have no confidence, whose principles are subversive of our liberties, whose aim is to exercise lordship over us, and share among themselves the public wealth, — men who are ready to serve any master, and execute the most unrighteous decrees for high wages, — whose faces we never saw before, and whose interests and connections may be far divided from us by the wide Atlantic, — are to be set over us, as counsellors and judges, at the pleasure of those who have the riches and power of the nation in their hands, and whose noblest plan is to subjugate the colonies, first, and then the whole nation, to their will.

That we might not have it in our power to refuse the most absolute submission to their unlimited claims of authority, they have not only endeavored to terrify us with fleets and armies sent to our capital, and distressed and put an end to our trade, — particularly that important branch of it, the fishery,[1] — but at length attempted, by a sudden

---

[1] Mr. Sabine's learned "Report on the Principal Fisheries of the American Seas," 1853, is an invaluable contribution to American history. It is

march of a body of troops in the night,[1] to seize and destroy one of our magazines, formed by the people merely for their security, if, after such formidable military preparations on the other side, matters should be pushed to an extremity. By this, as might well be expected, a skirmish was brought on; and it is most evident, from a variety of concurring circumstances, as well as numerous depositions both of the prisoners taken by us at that time and our own men then on the spot only as spectators, that the fire began first on the side of the king's troops. At least five or six of our inhabitants were murderously killed by the regulars at Lexington before any man attempted to return the fire, and when they were actually complying with the command to disperse; and two more of our brethren were likewise killed at Concord bridge, by a fire from the king's soldiers, before [2] the engagement began on our side. But, whatever credit falsehoods transmitted to Great Britain from the other side may gain, the matter may be rested entirely on this: that he that arms himself to commit a robbery, and demands the traveller's purse by the terror of instant death, is the first aggressor, though the other should take the advantage of discharging his weapon first, and killing the robber.

The alarm was sudden, but in a very short time spread far and wide. The nearest neighbors in haste ran together to assist their brethren and save their country. Not more than three or four hundred met in season, and bravely

essential to a correct knowledge of American colonization, and of much of our subsequent history. — ED.

[1] April 18-19. — ED.

[2] Mr. Frothingham presents the results of an able and conscientious study of these events in his " History of the Siege of Boston," — " The best of our historic monographs." — Bancroft in Allibone. See also Mr. Henry B. Dawson's elaborate pages in " The Battles of the United States." — ED.

attacked and repulsed the enemies of liberty, who re-
treated with great precipitation. But, by the help of a
strong reïnforcement, notwithstanding a close pursuit and
continual loss on their side, they acted the part of robbers and savages, by burning,[1] plundering, and damaging
almost every house in their way to the utmost of their

[1] Rev. Isaac Mansfield, Jr., chaplain to General Thomas's regiment, in
his Thanksgiving Sermon " in the camp at Roxbury, November 23, 1775,"
says of the event of April 19th: " What but the hand of Providence preserved the school of the prophets from their ravage, who would have
deprived us of many advantages for moral or religious improvement? "
To this he adds the note following: " ' General Gage, as governor of this
province, issued his precepts for convening a General Assembly at Boston,
designing to enforce a compliance with Lord North's designing motion;
they were to be kept as prisoners in garrison, till, under the mouth of cannon and at the point of the bayonet, they should be reduced to a mean and
servile submission. To facilitate this matter, he was to send out a party
to take possession of a magazine at Concord. Presuming that this might
be done without opposition, the said party, upon their return from Concord, were to lay waste till they should arrive at Cambridge common;
there, after destroying the colleges"— seminaries of sedition — " and other
buildings, they were to throw up an entrenchment upon the said common,
their number was to be increased from the garrison, and the next morning
a part of the artillery to be removed and planted in the entrenchment
aforesaid. This astonishing manœuvre, it was supposed, would so effectually intimidate the constituents, that the General Assembly, by the compliance designed, would literally *represent* their constituents.' The author
is not at liberty to publish the channel through which he received the foregoing, but begs to assure the reader that it came so direct that he cannot
hesitate in giving credit to it. He recollects one circumstance which renders it highly probable: Lord Percy (on April 19), suspicious his progress
to Concord might be retarded by the plank of the bridge at Cambridge
being taken away, brought out from Boston several loads of plank, with
a number of carpenters; not finding occasion to use them, he carried them
on his way to Concord, perhaps about a mile and a half from the bridge;
about an hour after the plank were returned. If he had intended to
repass that river at night, he must have reserved the plank; if he designed
to stop in Cambridge, the plank must be an incumbrance. This conduct,
in returning the plank, may be accounted for upon supposition of the
foregoing plan of operation."— ED.

power, murdering the unarmed and helpless, and not regarding the weaknesses of the tender sex, until they had secured themselves beyond the reach of our terrifying arms.[a]

That ever-memorable day, the nineteenth of April, is the date of an unhappy war openly begun by the ministers of the king of Great Britain against his good subjects in this colony, and implicitly against all the other colonies. But for what? Because they have made a noble stand for their natural and constitutional rights, in opposition to the machinations of wicked men who are betraying their royal master, establishing Popery in the British dominions, and aiming to enslave and ruin the whole nation, that they may enrich themselves and their vile dependents with the public treasures and the spoils of America.

We have used our utmost endeavors, by repeated humble petitions and remonstrances, by a series of unanswerable reasonings published from the press, — in which the dispute has been fairly stated, and the justice of our opposition clearly demonstrated, — and by the mediation of some of the noblest and most faithful friends of the British constitution, who have powerfully plead our cause in Parliament, to prevent such measures as may soon reduce the body politic to a miserable, dismembered, dying trunk, though lately the terror of all Europe. But our

---

[a] Near the meeting-house in Menotomy [1] two aged, helpless men, who had not been out in the action, and were found unarmed in a house where the regulars entered, were murdered without mercy. In another house, in that neighborhood, a woman, in bed with a new-born infant about a week old, was forced by the threats of the soldiery to escape, almost naked, to an open outhouse; her house was then set on fire, but was soon extinguished by one of the children which had laid concealed till the enemy was gone. In Cambridge, a man of weak mental powers, who went out to gaze at the regular army as they passed, without arms or thought of danger, was wantonly shot at and killed by those inhuman butchers as he sat on a fence.

[1] Now West Cambridge. — ED.

king, as if impelled by some strange fatality, is resolved to reason with us only by the roar of his cannon and the pointed arguments of muskets and bayonets. Because we refuse submission to the despotic power of a ministerial Parliament, our own sovereign, to whom we have been always ready to swear true allegiance, — whose authority we never meant to cast off, who might have continued happy in the cheerful obedience of as faithful subjects as any in his dominions, — has given us up to the rage of his ministers, to be seized at sea by the rapacious commanders of every little sloop of war and piratical cutter, and to be plundered and massacred by land by mercenary troops, who know no distinction betwixt an enemy and a brother, between right and wrong, but only, like brutal pursuers, to hunt and seize the prey pointed out by their masters.

We must keep our eyes fixed on the supreme government of the Eternal King, as directing all events, setting up or pulling down the kings of the earth at his pleasure, suffering the best forms of human government to degenerate and go to ruin by corruption, or restoring the decayed constitutions of kingdoms and states by reviving public virtue and religion, and granting the favorable interpositions of his providence. To this our text leads us ; and, though I hope to be excused on this occasion from a formal discourse on the words in a doctrinal way, yet I must not wholly pass over the religious instruction contained in them.

Let us consider — that for the sins of a people God may suffer the best government to be corrupted or entirely dissolved, and that nothing but a general reformation can give good ground to hope that the public happiness will be restored by the recovery of the strength and perfection of the state, and that Divine Providence will interpose to fill every department with wise and good men.

Isaiah prophesied about the time of the captivity of the Ten Tribes of Israel, and about a century before the captivity of Judah. The kingdom of Israel was brought to destruction because its iniquities were full; its counsellors and judges were wholly taken away because there remained no hope of reformation. But the sceptre did not entirely depart from Judah, nor a lawgiver from between his feet, till the Messiah came; yet greater and greater changes took place in their political affairs : their government degenerated in proportion as their vices increased, till few faithful men were left in any public offices ; and at length, when they were delivered up for seventy years into the hands of the king of Babylon, scarce any remains of their original excellent civil polity appeared among them.

The Jewish government, according to the original constitution which was divinely established, if considered merely in a civil view, was a perfect republic. The heads of their tribes and elders of their cities were their counsellors and judges. They called the people together in more general or particular assemblies, — took their opinions, gave advice, and managed the public affairs according to the general voice. Counsellors and judges comprehend all the powers of that government ; for there was no such thing as legislative authority belonging to it, — their complete code of laws being given immediately from God by the hand of Moses. And let them who cry up the divine right of kings consider that the only form of government which had a proper claim to a divine establishment was so far from including the idea of a king, that it was a high crime for Israel to ask to be in this respect like other nations; and when they were gratified, it was rather as a just punishment of their folly, that they might feel the burdens of court pageantry, of which they were warned by a very striking description, than as a divine recommendation of kingly authority.

Every nation, when able and agreed, has a right to set up over themselves any form of government which to them may appear most conducive to their common welfare.[1] The civil polity of Israel is doubtless an excellent general model, allowing for some peculiarities; at least, some principal laws and orders of it may be copied to great advantage in more modern establishments.

When a government is in its prime, the public good engages the attention of the whole; the strictest regard is paid to the qualifications of those who hold the offices of the state; virtue prevails; everything is managed with justice, prudence, and frugality; the laws are founded on principles of equity rather than mere policy, and all the people are happy. But vice will increase with the riches and glory of an empire; and this gradually tends to corrupt the constitution, and in time bring on its dissolution. This may be considered not only as the natural effect of vice, but a righteous judgment of Heaven, especially upon a nation which has been favored with the blessings of religion and liberty, and is guilty of undervaluing them, and eagerly going into the gratification of every lust.

In this chapter the prophet describes the very corrupt state of Judah in his day, both as to religion and common morality, and looks forward to that increase of wicked-

---

[1] " Governments are instituted among men, deriving their just powers from the consent of the governed; . . . . it is the right of the people to alter or abolish it, and to institute a new government, laying its foundations on such principles, and organizing its powers in such form, as to them shall seem most likely to effect their safety and happiness."— Dec. of Ind., July 4th, 1776. — ED.

ness which would bring on their desolation and captivity. They were " a sinful nation, a people laden with iniquity, a seed of evil-doers, children that were corrupters, who had forsaken the Lord, and provoked the Holy One of Israel to anger." The whole body of the nation, from head to foot, was full of moral and political disorders, without any remaining soundness. Their religion was all mere ceremony and hypocrisy; and even the laws of common justice and humanity were disregarded in their public courts. They had counsellors and judges, but very different from those at the beginning of the commonwealth. Their princes were rebellious against God and the constitution of their country, and companions of thieves, — giving countenance to every artifice for seizing the property of the subjects into their own hands, and robbing the public treasury. Every one loved gifts, and followed after rewards; they regarded the perquisites more than the duties of their office; the general aim was at profitable places and pensions; they were influenced in everything by bribery; and their avarice and luxury were never satisfied, but hurried them on to all kinds of oppression and violence, so that they even justified and encouraged the murder of innocent persons to support their lawless power and increase their wealth. And God, in righteous judgment, left them to run into all this excess of vice, to their own destruction, because they had forsaken him, and were guilty of wilful inattention to the most essential parts of that religion which had been given them by a well-attested revelation from heaven.

The Jewish nation could not but see and feel the unhappy consequences of so great corruption of the state. Doubtless they complained much of men in power, and very heartily and liberally reproached them for their notorious misconduct. The public greatly suffered, and the

people groaned and wished for better rulers and better
management; but in vain they hoped for a change of men
and measures and better times when the spirit of religion
was gone, and the infection of vice was become universal.
The whole body being so corrupted, there could be no
rational prospect of any great reformation in the state, but
rather of its ruin, which accordingly came on in Jeremiah's
time. Yet if a general reformation of religion and morals
had taken place, and they had turned to God from all their
sins, — if they had again recovered the true spirit of their
religion, — God, by the gracious interpositions of his providence, would soon have found out ·methods to restore the
former virtue of the state, and again have given them men
of wisdom and integrity, according to their utmost wish,
to be counsellors and judges. This was verified in fact
after the nation had been purged by a long captivity, and
returned to their own land humbled and filled with zeal
for God and his law.

By all this we may be led to consider the true cause of
the present remarkable troubles which are come upon Great
Britain and these colonies, and the only effectual remedy.

We have rebelled against God. We have lost the true
spirit of Christianity, though we retain the outward profession and form of it. We have neglected and set light
by the glorious gospel of our Lord Jesus Christ, and his
holy commands and institutions. The worship of many
is but mere compliment to the Deity, while their hearts
are far from him. By many the gospel is corrupted into
a superficial system of moral philosophy, little better
than ancient Platonism; and, after all the pretended refinements of moderns in the theory of Christianity, very
little of the pure practice of it is to be found among those
who once stood foremost in the profession of the gospel.
In a general view of the present moral state of Great

Britain it may be said, "There is no truth, nor mercy, nor knowledge of God in the land. By swearing, and lying, and killing, and stealing, and committing adultery," their wickedness breaks out, and one murder after another is committed, under the connivance and encouragement even of that authority by which such crimes ought to be punished, that the purposes of oppression and despotism may be answered. As they have increased, so have they sinned; therefore God is changing their glory into shame. The general prevalence of vice has changed the whole face of things in the British government.

The excellency of the constitution has been the boast of Great Britain and the envy of neighboring nations. In former times the great departments of the state, and the various places of trust and authority, were filled with men of wisdom, honesty, and religion, who employed all their powers, and were ready to risk their fortunes and their lives, for the public good. They were faithful counsellors to kings; directed their authority and majesty to the happiness of the nation, and opposed every step by which despotism endeavored to advance. They were fathers of the people, and sought the welfare and prosperity of the whole body. They did not exhaust the national wealth by luxury and bribery, or convert it to their own private benefit or the maintenance of idle, useless officers and dependents, but improved it faithfully for the proper purposes — for the necessary support of government and defence of the kingdom. Their laws were dictated by wisdom and equality, and justice was administered with impartiality. Religion discovered its general influence among all ranks, and kept out great corruptions from places of power.

But in what does the British nation now glory? — In a mere shadow of its ancient political system, — in titles of

dignity without virtue, — in vast public treasures continually lavished in corruption till every fund is exhausted,
notwithstanding the mighty streams perpetually flowing
in, — in the many artifices to stretch the prerogatives of
the crown beyond all constitutional bounds, and make the
king an absolute monarch, while the people are deluded
with a mere phantom of liberty. What idea must we
entertain of that great government, if such a one can be
found, which pretends to have made an exact counterbalance of power between the sovereign, the nobles and
the commons, so that the three branches shall be an
effectual check upon each other, and the united wisdom of
the whole shall conspire to promote the national felicity,
but which, in reality, is reduced to such a situation that it
may be managed at the sole will of one court favorite?
What difference is there betwixt one[1] man's choosing, at
his own pleasure, by his single vote, the majority of those
who are to represent the people, and his purchasing in such
a majority, according to his own nomination, with money
out of the public treasury, or other effectual methods of
influencing elections? And what shall we say if, in the
same manner, by places, pensions, and other bribes, a
minister of the crown can at any time gain over a nobler
majority likewise to be entirely subservient to his purposes,
and, moreover, persuade his royal master to resign himself
up wholly to the direction of his counsels? If this should

---

[1] Mr. Burke, in his "Thoughts on the Present Discontents," 1770, said:
"The power of the crown, almost rotten and dead as prerogative, has
grown up anew, with much more strength, and far less odium, under the
name of *influence*," intrigue, and favoritism; and a few years later he
refers to the "not disavowed use which has been made of his Majesty's
name for the purpose of the most unconstitutional, corrupt, and dishonorable influence on the minds of the members of this Parliament that
ever was practised in this kingdom. No attention even to exterior decorum," etc. — ED.

be the case of any nation, from one seven years' end to another, the bargain and sale being made sure for such a period, would they still have reason to boast of their excellent constitution?[1] Ought they not rather to think it high time to restore the corrupted, dying state to its original perfection? I will apply this to the Roman senate under Julius Cæsar, which retained all its ancient formalities, but voted always only as Cæsar dictated. If the decrees of such a senate were urged on the Romans, as fraught with all the blessings of Roman liberty, we must suppose them strangely deluded if they were persuaded to believe it.

The pretence for taxing America has been that the nation contracted an immense debt for the defence of the American colonies, and that, as they are now able to contribute some proportion towards the discharge of this debt, and must be considered as part of the nation, it is reasonable they should be taxed, and the Parliament has a right to tax and govern them, in all cases whatever, by its own supreme authority. Enough has been already published on this grand controversy, which now threatens a final separation of the colonies from Great Britain. But can the amazing national debt be paid by a little trifling sum, squeezed from year to year out of America, which is continually drained of all its cash by a restricted trade with the parent country, and which in this way is taxed to the government of Britain in a very large proportion? Would it not be much superior wisdom, and sounder policy, for a distressed kingdom to retrench the vast unneces-

---

[1] This contemporary observation of the English government of that period shows the watchful eye of the colonists on the administration; and by it we can better appreciate their masterly conduct of public affairs, and their superiority over the British statesmen. England knew not her colonists, but she was known of them. — ED.

sary expenses continually incurred by its enormous vices;
to stop the prodigious sums paid in pensions, and to numberless officers, without the least advantage to the public;
to reduce the number of devouring servants in the great
family; to turn their minds from the pursuit of pleasure
and the boundless luxuries of life to the important interests of their country and the salvation of the commonwealth? Would not a reverend regard to the authority
of divine revelation, a hearty belief of the gospel of the
grace of God, and a general reformation of all those vices
which bring misery and ruin upon individuals, families, and
kingdoms, and which have provoked Heaven to bring the
nation into such perplexed and dangerous circumstances,
be the surest way to recover the sinking state, and make it
again rich and flourishing? Millions might annually be
saved if the kingdom were generally and thoroughly reformed; and the public debt, great as it is, might in a few
years be cancelled by a growing revenue, which now
amounts to full ten millions per annum, without laying
additional burdens on any of the subjects. But the
demands of corruption are constantly increasing, and will
forever exceed all the resources of wealth which the wit
of man can invent or tyranny impose.

Into what fatal policy has the nation been impelled, by
its public vices, to wage a cruel war with its own children in these colonies, only to gratify the lust of power
and the demands of extravagance! May God, in his great
mercy, recover Great Britain from this fatal infatuation,
show them their errors, and give them a spirit of reformation, before it is too late to avert impending destruction!
May the eyes of the king be opened to see the ruinous
tendency of the measures into which he has been led, and
his heart inclined to treat his American subjects with justice and clemency, instead of forcing them still further to

the last extremities! God grant some method may be found out to effect a happy reconciliation, so that the colonies may again enjoy the protection of their sovereign, with perfect security of all their natural rights and civil and religious liberties.

But, alas! have not the sins of America, and of New England in particular, had a hand in bringing down upon us the righteous judgments of Heaven? Wherefore is all this evil come upon us? Is it not because we have forsaken the Lord? Can we say we are innocent of crimes against God? No, surely. It becomes us to humble ourselves under his mighty hand, that he may exalt us in due time. However unjustly and cruelly we have been treated by man, we certainly deserve, at the hand of God, all the calamities in which we are now involved. Have we not lost much of that spirit of genuine Christianity which so remarkably appeared in our ancestors, for which God distinguished them with the signal favors of providence when they fled from tyranny and persecution into this western desert? Have we not departed from their virtues? Though I hope and am confident that as much true religion, agreeable to the purity and simplicity of the gospel, remains among us as among any people in the world, yet, in the midst of the present great apostasy of the nations professing Christianity, have not we likewise been guilty of departing from the living God? Have we not made light of the gospel of salvation, and too much affected the cold, formal, fashionable religion of countries grown old in vice, and overspread with infidelity? Do not our follies and iniquities testify against us? Have we not, especially in our seaports, gone much too far into the pride and luxuries of life? Is it not a fact, open to common observation, that profaneness, intemperance, unchastity, the love of pleasure, fraud, avarice, and other vices, are increasing among us from year to year? And have not even these young governments been in some measure infected with the corruptions of European courts? Has there been no flattery, no bribery, no artifices practised, to get into places of honor and profit, or carry a vote to serve a particular interest, without regard to right or wrong? Have our statesmen always acted with integrity, and every judge with impartiality, in the fear of God? In short, have all ranks of men showed regard to the divine commands, and joined to promote the Redeemer's kingdom and the public welfare? I wish we could more fully justify ourselves in all these respects. If such sins have not been so notorious among us as in older countries, we must nevertheless remember that the sins of a people who have been remarkable for the profession of godliness, are more aggravated by all the advantages and favors they have enjoyed, and will receive more speedy and signal punishment; as God says of Israel: "You only have I known of all the families of the earth, therefore will I punish you for all your iniquities.[a]

The judgments now come upon us are very heavy and distressing, and have fallen with peculiar weight on our capital, where, notwithstanding the plighted honor of the chief commander of the hostile troops, many of our brethren are still detained, as if they were captives;[1] and those that have been released have left the principal part of their substance, which is withheld, by arbitrary orders, contrary to an express treaty, to be plundered by the army.[b]

a Amos iii. 2.

b Soon after the battle at Concord, General Gage stipulated, with the selectmen of Boston, that if the inhabitants would deliver up their arms, to be depos-

1 One apology for this bad faith was, that if only tory interests remained in Boston the patriots would fire the town. It occasioned extreme anxiety and suffering. — Frothingham, 93–96. — ED.

Let me address you in the words of the prophet: " O Israel! return unto the Lord thy God, for thou hast fallen by thine iniquity." My brethren, let us repent, and implore the divine mercy ; let us amend our ways and our doings, reform everything which has been provoking to the Most High, and thus endeavor to obtain the gracious interpositions of Providence for our deliverance.

If true religion is revived by means of these public calamities, and again prevails among us, — if it appears in our religious assemblies, in the conduct of our civil affairs, in our armies, in our families, in all our business and conversation, — we may hope for the direction and blessing of the Most High, while we are using our best endeavors to preserve and restore the civil government of this colony, and defend America from slavery.

Our late happy government is changed into the terrors of military execution. Our firm opposition to the establishment of an arbitrary system is called rebellion, and we are to expect no mercy, but to yield property and life at discretion. This we are resolved at all events not to do, and therefore we have taken up arms in our own defence, and all the colonies are united in the great cause of liberty.

But how shall we live while civil government is dis-

ited in Fanueil Hall, and returned when circumstances would permit, they should have liberty to quit the town, and take with them their effects. They readily complied, but soon found themselves abused. With great difficulty, and very slowly, they obtain passes, but are forbidden to carry out anything besides household furniture and wearing apparel. Merchants and shopkeepers are obliged to leave behind all their merchandise, and even their cash is detained. Mechanics are not allowed to bring out the most necessary tools for their work. Not only their family stores of provisions are stopped, but it has been repeatedly and credibly affirmed that poor women and children have had the very smallest articles of this kind taken from them, which were necessary for their refreshment while they travelled a few miles to their friends; and that even from young children, in their mothers' arms, the cruel soldiery have taken the morsel of bread given to prevent their crying, and thrown it away. How much better for the inhabitants to have resolved, at all hazards, to defend themselves by their arms against such an enemy, than suffer such shameful abuse!

solved ?   What shall we do without counsellors and judges ?   A state of absolute anarchy is dreadful.   Submission to the tyranny of hundreds of imperious masters, firmly embodied against us, and united in the same cruel design of disposing of our lives and subsistence at their pleasure, and making their own will our law in all cases whatsoever, is the vilest slavery, and worse than death.

Thanks be to God that he has given us, as men, natural rights, independent on all human laws whatever, and that these rights are recognized by the grand charter of British liberties.   By the law of nature, any body of people, destitute of order and government, may form themselves into a civil society, according to their best prudence, and so provide for their common safety and advantage.   When one form is found by the majority not to answer the grand purpose in any tolerable degree, they may, by common consent, put an end to it and set up another, — only, as all such great changes are attended with difficulty and danger of confusion, they ought not to be attempted without urgent necessity, which will be determined always by the general voice of the wisest and best members of the community.

If the great servants of the public forget their duty, betray their trust, and sell their country, or make war against the most valuable rights and privileges of the people, reason and justice require that they should be discarded, and others appointed in their room, without any regard to formal resignations of their forfeited power.

It must be ascribed to some supernatural influence on the minds of the main body of the people through this extensive continent, that they have so universally adopted the method of managing the important matters necessary to preserve among them a free government by corresponding committees and congresses, consisting of the wisest and most disinterested patriots in America, chosen by the unbiased suffrages of the people assembled for that purpose in their several towns, counties, and provinces. So general agreement, through so many provinces of so large a country, in one mode of self-preservation, is unexampled in any history; and the effect has exceeded our most sanguine expectations. Universal tumults, and all the irregularities and violence of mobbish factions, naturally arise when legal authority ceases. But how little of this has appeared in the midst of the late obstructions of civil government! — nothing more than what has often happened in Great Britain and Ireland, in the face of the civil powers in all their strength; nothing more than what is frequently seen in the midst of the perfect regulations of the great city of London; and, may I not add, nothing more than has been absolutely necessary to carry into execution the spirited resolutions of a people too sensible to deliver themselves up to oppression and slavery. The judgment and advice of the continental assembly of delegates have been as readily obeyed as if they were authentic acts of a long-established Parliament. And in every colony the votes of a congress have had equal effect with the laws of great and general courts.

It is now ten months since[1] this colony has been deprived of the benefit of that government which was so long enjoyed by charter. They have had no General Assembly for matters of legislation and the public revenue; the courts of justice have been shut up,[2] and almost the

---

[1] Since July 17, 1774, when the General Court at Salem closed the door against the secretary sent by Governor Gage to dissolve the Assembly, chose Thomas Cushing, Samuel Adams, Robert Treat Paine, James Bowdoin, and John Adams, delegates to a congress of the colonies, passed resolves, and separated. — ED.

[2] The *power of public opinion in preserving order and safety* during the

whole executive power has ceased to act; yet order among the people has been remarkably preserved. Few crimes

period from the time when the king's courts and magistrates — all legal authority — ceased to act, till the accession of constitutional authority, — a phenomenon which excited the admiration of the world, — is finely illustrated in Mr. Freeman's account of the proceedings in Barnstable county, "on the first Tuesday of September," 1774. As there might be appeals from the Court of Common Pleas to the Superior Court, the Chief Justice of which, Hutchinson, had accepted a salary from the crown, the people suppressed the sessions of that court throughout the province, except in Boston, where they were not in power. Fifteen hundred of the people of Barnstable, Plymouth, and Bristol counties, thoroughly organized, met in front of the court-house, at Barnstable, and, through their conductor-in-chief, Dr. Nathaniel Freeman, of Sandwich, addressed Colonel Otis, the venerable Chief Justice: . . . "Our safety, all that is dear to us, and the welfare of unborn millions, have directed this movement to *prevent the court from being opened or doing any business.* We have taken all the consequences into consideration; we have weighed them well, and have formed this *resolution,* which we *shall not rescind.*" The Chief Justice then calmly but firmly replied: "This is a *legal* and a *constitutional* court; it has suffered no mutations; the juries have been drawn from the boxes as the law directs; and why would you interrupt its proceedings? — why do you make a leap before you get to the hedge?" Dr. Freeman responded: "*All this* has been considered. We do not appear out of any disrespect to this honorable court, nor do we apprehend that if you proceed to business you will do anything that we could censure. But, sir, from all the *decisions* of this court, of more than forty shillings' amount, an *appeal* lies; an appeal to what? — to a court holding office during the king's pleasure, — a court over which we have no control or influence, — a court paid out of the revenue that is *extorted* from us by the *illegal* and *unconstitutional* edict of foreign despotism, — and *there* the jury will be appointed by the *sheriff.* For *this reason* we have adopted this method of stopping the avenue through which business may otherwise pass to that tribunal, — well knowing that if they have no business they can do us no harm." The Chief Justice then said: "As is my duty, I now, in his Majesty's name, *order you immediately to disperse,* and give the court the opportunity to perform the business of the county." Dr. Freeman replied: "We thank your Honor for having done YOUR duty: WE SHALL CONTINUE TO PERFORM OURS." The court then turned and repaired to the house where they had put up.

This was supposed to be the first overt act of TREASON, done deliber-

have been committed, punishable by the judge; even former contentions betwixt one neighbor and another have

ately, in the face of day. The solemnity and sense of right which governed the people, and which was a characteristic of the revolutionary
period, was grandly exhibited in their code of regulations adopted on this
occasion. We give their own words:

"Whereas a strict adherence to virtue and religion is not only well-
pleasing in the sight of Almighty God, and highly commendable before
men, but hath a natural tendency to good order, and to lead mankind in
the paths of light and truth:

"Therefore, Resolved, That we will . . . avoid all kinds of intemperance by strong liquors, and no otherwise frequent the taverns than for
necessary entertainment and refreshment; that we will not swear pro-
fanely, or abuse our superiors, equals, or inferiors, by any ill or opprobri-
ous language; that we will not invade the property of any, or take of their
goods or estate without their leave or consent; that we will not offer violence
to any persons, or use any threatening words, otherwise than such as shall
be approved of and accounted necessary by our community for the accomplishing the errand we go upon; and that we will carefully observe an
orderly, circumspect, and civil behavior, as well towards strangers and
all others as towards those of our own fellowship.

"Resolved, That Messrs. Aaron Barlow, Nathaniel Briggs, James Foster,
Joseph Haskell, 3d, John Doty, Judah Sears, Jr., Stephen Wing, and
John Pitcher, be a committee to hear and determine all offences against
morality, decency, and good manners, that shall be complained of, . . .
with power to call before them, examine, acquit, or punish, according to
the nature and circumstances of the offence. . . . .

"Resolved, That we will, during the time of our said enterprise, aid,
protect, and support our said committee in the full and free discharge of
their duty and office, and use our most careful endeavors for the punishment of all offenders.

"And, forasmuch as these our public transactions are of a public nature,
and, as we apprehend, laudable; and as we have no private interest to
serve, or anything in view but the good of our *country* and its *common
cause*:

"Therefore, Voted, That these resolves be read once every day, at some
convenient time and place, during our transitory state and temporary fellowship, — so that our righteousness may plead our cause, and bear a public testimony that we are neither friends to mobs, or riots, or any other
wickedness or abomination.

"And, lastly, we Resolve, That we will yield all due respect and obedi-

ceased ; nor have fraud and rapine taken advantage of the imbecility of the civil powers.

The necessary preparations for the defence of our liberties required not only the collected wisdom and strength of the colony, but an immediate, cheerful application of the wealth of individuals to the public service, in due proportion, or a taxation which depended on general consent. Where was the authority to vote, collect, or receive the large sums required, and make provision for the utmost extremities ? A Congress succeeded to the honors of a General Assembly as soon as the latter was crushed by the hand of power. It gained all the confidence of the people. Wisdom and prudence secured all that the laws of the former constitution could have given ; and we now observe with astonishment an army of many thousands of well-disciplined troops suddenly assembled, and abundantly furnished with all necessary supplies, in defence of the liberties of America.

But is it proper or safe for the colony to continue much longer in such imperfect order ? Must it not appear rational and necessary, to every man that understands the various movements requisite to good government, that the many parts should be properly settled, and every branch of the legislative and executive authority restored to that order and vigor on which the life and health of the body

---

ence to those persons whom we shall choose and appoint for our officers and leaders," etc. — " History of Cape Cod," by Rev. Frederick Freeman, Boston, 1860; a work of great value and interest, of which chapters xix. xx. are *additional* to previous materials, and supply a passage in the moral history of the people the most difficult to be preserved.

Mr. Burke, in March, 1775, reflecting on this singular spectacle of a people remaining in perfect order without a public council, judges, or executive magistrates, said: " Obedience is what makes government, and not the names by which it is called; not the name of governor, as formerly, or *committee, as at present*." — ED.

politic depend? To the honorable gentlemen now met in this new congress as the fathers of the people, this weighty matter must be referred. Who knows but in the midst of all the distresses of the present war to defeat the attempts of arbitrary power, God may in mercy restore to us our judges as at the first, and our counsellors as at the beginning?

On your wisdom, religion, and public spirit, honored gentlemen, we depend, to determine what may be done as to the important matter of reviving the form of government, and settling all necessary affairs relating to it in the present critical state of things, that we may again have law and justice, and avoid the danger of anarchy and confusion. May God be with you, and by the influences of his Spirit direct all your counsels and resolutions for the glory of his name and the safety and happiness of this colony. We have great reason to acknowledge with thankfulness the evident tokens of the Divine presence with the former congress, that they were led to foresee present exigencies, and make such effectual provision for them. It is our earnest prayer to the Father of Lights that he would irradiate your minds, make all your way plain, and grant you may be happy instruments of many and great blessings to the people by whom you are constituted, to New England, and all the united colonies.

Let us praise our God[1] for the advantages already given us over the enemies of liberty, particularly that they have been so dispirited by repeated experience of the efficacy of our arms; and that, in the late action at Chelsea, when several hundreds of our soldiery, the greater part open to

---

[1] Governor Gage, in his proclamation of June 12, 1775, a few days after Dr. Langdon's sermon was preached, said: "To complete the horrid profanation of terms and of ideas, the name of God has been introduced in the pulpits to excite and justify devastation and massacre."— ED.

the fire of so many cannon, swivels, and muskets, from a battery advantageously situated, — from two armed cutters, and many barges full of marines, and from ships of the line in the harbor, — not one man on our side was killed, and but two or three wounded; when, by the best intelligence, a great number were killed and wounded on the other side, and one of their cutters was taken and burnt, the other narrowly escaping with great damage.[a]

If God be for us, who can be against us? The enemy has reproached us for calling on his name, and professing our trust in him. They have made a mock of our solemn fasts, and every appearance of serious Christianity in the land. On this account, by way of contempt, they call us saints; and that they themselves may keep at the greatest distance from this character, their mouths are full of horrid blasphemies, cursing, and bitterness, and vent all the rage of malice and barbarity. And may we not be confident that the Most High, who regards these things, will vindicate his own honor, and plead our righteous cause against such enemies to his government, as well as our liberties? O, may our camp be free from every accursed thing! May our land be purged from all its sins! May we be truly a holy people, and all our towns cities of righteousness!

---

[a] This action was in the night following the twenty-seventh current, after our soldiery had been taking off the cattle from some islands in Boston harbor. By the best information we have been able to procure, about one hundred and five of the king's troops were killed, and one hundred and sixty wounded, in the engagement.[1]

[1] Frothingham, pp. 109, 110, says this was magnified into a battle, and dwelt upon with great exultation throughout the colonies. The loss of the enemy was probably exaggerated. — Gordon, Letter xiv.

Mr. Mansfield, in his Thanksgiving Sermon at Roxbury, November 23, 1775, said: " Providence has likewise smiled upon the camp, in permitting so few fatal accidents, and evidently been its safeguard." He says: " I am informed that by means of upwards two thousand balls that have been thrown from the opposite lines, five men only have been taken off!

Then the Lord will be our refuge and strength, a very present help in trouble, and we shall have no reason to be afraid though thousands of enemies set themselves against us round about, — though all nature should be thrown into tumults and convulsions. He can command the stars in their courses to fight his battles, and all the elements to wage war with his enemies. He can destroy them with innumerable plagues, or send faintness into their hearts, so that the men of might shall not find their hands. In a variety of methods he can work salvation for us, as he did for his people in ancient days, and according to the many remarkable deliverances granted in former times to Great Britain and New England when popish machinations threatened both countries with civil and ecclesiastical tyranny.[a]

[a] When we consider the late Canada Bill, which implies not merely a toleration of the Roman Catholic religion (which would be just and liberal), but a firm establishment of it through that extensive province, now greatly enlarged to serve political purposes, by which means multitudes of people, subjects of Great Britain, which may hereafter settle that vast country, will be tempted, by all the attachments arising from an establishment, to profess that religion, or be discouraged from any endeavors to propagate reformed principles, have we not great reason to suspect that all the late measures respecting the colonies have originated from popish schemes of men who would gladly restore the race of Stuart, and who look on Popery as a religion most favorable to arbitrary power? It is a plain fact that despotism has an establishment in that province equally with the Roman Catholic Church. The governor, with a council very much under his power, has by his commission almost unlimited authority, free from the clog of representatives of the people. However agreeable this may be to the genius of the French, English subjects there will be discouraged from continuing in a country where both they and their posterity will be deprived of the greatest privileges of the British constitution, and in many respects feel the effects of absolute monarchy.

Lord Littleton, in his defence of this detestable statute, frankly concedes that I perceive likewise that by means of about three hundred balls, etc., thrown into this place"— Roxbury — " in the course of one month, viz., from September 3 to October 3, but two were wounded (one but slightly; the other died, after some time, of his wound), and no man was immediately killed! It is to be remarked further, that not one person was hurt, in the course of above three hundred shells being thrown to a fortress erected upon Ploughed Hill," in Charlestown. — ED.

May the Lord hear us in this day of trouble, and the name of the God of Jacob defend us, send us help from his sanctuary, and strengthen us out of Zion! We will rejoice in his salvation, and in the name of our God we will set up our banners. Let us look to him to fulfil all our petitions.

it is an establishment of the Roman Catholic religion, and that part of the policy of it was to provide a check upon the New England colonies. And the writer of an address of the people of Great Britain to the inhabitants of America, just published, expresses himself with great precision when he says "that statute gave toleration to English subjects." [1]

[1] See page xxxi. — ED.

A
S E R M O N

PREACHED BEFORE THE

HONORABLE COUNCIL,

AND THE HONORABLE

HOUSE OF REPRESENTATIVES

OF THE

COLONY of the MASSACHUSETTS-BAY,

IN

N E W-E N G L A N D.

MAY 29th, 1776.

BEING THE ANNIVERSARY FOR THE ELECTION OF
THE HONORABLE COUNCIL FOR THE COLONY.

By SAMUEL WEST, A. M.

PASTOR OF A CHURCH IN DARTMOUTH.

And I will reſtore thy judges as at the firſt, and thy coun-
ſellors as at the beginning : afterward thou ſhalt be
called the city of righteouſneſs, the faithful city, ISA.
4. 26. Their children alſo ſhall be as aforetime, and
their congregations ſhall be eſtabliſhed before me, and
I will puniſh all that oppreſs them : and their nobles
ſhall be of themſelves, and their governor ſhall proceed
from the midſt of them, JERE. 30. 20. 21. As free
and not uſing your liberty for a cloak of maliciouſneſs,
but as the ſervants of G O D, 1 PETER 2 16. The
beaſt that thou faweſt, ſhall aſcend out of the bottomleſs
pit, and go into perdition : and they that dwell on the
earth ſhall wonder, whoſe names were not written in
the book of life from the foundation of the world,
when they behold the beaſt, REV. 17. ver. 8.

B O S T O N :

PRINTED BY JOHN GILL, in QUEEN-STREET.

1 7 7 6.

IN COUNCIL, May 30, 1776.

On motion, Ordered, That Thomas Cushing, Benjamin Lincoln, and Moses Gill, Esquires, be a Committee to wait on Rev. Mr. West, and return him the thanks of the Board for his Sermon delivered yesterday before both Houses of Assembly; and to request a copy thereof for the press.

PEREZ MORTON, D. Secretary.

EDITOR'S PREFATORY NOTE.

THE "Provincial Congress," or provisional government, after General Gage was renounced, October 7, 1774, and before which President Langdon preached in 1775, was dissolved, by its own act, July 19, 1775, and on the same day was convened the *new* government, "The Honorable Council and the Honorable House of Representatives," before which the Rev. Mr. West now preached. This step in political progress was initiated in this way: In an address, May 16, 1775, to the American Congress at Philadelphia, — "the representative body of the continent,"— the Massachusetts "Congress" said: "We have made all the preparation for our necessary defence that our confused state would admit of; and, as the question equally affected our sister colonies and us, we have declined, though urged thereto by the most pressing necessity, to assume the reins of civil government without their advice and consent. . . . We are now compelled to raise an army, which, with the assistance of the other colonies, we hope, under the smiles of Heaven, will be able to defend us, and all America, from the further butcheries and devastations of our implacable enemies. . . . We hope you will favor us with your most explicit advice respecting the taking up and exercising the powers of civil government. . . . As the sword should, in all free states, be subservient to the civil powers, . . . we beg leave to suggest to your consideration the propriety of your taking the regulation and general direction of the army."

Upon consideration of this application, the Continental Congress, June 9, 1775, recommended to Massachusetts " to conform as near as may be to the spirit and substance of the charter; " to choose an assembly who should elect councillors, " which assembly and council should exercise the powers of government until a governor of his Majesty's appointment will consent to govern the colony according to its charter." This form was continued till the present constitution was adopted, in 1780, and John Hancock chosen governor. Their political ideas were happily expressed by the device on the *bills of public credit*, of August 18, 1775, which was the figure of an American, with a sword in his right hand, bearing Algernon Sydney's celebrated line, "*Ense petit placidam sub libertate quietem*," and in his left hand *Magna Charta ;* around the figure, "Issued in Defence of American Liberty." This, modified, is emblazoned on the shield of the "Commonwealth;" the motto is still retained; and thus Massachusetts displays in her state arms a memento of the cost of her liberty, and in the legend a perpetual memorial of her historical and political fellowship with that eminent school of republican statesmen of which Sydney, with Russell, was the glory, and whose "Discourses on Government" was, next after the Bible, the political text-book of the fathers of the Republic.

On the 2d of July, Washington entered Cambridge as commander-in-chief. The speech from the throne, October 26, 1775, announced to Parliament actual "rebellion"[1] in the colonies, and that the naval and land forces had been greatly augmented, and set forth the necessity of sufficient force to suppress it. A bill was introduced interdicting all trade with the thirteen united colonies, and authorizing the capture of their property on the ocean. The Continental Congress retaliated by issuing letters of marque to cruise against the subjects of Great Britain, and by permitting trade with all the world but Great Britain and Ireland.

The New England "Thanksgiving"— the glad observance of which is now extended to nearly all the States in the Union, even to the Pacific — was not omitted even in the gloomiest days of the struggle. The proclamation for that anniversary in Massachusetts, intervening half way between the "election-days" of 1775 and 1776, is here given, as the object of this volume is to reproduce the facts, thoughts, and emotions of the days of the Revolution, as then expressed, — for contemporary pictures are always the most faithful.

A PROCLAMATION

FOR A PUBLIC THANKSGIVING.

Although, in consequence of the unnatural, cruel, and barbarous Measures adopted and pursued by the British Administration, great and distressing Calamities are brought upon our oppressed Country, and on this

---

1 See pp. 75, note 1, and 93—95.

Colony in particular; we feel the dreadful Effects of Civil War, by which America is stained with the Blood of her valiant Sons, who have bravely fallen in the laudable Defence of our Rights and Privileges; — Our Capital, once the Seat of JUSTICE, Opulence, and Virtue, is unjustly wrested from its proper Owners, who are obliged to flee from the Iron Hand of Tyranny, or are held in the unrelenting Arms of Oppression; — Our Seaports greatly distressed, and Towns burnt by the Foes, who have acted the Part of barbarous Incendiaries. And although the wise and holy Governor of the World has in his righteous Providence sent Droughts into this Colony, and wasting Sickness into many of our Towns, yet we have the greatest Reason to adore and praise the Supreme Disposer of Events, who deals infinitely better with us than we deserve; and, amidst all his judgments, hath remembered Mercy, by causing the Voice of Health again to be heard amongst us: Instead of Famine, affording to an ungrateful People a Competency of the Necessaries and Comforts of Life; in remarkably preserving and protecting our Troops when in apparent Danger, while our Enemies, with all their boasted Skill and Strength, have met with Loss, Disappointment, and Defeat; — and, in the Course of his good Providence, the Father of Mercies hath bestowed upon us many other Favors, which call for our grateful Acknowledgments.

Therefore, We have thought fit, with the Advice of the Council and House of Representatives, to appoint THURSDAY, the Twenty-third Day of November Instant, to be observed as a Day of Public THANKSGIVING, throughout this Colony; hereby calling upon Ministers and People to meet for religious Worship on said Day, and devoutly to offer up their unfeigned Praises to Almighty GOD, the Source and benevolent Bestower of all Good, for his affording the necessary Means of Subsistence, though our Commerce has been prevented, and the Supplies from the Fishery been denied us; — That such a Measure of Health is enjoyed among us; — That the Lives of our Officers and Soldiers have been so remarkably preserved, while our Enemies have fell before them; — That the vigorous Efforts which have been used to excite Savage Vengeance of the Wilderness, and rouse the Indians to Arms, that an unavoidable Destruction might come upon our Frontiers, have been almost miraculously defeated; — That our unnatural Enemies, instead of Ravaging the Country with uncontrolled Sway, are confined within such narrow Limits, to their own Mortification and Distress, environed by an American Army, brave and determined; — That such a Band of Union, founded upon the best Principles, unites the American Colonies; — That our Rights and Privileges, both Civil and Religious, are so far preserved to us, notwithstanding all the Attempts of our barbarous Enemies to deprive us of them.

And to offer up humble and fervent Prayers to Almighty GOD, for the whole British Empire, especially for the UNITED AMERICAN COLO-NIES: — That he would bless our Civil Rulers and lead them into wise and Prudent Measures in this dark and difficult Day: — That he would endow our General Court with all that Wisdom which is profitable to direct: — That he would graciously Smile upon our Endeavors to restore Peace, preserve our Rights and Privileges, and hand them down to Posterity: — That he would give Wisdom to the American Congress equal to their important Station: — That he would direct the Generals and the American Armies, wherever employed, and give them Success and Victory: — That he would preserve and strengthen the harmony of the UNITED COLONIES: — That he would pour out his Spirit upon all Orders of Men through the Land, bring us to a hearty Repentance and Reformation; purify and sanctify all his Churches: — That he would make Ours Emanuel's Land: — That he would spread the Knowledge of the Redeemer through the whole Earth, and fill the World with his Glory. All servile Labor is forbidden on said Day.

GIVEN *under our hands at the Council Chamber in* WATERTOWN, this Fourth Day of November, in the Year of the LORD One Thousand Seven Hundred and Seventy-five.

By their Honors' Command,

PEREZ MORTON, DEP'Y SEC'RY.

JAMES OTIS,	BENJAMIN LINCOLN,
W. SPOONER,	MICHAEL FARLEY,
CALEB CUSHING,	JOSEPH PALMER,
JOSEPH GERRISH,	SAMUEL HOLTON,
JOHN WHITCOMB,	JABEZ FISHER,
JEDEDIAH FOSTER,	MOSES GILL,
JAMES PRESCOTT,	BENJAMIN WHITE.
ELDAD TAYLOR,	

God Save the People.

So the clouds of war gathered rapidly and heavily, and the Declaration of July Fourth sundered the colonies from the mother country, and they became a nation.

Boston having been evacuated by General Howe, March 17th, the present Legislature was convened, as in former days, in the old Town House, or State House, as it then began to be called. The sermon was preached, as of old, in the "old brick meeting-house" near by, on the site which had been dedicated to the worship of God ever since 1640. It is now occupied by " Joy's Building."

The preacher, Samuel West, minister of Dartmouth, was not behind his professional brethren in zeal for the welfare and liberty of his country, nor in vigorous defence of her rights, both in the pulpit and by the press. He was an able and acute reasoner, and distinguished in metaphysical speculations with the Edwardses, father and son. The present Discourse was specially devoted to a consideration of the true principles of government, and a close application of them to Britain and her colonies. He was a member of the convention for forming the Constitution of Massachusetts, and of that of 1788, which ratified the constitution of the United States. With him the patriot Otis —

" Favored man, by touch ethereal slain" —

resided for a while after his retirement. Dr. West was born at Yarmouth, on Cape Cod, March 4, 1730, a *subject* of George II., graduated at Harvard College in 1754, and died September 24, 1807, aged seventy-seven, a *citizen* of the United States.

The texts on the title-page of the sermon admirably exhibit the political hopes of that day, the wish for reconciliation and the reëstablishment of the old relations to the mother country, and the intensity of the times.

The councillors elected for the memorable year 1776 were —

For the late Colony of MASSACHUSETTS BAY:

Hon. JAMES BOWDOIN, Esq.;
ARTEMAS WARD, Esq.;
BENJ. GREENLEAF, Esq.;
CALEB CUSHING, Esq.;
JOHN WINTHROP, Esq.;
RICH. DERBY, JUN., Esq.;
THOMAS CUSHING, Esq.;
JOHN WHITCOMB, Esq.;
ELDAD TAYLOR, Esq.;

Hon. BENJAMIN LINCOLN, Esq.;
SAMUEL HOLTON, Esq.;
JABEZ FISHER, Esq.;
MOSES GILL, Esq.;
BENJ. WHITE, Esq.;
WM. PHILLIPS, Esq.;
BENJ. AUSTIN, Esq.;
EBEN. THAYER, JUN., Esq.;
FRANCIS DANE, Esq.

For the late Colony of NEW PLYMOUTH:

Hon. WM. SEVER, Esq.;   Hon. DAN. DAVIS, Esq.;
   WALTER SPOONER, Esq.;   JOS. CUSHING, Esq.

For the Province of MAINE:

Hon. JERE. POWELL, Esq.;   Hon. DAVID SEWELL, Esq.;
        Hon. BENJ. CHADBOURN, Esq.

For SAGADAHOCK:

Hon. JOHN TAYLOR, Esq.

AT LARGE:

Hon. HENRY GARDNER, Esq.;   Hon. DANIEL HOPKINS, Esq.

Previous to the election the following gentlemen, who were of the last Council, resigned their seats at the Board, viz.:

Hon. JAMES OTIS, Esq.;   Hon. ENOCH FREEMAN, Esq.;
   JOHN ADAMS, Esq.;   CHARLES CHAUNCY, Esq.;
   JEDEDIAH FOSTER, Esq.;   JOSEPH PALMER, Esq.

DISCOURSE VI.

ELECTION SERMON.

PUT THEM IN MIND TO BE SUBJECT TO PRINCIPALITIES AND POWERS, TO OBEY MAGISTRATES, TO BE READY TO EVERY GOOD WORK. — Titus iii. 1.

THE great Creator, having designed the human race for society, has made us dependent on one another for happiness. He has so constituted us that it becomes both our duty and interest to seek the public good; and that we may be the more firmly engaged to promote each other's welfare, the Deity has endowed us with tender and social affections, with generous and benevolent principles: hence the pain that we feel in seeing an object of distress; hence the satisfaction that arises in relieving the afflictions, and the superior pleasure which we experience in communicating happiness to the miserable. The Deity has also invested us with moral powers and faculties, by which we are enabled to discern the difference between right and wrong, truth and falsehood, good and evil: hence the approbation of mind that arises upon doing a good action, and the remorse of conscience which we experience when we counteract the moral sense and do that which is evil. This proves that, in what is commonly called a state of nature, we are the subjects of the divine law and government; that the Deity is our supreme magistrate, who has written his law in our hearts, and will reward or punish us according as we obey or disobey his commands. Had the

human race uniformly persevered in a state of moral rectitude, there would have been little or no need of any other
law besides that which is written in the heart, — for every
one in such a state would be a law unto himself. There
could be no occasion for enacting or enforcing of penal
laws; for such are "not made for the righteous man, but
for the lawless and disobedient, for the ungodly, and for
sinners, for the unholy and profane, for murderers of
fathers and murderers of mothers, for manslayers, for
whoremongers, for them that defile themselves with mankind, for men-stealers, for liars, for perjured persons, and if
there be any other thing that is contrary to" moral rectitude and the happiness of mankind. The necessity of
forming ourselves into politic bodies, and granting to our
rulers a power to enact laws for the public safety, and to
enforce them by proper penalties, arises from our being in
a fallen and degenerate state. The slightest view of the
present state and condition of the human race is abundantly sufficient to convince any person of common sense
and common honesty that civil government is absolutely
necessary for the peace and safety of mankind; and, consequently, that all good magistrates, while[1] they faithfully
discharge the trust reposed in them, ought to be religiously
and conscientiously obeyed. An enemy to good government is an enemy not only to his country, but to all mankind; for he plainly shows himself to be divested of those
tender and social sentiments which are characteristic of a
human temper, even of that generous and benevolent disposition which is the peculiar glory of a rational creature.
An enemy to good government has degraded himself
below the rank and dignity of a man, and deserves to be
classed with the lower creation.[2] Hence we find that wise
and good men, of all nations and religions, have ever incul-

---

[1] See pp. 72, 75-77. — ED.   [2] See pp. 69-74, and notes. — ED.

cated subjection to good government, and have borne their
testimony against the licentious disturbers of the public
peace.

Nor has Christianity been deficient in this capital point.
We find our blessed Saviour directing the Jews to render
to Cæsar the things that were Cæsar's; and the apostles
and first preachers of the gospel not only exhibited a good
example of subjection to the magistrate, in all things that
were just and lawful, but they have also, in several places
in the New Testament, strongly enjoined upon Christians
the duty of submission to that government under which
Providence had placed them. Hence we find that those
who despise government, and are not afraid to speak evil
of dignities, are, by the apostles Peter and Jude, classed
among those presumptuous, self-willed sinners that are reserved to the judgment of the great day. And the apostle
Paul judged submission to civil government to be a matter of such great importance, that he thought it worth his
while to charge Titus to put his hearers in mind to be submissive to principalities and powers, to obey magistrates,
to be ready to every good work; as much as to say, none
can be ready to every good work, or be properly disposed
to perform those actions that tend to promote the public
good, who do not obey magistrates, and who do not become
good subjects of civil government.[1] If, then, obedience to
the civil magistrates is so essential to the character of a
Christian, that without it he cannot be disposed to perform
those good works that are necessary for the welfare of
mankind, — if the despisers of governments are those presumptuous, self-willed sinners who are reserved to the
judgment of the great day, — it is certainly a matter of the
utmost importance to us all to be thoroughly acquainted

[1] See pp. 54-61. — ED.

with the nature and extent of our duty, that we may yield the obedience required; for it is impossible that we should properly discharge a duty when we are strangers to the nature and extent of it.

In order, therefore, that we may form a right judgment of the duty enjoined in our text, I shall consider the nature and design of civil government, and shall show that the same principles which oblige us to submit to government do equally oblige us to resist tyranny; or that tyranny and magistracy are so opposed to each other that where the one begins the other ends.[1] I shall then apply the present discourse to the grand controversy that at this day subsists between Great Britain and the American colonies.

That we may understand the nature and design of civil government, and discover the foundation of the magistrate's authority to command, and the duty of subjects to obey, it is necessary to derive civil government from its original, in order to which we must consider what "state all men are naturally in, and that is (as Mr. Locke observes) a state of perfect freedom to order all their actions, and dispose of their possessions and persons as they think fit, within the bounds of the law of nature, without asking leave or depending upon the will of any man." It is a state wherein all are equal, — no one having a right to control another, or oppose him in what he does, unless it be in his own defence, or in the defence of those that, being injured, stand in need of his assistance.

Had men persevered in a state of moral rectitude, every one would have been disposed to follow the law of nature, and pursue the general good. In such a state, the wisest and most experienced would undoubtedly be chosen to guide and direct those of less wisdom and experience than themselves, — there being nothing else that

[1] See pages 62, 67 note 1; 69, 74, note 1. — ED.

could afford the least show or appearance of any one's having the superiority or precedency over another; for the dictates of conscience and the precepts of natural law being uniformly and regularly obeyed, men would only need to be informed what things were most fit and prudent to be done in those cases where their inexperience or want of acquaintance left their minds in doubt what was the wisest and most regular method for them to pursue. In such cases it would be necessary for them to advise with those who were wiser and more experienced than themselves. But these advisers could claim no authority to compel or to use any forcible measures to oblige any one to comply with their direction or advice. There could be no occasion for the exertion of such a power; for every man, being under the government of right reason, would immediately feel himself constrained to comply with everything that appeared reasonable or fit to be done, or that would any way tend to promote the general good. This would have been the happy state of mankind had they closely adhered to the law of nature, and persevered in their primitive state.

Thus we see that a state of nature, though it be a state of perfect freedom, yet is very far from a state of licentiousness. The law of nature gives men no right to do anything that is immoral, or contrary to the will of God, and injurious to their fellow-creatures; for a state of nature is properly a state of law and government, even a government founded upon the unchangeable nature of the Deity, and a law resulting from the eternal fitness of things. Sooner shall heaven and earth pass away, and the whole frame of nature be dissolved, than any part, even the smallest iota, of this law shall ever be abrogated; it is unchangeable as the Deity himself, being a transcript of his moral perfections. A revelation,[1] pretending to be from God, that contradicts any part of natural law, ought immediately to be rejected as an imposture; for the Deity cannot make a law contrary to the law of nature without acting contrary to himself, — a thing in the strictest sense impossible, for that which implies contradiction is not an object of the divine power. Had this subject been properly attended to[2] and understood, the world had remained free from a multitude of absurd and pernicious principles, which have been industriously propagated by artful and designing men, both in politics and divinity. The doctrine of non-resistance and unlimited passive obedience to the worst of tyrants could never have found credit among mankind had the voice of reason been hearkened to for a guide, because such a doctrine would immediately have been discerned to be contrary to natural law.

In a state of nature we have a right to make the persons that have injured us repair the damages that they have done us; and it is just in us to inflict such punishment upon them as is necessary to restrain them from doing the like for the future, — the whole end and design of punishing being either to reclaim the individual punished, or to deter others from being guilty of similar crimes. Whenever punishment exceeds these bounds it becomes cruelty and revenge, and directly contrary to the law of nature. Our wants and necessities being such as to render it impossible in most cases to enjoy life in any tolerable degree without entering into society, and there being innumerable cases wherein we need the assistance of others, which if not afforded we should very soon perish; hence the law of nature requires that we should endeavor to help one another to the utmost of our power in all cases where our assist-

---

[1] See pages 67 note 1, 86 note a. — ED.   [2] See pages 53, 54. — ED.

ance is necessary.   It is our duty to endeavor always to
promote the general good; to do to all as we would be
willing to be done by were we in their circumstances; to
do justly, to love mercy, and to walk humbly before God.
These are some of the laws of nature which every man in
the world is bound to observe, and which whoever violates
exposes himself to the resentment of mankind, the lashes
of his own conscience, and the judgment of Heaven. This
plainly shows that the highest state of liberty subjects us
to the law of nature and the government of God.   The
most perfect freedom consists in obeying the dictates of
right reason, and submitting to natural law.   When a man
goes beyond or contrary to the law of nature and reason,
he becomes the slave of base passions and vile lusts; he
introduces confusion and disorder into society, and brings
misery and destruction upon himself. This, therefore, cannot be called a state of freedom, but a state of the vilest
slavery and the most dreadful bondage.   The servants of
sin and corruption are subjected to the worst kind of
tyranny in the universe.   Hence we conclude that where
licentiousness begins, liberty ends.

The law of nature is a perfect standard and measure of
action for beings that persevere in a state of moral rectitude; but the case is far different with us, who are in a
fallen and degenerate estate.   We have a law in our members which is continually warring against the law of the
mind, by which we often become enslaved to the basest
lusts, and are brought into bondage to the vilest passions.
The strong propensities of our animal nature often overcome the sober dictates of reason and conscience, and
betray us into actions injurious to the public and destructive of the safety and happiness of society.   Men of unbridled lusts, were they not restrained by the power of
the civil magistrate, would spread horror and desolation

all around them. This makes it absolutely necessary that
societies should form themselves into politic bodies, that
they may enact laws for the public safety, and appoint particular penalties for the violation of their laws, and invest
a suitable number of persons with authority to put in
execution and enforce the laws of the state, in order that
wicked men may be restrained from doing mischief to
their fellow-creatures, that the injured may have their
rights restored to them, that the virtuous may be encouraged in doing good, and that every member of society
may be protected and secured in the peaceable, quiet possession and enjoyment of all those liberties and privileges
which the Deity has bestowed upon him; i. e., that he
may safely enjoy and pursue whatever he chooses, that is
consistent with the public good. This shows that the end
and design of civil government cannot be to deprive men
of their liberty or take away their freedom; but, on the
contrary, the true design of civil government is to protect
men in the enjoyment of liberty.[1]

From hence it follows that tyranny and arbitrary power
are utterly inconsistent with and subversive of the very
end and design of civil government, and directly contrary
to natural law, which is the true foundation of civil government and all politic law. Consequently, the authority
of a tyrant is of itself null and void; for as no man can
have a right to act contrary to the law of nature, it is
impossible that any individual, or even the greatest number
of men, can confer a right upon another of which they
themselves are not possessed; i. e., no body of men can
justly and lawfully authorize any person to tyrannize
over and enslave his fellow-creatures, or do anything contrary to equity and goodness. As magistrates have no
authority but what they derive from the people, whenever

1 Pages 69, 78. — ED.

they act contrary to the public good, and pursue measures destructive of the peace and safety of the community, they forfeit their right to govern the people. Civil rulers and magistrates are properly of human creation; they are set up by the people to be the guardians of their rights, and to secure their persons from being injured or oppressed, — the safety of the public being the supreme law of the state, by which the magistrates are to be governed, and which they are to consult upon all occasions. The modes of administration may be very different, and the forms[1] of government may vary from each other in different ages and nations; but, under every form, the end of civil government is the same, and cannot vary: it is like the laws of the Medes and Persians — it altereth not.

Though magistrates are to consider themselves as the servants of the people, seeing from them it is that they derive their power and authority, yet they may also be considered as the ministers of God ordained by him for the good of mankind;[2] for, under him, as the Supreme Magistrate of the universe, they are to act: and it is God who has not only declared in his word what are the necessary qualifications of a ruler, but who also raises up and qualifies men for such an important station. The magistrate may also, in a more strict and proper sense, be said to be ordained of God, because reason, which is the voice of God, plainly requires such an order of men to be appointed for the public good. Now, whatever right reason requires as necessary to be done is as much the will and law of God as though it were enjoined us by an immediate revelation from heaven, or commanded in the sacred Scriptures.

From this account of the origin, nature, and design of civil government, we may be very easily led into a thor-

---

[1] Page 82. — ED.   [2] Pages 75-77. — ED.

ough knowledge of our duty; we may see the reason why we are bound to obey magistrates, viz., because they are the ministers of God for good unto the people. While, therefore, they rule in the fear of God, and while they promote the welfare of the state, — i. e., while they act in the character of magistrates, — it is the indispensable duty of all to submit to them, and to oppose a turbulent, factious, and libertine spirit, whenever and wherever it discovers itself. When a people have by their free consent conferred upon a number of men a power to rule and govern them, they are bound to obey them. Hence disobedience becomes a breach of faith; it is violating a constitution of their own appointing, and breaking a compact for which they ought to have the most sacred regard. Such a conduct discovers so base and disingenuous a temper of mind, that it must expose them to contempt in the judgment of all the sober, thinking part of mankind. Subjects are bound to obey lawful magistrates by every tender tie of human nature, which disposes us to consult the public good, and to seek the good of our brethren, our wives, our children, our friends and acquaintance; for he that opposes lawful authority does really oppose the safety and happiness of his fellow-creatures. A factious, seditious person, that opposes good government, is a monster in nature; for he is an enemy to his own species, and destitute of the sentiments of humanity.[1]

Subjects are also bound to obey magistrates, for conscience' sake, out of regard to the divine authority, and out of obedience to the will of God;[2] for if magistrates are the ministers of God, we cannot disobey them without being disobedient to the law of God; and this extends to all men in authority, from the highest ruler to the lowest officer in the state. To oppose them when in the exercise

---

[1] See p. 87, note. — ED.   [2] See p. 64. — ED.

of lawful authority is an act of disobedience to the Deity, and, as such, will be punished by him. It will, doubtless, be readily granted by every honest man that we ought cheerfully to obey the magistrate, and submit to all such regulations of government as tend to promote the public good; but as this general definition may be liable to be misconstrued, and every man may think himself at liberty to disregard any laws that do not suit his interest, humor, or fancy, I would observe that, in a multitude of cases, many of us, for want of being properly acquainted with affairs of state, may be very improper judges of particular laws, whether they are just or not. In such cases it becomes us, as good members of society, peaceably and conscientiously to submit, though we cannot see the reasonableness of every law to which we submit, and that for this plain reason: if any number of men should take it upon themselves to oppose authority for acts, which may be really necessary for the public safety, only because they do not see the reasonableness of them, the direct consequence will be introducing confusion and anarchy into the state.

It is also necessary that the minor part should submit to the major; e. g., when legislators have enacted a set of laws which are highly approved by a large majority of the community as tending to promote the public good, in this case, if a small number of persons are so unhappy as to view the matter in a very different point of light from the public, though they have an undoubted right to show the reasons of their dissent from the judgment of the public, and may lawfully use all proper arguments to convince the public of what they judge to be an error, yet, if they fail in their attempt, and the majority still continue to approve of the laws that are enacted, it is the duty of those few that dissent peaceably and for conscience' sake to submit to the public judgment, unless something is required of them which they judge would be sinful for them to comply with; for in that case they ought to obey the dictates of their own consciences rather than any human authority whatever.[1] Perhaps, also, some cases of intolerable oppression, where compliance would bring on inevitable ruin and destruction, may justly warrant the few to refuse submission to what they judge inconsistent with their peace and safety; for the law of self-preservation will always justify opposing a cruel and tyrannical imposition, except where opposition is attended with greater evils than submission, which is frequently the case where a few are oppressed by a large and powerful majority.[a] Except the above-named cases, the minor ought always to submit to the major; otherwise, there can be no peace nor harmony in society. And, besides, it is the major part of a community that have the sole right of establishing a constitution and authorizing magistrates; and consequently it is only the major part of the community that can claim the right of altering the constitution, and displacing the magistrates; for certainly common sense will tell us that it requires as great an authority to set aside a constitution as there was at first to establish it. The collective body, not a few individuals, ought to constitute the supreme authority of the state.

The only difficulty remaining is to determine when a people may claim a right of forming themselves into a

---

[a] This shows the reason why the primitive Christians did not oppose the cruel persecutions that were inflicted upon them by the heathen magistrates. They were few compared with the heathen world, and for them to have attempted to resist their enemies by force would have been like a small parcel of sheep endeavoring to oppose a large number of ravening wolves and savage beasts of prey. It would, without a miracle, have brought upon them inevitable ruin and destruction. Hence the wise and prudent advice of our Saviour to them is, " When they persecute you in this city, flee ye to another." [1]

[1] See p. 295. — ED.

body politic, and assume the powers of legislation. In order to determine this point, we are to remember that all men being by nature equal, all the members of a community have a natural right to assemble themselves together, and act and vote for such regulations as they judge are necessary for the good of the whole. But when a community is become very numerous, it is very difficult, and in many cases impossible, for all to meet together to regulate the affairs of the state; hence comes the necessity of appointing delegates to represent the people in a general assembly. And this ought to be looked upon as a sacred and inalienable right, of which a people cannot justly divest themselves, and which no human authority can in equity ever take from them, viz., that no one be obliged to submit to any law except such as are made either by himself or by his representative.

If representation and legislation are inseparably connected, it follows, that when great numbers have emigrated into a foreign land, and are so far removed from the parent state that they neither are or can be properly represented by the government from which they have emigrated, that then nature itself points out the necessity of their assuming to themselves the powers of legislation; and they have a right to consider themselves as a separate state from the other, and, as such, to form themselves into a body politic.

In the next place, when a people find themselves cruelly oppressed by the parent state, they have an undoubted right to throw off the yoke,[1] and to assert their liberty, if they find good reason to judge that they have sufficient power and strength to maintain their ground in defending their just rights against their oppressors; for, in this case, by the law of self-preservation, which is the first law of

1 See pp. 93-95. — ED.

nature, they have not only an undoubted right, but it is their indispensable duty, if they cannot be redressed any other way, to renounce all submission to the government that has oppressed them, and set up an independent state of their own, even though they may be vastly inferior in numbers · to the state that has oppressed them. When either of the aforesaid cases takes place, and more especially when both concur, no rational man, I imagine, can have any doubt in his own mind whether such a people have a right to form themselves into a body politic, and assume to themselves all the powers of a free state. For, can it be rational to suppose that a people should be subjected to the tyranny of a set of men[1] who are perfect strangers to them, and cannot be supposed to have that fellow-feeling for them that we generally have for those with whom we are connected and acquainted; and, besides, through their unacquaintedness with the circumstances of the people over whom they claim the right of jurisdiction, are utterly unable to judge, in a multitude of cases, which is best for them?

It becomes me not to say what particular form[2] of government is best for a community, — whether a pure democracy, aristocracy, monarchy, or a mixture of all the three simple forms. They have all their advantages and disadvantages, and when they are properly administered may, any of them, answer the design of civil government tolerably. Permit me, however, to say, that an unlimited, absolute monarchy, and an aristocracy not subject to the control of the people, are two of the most exceptionable forms of government: firstly, because in neither of them is there a proper representation of the people; and, sec-

[1] As, for instance, in the case in hand, the British Parliament and the American colonies. pp. 110, 206. — ED.

[2] See pp. 80, 81, 82. — ED.

ondly, because each of them being entirely independent
of the people, they are very apt to degenerate into tyranny.
However, in this imperfect state, we cannot expect to have
government formed upon such a basis but that it may be
perverted by bad men to evil purposes. A wise and good
man would be very loth to undermine a constitution that
was once fixed and established, although he might discover many imperfections in it; and nothing short of the
most urgent necessity would ever induce him to consent
to it; because the unhinging a people from a form of government to which they had been long accustomed might
throw them into such a state of anarchy and confusion as
might terminate in their destruction, or perhaps, in the
end, subject them to the worst kind of tyranny.

Having thus shown the nature, end, and design of civil
government, and pointed out the reasons why subjects are
bound to obey magistrates, — viz., because in so doing they
both consult their own happiness as individuals, and also
promote the public good and the safety of the state, — I
proceed, in the next place, to show that the same principles that oblige us to submit to civil government do also
equally oblige us, where we have power and ability, to
resist and oppose tyranny; and that where tyranny begins
government ends.[1]   For, if magistrates have no authority
but what they derive from the people; if they are properly
of human creation; if the whole end and design of their
institution is to promote the general good, and to secure to
men their just rights, — it will follow, that when they act
contrary to the end and design of their creation they
cease being magistrates, and the people which gave them
their authority have the right to take it from them again.
This is a very plain dictate of common sense, which uni-

[1] See pp. 73, 74, note 1; 93–96. — ED.

versally obtains in all similar cases; for who is there that, having employed a number of men to do a particular piece of work for him, but what would judge that he had a right to dismiss them from his service when he found that they went directly contrary to his orders, and that, instead of accomplishing the business he had set them about, they would infallibly ruin and destroy it? If, then, men, in the common affairs of life, always judge that they have a right to dismiss from their service such persons as counteract their plans and designs, though the damage will affect only a few individuals, much more must the body politic have a right to depose any persons, though appointed to the highest place of power and authority, when they find that they are unfaithful to the trust reposed in them, and that, instead of consulting the general good, they are disturbing the peace of society by making laws cruel and oppressive, and by depriving the subjects of their just rights and privileges. Whoever pretends to deny this proposition must give up all pretence of being master of that common sense and reason by which the Deity has distinguished us from the brutal herd.[1]

As our duty of obedience to the magistrate is founded upon our obligation to promote the general good, our readiness to obey lawful authority will always arise in proportion to the love and regard that we have for the welfare of the public; and the same love and regard for the public will inspire us with as strong a zeal to oppose tyranny as we have to obey magistracy. Our obligation to promote the public good extends as much to the opposing every exertion of arbitrary power that is injurious to the state as it does to the submitting to good and wholesome laws. No man, therefore, can be a good member of

[1] See pp. 71, 72. — ED.

the community that is not as zealous to oppose tyranny as he is ready to obey magistracy. A slavish submission to tyranny is a proof of a very sordid and base mind.[1] Such a person cannot be under the influence of any generous human sentiments, nor have a tender regard for mankind.

Further: if magistrates are no farther ministers of God than they promote the good of the community, then obedience to them neither is nor can be unlimited; for it would imply a gross absurdity to assert that, when magistrates are ordained by the people solely for the purpose of being beneficial to the state, they must be obeyed when they are seeking to ruin and destroy it. This would imply that men were bound to act against the great law of self-preservation, and to contribute their assistance to their own ruin and destruction, in order that they may please and gratify the greatest monsters in nature, who are violating the laws of God and destroying the rights of mankind. Unlimited submission and obedience is due to none but God alone. He has an absolute right to command; he alone has an uncontrollable sovereignty over us, because he alone is unchangeably good; he never will nor can require of us, consistent with his nature and attributes, anything that is not fit and reasonable; his commands are all just and good; and to suppose that he has given to any particular set of men a power to require obedience to that which is unreasonable, cruel, and unjust, is robbing the Deity of his justice and goodness, in which consists the peculiar glory of the divine character, and it is representing him under the horrid character of a tyrant.[2]

If magistrates are ministers of God only because the law of God and reason points out the necessity of such an institution for the good of mankind, it follows, that whenever they pursue measures directly destructive of the pub-

[1] P. 51. — ED. [2] See p. 95. — ED.

lic good they cease being God's ministers, they forfeit their
right to obedience from the subject, they become the pests [1]
of society, and the community is under the strongest obligation of duty,[2] both to God and to its own members, to
resist and oppose them, which will be so far from resisting
the ordinance of God that it will be strictly obeying his
commands.[3]   To suppose otherwise will imply that the
Deity requires of us an obedience that is self-contradictory
and absurd, and that one part of his law is directly contrary to the other; *i. e.*, while he commands us to pursue
virtue and the general good, he does at the same time require us to persecute virtue, and betray the general good,
by enjoining us obedience to the wicked commands of
tyrannical oppressors.   Can any one not lost to the principles of humanity undertake to defend such absurd sentiments as these? As the public safety is the first and grand
law of society, so no community can have a right to invest
the magistrate with any power or authority that will enable him to act against the welfare of the state and the
good of the whole.   If men have at any time wickedly
and foolishly given up their just rights into the hands of
the magistrate, such acts are null and void, of course ; to
suppose otherwise will imply that we have a right to invest the magistrate with a power to act contrary to the
law of God, — which is as much as to say that we are not
the subjects of divine law and government.   What has
been said is, I apprehend, abundantly sufficient to show that
tyrants are no magistrates,[4] or that whenever magistrates
abuse their power and authority to the subverting the public happiness, their authority immediately ceases, and that
it not only becomes lawful, but an indispensable duty to

1 See p. 78. — ED.   3 See p. 62, note 1. — ED.
2 See p. 83, note 1. — ED.   4 See p. 94, note a. — ED.

oppose them; that the principle of self-preservation, the affection and duty that we owe to our country, and the obedience we owe the Deity, do all require us to oppose tyranny.

If it be asked, Who are the proper judges [1] to determine when rulers are guilty of tyranny and oppression? I answer, the public. Not a few disaffected individuals, but the collective body of the state, must decide this question; for, as it is the collective body that invests rulers with their power and authority, so it is the collective body that has the sole right of judging whether rulers act up to the end of their institution or not. Great regard ought always to be paid to the judgment of the public. It is true the public may be imposed upon by a misrepresentation of facts; but this may be said of the public, which cannot always be said of individuals, viz., that the public is always willing to be rightly informed, and when it has proper matter of conviction laid before it its judgment is always right.

This account of the nature and design of civil government, which is so clearly suggested to us by the plain principles of common sense and reason, is abundantly confirmed by the sacred Scriptures, even by those very texts which have been brought by men of slavish principles to establish the absurd doctrine of unlimited passive obedience and non-resistance, as will abundantly appear by examining the two most noted texts that are commonly brought to support the strange doctrine of passive obedience. The first that I shall cite is in 1 Peter ii. 13, 14: "Submit yourselves to every ordinance of man," — or, rather, as the words ought to be rendered from the Greek, submit yourselves to every human creation, or human constitution, — "for the Lord's sake, whether it be to the king

---

[1] See p. 86, note a. — ED.

as supreme, or unto governors, as unto them that are sent by him for the punishment of evil-doers, and for the praise of them that do well."[1] Here we see that the apostle asserts that magistracy is of human creation or appointment; that is, that magistrates have no power or authority but what they derive from the people; that this power they are to exert for the punishment of evil-doers, and for the praise of them that do well; *i. e.*, the end and design of the appointment of magistrates is to restrain wicked men, by proper penalties, from injuring society, and to encourage and honor the virtuous and obedient. Upon this account Christians are to submit to them for the Lord's sake; which is as if he had said, Though magistrates are of mere human appointment, and can claim no power or authority but what they derive from the people, yet, as they are ordained by men to promote the general good by punishing evil-doers and by rewarding and encouraging the virtuous and obedient, you ought to submit to them out of a sacred regard to the divine authority; for as they, in the faithful discharge of their office, do fulfil the will of God, so ye, by submitting to them, do fulfil the divine command. If the only reason assigned by the apostle why magistrates should be obeyed out of a regard to the divine authority is because they punish the wicked and encourage the good, it follows, that when they punish the virtuous and encourage the vicious we have a right to refuse yielding any submission or obedience to them; *i. e.*, whenever they act contrary to the end and design of their institution, they forfeit their authority to govern the people, and the reason for submitting to them, out of regard to the divine authority, immediately ceases; and, they being only of human appointment, the authority which the peo-

---

1 Compare these pages with Dr. Mayhew's, in 1750, p. 23. — Ed.

ple gave them the public have a right to take from them, and to confer it upon those who are more worthy. So far is this text from favoring arbitrary principles, that there is nothing in it but what is consistent with and favorable to the highest liberty that any man can wish to enjoy; for this text requires us to submit to the magistrate no further than he is the encourager and protector of virtue and the punisher of vice ; and this is consistent with all that liberty which the Deity has bestowed upon us.[1]

The other text which I shall mention, and which has been made use of by the favorers of arbitrary government as their great sheet-anchor and main support, is in Rom. xiii., the first six verses: "Let every soul be subject to the higher powers; for there is no power but of God. The powers that be are ordained of God. Whosoever therefore resisteth the power, resisteth the ordinance of God ; and they that resist shall receive to themselves damnation; for rulers are not a terror to good works, but to the evil. Wilt thou then not be afraid of the power? Do that which is good, and thou shalt have praise of the same : for he is the minister of God to thee for good. But if thou do that which is evil, be afraid; for he beareth not the sword in vain : for he is the minister of God, a revenger to execute wrath upon him that doth evil. Wherefore ye must needs be subject not only for wrath, but also for conscience' sake. For, for this cause pay you tribute also; for they are God's ministers, attending continually upon this very thing." A very little attention, I apprehend, will be sufficient to show that this text is so far from favoring arbitrary government, that, on the contrary, it strongly holds forth the principles of true liberty. Subjection to the higher powers is enjoined by the apostle because there is no power but of God; the powers that be

[1] See p. 78. — ED.

are ordained of God; consequently, to resist the power is to resist the ordinance of God: and he repeatedly declares that the ruler is the minister of God. Now, before we can say whether this text makes for or against the doctrine of unlimited passive obedience, we must find out in what sense the apostle affirms that magistracy is the ordinance of God, and what he intends when he calls the ruler the minister of God.

I can think but of three possible senses in which magistracy can with any propriety be called God's ordinance, or in which rulers can be said to be ordained of God as his ministers. The first is a plain declaration from the word of God that such a one and his descendants are, and shall be, the only true and lawful magistrates: thus we find in Scripture the kingdom of Judah to be settled by divine appointment in the family of David. Or,

Secondly, By an immediate commission from God, ordering and appointing such a one by name to be the ruler over the people: thus Saul and David were immediately appointed by God to be kings over Israel. Or,

Thirdly, Magistracy may be called the ordinance of God, and rulers may be called the ministers of God, because the nature and reason of things, which is the law of God, requires such an institution for the preservation and safety of civil society. In the two first senses the apostle cannot be supposed to affirm that magistracy is God's ordinance, for neither he nor any of the sacred writers have entailed the magistracy to any one particular family under the gospel dispensation. Neither does he nor any of the inspired writers give us the least hint that any person should ever be immediately commissioned from God to bear rule over the people. The third sense, then, is the only sense in which the apostle can be supposed to affirm that the magistrate is the minister of God, and that magistracy is the ordinance of God; viz., that the nature and reason of things require such an institution for the preservation and safety of mankind. Now, if this be the only sense in which the apostle affirms that magistrates are ordained of God as his ministers, resistance must be criminal only so far forth as they are the ministers of God, *i. e.*, while they act up to the end of their institution, and ceases being criminal when they cease being the ministers of God, *i. e.*, when they act contrary to the general good, and seek to destroy the liberties of the people.

That we have gotten the apostle's sense of magistracy being the ordinance of God, will plainly appear from the text itself; for, after having asserted that to resist the power is to resist the ordinance of God, and they that resist shall receive to themselves damnation, he immediately adds, as the reason of this assertion, "For rulers are not a terror to good works, but to the evil. Wilt thou then not be afraid of the power? Do that which is good, and thou shalt have praise of the same: for he is the minister of God to thee for good. But if thou do that which is evil, be afraid; for he beareth not the sword in vain: for he is the minister of God, a revenger to execute wrath upon him that doth evil." Here is a plain declaration of the sense in which he asserts that the authority of the magistrate is ordained of God, viz., because rulers are not a terror to good works, but to the evil; therefore we ought to dread offending them, for we cannot offend them but by doing evil; and if we do evil we have just reason to fear their power; for they bear not the sword in vain, but in this case the magistrate is a revenger to execute wrath upon him that doeth evil: but if we are found doers of that which is good, we have no reason to fear the authority of the magistrate; for in this case, instead of being punished, we shall be protected and encouraged.

The reason why the magistrate is called the minister of God is because he is to protect, encourage, and honor them that do well, and to punish them that do evil; therefore it is our duty to submit to them, not merely for fear of being punished by them, but out of regard to the divine authority, under which they are deputed to execute judgment and to do justice. For this reason, according to the apostle, tribute is to be paid them, because, as the ministers of God, their whole business is to protect every man in the enjoyment of his just rights and privileges, and to punish every evil-doer.

If the apostle, then, asserts that rulers are ordained of God only because they are a terror to evil works and a praise to them that do well; if they are ministers of God only because they encourage virtue and punish vice; if for this reason only they are to be obeyed for conscience' sake; if the sole reason why they have a right to tribute is because they devote themselves wholly to the business of securing to men their just rights, and to the punishing of evil-doers, — it follows, by undeniable consequence, that when they become the pests of human society, when they promote and encourage evil-doers, and become a terror to good works, they then cease being the ordinance of God; they are no longer rulers nor ministers of God; they are so far from being the powers that are ordained of God that they become the ministers of the powers of darkness,[1] and it is so far from being a crime to resist them, that in many cases it may be highly criminal in the sight of Heaven to refuse resisting and opposing them to the utmost of our power; or, in other words, that the same reasons that require us to obey the ordinance of God, do equally oblige us, when we have power and opportunity, to oppose and resist the ordinance of Satan.

[1] See p. 73. — ED.

Hence we see that the apostle Paul, instead of being a friend to tyranny and arbitrary government, turns out to be a strong advocate for the just rights of mankind, and is for our enjoying all that liberty with which God has invested us ; for no power (according to the apostle) is ordained of God but what is an encourager of every good and virtuous action, — "Do that which is good, and thou shalt have praise of the same." No man need to be afraid of this power which is ordained of God who does nothing but what is agreeable to the law of God ; for this power will not restrain us from exercising any liberty which the Deity has granted us ; for the minister of God is to restrain us from nothing but the doing of that which is evil, and to this we have no right. To practise evil is not liberty, but licentiousness. Can we conceive of a more perfect, equitable, and generous plan of government than this which the apostle has laid down, viz., to have rulers appointed over us to encourage us to every good and virtuous action, to defend and protect us in our just rights and privileges, and to grant us everything that can tend to promote our true interest and happiness ; to restrain every licentious action, and to punish every one that would injure or harm us ; to become a terror of evil-doers ; to make and execute such just and righteous laws as shall effectually deter and hinder men from the commission of evil, and to attend continually upon this very thing ; to make it their constant care and study, day and night, to promote the good and welfare of the community, and to oppose all evil practices? Deservedly may such rulers be called the ministers of God for good. They carry on the same benevolent design towards the community which the great Governor of the universe does towards his whole creation. 'T is the indispensable duty of a people to pay tribute, and to afford an easy and comfortable subsistence to such rulers, because they are the ministers of God, who are continually laboring and employing their time for the good of the community. He that resists such magistrates does, in a very emphatical sense, resist the ordinance of God; he is an enemy to mankind, odious to God, and justly incurs the sentence of condemnation from the great Judge of quick and dead. Obedience to such magistrates is yielding obedience to the will of God, and, therefore, ought to be performed from a sacred regard to the divine authority.

For any one from hence to infer that the apostle enjoins in this text unlimited obedience to the worst of tyrants, and that he pronounces damnation upon those that resist the arbitrary measures of such pests of society, is just as good sense as if one should affirm, that because the Scripture enjoins us obedience to the laws of God, therefore we may not oppose the power of darkness; or because we are commanded to submit to the ordinance of God, therefore we may not resist the ministers of Satan. Such wild work must be made with the apostle before he can be brought to speak the language of oppression! It is as plain, I think, as words can make it, that, according to this text, no tyrant can be a ruler;[1] for the apostle's definition of a ruler is, that he is not a terror to good works, but to the evil; and that he is one who is to praise and encourage those that do well. Whenever, then, the ruler encourages them that do evil, and is a terror to those that do well, — i. e., as soon as he becomes a tyrant, — he forfeits his authority to govern, and becomes the minister of Satan, and, as such, ought to be opposed.

I know it is said that the magistrates were, at the time when the apostle wrote, heathens, and that Nero,[2] that monster of tyranny, was then Emperor of Rome; that therefore the apostle, by enjoining submission to the pow-

---

[1] See p. 67, note 1. — ED.   [2] See pp. 57 b, 61 a. — ED.

ers that then were, does require unlimited obedience to be yielded to the worst of tyrants. Now, not to insist upon what has been often observed, viz., that this epistle was written most probably about the beginning of Nero's reign, at which time he was a very humane and merciful prince, did everything that was generous and benevolent to the public, and showed every act of mercy and tenderness to particulars, and therefore might at that time justly deserve the character of the minister of God for good to the people, — I say, waiving this, we will suppose that this epistle was written after that Nero was become a monster of tyranny and wickedness; it will by no means follow from thence that the apostle meant to enjoin unlimited subjection to such an authority, or that he intended to affirm that such a cruel, despotic authority was the ordinance of God. The plain, obvious sense of his words, as we have already seen, forbids such a construction to be put upon them, for they plainly imply a strong abhorrence and disapprobation of such a character, and clearly prove that Nero,[1] so far forth as he was a tyrant, could not be the minister of God, nor have a right to claim submission from the people; so that this ought, perhaps, rather to be viewed as a severe satire upon Nero, than as enjoining any submission to him.

It is also worthy to be observed that the apostle prudently waived mentioning any particular persons that were then in power, as it might have been construed in an invidious light, and exposed the primitive Christians to the severe resentments of the men that were then in power. He only in general requires submission to the higher powers, because the powers that be are ordained of God. Now, though the emperor might at that time be such a

---

[1] See pp. 57, 61. — Ed.

tyrant that he could with no propriety be said to be ordained of God, yet it would be somewhat strange if there were no men in power among the Romans that acted up to the character of good magistrates, and that deserved to be esteemed as the ministers of God for good unto the people. If there were any such, notwithstanding the tyranny of Nero, the apostle might with great propriety enjoin submission to those powers that were ordained of God, and by so particularly pointing out the end and design of magistrates, and giving his definition of a ruler, he might design to show that neither Nero, nor any other tyrant, ought to be esteemed as the minister of God. Or, rather, — which appears to me to be the true sense, — the apostle meant to speak of magistracy in general, without any reference to the emperor, or any other person in power, that was then at Rome; and the meaning of this passage is as if he had said, It is the duty of every Christian to be a good subject of civil government, for the power and authority of the civil magistrate are from God; for the powers that be are ordained of God; *i. e.*, the authority of the magistrates that are now either at Rome or elsewhere is ordained of the Deity. Wherever you find any lawful magistrates, remember, they are of divine ordination. But that you may understand what I mean when I say that magistrates are of divine ordination, I will show you how you may discern who are lawful magistrates, and ordained of God, from those who are not. Those only are to be esteemed lawful magistrates, and ordained of God, who pursue the public good by honoring and encouraging those that do well and punishing all that do evil. Such, and such only, wherever they are to be found, are the ministers of God for good: to resist such is resisting the ordinance of God, and exposing yourselves to the divine wrath and condemnation.

In either of these senses the text cannot make anything in favor of arbitrary government. Nor could he with any propriety tell them that they need not be afraid of the power so long as they did that which was good, if he meant to recommend an unlimited submission to a tyrannical Nero; for the best characters were the likeliest to fall a sacrifice to his malice. And, besides, such an injunction would be directly contrary to his own practice, and the practice of the primitive Christians, who refused to comply with the sinful commands of men in power; their answer in such cases being this, We ought to obey God rather than men.[1] Hence the apostle Paul himself suffered many cruel persecutions because he would not renounce Christianity, but persisted in opposing the idolatrous worship of the pagan world.

This text, being rescued from the absurd interpretations which the favorers of arbitrary government have put upon it, turns out to be a noble confirmation of that free and generous plan of government which the law of nature and reason points out to us. Nor can we desire a more equitable plan of government than what the apostle has here laid down; for, if we consult our happiness and real good, we can never wish for an unreasonable liberty, viz., a freedom to do evil, which, according to the apostle, is the only thing that the magistrate is to refrain us from. To have a liberty to do whatever is fit, reasonable, or good, is the highest degree of freedom that rational beings can possess. And how honorable a station are those men placed in, by the providence of God, whose business it is to secure to men this rational liberty, and to promote the happiness and welfare of society, by suppressing vice and immorality, and by honoring and encouraging everything that is honorable, virtuous, and praiseworthy! Such magistrates ought to be

1 See p. 278. — ED.

honored and obeyed as the ministers of God and the servants of the King of Heaven. Can we conceive of a larger and more generous plan of government than this of the apostle? Or can we find words more plainly expressive of a disapprobation of an arbitrary and tyrannical government? I never read this text without admiring the beauty and nervousness of it; and I can hardly conceive how he could express more ideas in so few words than he has done. We see here, in one view, the honor that belongs to the magistrate, because he is ordained of God for the public good. We have his duty pointed out, viz., to honor and encourage the virtuous, to promote the real good of the community, and to punish all wicked and injurious persons. We are taught the duty of the subject, viz., to obey the magistrate for conscience' sake, because he is ordained of God; and that rulers, being continually employed under God for our good, are to be generously maintained by the paying them tribute; and that disobedience to rulers is highly criminal, and will expose us to the divine wrath. The liberty of the subject is also clearly asserted, viz., that subjects are to be allowed to do everything that is in itself just and right, and are only to be restrained from being guilty of wrong actions. It is also strongly implied, that when rulers become oppressive to the subject and injurious to the state, their authority, their respect, their maintenance, and the duty of submitting to them, must immediately cease; they are then to be considered as the ministers of Satan,[1] and, as such, it becomes our indispensable duty to resist and oppose them.

Thus we see that both reason and revelation perfectly agree in pointing out the nature, end, and design of government, viz., that it is to promote the welfare and happiness of the community; and that subjects have a right to

[1] See p. 73. — Ed.

do everything that is good, praiseworthy, and consistent with the good of the community, and are only to be restrained when they do evil and are injurious either to individuals or the whole community; and that they ought to submit to every law that is beneficial to the community for conscience' sake, although it may in some measure interfere with their private interest; for every good man will be ready to forego his private interest for the sake of being beneficial to the public. Reason and revelation, we see, do both teach us that our obedience to rulers is not unlimited, but that resistance is not only allowable, but an indispensable duty in the case of intolerable tyranny and oppression. From both reason and revelation we learn that, as the public safety is the supreme law of the state, — being the true standard and measure by which we are to judge whether any law or body of laws are just or not, — so legislators have a right to make, and require subjection to, any set of laws that have a tendency to promote the good of the community.

Our governors have a right to take every proper method to form the minds of their subjects so that they may become good members of society. The great difference that we may observe among the several classes of mankind arises chiefly from their education and their laws: hence men become virtuous or vicious, good commonwealthsmen or the contrary, generous, noble, and courageous, or base, mean-spirited, and cowardly, according to the impression that they have received from the government that they are under, together with their education and the methods that have been practised by their leaders to form their minds in early life. Hence the necessity of good laws to encourage every noble and virtuous sentiment, to suppress vice and immorality, to promote industry, and to punish idleness, that parent of innumerable

evils; to promote arts and sciences, and to banish ignorance from among mankind.

And as nothing tends like religion and the fear of God
to make men good members of the commonwealth, it is
the duty of magistrates to become the patrons and pro-
moters of religion and piety, and to make suitable laws for
the maintaining public worship, and decently supporting
the teachers of religion. Such laws, I apprehend, are absolutely necessary for the well-being of civil society. Such
laws may be made, consistent with all that liberty of conscience which every good member of society ought to be
possessed of;[1] for, as there are few, if any, religious societies among us but what profess to believe and practise all
the great duties of religion and morality that are necessary
for the well-being of society and the safety of the state, let
every one be allowed to attend worship in his own society,
or in that way that he judges most agreeable to the will
of God, and let him be obliged to contribute his assistance
to the supporting and defraying the necessary charges
of his own meeting. In this case no one can have any right
to complain that he is deprived of liberty of conscience,
seeing that he has a right to choose and freely attend that
worship that appears to him to be most agreeable to the
will of God; and it must be very unreasonable for him to
object against being obliged to contribute his part towards
the support of that worship which he has chosen. Whether
some such method as this might not tend, in a very eminent
manner, to promote the peace and welfare of society, I
must leave to the wisdom of our legislators to determine;

---

[1] *"Ought to be* possessed of." But who is to be the judge? — Mr. Backus,
Mr. West, or the Pope? Mr. Backus demanded the repeal of all laws
compelling the support of public worship, and that it should be left to the
voluntary support of the people. — ED.

be sure it would take off some of the most popular[1] objections against being obliged by law to support public worship while the law restricts that support only to one denomination.

But for the civil authority to pretend to establish [2] particular modes of faith and forms of worship, and to punish all that deviate from the standard which our superiors have set up, is attended with the most pernicious consequences to society. It cramps all free and rational inquiry, fills the world with hypocrites and superstitious bigots — nay, with infidels and skeptics; it exposes men of religion and conscience to the rage and malice of fiery, blind zealots, and dissolves every tender tie of human nature; in short, it introduces confusion and every evil work. And I cannot but look upon it as a peculiar blessing of Heaven that we live in a land where every one can freely deliver his sentiments upon religious subjects, and have the privilege of worshipping God according to the dictates of his own conscience,[3] without any molestation or disturbance, — a privilege which I hope we shall ever keep up and strenuously maintain.[4] No principles ought ever to be discountenanced by civil authority but such as tend to the subversion of the state. So long as a man is a good member of society, he is accountable to God alone for his religious sentiments; but when men are found disturbers of the public peace, stirring up sedition, or practising against the state, no pretence of religion or conscience

---

[1] At this time the Baptists, of whom the excellent, and able, and zealous Backus was the chief, were restless under the then legal obligations. Dr. West's proposed method was deemed by many a dangerous departure from the old paths, and the complete divorce was not effected till many years later, in 1834. — ED.

[2] See pp. 47–52; also p. 86, note a. — ED.

[3] See p. 68, note 1. — ED.   [4] See p. 58, note a. — ED.

ought to screen them from being brought to condign punishment. But then, as the end and design of punishment
is either to make restitution to the injured or to restrain
men from committing the like crimes for the future, so,
when these important ends are answered, the punishment
ought to cease; for whatever is inflicted upon a man under
the notion of punishment after these important ends are
answered, is not a just and lawful punishment, but is
properly cruelty and base revenge.

From this account of civil government we learn that
the business of magistrates is weighty and important. It
requires both wisdom and integrity. When either are
wanting, government will be poorly administered; more
especially if our governors are men of loose morals and
abandoned principles; for if a man is not faithful to God
and his own soul, how can we expect that he will be faithful to the public? There was a great deal of propriety in
the advice that Jethro gave to Moses to provide able men,
— men of truth, that feared God, and that hated covetousness, — and to appoint them for rulers over the people. For
it certainly implies a very gross absurdity to suppose that
those who are ordained of God for the public good should
have no regard to the laws of God, or that the ministers
of God should be despisers of the divine commands.
David, the man after God's own heart, makes piety a necessary qualification in a ruler: "He that ruleth over men
(says he) must be just, ruling in the fear of God." It is
necessary it should be so, for the welfare and happiness of
the state; for, to say nothing of the venality and corruption, of the tyranny and oppression, that will take place
under unjust rulers, barely their vicious and irregular lives
will have a most pernicious effect upon the lives and manners of their subjects: their authority becomes despicable
in the opinion of discerning men. And, besides, with

what face can they make or execute laws against vices
which they practise with greediness? A people that have
a right of choosing their magistrates are criminally guilty
in the sight of Heaven when they are governed by caprice
and humor, or are influenced by bribery to choose magistrates that are irreligious men, who are devoid of sentiment, and of bad morals and base lives. Men cannot be
sufficiently sensible what a curse they may bring upon
themselves and their posterity by foolishly and wickedly
choosing men of abandoned characters and profligate lives
for their magistrates and rulers.[1]

We have already seen that magistrates who rule in the
fear of God ought not only to be obeyed as the ministers
of God, but that they ought also to be handsomely supported, that they may cheerfully and freely attend upon
the duties of their station; for it is a great shame and disgrace to society to see men that serve the public laboring
under indigent and needy circumstances; and, besides, it
is a maxim of eternal truth that the laborer is worthy of
his reward.

It is also a great duty incumbent on people to treat
those in authority with all becoming honor and respect, —
to be very careful of casting any aspersion upon their characters. To despise government, and to speak evil of dignities, is represented in Scripture as one of the worst of
characters; and it was an injunction of Moses, "Thou
shalt not speak evil of the ruler of thy people." Great
mischief may ensue upon reviling the character of good
rulers; for the unthinking herd of mankind are very apt
to give ear to scandal, and when it falls upon men in
power, it brings their authority into contempt, lessens their
influence, and disheartens them from doing that service to

[1] See p. 69, note 1. — ED.

the community of which they are capable; whereas, when they are properly honored, and treated with that respect which is due to their station, it inspires them with courage and a noble ardor to serve the public: their influence among the people is strengthened, and their authority becomes firmly established. We ought to remember that they are men like to ourselves, liable to the same imperfections and infirmities with the rest of us, and therefore, so long as they aim at the public good, their mistakes, misapprehensions, and infirmities, ought to be treated with the utmost humanity and tenderness.

But though I would recommend to all Christians, as a part of the duty that they owe to magistrates, to treat them with proper honor and respect, none can reasonably suppose that I mean that they ought to be flattered[1] in their vices, or honored and caressed while they are seeking to undermine and ruin the state; for this would be wickedly betraying our just rights, and we should be guilty of our own destruction. We ought ever to persevere with firmness and fortitude in maintaining and contending for all that liberty that the Deity has granted us. It is our duty to be ever watchful over our just rights, and not suffer them to be wrested out of our hands by any of the artifices of tyrannical oppressors. But there is a wide difference between being jealous of our rights, when we have the strongest reason to conclude that they are invaded by our rulers, and being unreasonably suspicious of men that are zealously endeavoring to support the constitution, only because we do not thoroughly comprehend all their designs. The first argues a noble and generous mind; the other, a low and base spirit.

Thus have I considered the nature of the duty enjoined in the text, and have endeavored to show that the same

---

[1] See pp. 97–103. — ED.

principles that require obedience to lawful magistrates do also require us to resist tyrants; this I have confirmed from reason and Scripture.

It was with a particular view to the present unhappy controversy that subsists between us and Great Britain that I chose to discourse upon the nature and design of government, and the rights and duties both of governors and governed, that so, justly understanding our rights and privileges, we may stand firm in our opposition to ministerial tyranny, while at the same time we pay all proper obedience and submission to our lawful magistrates; and that, while we are contending for liberty, we may avoid running into licentiousness; and that we may preserve the due medium between submitting to tyranny and running into anarchy. I acknowledge that I have undertaken a difficult task; but, as it appeared to me, the present state of affairs loudly called for such a discourse; and, therefore, I hope the wise, the generous, and the good, will candidly receive my good intentions to serve the public. I shall now apply this discourse to the grand controversy that at this day subsists between Great Britain and the American colonies.

And here, in the first place, I cannot but take notice how wonderfully Providence has smiled upon us by causing the several colonies to unite [1] so firmly together against the tyranny of Great Britain, though differing from each other in their particular interest, forms of government, modes of worship, and particular customs and manners, besides several animosities that had subsisted among them. That, under these circumstances, such a union should take place as we now behold, was a thing that might rather have been wished than hoped for.

And, in the next place, who could have thought that,

[1] See p. 218. — ED.

when our charter was vacated, when we became destitute
of any legislative authority, and when our courts of justice
in many parts of the country were stopped, so that we
could neither make nor execute laws upon offenders, —
who, I say, would have thought, that in such a situation
the people should behave so peaceably, and maintain such
good order and harmony among themselves? This is a
plain proof that they, having not the civil law to regulate
themselves by, became a law unto themselves; and by
their conduct they have shown that they were regulated
by the law of God written in their hearts. This is the
Lord's doing, and it ought to be marvellous in our eyes.[1]

From what has been said in this discourse, it will appear
that we are in the way of our duty in opposing the tyranny
of Great Britain; for, if unlimited submission is not due
to any human power, if we have an undoubted right to
oppose and resist a set of tyrants[2] that are subverting our
just rights and privileges, there cannot remain a doubt in
any man, that will calmly attend to reason, whether we
have a right to resist and oppose the arbitrary measures of
the King and Parliament; for it is plain to demonstration,
nay, it is in a manner self-evident, that they have been and
are endeavoring to deprive us not only of the privileges
of Englishmen, and our charter rights, but they have endeavored to deprive us of what is much more sacred, viz.,
the privileges of men and Christians;[a] i. e., they are robbing us of the inalienable rights that the God of nature
has given us as men and rational beings, and has confirmed

[a] The meaning is not that they have attempted to deprive us of liberty of conscience, but that they have attempted to take away those rights which God has
invested us with as his creatures and confirmed in his gospel, by which believers
have a covenant right to the good things of this present life and world.

[1] See note 1, p. 206. — ED.

[2] This was very plain English for the British Parliament to read, and
shocking to Oxford divines. — ED.

to us in his written word as Christians and disciples of
that Jesus who came to redeem us from the bondage of
sin and the tyranny of Satan, and to grant us the most
perfect freedom, even the glorious liberty of the sons
and children of God; that here they have endeavored to
deprive us of the sacred charter of the King of Heaven.
But we have this for our consolation: the Lord reigneth;
he governs the world in righteousness, and will avenge the
cause of the oppressed when they cry unto him. We
have made our appeal to Heaven, and we cannot doubt
but that the Judge of all the earth will do right.

Need I upon this occasion descend to particulars? Can
any one be ignorant what the things are of which we complain? Does not every one know that the King and Parliament have assumed the right to tax us without our
consent? And can any one be so lost to the principles of
humanity and common sense as not to view their conduct
in this affair as a very grievous imposition? Reason and
equity require that no one be obliged to pay a tax that he
has never consented to, either by himself or by his representative. But, as Divine Providence has placed us at so
great a distance from Great Britain that we neither are
nor can be properly represented in the British Parliament,
it is a plain proof that the Deity designed that we should
have the powers of legislation and taxation among ourselves; for can any suppose it to be reasonable that a set
of men that are perfect strangers to us should have the
uncontrollable right to lay the most heavy and grievous
burdens upon us that they please, purely to gratify their
unbounded avarice and luxury? Must we be obliged to
perish with cold and hunger to maintain them in idleness,
in all kinds of debauchery and dissipation? But if they
have the right to take our property from us without our
consent, we must be wholly at their mercy for our food

and raiment, and we know by sad experience that their tender mercies are cruel.

But because we were not willing to submit to such an unrighteous and cruel decree, — though we modestly complained and humbly petitioned for a redress of our grievances, — instead of hearing our complaints, and granting our requests, they have gone on to add iniquity to transgression, by making several cruel and unrighteous acts. Who can forget the cruel act to block up the harbor of Boston,[1] whereby thousands of innocent persons must have been inevitably ruined had they not been supported by the continent? Who can forget the act for vacating our charter, together with many other cruel acts which it is needless to mention? But, not being able to accomplish their wicked purposes by mere acts of Parliament, they have proceeded to commence [2] open hostilities against us, and have endeavored to destroy us by fire and sword. Our towns they have burnt,[3] our brethren they have slain, our vessels they have taken, and our goods they have spoiled. And, after all this wanton exertion of arbitrary power, is there the man that has any of the feeling of humanity left who is not fired with a noble indignation against such merciless tyrants, who have not only brought upon us all the horrors of a civil war, but have also added a piece of bar-

---

[1] No class in the community rendered more efficient service to their country than did the seamen, especially at the commencement of the war. Mr. Sabine's Report on the Fisheries contains a most interesting chapter — pp. 198–210 — on the "Public Services and Character of Fishermen." Newport, R. I., Marblehead, and Boston seamen did invaluable service. See also Lossing's Field Book of the Revolution, ii. 88, and Arnold's History of Rhode Island, ii. 386; Cooper's Naval History, London ed., 1839, i. 286. — ED.

[2] They shed the first blood at Lexington, April 19th. — ED.

[3] Charlestown, burnt June 17, and Falmouth, October 18. See Frothingham's History, and Willis's History of Portland, ii. chap. 8. — ED.

barity unknown to Turks and Mohammedan infidels, yea, such as would be abhorred and detested by the savages of the wilderness, — I mean their cruelly forcing our brethren whom they have taken prisoners, without any distinction of whig or tory, to serve on board their ships of war,[1] thereby obliging them to take up arms against their own countrymen, and to fight against their brethren, their wives, and their children, and to assist in plundering their own estates! This, my brethren, is done by men who call themselves Christians, against their Christian brethren, — against men who till now gloried in the name of Englishmen, and who were ever ready to spend their lives and fortunes in the defence of British rights. Tell it not in Gath, publish it not in the streets of Askelon, lest it cause our enemies to rejoice and our adversaries to triumph! Such a conduct as this brings a great reproach upon the profession of Christianity; nay, it is a great scandal even to human nature itself.

It would be highly criminal not to feel a due resentment against such tyrannical monsters. It is an indispensable duty, my brethren, which we owe to God and our country, to rouse up and bestir ourselves, and, being animated with a noble zeal for the sacred cause of liberty, to defend our lives and fortunes, even to the shedding the last drop of blood. The love of our country, the tender affection that we have for our wives and children, the regard we ought to have for unborn posterity, yea, everything that is dear and sacred, do now loudly call upon us to use our best endeavors to save our country. We must beat our ploughshares into swords, and our pruning-hooks into spears, and learn the art of self-defence against our

[1] "It is, in truth, nothing more than the old, and, as I thought, exploded problem of tyranny, which proposes to beggar its subjects into submission."— Edmund Burke, 1775. — ED.

enemies.[1] To be careless and remiss, or to neglect the cause of our country through the base motives of avarice and self-interest, will expose us not only to the resent-

---

[1] A large octavo pamphlet of thirty-one pages —" The Manual Exercises, as ordered by his Majesty in 1764, together with Plans and Explanations of the method generally practised at Reviews and Field-Days. Massachusetts Bay: Boston. Printed and sold by Isaiah Thomas at his Printing-office, near the Mill-Bridge "— was recommended by the " Provincial Congress at Cambridge, October 20, 1774, ... as the best calculated for appearance and defence." Another pamphlet of fifteen pages — " Rules and Regulations for the Massachusetts Army. Salem: Printed by Samuel and Ebenezer Hall. 1775"—begins thus: " In Provincial Congress, Concord, April 5th, 1775. Whereas the Lust of Power which of old oppressed, persecuted, and exiled our pious and virtuous ancestors from their fair possessions in Britain, now pursues, with tenfold severity, us, their guiltless children, who are unjustly and wickedly charged with Licentiousness, Sedition, Treason, and Rebellion; and being deeply impressed with a Sense of the almost incredible Fatigues and Hardships our venerable Progenitors encountered, who fled from Oppression for the sake of civil and religious Liberty for themselves and their offspring, and began a settlement here on bare Creation, at their own expense; and having seriously considered the Duty we owe to God, to the Memory of such invincible Worthies, to the King, to Great Britain, our Country, ourselves and Posterity, do think it an indispensable Duty, by all lawful Ways and Means in our Power, to recover, maintain, defend, and preserve the free exercise of all those civil and religious Rights and Liberties for which many of our Forefathers fought, bled, and died, and to hand them down entire for the free Enjoyment of the latest Posterity; " and they " recommend " fifty-three articles for the regulation of " the Army that may be raised," etc. Article one is that " all officers and soldiers . . . . shall diligently frequent Divine Service and Sermons."

The whole is " signed by order of the Provincial Congress.

"JOHN HANCOCK, President."

How perfectly Cromwellian is all this! These soldiers were freemen; they chose the delegates to that very congress; from the lips of their own chosen pastors flowed fervid appeals, like that in the text, to which they constantly listened, and which they drank in till their souls were kindled. Could George III. and his mercenary Hessians conquer such soldiers, who fought not for money, but for their homes, — yes, and for us, — with Bibles in their pockets, and faith in their hearts, and English Puritan blood in their veins? — ED.

ments of our fellow-creatures, but to the displeasure of God Almighty; for to such base wretches, in such a time as this, we may apply with the utmost propriety that passage in Jeremiah xlviii. 10: " Cursed be he that doth the work of the Lord deceitfully, and cursed be he that keepeth back his sword from blood." To save our country from the hands of our oppressors ought to be dearer to us even than our own lives, and, next the eternal salvation of our own souls, is the thing of the greatest importance, — a duty so sacred that it cannot justly be dispensed with for the sake of our secular concerns. Doubtless for this reason God has been pleased to manifest his anger against those who have refused to assist their country against its cruel oppressors. Hence, in a case similar to ours, when the Israelites were struggling to deliver themselves from the tyranny of Jabin, the king of Canaan, we find a most bitter curse denounced against those who refused to grant their assistance in the common cause; see Judges v. 23: " Curse ye Meroz, said the angel of the Lord, curse ye bitterly the inhabitants thereof; because they came not to the help of the Lord, to the help of the Lord against the mighty."

Now, if such a bitter curse is denounced against those who refused to assist their country against its oppressors, what a dreadful doom are those exposed to who have not only refused to assist their country in this time of distress, but have, through motives of interest or ambition, shown themselves enemies to their country by opposing[1] us in

[1] About this time — March 31st — Washington wrote of these men: " One or two have done what a great number ought to have done long ago — committed suicide. By all accounts there never existed a more miserable set of beings than these wretched creatures now are. Taught to believe that the power of Great Britain was superior to all opposition, and, if not, that foreign aid was at hand, they were even higher and more insulting in

the measures that we have taken, and by openly favoring the British Parliament! He that is so lost to humanity as to be willing to sacrifice his country for the sake of avarice or ambition, has arrived to the highest stage of wickedness that human nature is capable of, and deserves a much worse name than I at present care to give him. But I think I may with propriety say that such a person has forfeited his right to human society, and that he ought to take up his abode, not among the savage men, but among the savage beasts of the wilderness.

Nor can I wholly excuse from blame those timid persons who, through their own cowardice, have been induced to favor our enemies, and have refused to act in defence of their country; for a due sense of the ruin and destruction that our enemies are bringing upon us is enough to raise such a resentment in the human breast that would, I should think, be sufficient to banish fear from the most timid make. And, besides, to indulge cowardice in such a cause argues a want of faith in God; for can he that firmly believes and relies upon the providence of God doubt whether he will avenge the cause of the injured when they apply to him for help? For my own part, when I consider the dispensations of Providence towards this land ever since our fathers first settled in Plymouth, I find abundant reason to conclude that the great Sovereign of the universe has planted a vine in this American wilderness which he has caused to take deep root, and it has

their opposition than the regulars. When the order issued, therefore, for embarking the troops in Boston, no electric shock, no sudden explosion of thunder, in a word, not the last trump, could have struck them with greater consternation. They were at their wits' end; and, conscious of their black ingratitude, they chose to commit themselves, in the manner I have above described, to the mercy of the waves, at a tempestuous season, rather than meet their offended countrymen." — ED.

filled the land, and that he will never suffer it to be plucked up or destroyed.

Our fathers fled [1] from the rage of prelatical tyranny and persecution, and came into this land in order to enjoy liberty of conscience, and they have increased to a great people. Many have been the interpositions of Divine Providence on our behalf, both in our fathers' days and ours; and, though we are now engaged in a war with Great Britain, yet we have been prospered in a most wonderful manner. And can we think that he who has thus far helped us will give us up into the hands of our enemies? Certainly he that has begun to deliver us will continue to show his mercy towards us, in saving us from the hands of our enemies: he will not forsake us if we do not forsake him. Our cause is so just and good that nothing can prevent our success but only our sins. Could I see a spirit of repentance and reformation prevail through the land, I should not have the least apprehension or fear of being brought under the iron rod of slavery, even though all the powers of the globe were combined against us. And though I confess that the irreligion and profaneness which are so common among us gives something of a damp to my spirits, yet I cannot help hoping, and even believing, that Providence has designed this continent for to be the asylum of liberty and true religion; for can we suppose that the God who created us free agents, and designed that we should glorify and serve him in this world that we might enjoy him forever hereafter, will suffer liberty and true religion to be banished from off the face of the earth? But do we not find that both religion and liberty seem to be expiring and gasping for life in the other continent? — where, then, can they find a harbor or place of refuge but in this?

[1] See pp. x.—xii. — ED.

There are some [1] who pretend that it is against their consciences to take up arms in defence of their country; but can any rational being suppose that the Deity can require us to contradict the law of nature which he has written in our hearts, a part of which I am sure is the principle of self-defence, which strongly prompts us all to oppose any power that would take away our lives, or the lives of our friends? Now, for men to take pains to destroy the tender feelings of human nature, and to eradicate the principles of self-preservation, and then to persuade themselves that in so doing they submit to and obey the will of God, is a plain proof how easily men may be led to pervert the very first and plainest principles of reason and common sense, and argues a gross corruption of the human mind. We find such persons are very inconsistent with themselves; for no men are more zealous to defend their property, and to secure their estates from the encroachments of others, while they refuse to defend their persons, their wives, their children, and their country, against the assaults of the enemy. We see to what unaccountable lengths men will run when once they leave the plain road of common sense, and violate the law which God has written in the heart. Thus some have thought they did God service when they unmercifully butchered and destroyed the lives of the servants of God; while others, upon the contrary extreme, believe that they please God while they sit still and quietly behold their friends and brethren killed by their unmerciful enemies, without endeavoring to defend or rescue them. The one is a sin of omission, and the other is a sin of commission, and it may perhaps be difficult to say, under certain circumstances, which is the most

---

[1] " Whereas the people called Quakers profess themselves conscientiously scrupulous of attending in arms at military musters," they were exempted by a statute of 1763. — ED.

criminal in the sight of Heaven. Of this I am sure, that they are, both of them, great violations of the law of God.

Having thus endeavored to show the lawfulness and necessity of defending ourselves against the tyranny of Great Britain, I would observe that Providence seems plainly to point to us the expediency, and even necessity, of our considering ourselves as an independent state.[1] For, not to consider the absurdity implied in making war against a power to which we profess to own subjection, to pass by the impracticability of our ever coming under subjection to Great Britain upon fair and equitable terms, we may observe that the British Parliament has virtually declared us an independent state by authorizing their ships of war to seize all American property, wherever they can find it, without making any distinction between the friends of administration and those that have appeared in opposition to the acts of Parliament. This is making us a distinct nation from themselves. They can have no right any longer to style us rebels; for rebellion implies a particular faction risen up in opposition to lawful authority, and, as such, the factious party ought to be punished, while those that remain loyal are to be protected. But when war is declared against a whole community without distinction, and the property of each party is declared to be seizable, this, if anything can be, is treating us as an independent state. Now, if they are pleased to consider us as in a state of independency, who can object against our considering ourselves so too?

But while we are nobly opposing with our lives and estates the tyranny of the British Parliament, let us not forget the duty which we owe to our lawful magistrates; let us never mistake licentiousness for liberty. The more we

[1] Within forty days, July 4th, came the "Declaration of Independence." — ED.

understand the principles of liberty, the more readily shall we yield obedience to lawful authority; for no man can oppose good government but he that is a stranger to true liberty. Let us ever check and restrain the factious disturbers of the peace; whenever we meet with persons that are loth to submit to lawful authority, let us treat them with the contempt which they deserve, and ever esteem them as the enemies of their country and the pests of society. It is with peculiar pleasure that I reflect upon the peaceable behavior of my countrymen at a time when the courts of justice were stopped and the execution of laws suspended. It will certainly be expected of a people that could behave so well when they had nothing to restrain them but the laws written in their hearts, that they will yield all ready and cheerful obedience to lawful authority. There is at present the utmost need of guarding ourselves against a seditious and factious temper; for when we are engaged with so powerful an enemy from without, our political salvation, under God, does, in an eminent manner, depend upon our being firmly united together in the bonds of love to one another, and of due submission to lawful authority. I hope we shall never give any just occasion to our adversaries to reproach us as being men of turbulent dispositions and licentious principles, that cannot bear to be restrained by good and wholesome laws, even though they are of our own making, nor submit to rulers of our own choosing. But I have reason to hope much better things of my countrymen, though I thus speak. However, in this time of difficulty and distress, we cannot be too much guarded against the least approaches to discord and faction. Let us, while we are jealous of our rights, take heed of unreasonable suspicions and evil surmises which have no proper foundation; let us take heed lest we hurt the cause of liberty by speaking evil of the ruler of the people.

Let us treat our rulers with all that honor and respect which the dignity of their station requires; but let it be such an honor and respect as is worthy of the sons of freedom to give. Let us ever abhor the base arts that are used by fawning parasites and cringing courtiers, who by their low artifices and base flatteries obtain offices and posts which they are unqualified to sustain, and honors of which they are unworthy, and oftentimes have a greater number of places assigned them than any one person of the greatest abilities can ever properly fill, by means of which the community becomes greatly injured, for this reason, that many an important trust remains undischarged, and many an honest and worthy member of society is deprived of those honors and privileges to which he has a just right, whilst the most despicable, worthless courtier is loaded with honorable and profitable commissions. In order to avoid this evil, I hope our legislators will always despise flattery as something below the dignity of a rational mind, and that they will ever scorn the man that will be corrupted or take a bribe. And let us all resolve with ourselves that no motives of interest, nor hopes of preferment, shall ever induce us to act the part of fawning courtiers towards men in power. Let the honor and respect which we show our superiors be true and genuine, flowing from a sincere and upright heart.

The honors that have been paid to arbitrary princes have often been very hypocritical and insincere. Tyrants have been flattered in their vices, and have often had an idolatrous reverence paid them.[1] The worst princes have been the most flattered and adored; and many such, in the pagan world, assumed the title of gods, and had divine honors paid them. This idolatrous reverence has ever been the inseparable concomitant of arbitrary power and

[1] See pp. 98, 99, 100. — Ed.

tyrannical government; for even Christian princes, if they
have not been adored under the character of gods, yet the
titles given them strongly savor of blasphemy, and the
reverence paid them is really idolatrous. What right has
a poor sinful worm of the dust to claim the title of his
most sacred Majesty? Most sacred certainly belongs only
to God alone, — for there is none holy as the Lord, — yet
how common is it to see this title given to kings! And
how often have we been told that the king can do no
wrong![1] Even though he should be so foolish and wicked
as hardly to be capable of ever being in the right, yet still
it must be asserted and maintained that it is impossible for
him to do wrong!

The cruel, savage disposition of tyrants, and the idolatrous reverence that is paid them, are both most beautifully
exhibited to view by the apostle John in the Revelation,
thirteenth chapter, from the first to the tenth verse, where
the apostle gives a description of a horrible wild beast[a]

[a] Wild beast. By the beast with seven heads and ten horns I understand the
tyranny of arbitrary princes, viz., the emperors and kings of the Eastern and
Western Roman Empire, and not the tyranny of the Pope and clergy; for the
description of every part of this beast will answer better to be understood of
political than of ecclesiastical tyrants. Thus the seven heads are generally interpreted to denote the several forms of Roman government; the ten horns are
understood of the ten kingdoms that were set up in the Western Empire; and
by the body of the beast it seems most natural to understand the Eastern, or
Greek Empire, for it is said to be like a leopard. This image is taken from Daniel vii. 6, where the third beast is said to be like a leopard. Now, by the third
beast in Daniel is understood, by the best interpreters, the Grecian Monarchy.
It is well known that John frequently borrows his images from Daniel, and I
believe it will be found, upon a critical examination of the matter, that whenever he does so he means the same thing with Daniel; if this be true (as I am
fully persuaded it is), then, by the body of this beast being like a leopard in the
Revelation of John, is to be understood the Eastern, or Greek Empire, which
was that part of the old Roman Empire that remained whole for several ages
after the Western Empire was broken into ten kingdoms. Further: after the
beast was risen it is said that the dragon gave him his seat. Now, by the dragon
is meant the devil, who is represented as presiding over the Roman Empire in its
pagan state; but the seat of the Roman Empire in its pagan state was Rome.
Here, then, is a prophecy that the emperor of the East should become possessed

[1] See p. 94, note a. — ED.

which he saw rise out of the sea, having seven heads and
ten horns, and upon his heads the names of blasphemy.
By heads are to be understood forms of government, and
by blasphemy, idolatry; so that it seems implied that there
will be a degree of idolatry in every form of tyrannical
government. This beast is represented as having the body
of a leopard, the feet of a bear, and the mouth of a lion;
i. e., a horrible monster, possessed of the rage and fury of
the lion, the fierceness of the bear, and the swiftness of the
leopard to seize and devour its prey. Can words more
strongly point out, or exhibit in more lively colors, the
exceeding rage, fury, and impetuosity of tyrants, in their
destroying and making havoc of mankind? To this beast
we find the dragon gave his power, seat, and great authority; *i. e.*, the devil constituted him to be his vicegerent
on earth; this is to denote that tyrants are the ministers
of Satan, ordained by him for the destruction of mankind.

Such a horrible monster, we should have thought, would
have been abhorred and detested of all mankind, and that

of Rome, which exactly agrees with what we know from history to be fact; for
the Emperor Justinian's generals having expelled the Goths out of Italy, Rome
was brought into subjection to the emperor of the East, and was for a long time
governed by the emperor's lieutenant, who resided at Ravenna. These considerations convince me that the Greek Empire, and not the Pope and his clergy,
is to be understood by the body of the beast, which was like a leopard. And
what further confirms me in this belief is, that it appears to me that the Pope
and the papal clergy are to be understood by the second beast which we read
of in Revelation xiii. 11—17, for of him it is said that "he had two horns like a
lamb." A lamb, we know, is the figure by which Jesus Christ is signified in the
Revelation and many other parts of the New Testament. The Pope claims both
a temporal and spiritual sovereignty, denoted by the two horns, under the character of the vicar of Jesus Christ, and yet, under this high pretence of being
the vicar of Jesus Christ, he speaks like a dragon; *i. e.*, he promotes idolatry in
the Christian Church, in like manner as the dragon did in the heathen world.
To distinguish him from the first beast, he is called (Revelation xix.) "the false
prophet that wrought miracles;" *i. e.*, like Mahomet, he pretends to be a lawgiver, and claims infallibility, and his emissaries endeavor to confirm this doctrine by pretended miracles. How wonderfully do all these characters agree to
the Pope! Wherefore I conclude that the second, and not the first beast, denotes
the tyranny of the Pope and his clergy.

all nations would have joined their powers and forces together to oppose and utterly destroy him from off the face of the earth; but, so far are they from doing this, that, on the contrary, they are represented as worshipping him (verse 8) : " And all that dwell on the earth shall worship him," viz., all those "whose names are not written in the Lamb's book of life;" *i. e.*, the wicked world shall pay him an idolatrous reverence, and worship him with a godlike adoration. What ᵢcan in a more lively manner show the gross stupidity and wickedness of mankind, in thus tamely giving up their just rights into the hands of tyrannical monsters, and in so readily paying them such an unlimited obedience as is due to God alone ?

We may observe, further, that these men are said (verse 4) to " worship the dragon ; "—not that it is to be supposed that they, in direct terms, paid, divine homage to Satan, but that the adoration paid to the beast, who was Satan's vicegerent, did ultimately centre in him. Hence we learn that those who pay an undue and sinful veneration to tyrants are properly the servants of the devil; they are worshippers of the prince of darkness, for in him all that undue homage and adoration centres that is given to his ministers. Hence that terrible denunciation of divine wrath against the worshippers of the beast and his image : " If any man worship the beast and his image, and receive his mark in his forehead, or in his hand, the same shall drink of the wine of the wrath of God which is poured out without mixture into the cup of his indignation, and he shall be tormented with fire and brimstone in the presence of the holy angels, and in the presence of the Lamb ; and the smoke of their torment ascendeth for ever and ever : and they have no rest day nor night, who worship the beast and his image, and who receive the mark of

his name."[a]   We have here set forth in the clearest manner, by the inspired apostle, God's abhorrence of tyranny
and tyrants, together with the idolatrous[1] reverence that
their wretched subjects are wont to pay them, and the
awful denunciation of divine wrath against those who are
guilty of this undue obedience to tyrants.

Does it not, then, highly concern us all to stand fast in
the liberty wherewith Heaven hath made us free, and to
strive to get the victory over the beast and his image —
over every species of tyranny?   Let us look upon a freedom from the power of tyrants as a blessing that cannot
be purchased too dear, and let us bless God that he has so
far delivered us from that idolatrous reverence which men
are so very apt to pay to arbitrary tyrants; and let us
pray that he would be pleased graciously to perfect the
mercy he has begun to show us by confounding the devices
of our enemies and bringing their counsels to nought, and
by establishing our just rights and privileges upon such a
firm and lasting basis that the powers of earth and hell
shall not prevail against it.

Under God, every person in the community ought to
contribute his assistance to the bringing about so glorious
and important an event; but in a more eminent manner
does this important business belong to the gentlemen that
are chosen to represent the people in this General Assembly, including those that have been appointed members of
the Honorable Council Board.

Honored fathers, we look up to you, in this day of calamity and distress, as the guardians of our invaded rights,
and the defenders of our liberties against British tyranny.
You are called, in Providence, to save your country from

a Rev. xiv. 9, 10.

1 See pp. 48, note 1; 49, note 1; 98. — ED.

ruin. A trust is reposed in you of the highest importance to the community that can be conceived of, its business the most noble and grand, and a task the most arduous and difficult to accomplish that ever engaged the human mind — I mean as to things of the present life. But as you are engaged in the defence of a just and righteous cause, you may with firmness of mind commit your cause to God, and depend on his kind providence for direction and assistance. You will have the fervent wishes and prayers of all good men that God would crown all your labors with success, and direct you into such measures as shall tend to promote the welfare and happiness of the community, and afford you all that wisdom and prudence which is necessary to regulate the affairs of state at this critical period.

Honored fathers of the House of Representatives : We trust to your wisdom and goodness that you will be led to appoint such men to be in council whom you know to be men of real principle, and who are of unblemished lives ; that have shown themselves zealous and hearty friends to the liberties of America; and men that have the fear of God before their eyes ; for such only are men that can be depended upon uniformly to pursue the general good.

My reverend fathers and brethren in the ministry will remember that, according to our text, it is part of the work and business of a gospel minister[1] to teach his hearers the duty they owe to magistrates. Let us, then, endeavor to explain the nature of their duty faithfully, and show them the difference between liberty and licentiousness; and, while we are animating them to oppose tyranny and arbitrary power, let us inculcate upon them the duty of yielding due obedience to lawful authority. In order to the right and faithful discharge of this part

[1] See pp. 47, 53, 54. — Ed.

of our ministry, it is necessary that we should thoroughly study the law of nature, the rights of mankind, and the reciprocal duties of governors and governed. By this means we shall be able to guard them against the extremes of slavish submission to tyrants on one hand, and of sedition and licentiousness on the other. We may, I apprehend, attain a thorough acquaintance with the law of nature and the rights of mankind, while we remain ignorant of many technical terms of law, and are utterly unacquainted with the obscure and barbarous Latin that was so much used in the ages of popish darkness and superstition.[1]

To conclude : While we are fighting for liberty, and striving against tyranny, let us remember to fight the good

[1] " The old forms of writs and legal process — the authority of ' The State,' ' The Commonwealth,' or ' The People,' being substituted for that of the king — were still retained in all the states; and, out of a pedantic spirit of imitation on the part of the lawyers, in spite of the efforts of the state Legislatures to give greater simplicity to legal proceedings, the forms and practice of the courts, even subsequently to the Revolution, were made more and more to conform to English technicalities. This spirit on the part of the lawyers, who formed a very influential portion of every state Legislature, proved a serious obstacle to all attempted reforms and simplifications of the law." — Hildreth's History of the United States, vol. iii., 380, 381.

By recent legislation in England and in several of the United States, on the subject of evidence, a vast accumulation of legal subtleties and refinements, tending to hinder, if not to frustrate justice, has been thrown aside among the rubbish of the past, — curious and useless learning. Much has been done to simplify the conveyance of real estate, and divest it of the encumbrances which originated in early times and another condition of society ; and to secure to women their rights to property, by sweeping away the *fictions* which reminded us of former barbarity; and *special pleading* is added to the magnificent hecatomb. In review it seems as if the intent had been, first, to drive the parties out of court, but, if they were smart enough to keep in, next to prevent justice between them, if the subtlest logic and ingenuity, spun out to the thinnest though gravest nonsense, could do it. — ED.

fight of faith, and earnestly seek to be delivered from that bondage of corruption which we are brought into by sin, and that we may be made partakers of the glorious liberty of the sons and children of God: which may the Father of Mercies grant us all, through Jesus Christ. AMEN.

A

SERMON

PREACHED BEFORE THE

HONORABLE COUNCIL,

AND THE HONORABLE

HOUSE OF REPRESENTATIVES,

OF THE

STATE of MASSACHUSETTS-BAY,

IN

NEW-ENGLAND,

AT

BOSTON,

MAY 27, 1778.

BEING THE ANNIVERSARY FOR THE ELECTION
OF THE HONORABLE COUNCIL.

By PHILLIPS PAYSON, A. M.

PASTOR OF A CHURCH IN CHELSEA.

BOSTON: *N. E.*

PRINTED BY JOHN GILL, PRINTER TO THE
GENERAL ASSEMBLY.

M. DCC. LXXVIII.

STATE OF MASSACHUSETTS-BAY, COUNCIL CHAMBER, May 28, 1778.

Ordered, That Moses Gill, Henry Gardner, and Timothy Danielson, Esquires, be a Committee to wait on the Rev. Mr. Samuel Phillips Payson, and return him the thanks of the Board for his Sermon delivered yesterday before both Houses of Assembly; and request a copy thereof for the press.

JOHN AVERY, D. Secretary.

EDITOR'S PREFATORY NOTE.

In a note to Lord North, dated February 4, 1774, George III. wrote that "General Gage, though just returned from Boston, expresses his willingness to go back at a day's notice, if convenient measures are adopted. He says they will be lions while we are lambs; but if we take the resolute part, they will undoubtedly prove very meek. Four regiments, sent to Boston, will, he thinks, be sufficient to prevent any disturbance. All men now feel that the fatal compliance in 1766 has increased the pretensions of the Americans to thorough independence."

Generals Howe, Clinton, and Burgoyne, going into Boston, May 25, 1774, asked the skipper of a packet, outward bound, what news there was. He replied that Boston was surrounded by ten thousand country people. "What!" Burgoyne exclaimed, "ten thousand peasants keep five thousand king's troops shut up! Well, let *us* get in, and we'll soon find elbow-room." The presumptuous and confident general was soon to find snug quarters among those same "peasants," with hardly enough of "elbow-room" for comfortable reflection.[1]

On the 17th of October, 1777, at Saratoga, General Burgoyne surrendered his sword to General Gates. "After dinner, the American army was drawn up, in parallel lines, on each side of the road, extending nearly a mile. Between these victorious troops the British, with light infantry in front, and escorted by a company of light dragoons, preceded by two mounted officers bearing the American flag, marched to the lively tune of

---

[1] Frothingham's Siege of Boston, 114. Mr. F. says that Burgoyne loved a joke, and used to relate that, "while a prisoner of war, he was received with great courtesy by the Boston people as he stepped from the Charlestown ferry-boat, but he was really annoyed when an old lady, perched on a shed above the crowd, cried out, at the top of a shrill voice, 'Make way! make way! — the general's coming! Give him elbow-room!'"

Yankee Doodle." [1] General Burgoyne glittered in his uniform. Gates was in his plain blue frock, and each of the American soldiers had on "the clothes which he wore in the fields, the church, or the tavern. They stood, however, like soldiers, well arranged, and with a military air, in which there was but little to find fault with. All the muskets had bayonets, and the sharp-shooters had rifles. The men all stood so still that we were filled with wonder. Not one of them made a single motion, as if he would speak with his neighbor. Nay, more, all the lads that stood there in rank-and-file kind nature had formed so trim, so slender, so nervous, that it was a pleasure to look at them, and we were all surprised at the sight of such a handsome, well-formed race. In all earnestness," says the same Hessian officer,[2] " English America surpasses the most of Europe in the growth and looks of its male population. The whole nation has a natural talent for war and a soldier's life."

The ministry were assailed in Parliament for their employment of the Indians against the Americans. One of the secretaries defended it, concluding, "It is perfectly justifiable to use all the means that God and nature have put into our hands."—"That God and nature put into our hands!" repeated Chatham, with contemptuous abhorrence; "I know not what idea that lord may entertain of God and nature, but I know that such abominable principles are equally abhorrent to religion and humanity. What! attribute the sacred sanction of God and nature to the massacre of the Indian scalping-knife! — to the cannibal and savage torturing, murdering, roasting, and eating — literally, my lords, *eating* — the mangled victims of his barbarous battles! . . . The abominable principles, and this most abominable avowal of them, demand most decisive indignation. I call upon *that right reverend bench*,"— pointing to the bishops, — " *those holy ministers of the gospel, and pious pastors of the church*, — I conjure them to join in the holy work, and to vindicate the religion of their God." That appeal was in vain. The chief of that bench was at the head of the " Society for the Propagation of *their* Gospel in Foreign Parts" in America; the end justified the means; and, beside, implicit obedience was their "badge." [3] Mayhew had denounced their principles and object in 1750 and afterward. They knew the utter hostility of America [4] to their rule, and their only hope now was in violence. [5]

---

1 Lossing's Field Book of the Revolution, i. 81.
2 Irving's Washington, Lond. Ed., vol. iii. 905.   3 See p. 42.
4 See pp. xxix., 41, 44, 52, 88, 100, 108, 109, 110, 160, 175, 195, 197, 218.
5 See pp. xxxi., xxxii., and Peters' letter, p. 195.

The glad news from Saratoga was like the noonday sun on the gloom and heaviness, engendered by continued reverses and suffering, pervading the colonies; it strengthened the heart of Washington, infused new life into the legislative councils, inspirited the people; and in the providential ordering of events, which human foresight or prudence could not have anticipated or prevented, and on which hinged the great issue, the faith of all was confirmed that God was with them, as he had been with their fathers. An incident, close in time with this auspicious and splendid achievement, illumines the record of our history, and by its light we may see the source of that marvellous strength in weakness, and endurance in trial, which George III., Lord North, and that "right reverend bench" could never comprehend, nor their wit or power overcome. It was an order of Congress, directing the Committee of Commerce to import twenty thousand copies of the Bible, the great political text-book of the patriots.[1]

The enormous and unavailing expenditures of England against her colonies, the failure of her generals, of greatest reputation and success in Europe, in their American campaigns, and the animation and good cheer of the patriot heart, dispirited the tories, the "friends of government."

On the 15th of November, the thirteen colonies confederated under the style of "The United States of America," and presented a consolidated front to George III., who might see on their national coin, not his own now hated and discarded royal effigy, but the motto "We are one," which, passing from palm to palm, linked every heart in one united whole. In the midst of this prosperity, on the recommendation of Congress, the 18th day of December was observed as a day of solemn thanksgiving and praise throughout the United States.

On the sixth of February, 1778, France — hesitating till after the tidings of the capture of General Burgoyne, giving decisive evidence of the vigor of the American character, and of their ultimate success — formed an alliance with the "United States," as an independent nation, and from this time there was a feeling that the question was not as to the final result of the war, but only how long George III. would persist in fighting, and how long England would endure his blind obstinacy and folly. As in the other colonies, or "states," as they now were, so in Massachusetts, old ties and authorities being thrown aside, and new governments being only in inception, it was a period when executive authority and decision were most needed, and yet were weakest; and the disorder of anarchy and revolution

1 See p. 262.

were averted only by the virtue and intelligence of the people, demonstrating the truth that " where the spirit of liberty is found in its genuine vigor, it produces its genuine effects, . . . and can never endanger a state unless its root and source is corrupted." A constitution, agreed upon by a State Convention, February 28, 1778, was then before the people for their consideration, and Mr. Payson's Sermon, appropriate to the time, had particular reference to the subject of government. Its practical wisdom, its profound observations on man, on the dangers and safeguards of liberty, on religion, morality, and education, rather than large statistics of material wealth, as the greatest good, and the true test of prosperity — on the character and requisites of good magistracy, and on the difficulties of free institutions, all are treated on such broad and comprehensive principles of universal and perpetual truth, that his sermon is adapted to all times, and may be pondered, perhaps, with peculiar advantage at this day.

The preacher, Rev. Samuel Phillips Payson, son of Rev. Phillips Payson, of Walpole, Massachusetts, was born January 18, 1736, educated at Harvard College, 1754, ordained at Chelsea, October 26, 1757, and died January 11, 1801, aged sixty-four, after a life of great value to his own people and to his country. He was of a family noted in many generations for piety and usefulness. The name of Phillips is identified with venerable institutions of learning, and that of Payson is dear to the Christian world. Mr. Payson was distinguished as a classical scholar, for his studies in natural philosophy and astronomy, and for his fidelity as a Christian pastor and teacher, but has, perhaps, a stronger claim to our grateful remembrance as a high-minded patriot in the days of his country's peril, difficulty, and darkness. We find in the pages of his friend Gordon's History of the Revolution an incident illustrative of the times and of his character. It is this: The British forces, on their inglorious retreat towards Boston, after their raid at Lexington and Concord, suffered from the fire of the provincial sharp-shooters. A few of these, headed by Mr. Payson, who till now had been extremely moderate, attacked a party of twelve soldiers, carrying stores to the retreating troops, killed one, wounded several, made the whole prisoners, and gained possession of their arms and stores, without any loss whatever to themselves. The preacher suited the action to the word and the word to the action, in his part of the national tragedy.

DISCOURSE VII.

ELECTION SERMON.

BUT JERUSALEM, WHICH IS ABOVE, IS FREE, WHICH IS THE MOTHER OF US ALL. SO THEN, BRETHREN, WE ARE NOT CHILDREN OF THE BOND WOMAN, BUT OF THE FREE. — Gal. iv. 26, 31.

It is common for the inspired writers to speak of the gospel dispensation in terms applicable to the heavenly world, especially when they view it in comparison with the law of Moses. In this light they consider the church of God, and good men upon earth, as members of the church and family of God above, and liken the liberty of Christians to that of the citizens of the heavenly Zion. We doubt not but the Jerusalem above, the heavenly society, possesses the noblest liberty to a degree of perfection of which the human mind can have no adequate conception in the present state. The want of that knowledge and rectitude they are endowed with above renders liberty and government so imperfect here below.

Next to the liberty of heaven is that which the sons of God, the heirs of glory, possess in this life, in which they are freed from the bondage of corruption, the tyranny of evil lusts and passions, described by the apostle " by being made free from sin, and becoming the servants of God." These kinds of liberty are so nearly related, that the latter is considered as a sure pledge of the former; and therefore all good men, all true believers, in a special sense are

children of the free woman, heirs of the promise. This
religious or spiritual liberty must be accounted the greatest
happiness of man, considered in a private capacity. But
considering ourselves here as connected in civil society,
and members one of another, we must in this view esteem
civil liberty as the greatest of all human blessings. This
admits of different degrees, nearly proportioned to the
morals, capacity, and principles of a people, and the mode
of government they adopt; for, like the enjoyment of
other blessings, it supposes an aptitude or taste in the possessor. Hence a people formed upon the morals and principles of the gospel are capacitated to enjoy the highest
degree of civil liberty, and will really enjoy it, unless prevented by force or fraud.

Much depends upon the mode and administration of
civil government to complete the blessings of liberty; for
although the best possible plan of government never can
give an ignorant and vicious people the true enjoyment of
liberty, yet a state may be enslaved though its inhabitants
in general may be knowing, virtuous, and heroic. The
voice of reason and the voice of God both teach us that
the great object or end of government is the public good.
Nor is there less certainty in determining that a free and
righteous government originates from the people, and is
under their direction and control; and therefore a free,
popular model of government — of the republican kind —
may be judged the most friendly to the rights and
liberties of the people, and the most conducive to the
public welfare.

On account of the infinite diversity of opinions and
interests, as well as for other weighty reasons, a government altogether popular, so as to have the decision of
cases by assemblies of the body of the people, cannot be
thought so eligible; nor yet that a people should dele-

gate their power and authority to one single man, or to one body of men, or, indeed, to any hands whatever, excepting for a short term of time.[1] A form of government may be so constructed as to have useful checks in the legislature, and yet capable of acting with union, vigor, and despatch, with a representation equally proportioned, preserving the legislative and executive branches distinct, and the great essentials of liberty be preserved and secured. To adjust such a model[a] is acknowledged to be a nice and difficult matter;[2] and, when adjusted, to render it respectable, permanent, and quiet, the circumstances of the state, and the capacities and morals both of rulers and people, are not only of high importance, but of absolute necessity.

[a] The form or constitution of government that has been submitted to the people of this state so amply secures the essentials of liberty, places and keeps the power so entirely in the hands of the people, is so concise and explicit, and makes such an easy step from the old to the new form, that it may justly be considered as a high evidence of the abilities of its compilers; and if it should not be complied with, it is very probable we never shall obtain a better.

[1] "Sometimes it is said that man cannot be trusted with the government of himself; can he, then, be trusted with the government of others? Or have we found angels, in the form of kings, to govern him? Let history answer this question." — Jefferson. 1801. — ED.

[2] "A Constitution and Form of Government for the State of Massachusetts Bay, agreed upon by the Convention of said State, February 28, 1778, to be laid before the several Towns and Plantations in said State for their approbation or disapprobation," a pamphlet of twenty-three pages, was distributed among the towns, by vote of the House of Representatives, March 4, 1778. The constitution was rejected. Ten thousand votes were against it, two thousand votes in its favor; one hundred and twenty towns made no returns. It contained no bill of rights; did not properly separate the legislative, judicial, and executive functions; "allowed" the free exercise and enjoyment of religious worship, whereas that is an inalienable right; did not provide an equal representation; and many other objections were stated. It was thought best to postpone the framing of a constitution till more peaceful and settled times, and that it should then be done by delegates specially chosen for the service. Barry's History of Massachusetts, iii. ch. v., gives a very clear account of the subject. — ED.

It by no means becomes me to assume the airs of a dictator, by delineating a model of government; but I shall ask the candid attention of this assembly to some things respecting a state, its rulers and inhabitants, of high importance, and necessary to the being and continuance of such a free and righteous government as we wish for ourselves and posterity, and hope, by the blessing of God, to have ere long established.

In this view, it is obvious to observe that a spirit of liberty should in general prevail among a people; their minds should be possessed with a sense of its worth and nature. Facts and observation abundantly teach us that the minds of a community, as well as of individuals, are subject to different and various casts and impressions. The inhabitants of large and opulent empires and kingdoms are often entirely lost to a sense of liberty, in which case they become an easy prey to usurpers and tyrants. Where the spirit of liberty is found in its genuine vigor it produces its genuine effects; urging to the greatest vigilance and exertions, it will surmount great difficulties; [so] that it is no easy matter to deceive or conquer a people determined to be free. The exertions and effects of this great spirit in our land have already been such as may well astonish the world; and so long as it generally prevails it will be quiet with no species of government but what befriends and protects it. Its jealousy for its safety may sometimes appear as if verging to faction; but it means well, and can never endanger a state unless its root and source is corrupted.

Free republican governments have been objected to, as if exposed to factions from an excess of liberty. The Grecian states are mentioned for a proof, and it is allowed that the history of some of those commonwealths is little else but a narration of factions; but it is justly denied that the true spirit of liberty produced these effects. Violent and opposing parties,[1] shaking the pillars of the state, may arise under the best forms of government. A government, from various causes, may be thrown into convulsions, like the Roman state in its latter periods, and, like that, may die of the malady. But the evils which happen in a state are not always to be charged upon its government, much less upon one of the noblest principles that can dwell in the human breast. There are diseases in government, like some in the human body, that lie undiscovered till they become wholly incurable.

The baneful effects of exorbitant wealth, the lust of power, and other evil passions, are so inimical to a free, righteous government, and find such an easy access to the human mind, that it is difficult, if possible, to keep up the spirit of good government, unless the spirit of liberty prevails in the state. This spirit, like other generous growths of nature, flourishes best in its native soil. It has been engrafted, at one time and another, in various countries: in America it shoots up and grows as in its natural soil. Recollecting our pious ancestors, the first settlers of the country,—nor shall we look for ancestry beyond that period,[2]—and we may say, in the most literal sense, we

---

[1] "Let me warn you in the most solemn manner against the baneful effects of the spirit of party generally. . . . In governments of the popular form it is seen in its greatest rankness, and is truly their worst enemy; . . . in governments purely elective it is a spirit not to be encouraged. From their natural tendency it is certain there will always be enough of that spirit for every salutary purpose; and, there being such constant danger of excess, the effort ought to be, by force of public opinion, to mitigate and assuage it. A fire not to be quenched, it demands a uniform vigilance to prevent its bursting into a flame, lest, instead of warming, it should consume."—Washington.—ED.

[2] It is a mistaken pride and a fallacy which would lead us not to look for our origin beyond the Atlantic. We cannot know ourselves or our history without this. America, isolated from the Old World bravely warring

are children, not of the bond woman, but of the free. It may hence well be expected that the exertions and effects of American liberty should be more vigorous and complete. It has the most to fear from ignorance and avarice; for it is no uncommon thing for a people to lose sight of their liberty in the eager pursuit of wealth, as the states of Holland have done; and it will always be as easy to rob an ignorant people of their liberty as to pick the pockets of a blind man.

The slavery of a people is generally founded in ignorance of some kind or another; and there are not wanting such facts as abundantly prove the human mind may be so sunk and debased, through ignorance and its natural effects, as even to adore its enslaver, and kiss its chains. Hence knowledge and learning may well be considered as most essentially requisite to a free, righteous government.

against and slowly upheaving and overturning hereditary wrong, was exclusively appropriated by the advance guard of Christian humanity, by actual possession, at Plymouth, in 1620; and the spirit of liberty, freed from hoary hindrances, vigorously put forth her strength and glory. But liberty was not born here; and we cannot learn her lineage, nor that of our Puritan ancestors, — her devotees, — nor appreciate the cost and wealth of our inheritance, without the study of English history, and civilization, and of the Reformation; for the fruits of all this were simply transplanted to our shores by the *children* of those who wrought it. Alfred is ours, and Runnemede, and Edward VI., and Elizabeth; Raleigh, Bacon, and Shakspeare; Hampden, Milton, Cromwell, Sydney, yes, and "King Charles the martyr," are ours; and it is our glory that we continue the roll with the magnificent names of Washington, Franklin, and Edwards, — an earnest, may we hope, of our future.

The beautiful opening of Gibbon's "Memoirs of my Life and Writings," written in his usual philosophical vein, is a charming passage for all those who feel that "lively desire of knowing and of recording our ancestors," which "so generally prevails, that it must depend on the influence of some common principle in the minds of men." "Remember from whom you sprang," exclaimed John Hancock, when he proposed a general Colonial Congress. — ED.

A republican government and science mutually promote and support each other. Great literary acquirements are indeed the lot of but few, because but few in a community have ability and opportunity to pursue the paths of science; but a certain degree of knowledge is absolutely necessary to be diffused through a state for the preservation of its liberties and the quiet of government.

Every kind of useful knowledge will be carefully encouraged and promoted by the rulers of a free state, unless they should happen to be men of ignorance themselves; in which case they and the community will be in danger of sharing the fate of blind guides and their followers. The education of youth, by instructors properly qualified,[a] the establishment of societies for useful arts and sciences, the encouragement of persons of superior abilities, will always command the attention of wise rulers.

The late times of our glorious struggle have not indeed been favorable to the cause of education in general, though much useful knowledge of the geography of our country, of the science of arms, of our abilities and strength, and of our natural rights and liberties, has been acquired; great improvements have also been made in several kinds of manufactory.[1] But our security and the public welfare

[a] The want of proper instructors, and a proper method of instructing, are the reason that what we call common education, or school-learning, is generally so imperfect among us. Youth should always be taught by strict rule in reading, writing, and speaking, and so in all parts of their education. By this means the advantages of their education will commonly increase with their age, that by a little application in their riper years persons may raise a useful superstructure from a small foundation that was well laid at school in their earlier days. It would be of eminent service if instructors would more generally endeavor to fix in the minds of their scholars the rules of reading, of spelling, of writing, or of whatever branch of knowledge they teach.

[1] To the colonies, fringing the Atlantic, and hemmed in by primeval forests, the command to primitive man seemed to be uttered anew: "And God blessed them; and God said unto them, Be fruitful and multiply, and replenish the earth and subdue it; and have dominion over the fish of the

require yet greater exertions to promote education and useful knowledge. Most of the internal difficulties of a state commonly arise from ignorance, that general source of error. The growls of avarice and curses of clowns will generally be heard when the public liberty and safety call for more generous and costly exertions. Indeed, we may never expect to find the marks of public virtue, the efforts of heroism, or any kind of nobleness, in a man who has no idea of nobleness and excellency but what he hoards up in his barn or ties up in his purse.

It is readily allowed there have not been wanting statesmen and heroes of the generous growth of nature, though instances of this sort are not so common. But if these had been favored with the improvements of art, they would have appeared to much greater advantage, and with brighter lustre. Nothing within the compass of human

---

sea;" and " a man was famous according as he had lifted up axes on the thick trees." Their thrift was in the saw-mill, the ship-yard, the fisheries, commerce, and, last of all, agriculture; and their interest, as well as that of England, was to exchange their staples for the manufactures of the mother country. But the industry and increase of one hundred and fifty years had wrought a change in the condition and wants of the people, so that the more compact populations naturally turned to handicraft, and the new political relations quickened this action. Educated labor made rapid progress in new devices for economy of time and industry. It was encouraged by legislation, and stimulated by the desire of independence. " The great improvements and discoveries" of that day would now excite a smile, perhaps. The first cotton-mill in America, established at Beverly in 1788, was visited by Washington, in his tour through the country, in 1789. A periodical of the day described it as " a complete set of machines for carding and spinning cotton, which *answered the warmest expectations of the proprietors.* The spinning-jenny spins sixty threads at a time, and with the carding-machine *forty pounds of cotton can be well carded per day.* The warping-machine and the other tools and machinery are complete, performing their various operations to *great advantage, and promise much benefit to the public*, and emolument to the patriotic adventurers."— Stone's Beverly, 1843, p. 85. — ED.

ability is of that real weight and importance as the education of youth — the propagation of knowledge.[1] Despotism and tyranny want nothing but wealth and force, but liberty and order are supported by knowledge and virtue.

I shall also mention the love of our country, or public virtue, as another essential support of good government and the public liberties. No model of government whatever can equal the importance of this principle, nor afford proper safety and security without it. Its object being the approbation of conscience, and its motive to exertion being the public welfare, hence it can only dwell in superior minds, elevated above private interest and selfish views. It does that for the public which domestic affection does among real friends; but, like other excellences, is more frequently pretended to than possessed.

In the ancient Roman republic it was the life and soul of the state which raised it to all its glory, being always awake to the public defence and good; and in every state it must, under Providence, be the support of government, the guardian of liberty, or no human wisdom or policy can support and preserve them. Civil society cannot be maintained without justice, benevolence, and the social virtues. Even the government of the Jerusalem above could not render a vicious and abandoned people quiet and happy. The children of the bond woman, slaves to vice, can never be free. If the reason of the mind,

[1] " Patronize every rational effort to encourage schools, colleges, universities, academies, and every institution for propagating knowledge, virtue, and religion among all classes of the people, not only for their benign influence on the happiness of life in all its stages and classes, and of society in all its forms, but as the only means of preserving our constitution from its natural enemies, the spirit of sophistry, the spirit of party, the spirit of intrigue, the profligacy of corruption, and the pestilence of foreign influence, which is the angel of destruction to elective governments."— President Adams's Inaugural, 1797. — ED.

man's immediate rule of conduct, is in bondage to corruption, he is verily the worst of slaves. Public spirit,
through human imperfection, is in danger of degenerating
to selfish passion, which has a malignant influence on
public measures. This danger is the greater because the
corruption is not commonly owned, nor soon discerned.
Such as are the most diseased with it are apt to be the
most insensible to their error.

The exorbitant wealth of individuals has a most baneful
influence on public virtue, and therefore should be carefully guarded against. It is, however, acknowledged to
be a difficult matter to secure a state from evils and mischiefs from this quarter; because, as the world goes, and
is like to go, wealth and riches will have their commanding influence. The public interest being a remoter object
than that of self, hence persons in power are so generally
disposed to turn it to their own advantage. A wicked
rich man, we see, soon corrupts a whole neighborhood, and
a few of them will poison the morals of a whole community. This sovereign power of interest seems to have
been much the source of modern politics abroad, and has
given birth to such maxims of policy as these, viz., that
" the wealth of a people is their truest honor," that "every
man has his price," [1] that " the longest purse, and not the
longest sword, will finally be victorious." But we trust and
hope that American virtue will be sufficient to convince
the world that such maxims are base, are ill-founded, and
altogether unfit and improper to influence and lead in
government. In the infancy of states there is not commonly so much danger of these mischiefs, because the love

---

[1] Robert Walpole, Earl of Orford, is the reputed author of the saying
that *all men have their price;* but his biographer, Archdeacon Cox,
says the words were " all *those* men," speaking of a particular party in
opposition. — ED.

of liberty and public virtue are then more general and vigorous; but the danger is apt to increase with the wealth of individuals. These observations are founded upon such well-known facts, that the rulers of a free state have sufficient warning to guard against the evils. The general diffusion of knowledge is the best preservative against them, and the likeliest method to beget and increase that public virtue, which, under God, will prove, like the promises of the gospel, an impregnable bulwark to the state.[1]

I must not forget to mention religion, both in rulers and people, as of the highest importance to the public. This is the most sacred principle that can dwell in the human breast. It is of the highest importance to men, — the most perfective of the human soul. The truths of the gospel are the most pure, its motives the most noble and animating, and its comforts the most supporting to the mind. The importance of religion to civil society and government is great indeed, as it keeps alive the best sense of moral obligation, a matter of such extensive utility, especially in respect to an oath, which is one of the principal instruments of government. The fear and reverence of God, and the terrors of eternity, are the most powerful restraints upon the minds of men; and hence it is of special importance in a free government, the spirit of which being always friendly to the sacred rights of conscience, it will hold up the gospel as the great rule of faith and practice.[2] Established modes and usages in

---

[1] " It is substantially true that virtue, or morality, is a necessary spring of popular government. Promote, then, as an object of primary importance, institutions for the *general diffusion of knowledge.*"—Washington. — ED.

[2] " Of all the dispositions and habits which lead to political prosperity, *religion and morality* are indispensable supports. In vain would that man

religion, more especially the stated public worship of God, so generally form the principles and manners of a people, that changes or alterations in these, especially when nearly conformed to the spirit and simplicity of the gospel, may well be esteemed very dangerous experiments in government. For this, and other reasons, the thoughtful and wise among us trust that our civil fathers, from a regard to gospel worship and the constitution of these churches, will carefully preserve them, and at all times guard against every innovation that might tend to overset the public worship of God, though such innovations may be urged from the most foaming zeal. Persons of a gloomy, ghostly, and mystic cast, absorbed in visionary scenes, deserve but little notice in matters either of religion or government. Let the restraints of religion once be broken down, as they infallibly would be by leaving the subject of public worship to the humors of the multitude,[1] and we might well defy all human wisdom and power to support and preserve order and government in the state. Human conduct and character can never be better formed

---

claim the tribute of patriotism who should labor to subvert these *great pillars of human happiness,* these primest props of the duties of men and citizens. The mere politician, equally with the pious man, ought to respect and to cherish them. A volume could not trace all their connections with private and public felicity. Let it be simply asked, where is the security for property, for reputation, for life, if the sense of religious obligation desert the oaths which are the instruments of investigation in courts of justice? And let us with caution indulge the supposition that morality can be maintained without religion. Whatever may be conceded to the influence of refined education on minds of peculiar structure, reason and experience both forbid us to expect that national morality can prevail in exclusion of religious principles."—Washington's Farewell. — Ed.

1 This strong language was not considered extravagant. By "the humors of the multitude," so much dreaded, was meant simply leaving public worship to the *voluntary* support of the community, by which it is now sustained. See p. 181, note 1. — Ed.

than upon the principles of our holy religion; they give the justest sense, the most adequate views, of the duties between rulers and people, and are the best principles in the world to carry the ruler through the duties of his station; and in case a series of faithful services should be followed with popular censure, as may be the case, yet the religious ruler will find the approbation of his conscience a noble reward.

Many other things might be mentioned as circumstances much in favor of a free government and public liberty, as where the inhabitants of a state can, in general, give their suffrages in person, and men of abilities are dispersed in the several parts of a state capable of public office and station; especially if there is a general distribution of property, and the landed interest not engrossed by a few, but possessed by the inhabitants in general through the state. Things of this nature wear a kind aspect. But, for the preservation and permanence of the state, it is of still higher importance that its internal strength be supported upon the great pillars of capacity, defence, and union. The full liberty of the press — that eminent instrument of promoting knowledge, and great palladium of the public liberty — being enjoyed, the learned professions directed to the public good, the great principles of legislation and government, the great examples and truths of history, the maxims of generous and upright policy, and the severer truths of philosophy investigated and apprehended by a general application to books, and by observation and experiment, — are means by which the capacity of a state will be strong and respectable, and the number of superior minds will be daily increasing. Strength, courage, and military discipline being, under God, the great defence of a state, as these are cultivated and improved the public defence will increase; and if there is added to these a general union, a spirit of harmony, the internal strength and beauty of the state will be great indeed. The variety and freedom of opinion is apt to check the union of a free state; and in case the union be interrupted merely from the freedom of opinion, contesting for real rights and privileges, the state and its government may still be strong and secure, as was, in fact, the case in ancient Rome, in the more disinterested periods of that republic. But if parties and factions, arising from false ambition, avarice, or revenge, run high, they endanger the state, which was the case in the latter periods of the republic of Rome. Hence the parties in a free state, if aimed at the public liberty and welfare, are salutary; but if selfish interest and views are their source, they are both dangerous and destructive.

The language of just complaint, the voice of real grievance, in most cases may easily be distinguished from the mere clamor of selfish, turbulent, and disappointed men. The ear of a righteous government will always be open to the former; its hand with wisdom and prudence will suppress the latter. And, since passion is as natural to men as reason, much discretion should be used to calm and quiet disaffected minds. Coërcives in government should always be held as very dangerous political physic: such as have gone into the practice have commonly either killed or lost their patients.

A spirit of union is certainly a most happy omen in a state, and, upon righteous principles, should be cultivated and improved with diligence. It greatly strengthens public measures, and gives them vigor and dispatch; so that but small states, when united, have done wonders in defending their liberties against powerful monarchs. Of this we have a memorable example in the little state of Athens, which destroyed the fleet of Xerxes, consisting of a thousand ships, and drove Darius with his army of three hundred thousand men out of Greece.

It must not be forgotten that much, very much, depends upon rulers to render a free government quiet, permanent, and respectful; they ought therefore, in an eminent degree, to possess those virtues and abilities which are the source and support of such a government.[1] The modern maxims of policy abroad, the base arts of bribery and corruption, of intrigue and dissimulation, will soon be productive of evils and mischiefs in the state ; and, since a corruption of manners almost necessarily follows a corruption of policy, the rulers of a free state ought to be influenced by the most generous and righteous principles and views. Ignorant and designing men should be kept from public offices in the state, as the former will be dupes to the ambitious, and the latter will be likely to prove the instruments of discord. Men, upon their first promotion, commonly act and speak with an air of meekness and diffidence, which however may consist with firmness and resolution. The practice of power is apt to dissipate these humble airs ; for this and other reasons it may generally be best not to continue persons a long time in places of honor and emolument.

The qualities of a good ruler may be estimated from the nature of a free government. Power being a delegation, and all delegated power being in its nature subordinate and limited, hence rulers are but trustees, and government a trust ; therefore fidelity is a prime qualification in a ruler ; this, joined with good natural and acquired abilities, goes far to complete the character. Natural disposition that is benevolent and kind, embellished with the graceful modes of address, agreeably strike the mind, and hence, in preference to greater real abilities, will commonly carry the votes

[1] See p. 69, note 1, p. 86, note a, pp. 162, 168. — ED.

of a people. It is, however, a truth in fact, that persons of this cast are subject to a degree of indolence, from which arises an aversion to those studies which form the great and active patriot. It is also a temper liable to that flexibility which may prove prejudicial to the state. A good acquaintance with mankind, a knowledge of the leading passions and principles of the human mind, is of high importance in the character before us; for common and well-known truths and real facts ought to determine us in human matters. We should take mankind as they are, and not as they ought to be or would be if they were perfect in wisdom and virtue. So, in our searches for truth and knowledge, and in our labors for improvement, we should keep within the ken or compass of the human mind. The welfare of the public being the great object of the ruler's views, they ought, of consequence, to be discerning in the times — always awake and watchful to the public danger and defence. And in order that government may support a proper air of dignity, and command respect, the ruler should engage in public matters, and perform the duties of his office, with gravity and solemnity of spirit. With wisdom he will deliberate upon public measures; and, tenacious of a well-formed purpose and design, he will pursue it with an inflexible stability. Political knowledge, a sense of honor, an open and generous mind, it is confessed, will direct and urge a ruler to actions and exertions beneficial to the state; and if, added to these, he has a principle of religion and the fear of God, it will in the best manner fit him for the whole course of allotted duty. The greatest restraints, the noblest motives, and the best supports arise from our holy religion. The pious ruler is by far the most likely to promote the public good. His example will have the most happy influence; his public devotions will not only be acts of worship and homage to

God, but also of charity to men. Superior to base passions and little resentments, undismayed by danger, not awed by threatenings, he guides the helm in storm and tempest, and is ready, if called in providence, to sacrifice his life for his country's good. Most of all concerned to approve himself to his God, he avoids the subtle arts of chicanery, which are productive of so much mischief in a state ; exercising a conscience void of offence, he has food to eat which the world knows not of, and in the hour of his death — that solemn period — has a hope and confidence in God, which is better than a thousand worlds.

A state and its inhabitants thus circumstanced in respect to government, principle, morals, capacity, union, and rulers, make up the most striking portrait, the liveliest emblem of the Jerusalem that is above, that this world can afford. That this may be the condition of these free, independent, and sovereign states of America, we have the wishes and prayers of all good men. Indulgent Heaven seems to invite and urge us to accept the blessing. A kind and wonderful Providence has conducted us, by astonishing steps, as it were, within sight of the promised land. We stand this day upon Pisgah's top, the children of the free woman, the descendants of a pious race, who, from the love of liberty and the fear of God, spent their treasure and spilt their blood. Animated by the same great spirit of liberty, and determined, under God, to be free, these states have made one of the noblest stands against despotism and tyranny that can be met with in the annals of history, either ancient or modern. One common cause, one common danger, and one common interest, has united and urged us to the most vigorous exertions. From small beginnings, from great weakness, — impelled from necessity and the tyrant's rod, but following the guidance of Heaven, — we have gone through a course of noble and heroic actions, with minds superior to the most virulent menaces, and to all the horrors of war; for we trusted in the God of our forefathers. We have been all along the scorn and derision of our enemies, but the care of Heaven, the charge of God; and hence our cause and union, like the rising sun, have shone brighter and brighter. Thanks be to God! we this day behold in the fulness of our spirit the great object of our wishes, of our toils and wars, brightening in our view. The battles we have already fought, the victories[a] we have won, the pride of tyranny that must needs have been humbled, mark the characters of the freemen of America with distinguished honor, and will be read with astonishment by generations yet unborn.

The lust of dominion is a base and detested principle, the desire of revenge is an infernal one; and the former, if opposed, commonly produces the latter. From these our enemies seem to have taken their measures, and hence have treated us with the greatest indignities, reproaches, insults, and cruelties that were ever heaped upon a people when struggling for their all. The remembrance of these things can never be lost. And although, under God, American wisdom and valor have hitherto opposed and baffled both their force and fraud, and we trust ever will, yet justice to our cause, to ourselves, and to our posterity, as well as a most righteous resentment, absolutely forbid

---

a The memorable and complete victory obtained over General Burgoyne and his whole army will not only immortalize the character of the brave General Gates and the officers and troops under his command, but, considering the immense expense Britain would be at in replacing such an army in America, together with other reasons, renders it highly probable it may prove one of the capital events that decides the war and establishes the independency of these states.[1]

1 See the Prefatory Note. A very full and complete account of this event in every view is presented in Lossing's Field Book of the Revolution, vol. i., chaps. ii. iii. Read, also, Dawson's Battles of the United States, Book I., ch. xxv. — ED.

that anything should pacify our minds short of a full and perfect independence. This, supported by the wisdom, virtue, and strength of the continent, must be our great charter of liberty. Nature has given us the claim, and the God of nature appears to be helping us to assert and maintain it. I am led to speak upon this point with the greatest confidence, from the late measures and resolves of that august assembly, the American Congress, which were so circumstanced and timed as must, with their general conduct, raise a monument to their fame that will bid defiance even to the devouring hand of time itself.[1]

We must be infidels, the worst of infidels, to disown or disregard the hand that has raised us up such benevolent and powerful assistants in times of great distress. How wonderful that God, who in ancient times " girded Cyrus with his might," should dispose his most Christian Majesty the king of France to enter into the most open and generour alliance [2] with these independent states! — an event in providence which, like the beams of the morning, cheers and enlivens this great continent. We must cherish the feelings of gratitude to such friends in our distress; we must hold our treaties sacred and binding.

Is it possible for us to behold the ashes, the ruins, of large and opulent towns that have been burnt in the most wanton manner, to view the graves of our dear countrymen whose blood has been most cruelly spilt, to hear the cries and screeches of our ravished matrons and virgins that had the misfortune to fall into the enemies' hands, and think of returning to that cruel and bloody power which has done all these things? No! We are not to suppose such a thought can dwell in the mind of a free, sensi-

[1] See Prefatory Note — " Confederation."— ED.

[2] By treaty of February 6, 1778. War between England and France followed close after, March 13th. — ED.

ble American. The same feelings in nature that led a Peruvian prince to choose *the other place*, must also teach us to prefer connections with any people on the globe rather than with those from whom we have experienced such unrighteous severities and unparalleled cruelties.

It seems as if a little more labor and exertion will bring us to reap the harvest of all our toils; and certainly we must esteem the freedom and independency of these states a most ample reward for all our sufferings. In preference to all human affairs our cause still merits, and ever has done, the most firm and manly support. In this, the greatest of all human causes, numbers of the virtuous Americans have lost their all. I recall my words — they have not lost it; no, but, from the purest principles, have offered it up in sacrifice upon the golden altar of liberty. The sweet perfumes have ascended to heaven, and shall be had in everlasting remembrance.

In this stage of our struggle we are by no means to indulge to a supine and dilatory spirit, which might yet be fatal, nor have we to take our resolutions from despair. Far from this, we have the noblest motives, the highest encouragements. I know the ardor of the human mind is apt in time to abate, though the subject be ever so important; but surely the blood of our friends and countrymen, still crying in our ears, like the souls of the martyrs under the altar, must arouse and fire every nobler passion of the mind. Moreover, to anticipate the future glory of America from our present hopes and prospects is ravishing and transporting to the mind. In this light we behold our country, beyond the reach of all oppressors, under the great charter of independence, enjoying the purest liberty; beautiful and strong in its union; the envy of tyrants and devils, but the delight of God and all good men; a refuge to the oppressed; the joy of the earth;

each state happy in a wise model of government, and abounding with wise men, patriots, and heroes ; the strength and abilities of the whole continent, collected in a grave and venerable council, at the head of all, seeking and promoting the good of the present and future generations. Hail, my happy country, saved of the Lord! Happy land, emerged from the deluges of the Old World, drowned in luxury and lewd excess! Hail, happy posterity, that shall reap the peaceful fruits of our sufferings, fatigues, and wars! With such prospects, such transporting views, it is difficult to keep the passions or the tongue within the bounds of Christian moderation. But far be it from us to indulge vain-glory, or return railing for railing, or to insult our foes; we cultivate better principles of humanity and bravery, and would much rather cherish the feelings of pity, especially to those of our enemies of better minds, whose names, with the baser, may appear in the pages of impartial history with indelible blemish. We wish, from the infatuation, and wickedness, and fate of our enemies, the world would learn lessons in wisdom and virtue ; that princes would learn never to oppress their subjects ; that the vaunting generals of Britian would learn never more to despise and contemn their enemy, nor prove blasphemers of God and religion. We wish the whole world may learn the worth of liberty. And may the inhabitants of these states, when their independence and freedom shall be completed, bless God for ever and ever; for thine, O Lord, is the power, and the glory, and the victory.

But, under our raised expectations of seeing the good of God's chosen, let us think soberly, let us act wisely. The public still calls aloud for the united efforts both of rulers and people ; nor have we as yet put off the harness. We have many things amiss among ourselves that need to be reformed, — many internal diseases to cure, and secret internal enemies to watch against, who may aim a fatal blow while making the highest pretensions to our cause; for plausible pretences are common covers to the blackest designs. We wish we had more public virtue, and that people would not be so greedy of cheating themselves and their neighbors. We wish for much greater exertions to promote education, and knowledge, and virtue, and piety. But in all states there will be such as want no learning, no government, no religion at all.

For the cure of our internal political diseases, and to promote the health and vigor, the defence and safety, of the state, our eyes, under God, are directed to our rulers; and, from that wisdom and prudence with which they have conducted our public affairs in the most trying times, we have the highest encouragement to look to them.

As a token of unfeigned respect, the honorable gentlemen of both Houses of Assembly present will permit me, by way of address, to observe, that the freemen of this state, by delegating their powers to you, my civil fathers, have reposed the greatest trust and confidence in you, from whence, we doubt not but you are sensible, arises the most sacred obligation to fidelity. Preserving a constant sense of this, and keeping the public welfare as your great object in view, we trust you will never be wanting in your best endeavors and most vigorous exertions to defend and deliver your country. The matters of the war will undoubtedly, at present, claim your first and principal attention, — always esteeming its great object, the liberty of your country, of more inestimable value than all the treasure of the world; and therefore, to obtain and secure it, no necessary charges or costs are to be spared. The internal matters of the state that claim your attention, though they may pass a severe scrutiny, will be noticed with all justice and impartiality;

and in the choice of a Council, — that important branch of our Legislature from which we have experienced such eminent services — of which branch, or one nearly similar, we hope this state will never be destitute, — in this choice, persons of known ability, of public virtue and religion, and possessed of the spirit of liberty, will have the preference.[1]

The burdens of your station are always great, and in these times are much increased; but you have the best of motives for exertion, — you have the consolation which arises from the fullest assurance of the justice of our cause; you have the unceasing prayers of good men; more than all these, you have the countenance and smiles of Heaven: with unceasing ardor, therefore, you will strive to be laborers together with God.

---

[1] COUNCILLORS FOR 1778.

For the old Colony of MASSACHUSETTS BAY :

Hon. ARTEMAS WARD, Esq.;
BENJ. GREENLEAF, Esq.;
CALEB CUSHING, Esq.;
THOMAS CUSHING, Esq.;
JABEZ FISHER, Esq.;
BENJ. WHITE, Esq.;
BENJ. AUSTIN, Esq.;
DANIEL HOPKINS, Esq.;
FRANCIS DANA, Esq.;

Hon. TIMOTHY EDWARDS, Esq.;
OLIVER PRESCOTT, Esq.;
JOSIAH STONE, Esq.;
TIMOTHY DANIELSON, Esq.;
OLIVER WENDELL, Esq.;
SAMUEL NILES, Esq.;
JOHN PITTS, Esq.;
ELEAZER BROOKS, Esq.;
SAMUEL BAKER, Esq.

For the late Colony of NEW PLYMOUTH :

Hon. WM. SEVER, Esq.;
WALTER SPOONER, Esq.;

Hon. DAN. DAVIS, Esq.;
NATHAN CUSHING, Esq.

For the late Province of MAINE :

Hon. JERE. POWELL, Esq.;
Hon. JEDEDIAH PREBBLE, Esq.;
Hon. JOSEPH SIMPSON, Esq.

For SAGADAHOCK :

Hon. HENRY GARDNER, Esq.

AT LARGE :

Hon. MOSES GILL, Esq.;
Hon. ABRAHAM FULLER, Esq.

— ED.

As nothing will be omitted that the good of the state calls for, we expect to see greater exertions in promoting the means of education and knowledge[a] than ever have yet been made among us. You will especially allow me, my fathers, to recommend our college, so much the glory of our land, to your special attention and most generous encouragements; for everything that is excellent and good that we hope and wish for in future, in a most important and essential sense, is connected with and depends upon exertions and endeavors of this kind. I need not observe, the leaders and rulers in our glorious cause have a fair opportunity of transmitting their names to posterity with characters of immortal honor. With my whole soul, I wish you the blessing of God, and the presence and guidance of his Holy Spirit.

My hearers, let us all hearken to the calls of our country, to the calls of God, and learn those lessons in wisdom which are so forcibly inculcated upon us in these times, and by such wonderful measures in Providence. From a sacred regard both to the goodness and severity of God, let us follow the guidance of his providence, and in the way of duty leave ourselves and all events with God. Remembering that Jerusalem which is above is the mother of us all, that we are children " not of the bond woman, but of the free," let us stand fast in the liberty where-

---

[a] In matters of science we have a most ample field open for improvement. To complete the geography of our country, to improve in the arts of agriculture and manufacture, and of physic, and other branches of science, are great objects that demand our special attention, and to obtain which an uninterrupted course of observation and experiment ought to be kept up. And if our General Assembly would form, and establish upon generous principles, a Society of Arts and Sciences [1] in this state, they would most certainly do great honor to themselves, and most eminent service to the public.

[1] The American Academy of Arts and Sciences was incorporated in 1780, and Mr. Payson was a valued contributor to its " Transactions."— ED.

with Christ hath made us free, and be not entangled again with the yoke of bondage. Imitating the virtue, the piety, the love of liberty, so conspicuous in our pious ancestors, like them let us exert ourselves for the good of posterity. With diligence let us cultivate the spirit of liberty, of public virtue, of union and religion, and thus strengthen the hands of government and the great pillars of the state. Our own consciences will reproach us, and the world condemn us, if we do not properly respect, and obey, and reverence the government of our own choosing. The eyes of the whole world are upon us in these critical times, and, what is yet more, the eyes of Almighty God. Let us act worthy of our professed principles, of our glorious cause, that in some good measure we may answer the expectations of God and of men. Let us cultivate the heavenly temper, and sacredly regard the great motive of the world to come. And God of his mercy grant the blessings of peace may soon succeed to the horrors of war, and that from the enjoyment of the sweets of liberty here we may in our turn and order go to the full enjoyment of the nobler liberties above, in that New Jerusalem, that city of the living God, that is enlightened by the glory of God and of the Lamb. AMEN.

A

SERMON

PREACHED BEFORE THE

HONORABLE COUNCIL,

AND THE HONORABLE

HOUSE OF REPRESENTATIVES

OF THE

STATE OF MASSACHUSETTS-BAY,

IN

NEW-ENGLAND,

MAY 31, 1780.

BEING THE ANNIVERSARY FOR THE ELECTION
OF THE HONORABLE COUNCIL.

BY SIMEON HOWARD, A. M.

Paſtor of the Weſt Church in BOSTON.

N. B. Several paſſages omitted in preaching are now
inſerted in the publication of this diſcourſe.

BOSTON, NEW-ENGLAND:

Printed by JOHN GILL, in COURT-STREET.

MDCCLXXX.

EDITOR'S PREFATORY NOTE.

"At the commencement of the dispute, in the first effusions of their zeal, and looking upon the service to be only temporary, the American officers entered into it without paying any regard to pecuniary or selfish considerations. . . . . . It is not, indeed, consistent with reason or justice to expect that one set of men should make a sacrifice of property, domestic ease, and happiness, encounter the rigors of the field, the perils and vicissitudes of war, to obtain those blessings which every citizen will enjoy in common with them, without some adequate compensation. It must also be a comfortless reflection to any man, that, after he may have contributed to securing the rights of his country at the risk of his life and the ruin of his fortune, there would be no provision made to prevent himself and family from sinking into indigence and wretchedness." These were among the reflections presented by Washington, in January, 1778, to a committee of Congress on the causes of the numerous defects in the military establishment. He recommended a "half-pay establishment," or life pension to the officers after the close of the war. "Besides," he added, "adopting some methods to make the provision for officers equal to their present emergencies, a due regard should be paid to futurity. Nothing, in my opinion, would serve more powerfully to reänimate their languishing zeal, and interest them thoroughly in the service, than a half-pay establishment. This would not only dispel the apprehension of personal distress, at the termination of the war, from having thrown themselves out of professions and employments they might not have it in their power to resume, but would, in a great degree, relieve the painful anticipation of leaving their widows and orphans a burden on the charity of their country, should it be their lot to fall in its defence." May 15th, 1778, Congress passed resolves which for a time relieved the distresses of the army; but the inability of the public to perform their engagements, and the depression of public credit in subsequent years, "caused such discontents and uneasiness, that alarming consequences were feared." If the national and state credit should *now* be depreciated "sixty for one of specie, and even government take it at forty for one,"— its condition in 1780, — or seventy-five for one of specie, or even one hundred and twenty for one, as was the case in 1781, and this distress be in the midst of war against the greatest power in Christendom, and the evil be aggravated by the timid, sordid, and unscrupulous who infest every community, and the future be darkened by an uncertainty discouraging to even the most hopeful and patriotic, even in success,[1] — all this would fail to impress us with the actual distress of that period. The terrible experience of the inefficiency of the "confederacy," having authority over states only, and not over the people, — the individuals of the nation, — was the cause of its abandonment, and the adoption of the present Constitution, beginning, — "WE, the people of the United States."

The author of the following discourse needs no other memorial of his generous mind, sound judgment, and enlightened principles, than may be found in his own pages. He fitly succeeded the gospel minister and patriot, the Rev. Dr. Mayhew, in his pastorate of the West Church of Boston, May 6, 1767, and was distinguished for the gentle virtues, mildness, benevolence, charity; yet, says Dr. Allen, "he heartily engaged in promoting the American Revolution, and participated in the joy experienced on the acknowledgment of our Independence." He was a native of Bridgewater, Massachusetts, born May 10, 1733, graduated at Harvard College in 1758, and, after a prosperous ministry of thirty-seven years, died August 13, 1804, and was succeeded by the Rev. Dr. Lowell. The present constitution of Massachusetts was now before the people, waiting for their adoption, and Mr. Howard's sermon was a consideration of the principles of free civil government, and of the character and conduct of civil rulers essential to its administration. The constitution was adopted by the popular vote, but not with unanimity. The government was organized October 25, 1780, and John Hancock was chosen the first governor. [2]

---

[1] Congress, in its appeal to the states, September 13th, 1779, declared that "that period had past" when honest men could doubt of the success of the Revolution. The greatness of Washington, the immense cost of our liberty, the intolerable wrongs and cruelties of the war, cannot be appreciated without a study of the financial history of the Revolution — the most painful and gloomy, yet one of the most instructive chapters in our history. — See Ramsay, Marshall, Washington's Letters, and Felt's Massachusetts Currency.

[2] Barry's History of Massachusetts, iii. 177–182.

DISCOURSE VIII.

THOU SHALT PROVIDE OUT OF ALL THE PEOPLE ABLE MEN, SUCH AS FEAR GOD, MEN OF TRUTH, HATING COVETOUSNESS; AND PLACE SUCH OVER THEM TO BE RULERS. — Exodus xviii. 21.

ALMIGHTY God, who governs the world, generally carries on the designs of his government by the instrumentality of subordinate agents, hereby giving scope and opportunity to his creatures to become the ministers for good to one another, in the exercise of the various powers and capacities with which he has endowed them. Though, for the vindication of his honor, to dispel the darkness and give a check to the idolatry and vice which overspread the world, and in order to prepare mankind for the reception of a Saviour, to be manifested in due time, God was pleased to take the Jewish nation under his particular care and protection, and to become their political law-giver and head; yet he made use of the agency of some of that people in the administration of his government. The legislative power he seems to have reserved wholly to himself, there being no evidence that any of the rulers or assemblies of the people had authority to make laws; but the judicial and executive powers were intrusted with men. At the first institution of the government, Moses seems to have exercised the judicial authority wholly by himself. In this business he was employed from morning till evening, when Jethro, his father-in-law, the priest and prince of Midian, came to visit him. This wise man — for such he surely was — observed to Moses that this business was too heavy for him, and what he was not able to perform alone; and therefore advised him to appoint proper persons to bear the burden with him, provided it was agreeable to the divine will. Moses, it is said in the context, hearkened to the voice of his father-in-law, and did all that he had said. There can be no doubt but that God approved this measure, — though it was first suggested by a pagan, — otherwise it would not have been adopted. It seems, indeed, to have been highly expedient, and even necessary. From whence it appears that even in this government, which was so immediately the work of God, room was left for men to make such appointments as by experience should be found necessary for the due administration of it. The general plan was laid by God, and he was the sole legislator. This was necessary in that age of darkness, idolatry, and vice. Mankind seem to have been too ignorant and corrupt to form a constitution and a code of laws in any good measure adapted to promote their piety, virtue, and happiness; but God left many smaller matters to be regulated by the wisdom and discretion of the people. This is agreeable to a general rule of the divine conduct, which is, not to accomplish that in a supernatural or miraculous way which may be done by the exertion of human powers.

It is said in the context that, in compliance with the advice of Jethro, Moses chose able men, and made them rulers; but it is generally supposed that they were chosen by the people. This is asserted by Josephus, and plainly intimated by Moses in his recapitulatory discourse, recorded in the first chapter of Deuteronomy, where he says to the people, "I spake unto you, saying, I am not able to bear you myself alone : take ye wise men, and understanding, and known among your tribes, and I will make them rulers over you." So that these officers were without doubt elected by the people, though introduced by Moses into their office. And, indeed, the Jews always exercised this right of choosing their own rulers ; even Saul and David, and all their successors in the throne, were made kings by the voice of the people.ᵃ This natural and important right God never deprived them of, though they had shown so much folly and perverseness in rejecting him and desiring to have a king like the nations around them.

The business for which Jethro advised that these rulers should be chosen was, to decide the smaller and less difficult matters of controversy that arose among the people, while causes of greater consequence were to be brought before Moses; so that they were a sort of inferior judicial officers or judges of inferior courts. Though they were not officers of the highest dignity and authority in the state, yet the Midianitish sage advised that they should be " able men, such as fear God ; men of truth, hating covetousness ; " judging that such men only were fit for office. He has here in a few words pointed out to us what sort of men are proper to be put in authority, whether in a higher or lower station ; for if such qualifications are necessary for this inferior office, they must surely be more so for the higher and supreme offices in government. And the consideration of these qualifications is what I principally intend in the following discourse. But, before I enter upon this, I would give a little attention to two or three other points. Accordingly, I shall consider,

I. The necessity of civil government to the happiness of mankind.

ᵃ See 1 Sam. xi., xv.; 2 Sam. ii., iv., v., viii.

II. The right of the people to choose their own rulers.

III. The business of rulers in general.

These particulars being finished in a few words, I shall then,

IV. Particularly consider the qualifications pointed out in the text as necessary for civil rulers.

After which, the subject will be applied to the present occasion.

I. Let us consider the necessity of civil government for the happiness of mankind. Men have, in all ages and nations, been induced, by a sense of their wants and weaknesses, as well as by their love of society, to keep up some intercourse with one another. A man totally separated from his species would be less able to provide for himself than almost any other creature. Some sort of society, some intercourse with other men, is necessary to his happiness, if not to his very existence.

Suppose, then, a number of men living near together, and maintaining that intercourse which is necessary for the supply of their wants, but without any laws or government established among them by mutual consent, or in what is called a state of nature; — in this state every one has an equal right to liberty, and to do what he thinks proper. The love of liberty is natural to all. It appears the first, operates the most forcibly, and is extinguished the last of any of our passions. And this principle would lead every man to pursue and enjoy everything to which he had an inclination. Several persons would no doubt desire and pursue the same thing, which only one could enjoy; hence contests would arise, and, no one else having a right to interfere, they must be settled by the parties; but prejudice and self-love would render them partial judges, and probably prevent an amicable settlement, so that the dispute must at last be ended by the strongest arm, and thus the liberty of the weak would be destroyed by the power of the strong. Every unsuccessful competitor would think himself injured by another's seizing that to which, in his own opinion, he had an equal right, and would endeavor to obtain compensation. This would provoke retaliation, and naturally lead on to an endless reciprocation of injuries. The injured, who found himself unable to contend with his adversary, would call in the assistance of some more powerful combatant to avenge his cause. The aggressor, too, would endeavor to strengthen himself for defence, by associates; and thus parties would be formed for rapine, devastation, and murder, and the peaceful state of nature soon be exchanged for a number of little, contending tyrannies, or for one successful one that should swallow up all the rest. This would generally be the case where men should attempt to live without laws or government; nor can they any way secure themselves against all manner of violence and injuries from bad men but by uniting together in society, agreeing upon some universal rules to be observed by all; — that controversies shall be determined, not by the parties concerned, but by disinterested judges, and according to established rules; that their determinations shall be enforced by the joint power of the whole community, either in punishing the injurious or protecting the innocent.[1] Man is not to be trusted with his unbounded love of liberty, unless it is under some other restraint than what arises from his own reason or the law of God, — these, in many instances, would make but a feeble resistance to his lust or avarice; and he would pursue his liberty to the destruction of his fellow-creatures, if he was not restrained by human laws and punishment.

Let us next consider, —

[1] See pp. 86, note a; 280, 285. — Ed.

II. The right of the people to choose their own rulers.

No man is born a magistrate, or with a right to rule over his brethren. If this were the case, there must be some natural mark by which it might be known to whom this right belongs, or it could answer no end; but no man was ever known to come into the world with any such mark of superiority and dominion.[1] If a man, by the improvement of his reason and moral powers, becomes more wise and virtuous than his brethren, this renders him better qualified for authority than others; but still he is no magistrate or lawgiver till he is appointed such by the people.

Nor has one state or kingdom a right to appoint rulers for another. This would infer such a natural inequality in mankind as is inconsistent with the equal freedom of all. One state may, indeed, by virtue of its superior power, assume this right, and the weaker state may be obliged to submit to it for want of power to resist. But it is an unjust encroachment upon their liberty, which they ought to get rid of as soon as they can. It is a mark of tyranny on one side, and of inglorious slavery on the other.

The magistrate is properly the trustee of the people. He can have no just power but what he receives from them. To them he ought to be accountable for the use he makes of this power. But if a man may be invested with the power of government, which is the united power of the community, without their consent, how can they call

---

1 " Nature knew no right divine in man,
No ill could fear in God; and understood
A Sovereign Being but a sovereign good. . . . .
Who first taught souls enslaved, and realms undone,
The enormous faith of many made for one? . . . .
Force first made conquest, and that conquest, law;
Till Superstition taught the tyrant awe,
Then shared the tyranny, then lent it aid,
And gods of conquerors, slaves of subjects, made." POPE. — ED.

him to account? What check can they have upon him,
or what security for the enjoyment of anything which
he may see fit to deprive them of? They must in this
case be slaves. But as every people have a right to be
free, they must have a right of choosing their own rulers,
and appointing such as they think most proper; because
this right is so essential to liberty, that the moment a people are deprived of it they cease to be free. This, as has
been already observed, is a right which the Jews always
enjoyed. They elected their kings, generals, judges, and
other officers; though in some few instances God did expressly point out to them the person whom they ought to
choose, which, however, he has never done with any other
people.[1]

Let us now consider, —

III. The business of rulers in general.

And this is, to promote and secure the happiness of the
whole community. For this end only they are invested
with power, and only for this end it ought to be employed.
The apostle tells us that the magistrate is God's minister
for good to the people.[2] This is the sole end for which
God has ordained that magistrates should be appointed —
that they may carry on his benevolent purposes in promoting the good and happiness of human society; and
hence their power is said to be from God; that is, it is so
while they employ it according to his will. But when
they act against the good of society, they cannot be said
to act by authority from God, any more than a servant
can be said to act by his master's authority while he acts
directly contrary to his will. And no people, we may presume, ever elected a magistrate for any other end than
their own good; consequently, when a magistrate acts

---

[1] See p. 274. — ED.   [2] See pp. 75-77, 275. — ED.

against this end, he cannot act by authority from the people; so that he acts, in this case, without any authority either from God or man. He cannot, by any lawful authority, act against, but only for the good of society. This, in general, is the business of civil rulers. But there are a variety of ways and means by which they are to carry on this business, and accomplish the important end of their institution, which it is quite beyond my present design particularly to point out, though there may be occasion to suggest some of them in the progress of my discourse. Let us now consider, —

IV. The qualifications pointed out in the text as necessary for rulers.

1. They must be able men. God has made a great difference in men in respect of their natural powers, both of body and mind; to some he has given more, to others fewer talents. Nor is there perhaps a less difference in this respect arising from education. And though there are none but what may be good members of civil society, as well as faithful servants of God, yet every one has not abilities sufficient to make him a good civil ruler. "Woe unto thee, O land, when thy king is a child," says Solomon, hereby intimating that the happiness of a people depends greatly upon the character of its rulers, and that if they resemble children in weakness, ignorance, credulity, fickleness, etc., the people will of course be very miserable. By able men may be intended men of good understanding and knowledge, — men of clear heads, who have improved their minds by exercise, acquired a habit of reasoning, and furnished themselves with a good degree of knowledge, — men who have a just conception of the nature and end of government in general, of the natural rights of mankind, of the nature and importance of civil and religious liberty, — a knowledge of human nature, of the

springs of action, and the readiest way to engage and
influence the heart, — an acquaintance with the people to
be governed, their genius, their prejudices, their interest
with respect to other states, what difficulties they are
under, what dangers they are liable to, and what they
are able to bear and do. These things are ever to be
taken into consideration by legislators when they make
laws for the internal police of a people, and in their transactions with or respecting other states. It would be going
too far to say that an honest man cannot be a good ruler
unless he be of the first character for good sense, learning,
and knowledge ; but it will not be denied that the more
he excels in these things, the more likely he will be to rule
well. He will be better able to see what measures are
suited to the temper and genius of the people, and most
conducive to the end of his institution ; how to raise
necessary supplies for the expenses of government in
ways most easy and agreeable to the people ; how to
extricate them out of difficulties in which they may be
involved ; how to negotiate with foreign powers ; how
to prevent or mitigate the calamities of war by compro-
mising differences, or putting the people into a condition
to defend themselves and repel injuries ; in a word, how
to render them happy and respectable in peace, or formidable in war. These things require a very considerable
degree of penetration and knowledge.

As it is of great importance to the community that
learning and knowledge be diffused among the people in
general, it is proper that the government should take all
proper measures for this purpose — making provision for
the establishment and support of literary schools and colleges. But ignorant and illiterate men will not be likely
to be the patrons of learning ; unacquainted with its excellency and importance, and seeing no comeliness or

beauty in it, they will reject and despise it, as the Jews did the great Teacher of wisdom who came from God. It would not be strange if such men, entrusted with the government of a people, should wholly neglect to make any provision for the encouragement of literature. It is therefore proper that rulers should be men of understanding and learning, in order to their being disposed to give due encouragement and support to the teachers and professors of the liberal arts and sciences.[1]

It may be further observed, that weak and illiterate men at the head of a government will be likely to place in inferior and subordinate offices men of their own character, merely because they know no better.

But by "able men" may be intended men of courage, of firmness and resolution of mind, — men that will not sink into despondency at the sight of difficulties, or desert their duty at the approach of danger, — men that will hazard their lives in defence of the public, either against internal sedition or external enemies; that will not fear the resentment of turbulent, factious men; that will be a terror to evil-doers, however powerful, and a protection to the innocent, however weak; men that will decide seasonably upon matters of importance, and firmly abide by their decision, not wavering with every wind that blows. There are some men that will halt between two opinions, and hesitate so long when any question of consequence is

---

[1] Mr. Hildreth says that only the constitutions of Pennsylvania, North Carolina, Massachusetts, and the second constitution of New Hampshire, made any mention of the all-important subject of education; and in the two former states the clauses which required the Legislature to establish schools remained a dead letter. Jefferson attempted to introduce a system of common schools in Virginia, but did not succeed. Only New Hampshire, Massachusetts, Connecticut, and Maryland, could boast anything like a system of public education, and many years elapsed before their example was imitated. — History of the United States, iii. 385-395. — ED.

before them, and are so easily shaken from their purpose
when they have formed one, that they are on this account
very unfit to be intrusted with public authority.[1] Such
double-minded men will be unstable in all their ways;
their indecision in council will produce none but feeble and
ineffectual exertions; and this doubting and wavering in
the supreme authority must be prejudicial to the state,
and at some critical times may be attended with fatal consequences. Wise men will not indeed determine rashly,
but when the case requires it they will resolve speedily,
and act with vigor and steadiness.[1]

By "able men" may be further intended men capable
of enduring the burden and fatigue of government, — men
that have not broken or debilitated their bodies or minds
by the effeminating pleasures of luxury, intemperance, or
dissipation. The supreme government of a people is
always a burden of great weight, though more difficult at
some times than others. It cannot be managed well without great diligence and application. Weak and effeminate
persons are therefore by no means fit to manage it. But
rulers should not only be able men, but,

2. "Such as fear God." The fear of God, in the language of Scripture, does not intend a slavish, superstitious
dread, as of an almighty, arbitrary, and cruel Being, but
that just reverence and awe of him which naturally arises
from a belief and habitual consideration of his glorious
perfections and providence, — of his being the moral governor of the world, a lover of holiness and a hater of vice,
who sees every thought and design as well as every action
of all his creatures, and will punish the impenitently vicious
and reward the virtuous. It is therefore a fear of offend-

---

[1] Promptness and decision were peculiarly necessary at that time in the
emergencies of the war. — ED.

ing him productive of obedience to his laws, and ever accompanied with hope in his mercy, and that filial love which is due to so amiable a character.

It is of great importance that civil rulers be possessed of this principle. It must be obvious to all that a practical regard to the rules of social virtue is necessary to the character of a good magistrate. Without this a man is unworthy of any trust or confidence. But no principle so effectually promotes and establishes this regard to virtue as the fear of God. A man may, indeed, from a regard to the intrinsic amiableness and excellency of virtue, from a mere sense of honor, from a love of fame, from a natural benevolence of temper, or from a prudent regard to his own temporal happiness, follow virtue when he is under no strong temptation to the contrary. But suppose him in a situation where he apprehends that temporal infamy and misery will be the certain consequence of his practising virtue, and temporal honor and happiness the consequence of his forsaking it, without any regard to God, as his ruler and judge, and can we expect that he will adhere to his duty? Will he sacrifice everything dear in this life in the cause of virtue, when he has no expectation of any reward for it beyond the grave? Will he deny himself a present gratification, without any prospect of being repaid either here or hereafter? Will he expose himself to reproach, poverty, and death, for the sake of doing good to mankind, without any regard to God as the rewarder of virtue or punisher of vice? This is not to be expected. We all love, and we ought to love, ourselves; and all wish to be happy. Why, then, should a man give up present ease and happiness for suffering and death in the cause of virtue, if he has no expectation that God will reward virtue? This would be acting against the principle of self-love, which is generally too powerful to be counter-acted.

But suppose a man to be habitually under the influence of this principle, — that is, to believe and duly consider God as his ruler and judge, who will hereafter reward virtue and punish vice with happiness and misery respectively, unspeakably greater than any to be enjoyed in this world, — and he may then, upon rational principles, and in consistency with his self-love, forego the greatest temporal good, and expose himself to the greatest temporal evil, in the cause of virtue; and we may reasonably expect that he will. Virtue will be his chief good; he will be attached to it as to his very being, with all the strength and ardor of his love and desire of happiness. The fear of God, therefore, is the most effectual and the only sure support of virtue in the world.

Men invested with civil powers are not, to be sure, less, but generally much more, exposed to temptations to violate their duty than other men. They have more frequent opportunities of committing injuries, and may do it with less fear of present punishment; and therefore stand in need of every possible restraint to keep them from abusing their power by deviating into the paths of vice.

It is further to be considered that the practice of piety, which is comprised in the fear of God, has a powerful tendency to ennoble and dignify the mind, and beget in it an abhorrence of everything mean and base; to inspire a magnanimity and fortitude of spirit that will support and carry it through the greatest dangers and difficulties; to refine and purify the heart, to disengage it from the vanities of the world, and beget that good-will and benevolence which are the brightest part of a virtuous character. Contemplating daily the perfections of the Deity, as displayed in the creation, government, and redemption of the world, must naturally tend to exalt the affections, and fix them upon divine things; to make us love and desire to imitate the moral character of God, and consequently to weaken the force of those lusts which are so apt to draw men aside and entice them into sin; to enliven every principle of virtue, and make us perfect, even as our Father in heaven is perfect.

It is also to be observed that the human mind is liable to mistake and err; that circumstances often occur, especially to those who are concerned in government, in which more wisdom is necessary than they are possessed of, even though they may be able men. In such cases we are directed to look up to God, the original and inexhaustible source of wisdom. Nor have we any reason to suspect that such applications will be in vain. God perfectly knows the human mind, and all the ways in which its views and determinations can be influenced, and he may, without infringing upon its moral liberty, by a powerful though imperceptible operation, put it into such a train of thinking as may give it a juster view and lead it to a wiser determination than it would otherwise have formed. There is, I apprehend, nothing in this supposition inconsistent with the principles of rational theology and natural religion. Nor, without supposing that God does thus interpose, is it easy to conceive how that part of the divine government which is in the hands of civil rulers should in all cases be adapted to the various circumstances of particular persons. But there is little reason to think that this light and direction will be granted to men who have no fear of God before their eyes, because, though they lack wisdom, they will not ask it of God, who giveth to all men liberally, and upbraideth not. And rulers being without this divine counsel, it will not be strange if, merely for this reason, their conduct is wrong and ill-judged, calculated in many instances not for the good, but the hurt of the people, and, it may be, at a critical time, for their utter destruction.

There can be no doubt but God often brings distress and ruin upon a sinful people through the ill-management of their rulers, given up to error and blindness. In the nineteenth chapter of Isaiah we have a prophecy of the overthrow of the kingdom of Egypt; and the infatuation of their rulers is mentioned as one of the immediate causes of this calamity. "The spirit of Egypt," says God, "shall fail, and I will destroy the counsel thereof." It is afterwards added, "Surely the princes of Zoan are fools, the counsel of the wise counsellors of Pharaoh is become brutish." And in the twenty-ninth chapter of the same book God threatens his own people that, for their hypocrisy and other wickedness, "the wisdom of their wise men shall perish, and the understanding of their prudent men shall be hid." In the same way, it is reasonable to suppose, God often brings his judgments upon other nations. And, therefore, if a people desire to have rulers of wise and understanding hearts, counselled and directed by Heaven, they should take care that they be men who fear God.

Let me observe, once more, that it is of great importance to their happiness that religion and virtue generally prevail among a people; and in order to this, government should use its influence to promote them. Rulers should encourage them, not only by their example, but by their authority; and the people should invest them with power to do this, so far as is consistent with the sacred and inalienable rights of conscience, which no man is supposed to give up, or may lawfully give up, when he enters into society. But, reserving these, the people may and ought to give up every right and power to the magistrate which will enable him more effectually to promote the common good, without putting it in his power essentially to injure it. He ought, therefore, to have power to punish all open acts of profaneness and impiety, as tending, by way of example, to destroy that reverence of God which is the only effectual support of moral virtue, and all open acts of vice, as prejudicial to society. He should have power to provide for the institution and support of the public worship of God, and public teachers of religion and virtue, in order to maintain in the minds of the people that reverence of God, and that sense of moral obligation, without which there can be no confidence, no peace or happiness in society.

Without such care in government, there is danger that the people will forget the God that is above, and abandon themselves to vice; or, to say the least, impiety and vice are much less likely to become general where such care is taken than where it is not. And God having, in the constitution of nature, made religion and virtue conducive, and even necessary, to the happiness of human society, he has thereby plainly taught us that it is the duty and business of society, as such, or of the civil magistrate, to do everything to promote them that may be done without injuring the rights of conscience. And no man who has full liberty of inquiring and examining for himself, of openly publishing and professing his religious sentiments, and of worshipping God in the time and manner which he chooses, without being obliged to make any religious profession, or attend any religious worship contrary to his sentiments, can justly complain that his rights of conscience are infringed.[1] And such liberty and freedom

---

[1] The scheme here indicated by Mr. Howard resembled that in the constitution of Maryland, which authorized a "general and equal tax" for the support of the Christian religion, to be applied to the maintenance of

every man may enjoy, though the government should require him to pay his proportion towards supporting public teachers of religion and morality.

Taking this care of religion is so plain and important a duty, that the government which should wholly neglect it would not only act a very unwise and imprudent part with respect to themselves, but be guilty of base ingratitude and a daring affront to Heaven.[1] By such conduct they would, as a community, in effect adopt the language of the profane fatalists mentioned by Job, who "say unto God, depart from us, for we desire not the knowledge of thy ways. What is the Almighty that we should serve him ? And what profit shall we have if we pray unto him ? " Now, although it is possible that rulers who have no religion themselves may enact proper laws to support it among the people, yet it is to be remembered that their example will have great influence, and, if that be irreligious and vicious, will in some measure defeat the good effects of their authority, and do more to spread corruption than that will to prevent it. It is therefore highly proper, in

such minister as the tax-payer should designate, or, if he preferred it, to the support of the poor. — Hildreth's U. S., iii. 383. See p. 298. — ED.

[1] A clear and concise summary of the early constitutional provisions in the several states on the subject of religion may be found in Mr. Hildreth's History of the United States, iii. 382–385. At the beginning of the Revolution, Congregationalism was the established religion in Massachusetts, New Hampshire, and Connecticut; the Church of England in all the southern colonies, and partially so in New York and New Jersey. The equality of all Protestant sects was recognized in Rhode Island, Pennsylvania, and Delaware; and of the Roman Catholics in the last two. The priests of the last-named sect were liable to perpetual imprisonment or death in Massachusetts and New York. In its history, principles, and sympathies, Catholicism was said to be subversive of free government; an enemy — open or concealed, as expedient in its progress — to free institutions, the printing-press, common schools, popular education, the Bible, and freedom of opinion and speech — the safeguards of liberty. — ED.

order to promote piety and good morals among the people, that rulers be men who fear God — who have a just sense of religion on their own minds, and conform to it in their lives.

It may be proper to add, that though the fear of God may exist where there is no knowledge or belief of Christianity, yet that the scheme of doctrines contained in the gospel is much better calculated than any other known to the world to produce and strengthen that divine principle. The plan of redemption which it unfolds for the fallen race of men exhibits the Deity in the most amiable light, as the perfection of love and benevolence. " The solemn scenes which it opens beyond the grave; the resurrection of the dead; the general judgment; the equal distribution of rewards and punishments to the good and bad, and the full completion of divine wisdom and goodness in the final establishment of order, perfection, and happiness," afford such motives to the love and reverence of God, and to the practice of all holiness and virtue, as can be drawn from no other scheme of religion ; and, therefore, a belief of the gospel of Christ may justly be considered as an important qualification for a civil ruler.

I might observe further, under this particular, that impious, immoral men at the head of government, and having authority to appoint subordinate officers, will probably make choice of men of their own character, and in this way be a means of spreading corruption, and of much injury to society.[1] But I must pass on to consider another qualification of rulers. For,

3. They must be men of truth.

This means men free from deceit and hypocrisy, guile, and falsehood, — men who will not, by flattery and cajoling, by falsehood and slandering a competitor, endeavor to

[1] See pp. 69, 70, 274. — ED.

get into authority; and who, when they are in, will conscientiously speak the truth in all their declarations and promises, and punctually fulfil all their engagements.

In treating with other states they will act with the same integrity which honest men do in their private affairs, and promise nothing but what they intend and think they shall be able to perform. Engagements already made to other powers they will honestly endeavor to fulfil, so far as it belongs to their department, without seeking or pretending a cause for failure when no such cause exists.[1]

They will show the same integrity and fidelity in their conduct towards individuals. They will not promise to any one what they have reason to think they cannot or do not intend to perform. Promises of government already made, the execution of which belongs to them, they will

---

[1] "I hold the maxim no less applicable to public than to private affairs, that 'honesty is always the best policy.' . . . . . Observe good faith and justice towards all nations; cultivate peace and harmony with all: religion and morality enjoin this conduct; and can it be good policy that does not equally enjoin it? It will be worthy of a free, enlightened, and, at no distant period, a great nation, to give to mankind the magnanimous and too novel example of a people always guided by an exalted justice and benevolence. Who can doubt that, in the course of time and things, the fruits of such a plan would richly repay any temporary advantages which might be lost by a steady adherence to it? Can it be that Providence has not connected the permanent felicity of a nation with its virtue? The experiment, at least, is recommended by every sentiment which ennobles human nature. Alas! is it rendered impossible by its vices?"— Washington's Farewell.

"The pretended depth and difficulty in matters of state is a mere cheat. From the beginning of the world to this day you never found a commonwealth where the leaders, having honesty enough, wanted skill enough to lead her to her true interest at home and abroad."— Harrington.

"The laws by which God governs the world must be quite altered, the course of nature must be reversed, before it can reasonably be hoped that unrighteous schemes will operate for the real advantage of a people."— Hemmenway.— ED.

look upon themselves bound to fulfil, if possible, that no man may be a sufferer by confiding in the public faith.

Civil rulers generally bind themselves expressly, and always implicitly, by accepting their office, faithfully to discharge the duties of it, — and a man of truth will pay a sacred regard to this engagement. He will not content himself with receiving the honors and emoluments of his office while he neglects the duties of it. Considering that he has solemnly bound himself to do this business, he will give the same care and attention to it that a prudent man in a private station does to his own particular concerns. A man of truth will not undertake an office for which he thinks himself incapable, because this would be promising to do what he is conscious he is incapable of doing; nor will he be instrumental of appointing others to offices for which he thinks them unqualified: this would be acting falsely; because, by the appointment, he declares that he thinks them qualified. Having solemnly engaged to use his power for the public good, he will never employ it in encouraging and supporting the enemies of his country, or carry on, under the mask of patriotism, measures to promote his own selfish and private views, or to screen and protect from public justice offenders against society. He will not employ his abilities to impose upon the understandings of others, and make the worse appear the better reason, in order to disguise truth and pervert justice. He will not suffer one man, or one part of the community, to be injured and robbed by another, when his office enables him to prevent it, because this would be violating his promise. In a word, he will to his utmost endeavor to answer the end of his institution by performing the duties of his station, and manifest by all his conduct that he is an honest, upright man. He will make no false pretences, he will put on no false appearances, but ever act with Christian simplicity and godly sincerity.

Such will be the conduct of men of truth, and such men only are proper to be entrusted with authority over a free people. Rulers of this character will be honored, beloved, and confided in by their countrymen, and respected by other nations; their subjects will be easy and happy, united together in the bonds of truth and love, and by their union able to defend themselves against invaders; their government, resting on the basis of truth and justice, will be firm and stable, revered and honored both at home and abroad. Whereas that deceit and hypocrisy, that falsehood and insincerity, that dissimulation and craftiness, which have so often dictated the measures of government in most of the nations of the earth, and which are expressly recommended to rulers by Machiavel, and inculcated, among other immoralities, as necessary parts of a good education, in the celebrated and much-admired letters of a late British nobleman to his son,[a] however they may sometimes succeed and procure some temporary advantages, will almost always weaken and disgrace the government which practises them,[b] by sapping the foundation of public credit, producing uneasy jealousies, disaffection, divisions, and contempt of authority among the people, and leading them by example to the practice of the same insincerity, falsehood, and dishonesty towards one another which they see in their rulers, and by rendering them infamous in the eyes of other nations, and perhaps raising up enemies to punish their perfidy.

And it may without doubt be asserted with truth, upon the principles both of natural religion and revelation, that that government which is directed by truth and integrity

[a] Lord Chesterfield.

[b] "There is no safety where there is no strength, no strength without union, no union without justice, no justice where faith and truth in accomplishing public and private engagements is wanting." — Sydney's discourses concerning government.

will bid the fairest to secure and promote the happiness of the community, however contrary this assertion may be to the principles and practices of modern courtiers and politicians. But I must proceed to the other qualification of a good ruler mentioned in the text, which is

4. "Hating covetousness." Covetousness, you all know, is an inordinate desire of riches, — such a desire as will make a man pursue them by unlawful means, and prevent his using them in a right manner. Hating covetousness is a strong expression to denote a freedom from this vicious temper, and a sense of its unreasonableness and turpitude.

That it is of great importance that civil rulers have this qualification will be evident on a little reflection.

Covetousness is a fruitful source of corruption. A man governed by this appetite will be guilty of any enormity for the sake of gratifying it. "They that will be rich fall into temptation and a snare, and into many foolish and hurtful lusts, which drown men in destruction and perdition ; for the love of money is the root of all evil." Almost all the oppression, fraud, and violence that has been done under the sun, has owed is rise and progress to covetousness. The indulgence of this vice debases the mind, and renders it incapable of anything generous and noble; contracts its views, destroys the principles of benevolence, friendship, and patriotism, and gives a tincture of selfishness to all its sentiments. It hardens the heart, and makes it deaf to the cries of distress and the dictates of charity ; it blinds and perverts the judgment, and disposes it to confound truth and falsehood, right and wrong.

A civil ruler, under the direction of this principle, will oppress and defraud his subjects whenever he has it in his power ; he will neglect the duties of his office whenever he can promote his private interest by the neglect ; he will enact laws to serve himself, not the community; and he will enact none that he thinks would be prejudicial to his private interest, however beneficial they might be to the public, however necessary for the support of justice and equity between man and man; he will pervert justice, and rob the innocent for bribes; he will discourage every measure that would occasion expense to himself, however salutary to his country. Rather than part with his money, he will see the arts and sciences, which are so ornamental and friendly to a community, languish, erudition starve, and the rising genius which promised glory to his country nipped in the bud by the cold hand of poverty; yea, religion itself, the greatest honor and blessing of society, he will see languish and die, rather than impart anything to support its cause. And having long looked upon riches in the same light that good men do upon religion, as his chief good, and feeling the same attachment to them which they do to that, he may, if required by laws already made to pay anything for its support, absurdly plead that it is against his conscience, strangely mistaking his love of money for the love of God, and his covetousness for his conscience; supposing, with those corrupters of religion mentioned by the apostle, "that gain is godliness." If he has a voice in the appointment of subordinate officers, he will sell his vote to the highest bidder, and appoint such as will be most subservient to his private interest, however unqualified for the office. In a word, all his conduct, all his reasoning and votes, will be tinctured by his selfish spirit; and in a critical time, when great expense is necessary for the public safety, he may by his parsimony be a means of the ruin of his country.

But a ruler who hates covetousness will conduct in a very different manner. He will never oppress or wrong the community; the public interest will be always safe in his hands; he will freely expend his time and his estate in discharging the duties of his office for the good of his country; he will be ever ready to promote good laws, though they deprive him of opportunities of making gain, and involve him in expense; he will devise liberal things, and cheerfully bear his part in the expense necessary to carry on every measure that promises advantage to his country; he will do all in his power to promote the liberal arts and sciences, manufactures, and all useful inventions, to encourage men of learning and genius, and to aid the cause of religion and virtue. In promoting men to places of trust, he will be influenced by no selfish, private views, but by a regard to the public good; no bribe will purchase his vote for an unfit man, and, hating covetousness himself, no consideration will induce him to give it for a sordid, avaricious wretch; he will neglect no measures necessary for the public safety and happiness for fear of parting with his money. In fine, all his conduct will bear the marks of his nobleness and liberality of sentiment, of his disinterestedness and public spirit.

I have now considered the several qualifications of a good ruler mentioned in the text; and they all appear necessary to form that character, whether in the legislative, executive, or judicial department. Nor is it easy to say in which they are most necessary, though it is not difficult to see that the want of any one of them in either must be prejudicial and dangerous to the community.

But I must now make some reflections upon the subject, and apply it to the present occasion. And,

1. What has been said of the necessity of government for the peace and happiness of mankind may lead us to reflect with shame upon the selfishness and corruption of our species, who, with all their rational and moral powers, can no otherwise be kept from injuring and de-

stroying one another than by superior force, or the fear of
temporal sufferings and punishment, and with whom you
are no longer safe than it is unsafe for them to hurt you.
This is a very humiliating consideration ; and, so far as we
know, there is no other order of creatures throughout the
boundless universe who, if left to their natural liberty,
would be so mischievous to one another as man.

2. This may also lead us to reflect, with pleasure and
gratitude to God, upon the steps which have been taken
by this people to frame a new constitution of government, and that a plan has been formed which appears, in
general, so well calculated to guard the rights and liberties, and promote the happiness of society, and which, it
is to be hoped, will soon be the foundation of our government, instead of that insecure basis upon which it now
rests.[1]

[1] The constitution framed by the convention Sept. 1, 1779—March 2,
1780, was adopted by the people, and the first Legislature under it assembled at Boston, October 25, 1780.

That " ALL MEN ARE BORN FREE AND EQUAL" was inserted in the
Declaration of Rights by the late Judge Lowell, father of Rev. Dr. Charles
Lowell, of the West Church, with express reference to the abolition of
slavery. It was simply *declaratory* of public opinion, which expressed
itself in our early laws, but with more force and distinctness, in later
years, from the pulpit and the press. I have found frequent and earnest
reference to the subject in the sermons of the period, from which this
volume is a selection.

The Rev. Dr. Hemmenway, in a profound discourse on " A CHRISTIAN
STATE," — Massachusetts Election, 1784, — alluding to a legal decision
then lately made by the Supreme Judicial Court in that commonwealth,
interpreting the clause, " All men are born free and equal," and involving
the existence of slavery, used these words : " We rejoice to find the right of
enslaving our fellow-men is absolutely disclaimed, ... is at length pro-
scribed, and is no longer suffered to live with us. And it is devoutly
wished that the turf may lie firm on its grave." Yet the system in Massachusetts seems to have partaken rather of the *spirit*, though not of the
form, of the old English relation of master and servant, or apprenticeship,

3. We may likewise see, from what has been said, how much it is the duty and interest of a people to pay due submission to the orders of government, and to endeavor unitedly to support its authority. Both rulers and subjects are perhaps too apt to consider their respective interests as distinct and separate, whereas they are in truth one and the same — the prosperity and happiness of the whole community. Everything done by subjects in obedience to and support of the just authority of government, is conducive to their own happiness ; and everything done by governors that is beneficial to the governed, is likewise so to themselves ; and it is from the mutual endeavors of both to serve each other that the prosperity of society must result. If rulers abuse their power they may destroy the happiness of the community, but this may be done as effectually by the subjects' refusing to obey and support the authority of government.[1] Nor may any people expect to enjoy all the blessings of society unless their government is preserved in due force and vigor.

4. We are reminded of the gratitude which we owe to God that he has not permitted the natural and important right which every society has of electing its own rulers to be wrested out of our hands, as is the case

than of unlimited ownership; for the courts sometimes recognized in them rights inconsistent with the latter.

It is worthy of note that no distinct provision on the subject of slavery appears in any state constitution, except that of Delaware, which provided that "no person hereafter imported from Africa ought to be held in slavery under any pretence whatever;" and that "no negro, Indian, or mulatto slave ought to be brought into this state for sale from any part of the world."—Hildreth's History of the United States, iii. 390, 391, 392. — ED.

[1] See pp. 87, 276. — ED.

in some other countries. Had Great Britain carried on without opposition the measures she was pursuing with us, we should probably in a little time have been wholly deprived of this privilege. She had already assumed an absolute right of appointing two brances of the Legislature.[1] These would have had the appointment of all judicial and military officers. And upon the same ground that she robbed us of the election of a governor formerly, and of councillors lately, she might have annihilated the House of Representatives ; or, if she had not done this in form, she might, by bribery and corruption, have rendered that House a mere tool to the servants of the crown, as is the case in that country.[2] It is therefore owing to the opposition which this people made to the measures of the British court, and to the blessing of God upon that opposition, that they have now a voice in appointing their own rulers ; otherwise our government might now have been in the hands of the weakest and most profligate favorites of that corrupt and infatuated court.

5. We are reminded how much it is the duty and interest of a people who are in the enjoyment of this right to

---

[1] The governor and council. — ED.

[2] Thomas Paine, in "The Crisis, Number III.," one of his popular political appeals in 1775, addressed " To the King," used this language: " Sir, it is not your rotten troop in the present House of Commons; it is not your venal, beggarly, pensioned lords; it is not your polluted, canting, prostituted bench of bishops; it is not your whole set of abandoned ministers, nor all your army of Scotch cut-throats, that can protect you from the people's rage." This not elegant but energetic appeal represents the contemporary feeling towards the British government, and was the language best suited to the times that " tried men's souls." The Earl of Chatham said, in the House of Peers, in 1770: " I do not say, my lords, that corruption lies *here*, or that corruption lies *there*; but if any gentleman in England were to ask me whether I thought both Houses of Parliament were bribed, I should laugh in his face, and say, '*Sir, it is not so!*' " See also p. 244, note 1. — ED.

exercise it with prudence and integrity. The people's appointing their own rulers will be no security for their good government and happiness if they pay no regard to the character of the men they appoint. A dunce or a knave, a profligate or an avaricious worldling, will not make a good magistrate because he is elected by the people. To make this right of advantage to the community, due attention must be paid to the abilities and moral character of the candidate. This is a consideration that concerns this people at large, as all have a voice in the election of our rulers, either personally or by their representatives. But upon this occasion it is proper to observe that it especially concerns the members of the honorable Council and House of Representatives here present, by whom the councillors for the ensuing year are this day to be elected. And I shall not, I hope, be thought to go beyond my line of duty [1] if I say that the electors ought not to give their votes at random, or from personal or private views. They act in this business in a public character, by virtue of power delegated to them by the people, to whom, as well as to God, the origin of all power, they are accountable for the use they make of it. Nor can they answer it to either, or even to their own consciences, if, through interested or party views, they advance to the council-board men unqualified for the important duties of that station. At such a critical time as the present, the want of wisdom or integrity in that House may be attended with the most fatal consequences. The advice of Jethro in the text demands the consideration of all those who are to bear a part in the elections of this day: " Provide out of all the people able men, such as fear God, — men of truth, hating covetousness." There never was a time when such men were more necessary at that board than the present. Nor would I

---

[1] See pp. xxv., xxix. — xxxviii., 47, 54. — ED.

entertain an opinion so dishonorable to my country as to suppose there are not such men in it; though I cannot, at the same time, entertain an idea so flattering as to suppose there are not many among us who fall far short of this character. It belongs to the present electors to distinguish, so far as they can, these characters one from the other, and to give their votes only for the former. Whoever considers the part which this Board has in legislation, — their authority in directing the military and naval force of the state, their being invested with the supreme executive power, and, in some important cases, with a supreme judicial power, — will be sensible that great wisdom, integrity, and fortitude are necessary for the right management of these powers. Should they be committed to men of small abilities and little knowledge, — men unacquainted with the nature of government, and with the circumstances of this state, — men void of integrity, of narrow, contracted views, governed by ambition, avarice, or some other selfish passion, — men of no fortitude and resolution, of dastardly, effeminate spirits, — should such men, I say, be intrusted with the great and important powers vested in the Council, what could be expected but that their public conduct would bear the marks of their ignorance, weakness, effeminacy, and selfishness, to the great injury and dishonor, if not to the ruin, of the Commonwealth? And though such men may be as fond of this station as those who are best qualified for it, and perhaps much fonder, yet it would be so far from rendering them truly honorable, that it would only render them the more infamous, by bringing into public view their vices and defects, while the electors of such men would fix an indelible stain upon their own characters, and inherit the curses of the present and future generations.

But men who have themselves been honored by the unbiased suffrages of their country must surely be too wise and virtuous thus to prostitute their votes; and it may, I hope, be taken for granted that knowledge and integrity, the fear of God, and a public spirit, will govern in the ensuing election, and such men be raised to the council-board as will do honor to that respectable station, to their electors, and themselves.[1]

I now beg leave, with all due deference and submission, to suggest a few things that may reasonably be expected of a General Court, composed of such men as the text describes, by the people who have invested them with this power and authority. It may be expected that they will give due attention to the public affairs committed to their care. By accepting a seat in either House, a man does, implicitly at

[1] COUNCILLORS FOR 1780.

For the old Colony of MASSACHUSETTS BAY:

† Hon. JAMES BOWDOIN, Esq.;   Hon. SAMUEL NILES, Esq.;
THOMAS CUSHING, Esq.;   SAMUEL BAKER, Esq.;
JABEZ FISHER, Esq.;   JOHN PITTS, Esq.;
SAMUEL HOLTON, Esq.;   † ELEAZER BROOKS, Esq.;
MOSES GILL, Esq.;   AARON WOOD, Esq.;
† BENJ. AUSTIN, Esq.;   † STEPHEN CHOATE, Esq.;
TIMOTHY DANIELSON, Esq.;   † CALEB STRONG, Esq.;
JOSIAH STONE, Esq.;   † WILLIAM WHITING, Esq.;
ABRAHAM FULLER, Esq.;   † JOSEPH DORR, Esq.

For the late Colony of NEW PLYMOUTH:

Hon. WALTER SPOONER, Esq.;   Hon. NATHAN CUSHING, Esq.;
DAN. DAVIS, Esq.;   THOMAS DURFEE, Esq.

For the late Province of MAINE:

Hon. JERE. POWELL, Esq.;   Hon. EDWARD CUTT, Esq.;
Hon. JOSEPH SIMPSON, Esq.

For SAGADAHOCK:

Hon. HENRY GARDNER, Esq.

AT LARGE:

† Hon. ROBERT TREAT PAINE, ESQ.;   Hon. BENJAMIN WHITE, Esq.

† Not of the Board the last year.

— ED.

least, solemnly engage to attend to the business which is there to be transacted. Nor do I see how he can with any propriety be called a man of truth who, after such engagement, neglects that business, for the sake of going to his farm, his merchandise, or his pleasure. It appears to me that such neglect argues great unfaithfulness in the delinquents, and it may be attended with very pernicious consequences. Individuals may, and often do, plead in excuse for this, that the business may be done without them; but they ought to remember that every one has an equal right to excuse himself by this plea, and if all should do so, the concerns of the public must be wholly neglected. But it may be justly expected that our civil rulers will take due care to provide for the public defence. Notwithstanding the great exertions we have already made, and the great things which God has done for us, we must still contend with the enemies of our rights and liberties, or become their abject slaves. And it depends in a great measure upon our public rulers, under God, whether we shall contend with success or not. It is by their seasonable and prudent measures that an army is to be provided and furnished with necessaries to oppose the enemy; and it must be the wish of every true American that nothing may be omitted which can be done to support and render successful so important a cause, — a cause so just in the sight of God and man, which Heaven has so remarkably owned, and all wise and good men approved, — a cause which not only directly involves in it the rights and liberties of America, but in which the happiness of mankind is so nearly concerned, — for in this extensive light I have always considered the cause in which we are contending. Should our enemies finally prevail, and establish that absolute dominion over us at which they aim, they would not only render us the most miserable of all nations, but probably be able, by the riches and forces of America, to triumph over the arms of France and Spain, and carry their conquests to every corner of the globe; nor can we doubt but that they would carry them wherever there was wealth to tempt the enterprise. The noble spirit of liberty which has arisen in Ireland[1] would be instantly crushed, and the brave men who have appeared foremost in its support be rewarded with an axe or a halter. The few advocates for this suffering cause in Britain would be hunted and persecuted as enemies to government, and be obliged in despair to abandon her interest. And in every country where this event should be known the friends of liberty would be disheartened, and, seeing her in the power of her enemies, forsake her, as the disciples of Christ did their Master; so that our being subdued to the will of our enemies might, in its consequences, be the banishment of liberty from among mankind. The heaven-born virgin, seeing her votaries slain, her altars overthrown, and her temples demolished, and finding no safe habitation on earth, would be obliged, like the great patron of liberty the First-born of God, to ascend to her God and our God, her Father and our Father, from whom she was sent to bless mankind, leaving an ungrateful world, after she had, like him, been "rejected and despised of men," in slavery and misery, till with him she shall again descend to reign and triumph on earth. Such might be the consequence should the arms of Britain triumph over us. Whereas, if America preserves her freedom, she will be an asylum for the oppressed and persecuted of every country; her example and

---

[1] Towards the close of the American war there sprang up in Ireland a large party, who declared that no power on earth could bind Ireland but its own king, lords, and commons. January 1, 1800, the separate legislature of Ireland being suppressed, its legislative union with Great Britain was effected. — ED.

success will encourage the friends and rouse a spirit of liberty through other nations, and will probably be the means of freedom and happiness to Ireland, and perhaps in time to Great Britain, and many other countries. So that our contest is not merely for our own families, friends, and posterity, but for the rights of humanity, for the civil and religious privileges of mankind. We have surely, then, a right to expect that the government of this state will neglect no measure that is necessary on their part to aid so interesting a cause, whatever difficulties or expense may attend it; and I hope it may with equal confidence be expected that the people will cheerfully lend their arms and bear the expense that may be required for so glorious a purpose. Great expense must, without doubt, be necessary to carry on our defence; but whoever is disposed on this account to give up the dispute, proves himself totally unworthy of the liberty for which we are contending.

As the support, or rather the recovery, of the public credit is absolutely necessary to our having a respectable army in the field, as well as to our internal peace and prosperity, it may be expected that this government will not be wanting in any measure for this purpose which wisdom and sound policy can suggest.

If by means of the depreciation of our paper currency, and any law of this state, many persons have suffered, and are still liable to suffer great injury, — if this injustice falls principally upon widows and fatherless children, and such others as are least able to support themselves under the loss, — this surely is an evil that ought speedily to be redressed; and, if it be possible, compensation should be made to the sufferers by those who have grown rich by this iniquity. And as the General Court of the last year did with great justice make an allowance for the depreciation of the currency, in fixing their own wages, and in some other instances, it may justly be expected that the honorable court of this year will go on to extend this justice to every part of the community, and order the same allowance to be made in discharging all debts and contracts, however their private interests may be thereby affected.

The large taxes now levying, and to be levied, make it peculiarly proper that great care should be taken in fixing the proportion which the different parts of the community are respectively to pay; and we have a right to expect that our honored fathers who are to guard the rights of the whole will not require any particular part to bear a greater proportion of this burden than is just, considering its ability and circumstances.

Liberty and learning are so friendly to each other, and so naturally thrive and flourish together, that we may justly expect that the guardians of the former will not neglect the latter. The good education of children is a matter of great importance to the commonwealth. Youth is the time to plant the mind with the principles of virtue, truth and honor, the love of liberty and of their country, and to furnish it with all useful knowledge; and though in this business much depends upon parents, guardians, and masters, yet it is incumbent upon the government to make provision for schools and all suitable means of instruction. Our college justly claims the patronage and assistance of the state, in return for the able men with which she has furnished the public,[1] not to observe that her present suffering and low state renders her an object of pity. By the well-known depreciation, she, as well as many of her sons in the ministry, have lost a great part of their income, — she and they having in this respect had the same hard lot with widows and orphans.[2] Nor will I suppose that we shall ever have a General Court of so little love to their

1 See p. xxxiv. — ED.   2 See page 368, note 1. — ED.

country, or so little sensible of the importance of literature to its virtue, liberty, and happiness — so barbarous and savage as to suffer her, or any of her family, to languish in poverty, or to want what is necessary to their making a decent and honorable appearance.[1]

If anything can be done by government to discourage prodigality and extravagance, vain and expensive amusements and fantastic foppery, and to encourage the opposite virtues, we may reasonably hope it will not be neglected. The fondness of our countrymen — or, shall I say, country-women? — for showy and useless ornaments, and other articles of luxury, has been remarked by a gentleman in Europe, of great eminence for political wisdom, as very unbecoming our present circumstances. This is a folly that bodes ill to the public, and it must be the wish of every wise and good man that it were laid aside. Men in authority, if they can do no more, may at least discountenance it by their example, and this will not be without its good effect.

Finally, our political fathers will not fail to do all they can to promote religion and virtue through the community, as the surest means of rendering their government easy and happy to themselves and the people. For this purpose they will watch over their morals with the same affectionate and tender care that a pious and prudent parent watches over his children, and, by all the methods which love to God and man can inspire and wisdom point out, endeavor to check and suppress all impiety and vice, and lead the people to the practice of that righteousness which exalteth a nation. If any new laws are wanting, or more care in the execution of laws already made, for discouraging profaneness, intemperance, lewdness, extravagant gaming, extortion, fraud, oppression, or any other

[1] See pp. 335, 352, 367. — ED.

vice, they will take speedy care to supply this defect, and render themselves a terror to evil-doers, as well as an encouragement to such as do well. They will promote to places of trust men of piety, truth, and benevolence. Nor will they fail to exhibit in their own lives a fair example of that piety and virtue which they wish to see practised by the people. They will show that they are not ashamed of the gospel of Christ, by paying a due regard to his sacred institutions, and to all the laws of his kingdom. Magistrates may probably do more in this way than in any other, and perhaps more than any other order of men, to preserve or recover the morals of a people. The manners of a court are peculiarly catching, and, like the blood in the heart, quickly flow to the most distant members of the body. If, therefore, rulers desire to see religion and virtue flourish in the community over which they preside, they must countenance and encourage them by their own example. And to excite them to this, I must not omit to observe that, though the fear of God, a regard to truth, and a hatred of covetousness, are necessary to form the character of a good ruler, they are, if possible, still more necessary to form the character of a good man, and secure the approbation of God, the Judge of all; for to him magistrates, in common with other men, are accountable. Nor does he regard the persons of princes any more than of their subjects. If they are impious and vicious, if they abuse their power, they may bring great misery upon other men, but they will surely bring much greater upon themselves. The eye of Heaven surveys all their counsels, designs, and actions; and the day is coming when these shall all be made manifest, and every one receive according to his works. Happy they who in that day shall be found faithful, for they shall lift up their heads with confidence, and, amidst applauding angels, enter into they joy of their Lord; while those who have oppressed and injured the people by their power, and corrupted them by their example, shall be covered with shame and confusion, and sentenced to that place of blackness and darkness, where there is weeping, and wailing, and gnashing of teeth!

Let me now conclude by reminding this assembly in general that it concerns us all to fear God, and to be men of truth, hating covetousness. The low and declining state of religion and virtue among us is too obvious not to be seen, and of too threatening an aspect not to be lamented, by all the lovers of God and their country. Though our happiness as a community depends much upon the conduct of our rulers, yet it is not in the power of the best government to make an impious, profligate people happy. How well soever our public affairs may be managed, we may undo ourselves by our vices. And it is from hence, I apprehend, that our greatest danger arises. That spirit of infidelity, selfishness, luxury, and dissipation, which so deeply marks our present manners, is more formidable than all the arms of our enemies. Would we but reform our evil ways, humble ourselves under the corrections, and be thankful for the mercies of Heaven; revive that piety and public spirit, that temperance and frugality, which have entailed immortal honor on the memory of our renowned ancestors; we might then, putting our trust in God, humbly hope that our public calamities would be soon at an end, our independence established, our rights and liberties secured, and glory, peace, and happiness dwell in our land. Such happy effects to the public might we expect from a general reformation.

But let every one remember that, whatever others may do, and however it may fare with our country, it shall surely be well with the righteous; and when all the mighty states and empires of this world shall be dissolved, and pass away "like the baseless fabric of a vision," they shall enter into the kingdom of their Father, which cannot be moved, and, in the enjoyment and exercise of perfect peace, liberty, and love, shine forth as the sun forever and ever.

The UNITED STATES elevated to Glory and Honor.

A

S E R M O N,

Preached before

His E x c e l l e n c y

JONATHAN TRUMBULL, Esq L.L.D.

Governor and Commander in Chief,

And the H o n o r a b l e

The GENERAL ASSEMBLY

O F

The State of CONNECTICUT,

Convened at Hartford,

At the

Anniverſary E l e c t i o n,

May 8th, 1783.

By E z r a S t i l e s, D. D.

P r e s i d e n t o f Y a l e - C o l l e g e.

N E W - H A V E N:

Printed by THOMAS & SAMUEL GREEN.

M,DCC,LXXXIII.

At a General Assembly of the Governor and Company of the State of Connecticut, holden at Hartford on the second Thursday of May, Anno Dom. 1783.

Ordered, That Roger Sherman, Esq., and Captain Henry Daggett return the thanks of this Assembly to the Reverend Doctor Ezra Stiles for his Sermon delivered before the Assembly on the 8th instant; and desire a copy thereof, that it may be printed.

A true copy of Record,

Examined by

GEORE WYLLYS, Secretary.

EDITOR'S PREFATORY NOTE.

PRESIDENT STILES was one of the most learned and high-minded men of his time. He was familiar with the lore of the Hebrew and Christian Church. He conversed and corresponded in Hebrew, Latin, and French, with facility, and was learned in the Oriental literature and antiquities connected with Biblical history. He taught in astronomy, chemistry, and philosophy. He and his friend Dr. Franklin were among the earliest statisticians in America, and his studies in this science exhibit the most comprehensive and enlightened views. That he was a thorough antiquary is manifest in his history of the Three Tyrannicides, and that he was a true son of New England appears in his saying that the day of the "martyrdom" of King Charles I. "ought to be celebrated as an anniversary thanksgiving that one nation on earth had so much fortitude and public justice as to make a royal tyrant bow to the sovereignty of the people."

By an extensive foreign correspondence he kept up with the progress of knowledge and discovery, to which he himself contributed. That he was a zealous and an understanding friend of civil and religious liberty, a man of practical knowledge and observation, a sagacious student of men and things, is apparent in his discourse on "Christian Union," 1760, as well as in this remarkable sermon of 1783, on the "United States elevated to Glory and Honor." Chancellor Kent said, at the Commencement at Yale College, in 1831: "President Stiles's zeal for civil and religious liberty was kindled at the altar of the English and New England Puritans, and it was animating and vivid. A more constant and devoted friend to the Revolution and independence of this country never existed. Take him for all in all, this extraordinary man was undoubtedly one of the purest and best gifted men of his age. Though he was uncompromising in his belief and vindication of the Protestant faith, he was nevertheless of the most charitable and catholic temper, resulting equally from the benevolence of his disposition and the spirit of the gospel." The Rev. Dr. Channing said of Dr. Stiles: "This country has not perhaps produced a more learned man. . . . . . His virtues were proportioned to his intellectual acquisition. . . . . . In his faith he was what is called a moderate Calvinist; but his heart was of no sect. . . . . . He desired to heal the wounds of the divided Church of Christ, not by a common creed, but by the spirit of love. . . . . . He wished to break every yoke, civil and ecclesiastical, from men's necks. To the influence of this distinguished man in the circle in which I was brought up, I may owe in part the indignation which I feel towards every invasion of human rights. In my earliest years I regarded no other human being with equal reverence." Nor did his zeal as a scholar lessen his fidelity as a pastor and preacher in his ministry at Newport, then second only to Boston in commerce.

Ezra Stiles, son of Rev. Isaac Stiles, was born in North Haven, Connecticut, December 10, 1727; graduated at Yale in 1747; delivered a Latin oration, in 1753, in memory of Dean Berkeley, and another at New Haven, in February, 1755, in honor of Dr. Franklin, with whom he had a life-long friendship. He was minister at Newport, Rhode Island, from 1755 to the beginning of the war of the Revolution, in 1777; became pastor of the North Church in Portsmouth, but was soon appointed President of Yale College, an office which he adorned; and died May 12th, 1795. The present edition of his Election Sermon is reprinted from the edition of 1783, at New Haven. It was reprinted in London, as a literary curiosity, in all the luxury and splendor of large paper and bold type. — Sparks's American Biography, xvi. 78; Sprague's Annals, i. 470, 479; Dr. Park's Life of Hopkins.

DISCOURSE IX.

AND TO MAKE THEE HIGH ABOVE ALL NATIONS WHICH HE HATH MADE, IN
PRAISE, AND IN NAME, AND IN HONOR; AND THAT THOU MAYEST BE AN
HOLY PEOPLE UNTO THE LORD THY GOD. — Deut. xxvi. 19.

TAUGHT by the omniscient Deity, Moses foresaw and
predicted the capital events relative to Israel, through the
successive changes of depression and glory, until their final
elevation to the first dignity and eminence among the
empires of the world. These events have been so ordered
as to become a display of retribution and sovereignty; for,
while the good and evil hitherto felt by this people have
been dispensed in the way of exact national retribution,
their ultimate glory and honor will be of the divine sovereignty, with a "Not for your sakes do I this, saith the
Lord, be it known unto you, but for mine holy name's
sake."

However it may be doubted whether political communities are rewarded and punished in this world only, and
whether the prosperity and decline of other empires have
corresponded with their moral state as to virtue and vice,
yet the history of the Hebrew theocracy shows that the
secular welfare of God's ancient people depended upon
their virtue, their religion, their observance of that holy covenant which Israel entered into with God on the plains at
the foot of Nebo, on the other side Jordan. Here Moses,

the man of God, assembled three million of people, — the
number of the United States, — recapitulated and gave
them a second publication of the sacred jural institute,
delivered thirty-eight years before, with the most awful
solemnity, at Mount Sinai. A law dictated with sovereign
authority by the Most High to a people, to a world, a
universe, becomes of invincible force and obligation without any reference to the consent of the governed. It is
obligatory for three reasons, viz., its original justice and
unerring equity, the omnipotent Authority by which it is
enforced, and the sanctions of rewards and punishments.
But in the case of Israel he condescended to a mutual
covenant, and by the hand of Moses led his people to
avouch the Lord Jehovah to be their God, and in the most
public and explicit manner voluntarily to engage and covenant with God to keep and obey his law. Thereupon
this great prophet, whom God had raised up for so solemn
a transaction, declared in the name of the Lord that the
Most High avouched, acknowledged, and took them for a
peculiar people to himself; promising to be their God and
Protector, and upon their obedience to make them prosperous and happy.[a] He foresaw, indeed, their rejection of
God, and predicted the judicial chastisement of apostasy —
a chastisement involving the righteous with the wicked.
But, as well to comfort and support the righteous in every
age, and under every calamity, as to make his power known
among all nations, God determined that a remnant should
be saved. Whence Moses and the prophets, by divine
direction, interspersed their writings with promises that
when the ends of God's moral government should be
answered in a series of national punishments, inflicted for
a succession of ages, he would, by his irresistible power
and sovereign grace, subdue the hearts of his people to a

a Deut. xxix. 10, 14; xxx. 9, 19.

free, willing, joyful obedience; turn their captivity; recover and gather them "from all the nations whither the Lord had scattered them in his fierce anger; bring them into the land which their fathers possessed ; and multiply them above their fathers, and rejoice over them for good, as he rejoiced over their fathers.[a]   Then the words of Moses, hitherto accomplished but in part, will be literally fulfilled, when this branch of the posterity of Abraham shall be nationally collected, and become a very distinguished and glorious people, under the great Messiah, the Prince of Peace.   He will then "make them high above all nations which he hath made, in praise, and in name, and in honor, and they shall become a holy people unto the Lord their God."

I shall enlarge no further upon the primary sense and literal accomplishment of this and numerous other prophecies respecting both Jews and Gentiles in the latter-day glory of the church ; for I have assumed the text only as introductory to a discourse upon the political welfare of God's American Israel, and as allusively prophetic of the future prosperity and splendor of the United States.   We may, then, consider —

I. What reason we have to expect that, by the blessing of God, these States may prosper and flourish into a great American Republic, and ascend into high and distinguished honor among the nations of the earth.   "To make thee high above all nations which he hath made, in praise, and in name, and in honor."

II. That our system of dominion and civil polity would be imperfect without the true religion ; or that from the diffusion of virtue among the people of any community would arise their greatest secular happiness : which will terminate in this conclusion, that holiness ought to be the end of all civil government. " That thou mayest be a holy people unto the Lord thy God."

I. The first of these propositions will divide itself into two branches, and lead us to show,

1. Wherein consists the true political welfare and prosperity, and what the civil administration necessary for the elevation and advancement of a people to the highest secular glory.

2. The reasons rendering it probable that the United States will, by the ordering of Heaven, eventually become this people. But I shall combine these together as I go along.

Dominion is founded in property, and resides where that is, whether in the hands of the few or many. The dominion founded in the feudal tenure of estate is suited to hold a conquered country in subjection, but is not adapted to the circumstances of free citizens. Large territorial property vested in individuals is pernicious to society. Civilians, in contemplating the principles of government, have judged superior and inferior partition of property necessary in order to preserve the subordination of society and establish a permanent system of dominion. This makes the public defence the interest of a few landholders only.

A free tenure of lands, an equable distribution of property, enters into the foundation of a happy state, — so far, I mean, as that the body of the people may have it in their power, by industry, to become possessed of real freehold, fee-simple estate ; for connected with this will be a general spirit and principle of self-defence — defence of our property, liberty, country. This has been singularly verified in New England, where we have realized the capital ideas of Harrington's Oceana.[1]

<hr />

[1] " The Commonwealth of Oceana," by James Harrington, Chief of the Commonwealth Club, was published in 1656, when Cromwell was in the

But numerous population, as well as industry, is necessary towards giving value to land, to judiciously partitioned territory. The public weal requires the encouragement of both. A very inconsiderable value arose from the sparse, thin settlement of the American aboriginals, of whom there are not fifty thousand souls on this side the Mississippi. The Protestant Europeans have generally bought the native right of soil, as far as they have settled, and paid the value ten-fold, and are daily increasing the value of the remaining Indian territory a thousand-fold; and in this manner we are a constant increasing revenue to the sachems and original lords of the soil. How much must the value of lands reserved to the natives of North and South America be increased to remaining Indians by the inhabitation of two or three hundred millions of Europeans?

Heaven hath provided this country, not indeed derelict, but only partially settled, and consequently open for the reception of a new enlargement of Japheth. Europe was settled by Japheth; America is settling from Europe: and perhaps this second enlargement bids fair to surpass the first; for we are to consider all the European settlements of America collectively as springing from and transfused with the blood of Japheth. Already for ages has Europe arrived to a plenary, if not declining, population of one hundred millions; in two or three hundred years this second enlargement may cover America with three times that number, if the present ratio of increase continues with

meridian. The American Republic was born of the English Commonwealth. The lineage is clear; and this reference by President Stiles to Harrington's schemes is one of many beautiful illustrations of the fact, which come up to the surface along the current of literature, and remain, as buoys, to mark the channel down which have flowed the great hopes of former days to become the verities of our own. — ED.

the enterprising spirit of Americans for colonization and
removing out into the wilderness and settling new countries, and if Spain and Portugal should adopt that wise
regulation respecting the connection of the sexes which
would give a spring to population within the tropics equal
to that without. There may now be three or four millions
of whites, or Europeans, in North and South America, of
which one-half are in rapid increase, and the rest scarcely
keeping their number good without supplies from the
parent states. The number of French, Spaniards, Dutch,
and Portuguese may be one million souls in all America, although they have transfused their blood into twice
that number of Indians. The United States may be two
million souls, whites, which have been an increase upon
perhaps fewer than twenty or thirty thousand families
from Europe. Can we contemplate their present, and
anticipate their future increase, and not be struck with
astonishment to find ourselves in the midst of the fulfil-
ment of the prophecy of Noah? May we not see that we
are the object which the Holy Ghost had in view four
thousand years ago, when he inspired the venerable patriarch with the visions respecting his posterity? How
wonderful the accomplishments in distant and disconnected ages! While the principal increase was first in
Europe, westward from Scythia, the residence of the
family of Japheth, a branch of the original enlargement,
extending eastward into Asia, and spreading round to the
southward of the Caspian, became the ancient kingdoms
of Media and Persia:[a] and thus he dwelt in the tents
of Shem. Hence the singular and almost identical affinity between the Persic and Teutonic languages, through
all ages, to this day. And now the other part of the
prophecy is fulfilling in a new enlargement, not in the

a Jos. Ant., lib. i. c. 6.

tents of Shem, but in a country where Canaan shall be his servant, at least unto tribute.

I rather consider the American Indians as Canaanites of the expulsion of Joshua,[1] some of which, in Phœnician ships, coasted the Mediterranean to its mouth, as appears from an inscription which they left there. Procopius, who was born in Palestine, a master of the Phœnician and other oriental languages, and the historiographer of the great Belisarius, tells us that at Tangier he saw and read an inscription upon two marble pillars there, in the ancient Phœnician — not the then modern Punic — letter, "We are they who have fled from the face of Joshua the robber, the son of Nun." [a] Bochart and Selden conjecture the very Punic itself. Plato, Ælian, and Diodorus Siculus narrate voyages into the Atlantic Ocean thirty days west from the Pillars of Hercules, to the island of Atlas. This inscription, examined by Procopius, suggests that the Canaanites, in coasting along from Tangier, might soon get into the trade winds and be undesignedly wafted across the Atlantic, land in the tropical regions, and commence the settlements of Mexico and Peru. Another branch of the Canaanitish expulsions might take the resolution of the ten tribes, and travel north-eastward to where never man dwelt, become the Tchuschi and Tungusi Tartars about Kamschatka and Tscukotskoinoss, in the northeast of Asia; thence, by water, passing over from island to island through the Northern Archipelago, to America, became the scattered Sachemdoms of these northern regions. It is now known that Asia is separated by water

[a] Ibi ex albis lapidibus constant COLUMNÆ DUÆ prope magnum fontem erectæ, Phœnicios habentes characteres insculptos, qui Phœcicum lingua sic sonant: NOS II SUMUS QUI FUGERUNT A FACIE JOSHUÆ PRÆDONIS FILII NAUE. — Evagr. Hist. ecc. l. 4, c. 18. Procop. Vandalic, l. 8.

[1] See Gookin's Historical Collections of the Indians, in Massachusetts Historical Collections, i. 144. — ED.

from America, as certainly appears from the Baron Dul-
feldt's voyage round the north of Europe into the Pacific
Ocean, A. D. 1769. Amidst all the variety of national
dialects, there reigns a similitude in their language, as
there is also in complexion and beardless features, from
Greenland to Del Fuego, and from the Antilles to Otaheite,
which show them to be one people.

A few scattered accounts, collected and combined together, may lead us to two certain conclusions:[1] 1. That
all the American Indians are one kind of people; 2. That
they are the same as the people in the northeast of Asia.

An Asiatic territory, three thousand miles long and
fifteen hundred wide, above the fortieth degree of latitude,
to the hyperborean ocean, contains only one million of
souls, settled as our Indians, as appears from the numera-
tions and estimates collected by M. Müller and other
Russian academicians in 1769. The Koreki, Jakuhti, and
Tungusij, living on the eastern part of this territory next
to America, are naturally almost beardless, like the Samoieds in Siberia, the Ostiacs and Calmucks, as well as the
American Indians,— all these having also the same custom
of plucking out the few hairs of very thin beards. They
have more similar usages, and fewer dissimilar ones, than
the Arabians of the Koreish tribe and Jews who sprang
from Abraham, or than those that subsist among European
nations who sprang from one ancestor, or those Asiatic
nations which sprang from Shem. The portrait-painter,
Mr. Smibert,[2] who accompanied Dr. Berkeley, then Dean

---

[1] The learned and judicious paper, by Samuel Foster Haven, Esq., of the
American Antiquarian Society, published by the Smithsonian Institute in
1856, gives an elaborate view of the "General Opinions respecting the Origin
of Population in the New World," with a critical account of the literature
upon this subject. — ED.

[2] Smibert's picture of Dr. Berkeley and his family is in possession of
Yale College. — ED.

of Derry, and afterward Bishop of Cloyne, from Italy to America in 1728, was employed by the Grand Duke of Tuscany, while at Florence, to paint two or three Siberian Tartars, presented to the duke by the Czar of Russia. This Mr. Smibert, upon his landing at Narraganset Bay with Dr. Berkeley, instantly recognized the Indians here to be the same people as the Siberian Tartars whose pictures he had taken. Moravian Indians from Greenland and South America have met those in our latitude at Bethlehem,[1] and have been clearly perceived to be the same people. The Kamschatdale Tartars have been carried over from Asia to America, and compared with our Indians, and found to be the same people. These Asiatic Tartars, from whom the American aboriginals derived, are distinct from and far less numerous than the Mongul and other Tartars which for ages, under Tamerlane and other chieftains, have deluged and overrun the southern ancient Asiatic empires. Attending to the rational and just deductions from these and other disconnected data[2] combined together, we may perceive that all the

---

[1] Moravian settlement of Pennsylvania. — ED.

[2] By his foreign correspondence Dr. Stiles was assiduous in learning the progress of discovery on the northwest coast of America. This collection of data, the bases of his "certain" deduction, well illustrate his intellectual life, his untiring acquisitiveness, — for he gathered the facts more from observation than from books, — his systemization, and his penetration and judgment. His theory is adopted by Dr. Charles Pickering, of the United States Exploring Expedition, who says: "I confess it was only on actually visiting the North Pacific that the whole matter seemed open to my view." He describes the islands of the Aleutian group, the countless inlets and channels connecting the two continents, and says, "Where, then, shall Asia end and America begin?"— "Races of Man," Bohn's Ed., 1854, p. 296.

> "The invention all admired, and each how he
> To be th' inventor missed; *so easy it seemed,*
> *Once found,* which yet, unfound, most would have thought
> Impossible." — MILTON.
>   — ED.

Americans are one people — that they came hither certainly from the northeast of Asia; probably, also, from the Mediterranean; and if so, that they are Canaanites, though arriving hither by different routes. The ocean current from the north of Asia might waft the beardless Samoieds or Tchuschi from the mouth of Jenesea or the Oby, around Nova Zembla to Greenland, and thence to Labrador, many ages after the refugees from Joshua might have colonized the tropical regions. Thus Providence might have ordered three divisions of the same people from different parts of the world, and perhaps in very distant ages, to meet together on this continent, or " our island," as the Six Nations call it, to settle different parts of it, many ages before the present accession of Japheth, or the former visitation of Madoc, 1001, or the certain colonization from Norway, A. D. 1001, as well as the certain Christianizing of Greenland in the ninth century, not to mention the visit of still greater antiquity by the Phœnicians, who charged the Dighton[1] rock, and other rocks in Narraganset Bay, with Punic inscriptions, remaining to this day; — which last I myself have repeatedly seen and taken off at large, as did Professor Sewall. He has lately transmitted a copy of this inscription to M. Gebelin, of the Parisian Academy of Sciences, who, comparing them with the Punic paleography, judges them Punic, and has interpreted them as denoting that the ancient Carthaginians once visited these distant regions.

Indians are numerous in the tropical regions; not so

---

[1] Dr. Stiles resided at Dighton for a while, after the war began, Newport being open to the enemy from the sea. The result of Mr. Schoolcraft's more careful study of the Dighton inscription is, that it is simply of Indian origin. The *Mananas* " inscription," coast of Maine, has excited a like interest. From a personal examination of it, in August, 1855, I believe that the Hand which made the rock made the " inscription."— ED.

elsewhere. Baron la Hontan, the last century, and Mr. Carver so lately as 1776 and 1777, travelled northwest beyond the sources of the Mississippi. From their observations it appears that the ratio of Indian population, in the very heart of the continent, is similar to that on this side of the Mississippi. By an accurate numeration made in 1766, and returned into the plantation office in London, it appeared that there were not forty thousand souls, Indians, from the Mississippi to the Atlantic, and from Florida to the Pole. According to Mr. Carver, there are about thirty,[a] and certainly not forty, Indian tribes west of the Senecas and Six Nation confederacy, and from the Mississippi and Ohio northward to Hudson's Bay, and from Niagara to the Lake of the Woods. The chiefs of all these speak the Chippeway language. And perhaps all the remaining territory north of New Spain, and even on this side the northern tropic, and northwestward to Asia, will not exhibit five times that number, at highest.

Partly by actual numeration, and partly by estimate, the Indians in the Spanish dominions in America are considered as a million souls in New Spain, and a million and one-half in Peru; or two or three million souls in the whole. And perhaps this would fully comprehend those of Paraguay and the Portuguese provinces. In my opinion, great defalcation must be made from these numbers. The aboriginals have been injudiciously estimated at twenty millions; but I believe they never exceeded two or three million souls in all North and South America, since the days of Columbus.

The European population so surpasses them already, that, of whatever origin, they will eventually be, as the most of them have already become, servants unto Japheth. Six hundred and twelve thousand Indians pay tribute in

[a] Carver's Trav., p. 415.

Peru. We are increasing with great rapidity; and the Indians, as well as the million Africans in America, are decreasing as rapidly. Both left to themselves, in this way diminishing, may gradually vanish;[1] and thus an unrighteous slavery may at length, in God's good providence, be abolished, and cease in this land of liberty.

But, to return: The population of this land will probably become very great, and Japheth become more numerous millions in America than in Europe and Asia; and the two or three millions of the United States may equal the population of the oriental empires, which far surpasses that of Europe. There are reasons for believing that the English increase will far surpass others, and that the diffusion of the United States will ultimately produce the general population of America. The northern provinces of China spread for ages, and at length deluged the southern with a very numerous and accumulated population. "In the multitude of people is the king's honor."[a]

But a multitude of people, even the two hundred million[2] of the Chinese empire, cannot subsist without civil government. All the forms of civil polity have been tried by mankind, except one, and that seems to have been reserved in Providence to be realized in America. Most

---

[a] Prov. xiv. 28.

[1] The cotton-gin, invented about 1793–4, by ELI WHITNEY, a native of Westborough, Massachusetts, December 8, 1765, turned " the whole course of industry in the southern section of the Union," and the fate of " the million Africans," and their descendants of mingled blood. The total number of Indians in the United States territory was estimated, in 1853, at 400,764. The total number of slaves, in 1854, was 3,204,313. The shameless ingratitude and wrong to Whitney are narrated in " Silliman's Journal," January, 1832. — ED.

[2] The reader will readily excuse the omission of the author's long note on Chinese statistics, cited from Hatton's Geography, and Du Halde, v., p. 209. — ED.

of the states, of all ages, in their originals, both as to policy and property, have been founded in rapacity, usurpation, and injustice; so that in the contests recorded in history, the public right is a dubious question, — it being rather certain that it belongs to neither of the contending parties, — the military history of all nations being but a description of the wars and invasions of the mutual robbers and devastators of the human race. The invasion of the lawless Macedonian, who effected the dissolution of the Medo-Persian empire; the wide-spread Roman conquests; the inundation of the Goths and Vandals; the descents of the Tartars on China; the triumphs of Tamerlane, Ulugh-beg, and Aurengzebe; and the wide-spread domination of the impostor of Mecca, with his successors, the Caliphs and Mamelukes, down to Kouli-Kan, who dethroned his prince, and plundered India of two hundred millions sterling; — these, I say, with the new distribution of property and new erected policies, were all founded in unrighteousness and tyrannical usurpation. The real interest of mankind, and the public good, has been generally overlooked. It has really been very indifferent to the great cause of right and liberty which of the belligerent powers prevailed, — a Tangrolipix or a Mahomet, an Augustus or an Antony, a Scipio or a Hannibal, a Brennus or an Antiochus, — tyranny being the sure portion of the plebeians, be the victory as it should happen. These things have led some very enlightened as well as serious minds to a fixed conclusion and judgment against the right and legality of all wars. In the simplicity of my judgment, I have for years been of this opinion, except as to the offensive wars of Israel and defensive war of America. War, in some instances, especially defensive, has been authorized by Heaven. The blessing given by Melchisedec to Abraham, upon his return from the slaugh-

ter of Chelderlaomer and the kings of the East, justified
that holy patriarch. The war with Amelek, and the extir-
pation of the Canaanites by Joshua, were of God. The
location of the respective territories to the first nations,
was so of God as to give them a divine right defensively
to resist the Nimrods and Ninuses, the first invading tyrants of the ancient ages. The originally free and glorious republics of Greece had a right from God to withstand
the haughty claims of the Assyrian empire, which they
successfully resisted for ages, till the Roman power arose
behind them, and at length prostrated their liberties.

But after the spirit of conquest had changed the first
governments, all the succeeding ones have, in general,
proved one continued series of injustice, which has reigned
in all countries for almost four thousand years. These
have so changed property, laws, rights, and liberties, that
it has become impossible for the most sagacious civilians
to decide whose is the abstract political right in national
controversies; rather, we know that none of them have
any right. All original right is confounded and lost. We
can only say that there still remains in the body of the
people at large — the body of mankind, of any and every
generation — a power, with which they are invested by the
Author of their being, to wrest government out of the
hands of reigning tyrants, and originate new policies,
adapted to the conservation of liberty, and promoting the
public welfare. But what is the happiest form of civil
government, is the great question. Almost all the polities
may be reduced to hereditary dominion, in either a monarchy or aristocracy, and these supported by a standing
army. The Roman and Venetian senates were but a
hereditary aristocracy, with an elective head. The senatorial succession is preserved independent of the people.
True liberty is preserved in the Belgic and Hælvetic re-

publics, and among the nobles in the elective monarchy of Poland. For the rest of the world, the civil dominion, though often wisely administered, is so modelled as to be beyond the control of those for whose end God instituted government. But a democratical polity for millions, standing upon the broad basis of the people at large, amply charged with property, has not hitherto been exhibited.

Republics are democratical, aristocratical, or monarchical. Each of these forms admits of modifications, both as to hereditation and powers, from absolute government up to perfect liberty. Monarchy might be so limited, one would think, as to be a happy form, especially if elective; but both monarchy and aristocracy, when they become hereditary, terminate in the prostration of liberty. The greater part of the governments on earth may be termed monarchical aristocracies, or hereditary dominions independent of the people. The nobles and nabobs, being hereditary, will at first have great power; but the royal factions have not failed to intrigue this away from the nobles to the prince: the assembly of even hereditary nobles then become ciphers and nullities in dominion. The once glorious Cortes of Spain experienced this loss of power. It is next to an impossibility to tame a monarch; and few have ruled without ferocity. Scarcely shall we find in royal dynasties, in long line of princes, a few singularly good sovereigns — a few Cyruses, Antonini, Alfreds, Boroihmeses. Indeed, if we look over the present sovereigns of Europe, we behold with pleasure two young princes, the emperor,[1] and the monarch of France,[2] who seem to be raised up in Providence to make their people and mankind happy.

---

[1] See p. 464, note 1. — ED.

[2] Louis XVI., for the iniquities of his fathers, died upon the scaffold, January 21, 1793, aged thirty-eight. See p. 445, note 1. — ED.

A Ganganelli in the pontifical throne was a phœnix of ages, shone for his moment, and scarcely to be found again in the catalogue of a Platina.[1] We see enterprising literary and heroic talents in a Frederick III., and wisdom in a Poniatowski. I add no more. But when we contemplate the other European and Asiatic potentates, and especially the sovereigns of Delhi, Ispahaun, and Constantinople, one cannot but pity mankind whose lot is to be governed by despots of small abilities, immersed and rioting in the splendor of a luxurious effeminacy. Nor could government proceed were not the errors and desultory blunders of royalty frequently corrected by the circumspection of a Colao, a few sensible characters, venerable for wisdom, called up among the stated councillors of majesty.

Lord Bacon said that monarchy had a platform in nature; and, in truth, monarchical ideas reign through the universe. A monarchy conducted with infinite wisdom and infinite benevolence is the most perfect of all possible governments. The Most High hath delegated power and authority to subordinate monarchies, or sole ruling powers, in limited districts, throughout the celestial hierarchy, and through the immensity of the intellectual world; but, at the same time, he hath delegated and imparted to them wisdom and goodness adequate to the purposes of dominion ; and thence the government is, as it ought to be, absolute. But in a world or region of the universe where God has imparted to none either this superior power or adequate wisdom beyond what falls to the common share of humanity, it is absurd to look for such qualities in one man — not even in the man Moses, who shared the government of Israel with the senate of seventy. Therefore there is no foundation for monarchical government from supposed

1 See p. 466, note 1. — ED.

hereditary superiority in knowledge. If it be said that monarchs always have a council of state, consisting of the wisest personages, of whose wisdom they avail themselves in the government of empires, — not to observe that this is a concession indicating a deficiency of knowledge in princes, — it may be asked, Why not, then, consign and repose government into the hands of the national council, where always resides the superiority of wisdom? The supposed advantage of having one public head for all to look up to, and to concentre the attention, obedience, and affection of subjects, and to consolidate the empire, will not counterbalance the evils of arbitrary despotism and the usual want of wisdom in the sovereigns and potentates of the earth. For the hereditary successions in the dynasties of kings, in the effeminate families of the great, seem to be marked and accursed by Providence with deficient wisdom. And where is the wisdom of consigning government into such hands? Why not much better — since we for once have our option or choice — to commit the direction of the republic to a Wittena-gemot, or an aristocratical council of wise men? Should we call forth and dignify some family, either from foreign nations or from among ourselves, and create a monarch, whether a hereditary prince or protector for life, and seat him in supremacy at the head of Congress, soon, with insidious dexterity, would he intrigue, and secure a venal majority even of new and annual members, and, by diffusing a complicated and variously modified influence, pursue an accretion of power till he became absolute.

The celebrated historian Mrs. Catharine Macaulay,[1] that

---

[1] The eight volumes of Mrs. Macaulay's " History of England from the Accession of James I. to that of the Brunswick Line," appeared successively during the years 1763 to 1783. The high republican tone and noble zeal for liberty which distinguished this work, and the time of its publica-

ornament of the republic of letters, and the female Livy of the age, observes: " The man who holds supreme power for life will have a great number of friends and adherents, who are attached by interest to his interest, and who will wish for continuance of power in the same family. This creates the worst of factions, a government faction, in the state. The desire of securing to ourselves a particular unshared privilege is the rankest vice which infests humanity ; and a protector for life, instead of devoting his time and understanding to the great cares of government, will be scheming and plotting to secure the power, after his death, to his children, if he has any, if not, to the nearest of his kin. This principle in government has been productive of such bloodshed and oppression that it has inclined politicians to give preference to hereditary rather than elective monarchies; and, as the lesser evil, to consign the government of society to the increasing and at length unlimited sway of one family, whether the individuals of it should be idiots or madmen. It is an uncontroverted fact, that supreme power never can continue long in one family without becoming unlimited." [a]

We stand a better chance with aristocracy, whether hereditary or elective, than with monarchy. An unsystematical democracy and an absolute monarchy are equally detestable, equally a *magormissabib*, the terror to all around them. An elective aristocracy is preferable for America, as it is rather to be a council of nations [1] —

---

[a] Mrs. Macaulay's letter to the author, 1771.

tion, coïncident with the period of the Revolution, rendered the author a great favorite with the American patriots and scholars. Dr. Stiles's language was not an extravagant expression of her popularity in England or America. She visited Washington in 1785. He was one of her correspondents. After a remarkable and somewhat eccentric life, she died in 1791. — ED.

[1] See p. 458, and note 1. — ED.

agreeable to the humane, liberal, and grand ideas of Henry IV. and the patriot Sully — than a body in which resides authoritative sovereignty; for there is no real cession of dominion, no surrender or transfer of sovereignty to the national council, as each state in the confederacy is an independent sovereignty.[1]

In justice to human society it may perhaps be said of almost all the polities and civil institutions in the world, however imperfect, that they have been founded in and carried on with very considerable wisdom. They must have been generally well administered, — I say generally, — otherwise government could not proceed. This may be said even of those governments which carry great defects and the seeds of self-destruction and ruin in their constitution; for even an Ottoman or an Aurengzebe must establish and prescribe to himself a national constitution, a system of general laws and dominion. But the abstract rationale of perfect civil government remains still hidden among the desiderata of politics, having hitherto baffled the investigation of the best writers on government, the ablest politicians, and the sagest civilians. A well-ordered democratical aristocracy, standing upon the annual elections of the people, and revocable at pleasure, is the polity which combines the United States; and, from the nature of man and the comparison of ages, I believe it will approve itself the most equitable, liberal, and perfect.

With the people, especially a people seized of property, resides the aggregate of original power. They cannot, however, assemble from the territory of an empire, and must, therefore, if they have any share in government, represent themselves by delegation. This constitutes one order in legislature and sovereignty. It is a question whether there should be any other; to resolve which, it

---

[1] See p. 358, note 1. — ED.

may be considered that each of these delegates, or representatives, will be faithful conservators of local interests, but have no interest in attending extensively to the public, further than where all particular local interests are affected in common with that which one delegate represents in particular.

It should seem, then, that the nature of society dictates another, a higher branch, whose superiority arises from its being the interested and natural conservator of the universal interest. This will be a senatorial order, standing, not on local, but a general election of the whole body of the people. Let a bill, or law, be read, in the one branch or the other, every one instantly thinks how it will affect his constituents. If his constituents are those of one small district only, they will be his first care; if the people at large, their general or universal interest will be his first care, the first object of his faithful attention. If a senator, as in Delaware, stands on the election of only the same district as a deputy, the Upper House is only the repetition of the lower; if on the election of several counties combined, as in Virginia, each member of the Upper House stands and feels himself charged with a greater and more extensive care than a member of the House of Burgesses : not but that it is the duty of each deputy to attend to the general interest. Georgia, Pennsylvania,[1] and Jersey, have each a Senate or Legislature of one order only; for although in Jersey it seemeth otherwise, yet that interest which will determine a vote in one, will determine it in both Houses. The same is true of the two Carolinas.

The constitutions of Maryland and New York are

---

[1] The single legislature was a favorite idea with Dr. Franklin, and it is said that the high authority of his opinions in France aided its adoption there; and from the want of the Senate, or Upper House, as a great balance-wheel, came the horrors of the French Revolution. — ED.

founded in higher wisdom. The polity of Massachusetts is excellent, and truly grand; it retains, indeed, some of the shadows of royalty, which may give dignity, but never operate an essential mischief in the hands of a chief magistrate who is annually elected by the people at large. But Connecticut and Rhode Island have originally realized the most perfect polity as to a legislature. Any emendations and improvements may be made by the Assembly, with respect to the establishment of the law courts, and a constitutional privy council, which in all future time will be necessary to attend the chief magistrate in the ordinary civil administration. These things are remedied in Virginia, whose constitution seems to be imperfect in but one thing: its twenty-four senators, though elected from local districts, should be elected by the people at large, — being men of such public eminence, and of merit so illustrious, as to be known, not to a few only, but to all the tribes throughout the state. It establishes judges *quamdiu se bene gesserint*. It provides perfectly for legislation and law courts, for the militia, and for that continual administration of government, in absence of assemblies and while the judiciary tribunals are sitting, which must reside in and be uninterruptedly exercised at the head of sovereignty in every civil polity.

It gives me pleasure to find that public liberty is effectually secured in each and all the policies of the United States, though somewhat differently modelled. Not only the polity, or exterior system of government, but the laws and interior regulations of each state, are already excellent, surpassing the institutions of Lycurgus or Plato; and by the annual appeals to the public a power is reserved to the people to remedy any corruptions or errors in government. And even if the people should sometimes err, yet each assembly of the states, and the body of the people,

always embosom wisdom sufficient to correct themselves;
so that a political mischief cannot be durable. Herein we
far surpass any states on earth. We can correct ourselves,
if in the wrong. The Belgic states, in their federal capacity, are united by a perfect system, constituted by that
great prince, William of Nassau, and the compatriots of
that age; but they left the interior government of the jural
tribunals, cities, and provinces, as despotic and arbitrary as
they found them. So the elective monarchical republic
of Poland is an excellent constitution for the nobles, but
leaves despotism and tyranny, the portion and hard fate
of the plebeians, beyond what is to be found in any
part of Europe. Not so the American states; their interior as well as exterior civil and jural polities are so nearly
perfect, that the rights of individuals, even to numerous
millions, are guarded and secured.

The crown and glory of our confederacy is the amphic-
tyonic council[1] of the General Congress, standing on the
annual election of the united respective states, and revocable at pleasure. This lays the foundation of a permanent
union in the American Republic, which may at length
convince the world that, of all the policies to be found on
earth, not excepting the very excellent one of the Chinese
Empire, the most perfect one has been invented and
realized in America.

If, in the multitude of devices for improving and carrying our policy to greater perfection and a more permanent
and efficacious government, — if, I say, some elevated
geniuses should go into the ideas of monarchy, whether
hereditary or elective, and others think of a partition of

---

[1] Five years later, in 1788, James Madison, in the "Federalist," Nos. 18,
38, describes this celebrated institution, as "it bore a very instructive
analogy to the present confederation of the American Union." See p.
458, note 1. — ED.

the United States into three or four separate independent confederacies, perhaps, upon discussing the subject calmly and thoroughly, and finding that the policy which will at last take place must stand on plebeian election, they may at length be satisfied that the die is already cast, and the policy has taken its complexion for ages to come. Thus the nine bowls engraved with the map of dominion established the policy of the Chinese empire for near twenty ages.[a] The ancient division of the empire subsisted by means of these symbols of dominion, which passed in succession to the nine principal mandarins, or supreme governors under the imperial sovereignty; and this for the long tract from their first institution by the Emperor Yu, who reigned two thousand two hundred years before Christ, to Chey-lie-vang, who was contemporary with the great philosopher Menzius, three hundred years before Christ. So that symbol of union, the American flag, with its increasing stripes and stars, may have an equally combining efficacy for ages. The senatorial constitution and consulate of the Roman Empire lasted from Tarquin to Cæsar. The pragmatic sanction has probably secured the imperial succession in the House of Austria for ages. The Medo-Persian and Alexandrian empires, and that of Tamerlane, who reigned, A. D. 1400, from Smyrna to the Ganges, were, for obvious reasons, of short and transitory duration; but that of the Assyrian endured, without mutation, through a tract of one thousand three hundred years, from Semiramis to Sardanapalus. Nor was the policy of Egypt overthrown for a longer period, from the days of Mitzraim till the time of Cambyses and Amasis. Whatever mutations may arise in the United States, perhaps hereditary monarchy and a standing army will be the last.

a Du Halde, Hist. China.

Besides a happy policy as to civil government, it is necessary to institute a system of law and jurisprudence founded in justice, equity, and public right. The American codes of law, and the *lex non scripta*, the *senatus consulta*, and the common law, are already advanced to great perfection, — far less complicated and perplexed than the jural systems of Europe, where reigns a mixture of Roman, Gothic, Teutonic, Salic, Saxon, Norman, and other local or municipal law, controlled or innovated and confused by subsequent royal edicts and imperial institutions, superinducing the same mutation as did the imperatorial decrees of the Cæsars upon the ancient *jus civile*, or Roman law. A depuration from all these will take place in America, and our communication with all the world will enable us to bring home the most excellent principles of law and right to be found in every kingdom and empire on earth. These being adopted here may advance our systems of jurisprudence to the highest purity and perfection, — especially if hereafter some Fleta, Bracton, Coke, some great law genius, should arise, and, with vast erudition, and with the learned sagacity of a Trebonianus, reduce and digest all into one great jural system.

But the best laws will be of no validity unless the tribunals be filled with judges of independent sentiment, vast law knowledge, and of an integrity beyond the possibility of corruption. Even a Bacon should fall from his highest honors the moment he tastes the forbidden fruit. Such infamy and tremendous punishment should be connected with tribunal bribery, that a judge should be struck into the horror of an earthquake at the very thoughts of corruption. The legislatures have the institution and revocation of law; and the judges in their decisions are to be sacredly governed by the laws of the land.[1] Most of the states have judged it necessary, in order to keep the supreme law courts uninfluenced and uncorrupted tribunals, that the judges be honorably supported, and be fixed in office *quamdiu se bene gesserint.*

But I pass on to another subject, in which the welfare of a community is deeply concerned, — I mean the public revenues. National character and national faith depend on these. Every people, every large community, is able to furnish a revenue adequate to the exigencies of government. But this is a most difficult subject; and what the happiest method of raising it, is uncertain. One thing is certain, that however in most kingdoms and empires the people are taxed at the will of the prince, yet in America the people tax themselves, and therefore cannot tax themselves beyond their abilities. But whether the power of taxing be in an absolute monarchy a power independent of the people, or in a body elected by the people, one great error has, I apprehend, entered into the system of revenue and finance in almost all nations, viz., restricting the collection to money. Two or three millions can more easily be raised in produce than one million in money. This, collected and deposited in stores and magazines, would, by bills drawn upon these stores, answer all the expenditures of war and peace. The little imperfect experiment lately made here should not discourage us. In one country it has been tried with success for ages, — I mean in China, the wisest empire the sun hath ever shined upon. And here, if I recollect aright, not a tenth of the imperial revenues hath been collected in money. In rice, wheat, and millet only, are collected forty million of sacks, — one hundred and twenty each, — equal to eighty million

---

[1] In this connection read Mr. George Sumner's oration, Boston, July 4, 1859, pp. 10, 51–67. — ED.

bushels; in raw and wrought silk, one million pounds.
The rest is taken in salt, wines, cotton, and other fruits of
labor and industry, at a certain ratio per cent., and deposited in stores over all the empire. The perishable commodities are immediately sold, and the mandarins and
army are paid by bills on these magazines. In no part of
the world are the inhabitants less oppressed than there.
England has eleven hundred millions property, — real,
personal, and commercial, — and five million souls. Their
ordinary revenue has for many years been ten or twelve
millions; and during this war the national expenditures
have been annually twenty millions. A great part is raised
by excise; by the land tax not above a fifth or sixth,
although the annual rental of England is really sixty millions. The funded debt has arisen from one hundred and
twenty-three millions, A. D. 1775, to two hundred and
thirty millions, in 1783, and can never be paid.[1] It is unparalleled in the annals of empires that six or seven millions of people ever discharged so heavy a burden. The
Roman imperial debt was once — in the times of the
Cæsars — three hundred millions sterling, when the empire consisted of thirty million of people. One emperor
at his accession wiped out twenty millions, and the Goths
and Vandals settled the rest to the ruin of thousands.
May God preserve these States from being so involved!
The present war being over, the future increase of population and property will in time enable us with conven-
ience to discharge the heavy debt we have incurred in the
defence of our rights and liberties. The United States
have now two hundred and fifty millions of property,
pretty equally shared by two or three million people.

---

[1] The debt of Great Britain is £803,733,958. The population of the
British Islands is 27,000,000, and of all territory under British rule,
215,000,000. — ED.

And our national debt [a] is not ten million sterling, — which
is to the whole collectively as it would be for one man
possessing an estate of two hundred and fifty pounds in
land and stock to oblige himself to pay ten pounds. The
interest only of the British national debt, upon six or seven
million people, is above ten millions sterling annually; —
that is, greater than the whole national debt of the United
States upon half that number. Our population will soon
overspread the vast territory from the Atlantic to the
Mississippi, which in two generations will become a property superior to that of Britain. Thus posterity may
help to pay for the war [1] which we have been obliged to
fight out for them in our day. It will not, however, be
wise to consign to posterity so heavy a debt, lest they
should be tempted to learn, like other nations, the practice
of public injustice and broken national faith.

Another object of great attention in America will be
commerce. In order to form some ideas respecting it in
the United States, we may take a summary view of it
while we were in connection with Britain, and thence

---

[a] Forty-two millions of dollars at the peace.

[1] The gracious Providence which ordained Washington, no less created
Hamilton specially for the nation. His genius brought order out of chaos,
and created our permanent financial system. "At the time when our
government was organized, we were without funds, though not without
resources. To call them into action, and establish order in the finances,
Washington sought for splendid talents, for extensive information, and,
above all, he sought for sterling, incorruptible integrity. All these he
found in Hamilton."— Gouverneur Morris. " He smote the rock of the
national resources, and abundant streams of revenue gushed forth. He
touched the dead corpse of the public credit, and it sprang upon its
feet. The fabled birth of Minerva from the brain of Jove was hardly more
sudden or more perfect than the financial system of the United States as
it burst forth from the conception of Alexander Hamilton."— Daniel
Webster. See the admirable sketch of Hamilton and his Works in Allibone's Dictionary of Authors. — ED.

judge what it may be after we shall have recovered from
the shock of this war.

The British merchants represented that they received
some profit indeed from Virginia and South Carolina, as
well as the West Indies; but as for the rest of this continent, they were constant losers in trade. Mr. Glover has
candidly disclosed the truth; and he and other writers
enable us to form some ideas of the matter. It appears,
from an undecennary account laid before Parliament in
1776, that the state of commerce between England only
and English America, for the eleven years preceding hostilities, was thus:

Exports to the	Imports from the
Continental colonies, 26¾ mil. ster.	13¾ mil. ster.
West Indies, . . 14¼ " "	35¼ " " { mostly on acct. of the continental colonies.
Total, 41 " "	49

A commerce of twenty-six million exports, and only thirteen million imports, is self-annihilated and impossible.
The returns from the West Indies comprehended a great
part of the continental remittances. The American merchants, by a circuitous trade from this continent and from
Africa, remitted to London and Britain, by way of the
West Indies, in bills of exchange drawn on sugars, the
balance of what they seem to fall short in direct remittances on the custom-house books.

The whole American commerce monopolized by Great
Britain must be considered collectively, and was to England only in the above account forty-one million exports,
and forty-nine million imports. This, inclusive of the
twelve per cent. charged, amounted to a real annual profit
of thirty-two per cent. to the English merchants, in actual
remittances of the year, besides a standing American debt,
it is said, of six million, carrying interest. Well might

the British merchants sustain a loss in American bankrupt-
cies of a million a year — though probably at an average
not five or ten thousand — in so lucrative a trade.[1]   An
idea of the mercantile debt may be thus conceived.   There
is a district within the United States upon which the state
of European trade [2] at the commencement of hostilities
was thus; being chiefly carried on by foreign factorages —
a mode of commerce which the British merchants intended
to have been universal.   In the course of a systematical
trade had at length arisen a standing debt of a million
sterling, among about a quarter of a million of people.   To
feed this the British merchants sent over one quarter of a
million sterling annually ; for which, and collected debts,
they received in actual remittance half a million sterling
within the same year; *i. e.*, a quarter of a million returned
half a million, and fed or kept up a debt of one million,
paying to Britain an annual lawful interest ; the security
of all which complicated system stood upon American
mortgages.   This is true mercantile secret history.

If this specimen applied to all the States — and, God be
thanked! it does not — it would show not only the greatness and momentous importance of our trade to Europe,
but the necessity of legislative regulations in commerce,
to invalidate future foreign mortgages, and yet support
credit by the enforcement of punctual, speedy, and certain
payments, whether with profit or loss.   Without this no
permanent commerce can be supported.   I observed that
the above specimen may assist us.   It is not necessary for
every purpose to come to great exactness in capital estimates.   The total exterior commerce of Great Britain
with all the world is about twelve millions annually ; of

---

[1] See pp. 107, 127, note; 136. — ED.

[2] Boston and Newport were the great marts of foreign trade. — ED.

which five millions, or near half, was of American connection, and four millions of this directly American, as Mr. Glover asserts; and the real profit of the American trade was become to Britain equal to nearly half the benefit of her total exterior commerce to the whole world. The total of British exports to all the world, A. D. 1704, was only six millions and a half sterling. The American British trade, in its connections, returns, and profits, nearly equalled this, A. D. 1774. We were better to Britain than all the world was to her seventy years before. Despised as our commerce was, it is evident that, had the union continued, our increasing millions would soon have made remittances for more than the fewer millions of Britain could have manufactured for exportation; for the greater part of the manufactures of every country must be for domestic consumption. A specimen of this we have in the woollen manufacture. England grows eleven million fleeces a year, worth two million sterling, manufactured into eight million; of which six million is of domestic consumption, and two million only for exportation. When it is considered that a great part of this went to other countries, how weak must be the supposition that Britain clothed America; while America, from the beginning, in their own domestic manufactures, furnished nine-tenths of their apparel.

Our trade opens to all the world. We shall doubtless at first overtrade ourselves everywhere, and be in danger of incurring heavy mortgages, unless prevented.[1] The nations will not at first know how far they may safely trade with us. But commerce will find out its own sys-

---

[1] Child, Gee, Huske, and Glover wrote largely on American trade, and its value to England. Edmund Burke mastered its principles; and his speeches, especially that of 1775, contain much of the order observable in these pages of Dr. Stiles. — ED.

tem, and regulate itself in time. It will be governed on
the part of America by the cheapest foreign markets; on
the part of Europe, by our ability and punctuality of remittance. We can soon make a remittance of three or
four million a year, in a circuitous trade, exclusive of the
iniquitous African trade.[1] If Europe should indulge us
beyond this, our failures and disappointments might lay
the foundation of national animosities. Great wisdom is
therefore necessary to regulate the commerce of America.
The caution with which we are to be treated may occasion
and originate a commercial system among the maritime
nations on both sides of the Atlantic, founded in justice
and reciprocity of interest, which will establish the benevolence as well as the opulence of nations, and advance the
progress of society to civil perfection.

It is certainly for the benefit of every community that
it be transfused with the efficacious motives of universal
industry. This will take place if every one can enjoy the
fruits of his labor and activity unmolested. All the variety
of labor in a well-regulated state will be so ordered and
encouraged as that all will be employed, in a just proportion, in agriculture, mechanic arts, commerce, and the literary professions. It has been a question whether agriculture or commerce needs most encouragement in these
states. But the motives for both seem abundantly sufficient. Never did they operate more strongly than at present. The whole continent is [in] activity, and in the lively,
vigorous exertion of industry. Several other things call
for encouragement, as the planting of vineyards, and olive
yards, and cotton-walks; the raising of wool, planting

---

[1] The pulpits of Dr. Stiles and Dr. Hopkins, at Newport, R. I., — then the
headquarters of the African slave-trade, — afford models of apostolic fidelity in gospel preaching at "the sins of the times." They were Christian
heroes. See Dr. Park's Memoir of Samuel Hopkins, D. D., 1854. — ED.

mulberry trees, and the culture of silk; and, I add, establishing manufactories.[1] This last is necessary, very necessary — far more necessary, indeed, than is thought by many deep politicians. Let us have all the means possible of subsistence and elegance among ourselves, if we would be a flourishing republic of real independent dignity and glory.

Another thing tending to the public welfare is, removing causes of political animosities and civil dissension, promoting harmony, and strengthening the union among the several parts of this extended community.[2] In the memorable *bellum sociale* among the Romans, three hundred thousand of Roman blood fought seven hundred thousand brethren of the Italian blood. After a loss of sixty thousand, in disputing a trifling point of national honor, they pacificated the whole by an amnesty, and giving the city to the Italians.[a] We may find it a wise policy, a few years hence, under certain exceptions, to settle an amnesty and

---

[a] Vid. Velleius paterc.

[1] Hildreth, iii. 466. The imports from Great Britain in 1784 and 1785 amounted in value to thirty millions of dollars, while the exports did not exceed nine millions. This ruinous competition was checked by the law of 1789, proposed by Hamilton, for the encouragement of manufactures, to which the war of 1812 gave a fresh impulse. They have felt the fluctuations of party and of commerce, but the United States are now far advanced to the "real independent dignity" foreseen by Dr. Stiles in 1783. Arkwright and Whitney, Fulton and Watt, divide the honors in this noble competition of industry. See p. 335, note 1. — Ed.

[2] In a sermon, preached in 1760, on the conquest of Canada, Dr. Stiles said: "It is probable that in time there will be a Provincial Confederacy and a Common Council, and *this may in time terminate* in an Imperial Diet, when the imperial dominion will subsist, *as it ought*, in election." The sagacious author saw the "imperial dominion," as he called it in 1760, or "amnesty," as he termed it in 1783, consummated in the unanimous election of Washington in 1789 as President of the Republic — of "the people of the United States." This foreseeing, this repeated prediction, first of the *Confederacy*, and then of its "terminating" "in a few years" in the

circulate a brotherly affection among all the inhabitants of this glorious republic.   We should live henceforward in amity, as brothers inspired with and cultivating a certain national benevolence, unitedly glorying in the name of a Columbian or American, and in the distinguished honor and aggrandizement of our country; — like that ancient national affection which we once had for the parent state while we gloried in being a part of the British empire, and when our attachment and fidelity grew to an unexampled vigor and strength.   This appeared in the tender distress we felt at the first thoughts of the dissolution of this ancient friendship.   We once thought Britain our friend, and gloried in her protection.   But some demon[a] whispered folly into the present reign, and Britain forced upon America the tremendous alternative of the loss of liberty or the last appeal, either of which instantly alienated and dissolved our affection.   It was impossible to hesitate, and the affection is dissolved, never, never more to be recovered; like that between Syracuse and Athens, it is lost forever.   A political earthquake through the continent hath shook off America from Great Britain.   Oh, how painful and distressing the separation and dismemberment!   Witness, all ye patriotic breasts, all ye lovers of your country, once lovers of Great Britain — witness the tender sensations and heartfelt violence, the reluctant distress and sorrow, with which ye were penetrated, when, spurned from a parent's love, ye felt the conviction of the dire necessity of an everlasting parting to meet no more — never to be united again!

O, England! how did I once love thee! how did I once glory in thee! how did I once boast of springing

a Bute.

Union, is one of the most remarkable instances of political foresight and sagacity on record. — ED.

from thy bowels, though at four descents ago, and the nineteenth from Sir Adam of Knapton! In the rapturous anticipation of thine enlargement and reflourishing in this western world, how have I been wont to glory in the future honor of having thee for the head of the Britannico-American empire for the many ages till the millennium, when thy great national glory should have been advanced in then becoming a member of the universal empire of the Prince of Peace! And if perchance, in some future period, danger should have arisen to thee from European states, how have I flown on the wings of prophecy, with the numerous hardy hosts of thine[1] American sons inheriting thine ancient principles of liberty and valor, to rescue and reïnthrone the hoary, venerable head of the most glorious empire on earth! But now, farewell — a long farewell — to all this greatness! And yet even now, methinks, in such an exigency, I could leap the Atlantic, not into thy bosom, but to rescue an aged parent from destruction, and then return on the wings of triumph to this asylum of the world, and rest in the bosom of Liberty.[2]

[1] See pp. 130–135, 184, 185, 238. — ED.

[2] It is grand to find the magnanimous feelings and views of early times, briefly interrupted, again asserting their legitimate power in the leading minds of this day, and none would more enjoy and value the flow of good feeling and sound sense in the following passage than Washington and his associates:

" Of all countries known in history, the North American Republic is most conspicuously marked by the fusion, or rather the absence, of rank and social distinctions, by community of interests, by incessant and all-pervading intercommunication, by the universal diffusion of education, and the abundant facilities of access not only to the periodical conduits, but to the permanent reservoirs of knowledge. The condition of England is in all these respects closely assimilated to that of the United States; and not only the methods, but the instruments of popular instruction are fast becoming the same in both, and there is a growing conviction among the wise of the two great empires that the highest interests of both will be promoted by reciprocal good-will and unrestricted intercourse,

Moreover, as we have seen the wisdom of our ancestors in instituting a militia, so it is necessary to continue it. The Game Act, in the time of James I., insidiously disarmed the people of England.[1] Let us not be insidiously disarmed. In all our enlargements in colonization, in all our increasing millions, let the main body be exercised annually to military discipline, whether in war or peace. This will defend us against ourselves and against surrounding states. Let this be known in Europe, in every future age, and we shall never again be invaded from the other side of the Atlantic. "The militia[2] of this country," says General Washington, "must be considered as the palladium of our security and the first effectual resort in case of hostility."

Another thing necessary is a vigilance against corrup-

perilled by jealousies and estrangement. Favored, then, by the mighty elective affinities, the powerful harmonic attractions which subsist between the Americans and the Englishmen as brothers of one blood, one speech, one faith, we may reasonably hope that the Anglican tongue, on both sides of the Atlantic, as it grows in flexibility, comprehensiveness, expression, wealth, will also more and more clearly manifest the organic unity of its branches, and that national jealousies, material rivalries, narrow interests, will not disjoin and shatter that great instrument of social advancement which God made one, as he made one the spirit of the nation that uses it."— Marsh, "English Language in America," Lecture xxx., 1860. — Ed.

[1] By the Act 3d James I., 1606, persons of an annual landed revenue of £100 were empowered to seize all guns and sporting implements from any and all persons of an income of less than £40 a year, they being deemed unqualified for the enjoyment of cony and deer hunting. In those days the king called upon all of £40 a year to receive knighthood, or pay into his royal palm a fee for escaping the honor. Such were the hazards of having "£40 a year," or more or less; such the security of individual or popular rights; and such the boast of him who may hold his patent of nobility, temp. Jac. I. — Ed.

[2] The Constitution of the United States, 1789, provides that, "a well-regulated militia being necessary to the security of a free state, the right of the people to keep and bear arms shall not be infringed."— Ed.

tion in purchasing elections and in designations to offices
in the Legislatures and Congress, instituting such efficacious provisions against corruption as shall preclude the
possibility of its rising to any great height before it shall
be controlled and corrected.[1] Although, in every political
administration, the appointment to offices will ever be
considerably influenced by the sinister, private, personal
motives either of interest or friendship, yet the safety of
the state requires that this should not go too far. An
administration may indeed proceed tolerably when the
officers of a well-arranged system are in general ordinary
characters, provided there is a pretty good sprinkling of
men of wisdom interspersed among them. How much
more illustrious would it be if three quarters of the offices
of government were filled with men of ability, understanding, and patriotism! What an animation would it diffuse through a community if men of real merit in every
branch of business were sure of receiving the rewards and
honors of the state! That great and wise monarch, Olam

1 President Buchanan, whose many years and opportunities of observation and experience, early and late, give weight to his testimony both as
to fact and principle, in a letter of the 22d of November, 1858, wrote as
follows :

" I shall assume the privilege of advancing years in referring to another
growing and dangerous evil. In the last age, although our fathers, like
ourselves, were divided into political parties, which often had severe conflicts, yet we never heard, until a recent period, of the employment of money
to carry elections. Should this practice increase until the voters and their
representatives in the state and national legislatures shall become infected,
the fountain of free government will then be poisoned at its source, and
we must end, as history proves, in military despotism. A democratic
republic, all agree, cannot long survive unless sustained by public virtue.
When this is corrupted, and the people become venal, there is a canker at
the root of the tree of liberty, which must cause it to wither and die."

In a letter to the editor, in 1846, Hon. Henry Clay said of the system
indicated by the phrase "*To the victors belong the spoils,*" it is a "policy
which I fear may, in the end, prove disastrous to our institutions."— Ed.

Fodhla, the Alfred of Ireland, one thousand years before Christ, instituted an annual review and examination of all the achievements and illustrious characters in the realm; and, being approved by himself and the annual assembly of the nobles, he ordered their names and achievements to be enrolled in a public register of merit. This continued two thousand years, to the time of that illustrious chieftain, Brien O'Boroihme. This had an amazing effect. By this animation, the heroic, military, and political virtues, with civilization, and, I add, science and literature, ascended to an almost unexampled and incredible perfection in Ireland, ages before they figured in other parts of Europe, not excepting even Athens and Rome. I have a very great opinion of Hibernian merit, literary as well as civil and military, even in the ages before St. Patrick.

But to return: The cultivation of literature will greatly promote the public welfare. In every community, while provision is made that all should be taught to read the Scriptures, and the very useful parts of common education, a good proportion should be carried through the higher branches of literature. Effectual measures should be taken for preserving and diffusing knowledge among a people. The voluntary institution of libraries in different vicinities will give those who have not a liberal education an opportunity of gaining that knowledge which will qualify them for usefulness. Travels, biography, and history, the knowledge of the policies, jurisprudence, and scientific improvements among all nations, ancient and modern, will form the civilian, the judge, the senator, the patrician, the man of useful eminence in society. The colleges have been of singular advantage in the present day.[1] When Britain

[1] There are 124 colleges, 51 theological schools, 19 law schools, and 40 medical, in the United States. — American Almanac, 1860. The United

withdrew all her wisdom from America, this revolution
found above two thousand, in New England only, who
had been educated in the colleges, intermixed among
the people, and communicating knowledge among them.
Almost all of them have approved themselves useful;
and there have been some characters among us of the
first eminence for literature.[1] It would be for the public
emolument should there always be found a sufficient
number of men in the community at large of vast and
profound erudition, and perfect acquaintance with the
whole system of public affairs, to illuminate the public
councils, as well as fill the three learned professions with
dignity and honor.

I have thus shown wherein consists the true political
welfare of a civil community or sovereignty. The foundation is laid in a judicious distribution of property, and in a
good system of polity and jurisprudence, on which will
arise, under a truly patriotic, upright, and firm administration, the beautiful superstructure of a well-governed
and prosperous empire.

Already does the new constellation of the United States
begin to realize this glory. It has already risen to an
acknowledged sovereignty among the republics and kingdoms of the world. And we have reason to hope, and, I
believe, to expect, that God has still greater blessings in
store for this vine which his own right hand hath planted,
to make us high among the nations in praise, and in name,

States census of 1850 showed, at that date, an annual expenditure of
about $15,000,000 for newspapers and periodical literature, which, on a
probable estimate, "would cover a surface of one hundred square miles,
or constitute a belt of thirty feet around the earth, and weigh nearly
70,000,000 pounds." There were, at the same date, 15,615 other than private libraries, containing 4,636,411 volumes, much the larger portion of the
above being in the northern states. — ED.

1 See pp. xxxii., xxxiv., 43. — ED.

and in honor. The reasons are very numerous, weighty, and conclusive.

In our civil constitutions, those impediments are re-moved which obstruct the progress of society towards perfection, such, for instance, as respect the tenure of estates, and arbitrary government. The vassalage of dependent tenures, the tokens of ancient conquests by Goths and Tartars, still remain all over Asia and Europe. In this respect, as well as others, the world begins to open its eyes. One grand experiment, in particular, has lately been made. The present Empress of Russia, by granting lands in freehold, in her vast wildernesses of Vol-kouskile, together with religious liberty, has allured and already drafted from Poland and Germany a coloniza-tion of six hundred thousand souls in six years only, from 1762 to 1768.[a]

Liberty, civil and religious, has sweet and attractive charms. The enjoyment of this, with property, has filled the English settlers in America with a most amazing spirit, which has operated, and still will operate, with great energy. Never before has the experiment been so effectu-ally tried of every man's reaping the fruits of his labor and feeling his share in the aggregate system of power. The ancient republics did not stand on the people at large, and therefore no example or precedent can be taken from them. Even men of arbitrary principles will be obliged, if they would figure in these states, to assume the patriot so long that they will at length become charmed with the sweets of liberty.

Our degree of population is such as to give us reason to expect that this will become a great people. It is proba-ble that within a century from our independence the sun will shine on fifty millions of inhabitants in the United

a Marshal's Travels.

States.[1] This will be a great, a very great nation, nearly equal to half Europe. Already has our colonization extended down the Ohio, and to Koskaseah on the Mississippi. And if the present ratio of increase should be rather diminished in some of the other settlements, yet an accelerated multiplication will attend our general propagation, and overspread the whole territory westward for ages. So that before the millennium the English settlements in America may become more numerous millions than that greatest dominion on earth, the Chinese Empire. Should this prove a future fact, how applicable would be the text, when the Lord shall have made his American Israel high above all nations which he has made, in numbers, and in praise, and in name, and in honor!

I am sensible some will consider these as visionary, utopian ideas; and so they would have judged had they lived in the apostolic age, and been told that by the time of Constantine the Empire would have become Christian. As visionary that the twenty thousand souls which first settled New England should be multiplied to near a million in a century and a half.[2] As visionary that the Ottoman Empire must fall by the Russian. As visionary to the Catholics is the certain downfall of the pontificate.

---

[1] As deduced, by method of finite differences, from the census returns of 1830, '40, and '50, the population of the United States will be, in 1883, 56,992,000; and, on an assumed equi-rational law of increase, according to the returns of 1820, '30, '40, and '50, it will then be 60,146,000. — Mr. E. B. Elliott's MSS. Thus the official decennial enumerations more than justify the estimates made by Dr. Stiles from his comparatively crude data. Dr. Franklin made similar calculations. See Franklin's Works, edited by Jared Sparks, LL.D., ii., p. 319. There are now living some who will see the political centre of the Union near the Mississippi; and already the commerce of the great lakes exceeds the total foreign commerce of the United States. See Cooper's Cont. to Smithsonian Inst. 1858, paper on the region west of the Mississippi. — Ed.

[2] See p. 211, note 1. — Ed.

As utopian would it have been to the loyalists, at the battle of Lexington, that in less than eight years the independence and sovereignty of the United States should be acknowledged by four European sovereignties, one of which should be Britain herself. How wonderful the revolutions, the events of Providence! We live in an age of wonders; we have lived an age in a few years; we have seen more wonders accomplished in eight years than are usually unfolded in a century.

God be thanked, we have lived to see peace restored to this bleeding land, at least a general cessation of hostilities among the belligerent powers. And on this occasion does it not become us to reflect how wonderful, how gracious, how glorious has been the good hand of our God upon us, in carrying us through so tremendous a warfare! We have sustained a force brought against us which might have made any empire on earth to tremble; and yet our bow has abode in strength, and, having obtained help of God, we continue unto this day. Forced unto the last solemn appeal, America watched for the first blood; [1] this was shed by Britons on the nineteenth of April, 1775, which instantly sprung an army of twenty thousand into spontaneous existence, with the enterprising and daring, if imprudent, resolution of entering Boston and forcibly disburdening it of its bloody legions. Every patriot trembled till we had proved our armor, till it could be seen whether this hasty concourse was susceptible of exercitual arrangement, and could face the enemy with firmness. They early gave us the decided proof of this in the memorable battle of Bunker Hill.[a] We were satisfied. This instantly convinced us, and for the first time convinced Britons themselves, that Americans both would and could fight with

[a] June 17, 1775.

[1] See pp. 235, 237. — ED.

great effect. Whereupon Congress put at the head of this spirited army the only man on whom the eyes of all Israel were placed. Posterity, I apprehend, and the world itself, inconsiderate and incredulous as they may be of the dominion of Heaven, will yet do so much justice to the divine moral government as to acknowledge that this American Joshua was raised up by God, and divinely formed, by a peculiar influence of the Sovereign of the universe, for the great work of leading the armies of this American Joseph (now separated from his brethren), and conducting this people through the severe, the arduous conflict, to liberty and independence. Surprising was it with what instant celerity men ascended and rose into generals, and officers of every subordination, formed chiefly by the preparatory discipline of only the preceding year 1774,[1] when the ardor and spirit of military discipline was by Heaven, and without concert, sent through the continent like lightning. Surprising was it how soon the army was organized, took its formation, and rose into firm system and impregnable arrangement.

To think of withstanding and encountering Britain by land was bold, and much more bold and daring by sea; yet we immediately began a navy, and built ships of war with an unexampled expedition. It is presumed never was a thirty-five-gun ship before built quicker than that well-built, noble ship, the *Raleigh*,[2] which was finished from the keel and equipped for sea in a few months. Soon had we got, though small, a very gallant initial navy,

---

1 See pp. 193, 196, 214-220, 224, 251, 253, note. — ED.

2 " A fine twelve-pounder frigate," launched May 21, 1776, at Portsmouth, N. H. Her hull was completed in sixty days after her keel was laid. She was pierced for thirty-two guns. Nine weeks before the " Madison," of twenty-four guns, was launched at Sackett's Harbor, November 26, 1812, her timber was growing in the forest. — ED.

which fought gallantly, and wanted nothing but numbers of ships for successful operations against that superior naval force before which we fell. We have, however, exhibited proof to posterity and the world that a powerful navy may be originated, built, and equipped for service in a much shorter period than was before imagined. The British navy has been many centuries growing; and France, Holland, the Baltic powers, or any of the powers of this age, in twenty years may build navies of equal magnitude, if necessary for dominion, commerce, or ornament.

A variety of success and defeat hath attended our warfare both by sea and land. In our lowest and most dangerous estate, in 1776 and 1777, we sustained ourselves against the British army of sixty thousand troops, commanded by Howe, Burgoyne, and Clinton, and other the ablest generals Britain could procure throughout Europe, with a naval force of twenty-two thousand seamen in above eighty British men-of-war.[a] These generals we sent home, one after another, conquered, defeated, and convinced of the impossibility of subduing America. While oppressed by the heavy weight of this combined force, Heaven inspired us with resolution to cut the gordian knot, when the die was cast irrevocable in the glorious act of Independence. This was sealed and confirmed by God Almighty in the victory of General Washington at Trenton, and in the surprising movement and battle of Princeton, by which astonishing effort of generalship General Howe and the whole British army, in elated confidence and in open-mouthed march for Philadelphia, was instantly stopped,

[a] To lose America has cost Britain the loss of more than a hundred thousand men, and a hundred and twenty millions sterling in money. Mr. Thomas Pitt, from authentic documents, lately asserted in Parliament that only the first five years of this war had cost Britain five millions more than all the wars of the last age, including the splendid victories of the Duke of Marlborough.

remanded back, and cooped up for a shivering winter in the little borough of Brunswick. Thus God "turned the battle to the gate," and this gave a finishing to the foundation of the American Republic. This, with the Burgoynade at Saratoga by General Gates, and the glorious victory over the Earl of Cornwallis in Virginia, together with the memorable victory of Eutaw Springs, and the triumphant recovery of the southern states by General Greene, are among the most heroic acts and brilliant achievements which have decided the fate of America. And who does not see the indubitable interposition and energetic influence of Divine Providence in these great and illustrious events? Who but a Washington, inspired by Heaven, could have struck out the great movement and manœuvre at Princeton? To whom but the Ruler of the winds shall we ascribe it that the British reïnforcement, in the summer of 1777, was delayed on the ocean three months by contrary winds, until it was too late for the conflagrating General Clinton to raise the siege of Saratoga? What but a providential miracle detected the conspiracy of Arnold, even in the critical moment of the execution of that infernal plot, in which the body of the American army, then at West Point, with his Excellency General Washington himself, were to have been rendered into the hands of the enemy? Doubtless inspired by the Supreme Illuminator of great minds were the joint counsels of a Washington and a Rochambeau in that grand effort of generalship with which they deceived and astonished a Clinton, and eluded his vigilance, in their transit by New York and rapid marches for Virginia. Was it not of God that both the navy and army should enter the Chesapeake at the same time? Who but God could have ordained the critical arrival of the Gallic fleet, so as to prevent and defeat the British, and assist and coöperate with the combined armies in the siege and reduction of Yorktown? Should we not ever admire and ascribe to a Supreme Energy the wise and firm generalship displayed by General Greene when, leaving the active, roving Cornwallis to pursue his helter-skelter, ill-fated march into Virginia, he coolly and steadily went onwards, and deliberately, judiciously, and heroically recovered the Carolinas and the southern states?

How rare have been the defections and apostasies of our capital characters, though tempted with all the charms of gold, titles, and nobility! Whence is it that so few of our army have deserted to the enemy? Whence that our brave sailors have chosen the horrors of prison-ships and death, rather than to fight against their country? Whence that men of every rank have so generally felt and spoken alike, as if the cords of life struck unison through the continent? What but a miracle has preserved the union of the States, the purity of Congress, and the unshaken patriotism of every General Assembly? It is God, who has raised up for us a great and powerful ally,[1] — an ally which sent us a chosen army and a naval force; who sent us a Rochambeau and a Chastelleux,[2] and other characters of the first military merit and eminence, to fight side by side with a Washington and a Lincoln, and the intrepid Americans, in the siege and battle of Yorktown. It is God

[1] The gratitude due to France for the services rendered to us in our Revolution is considered in Letters iv.—vii. of "Pacificus"—Alexander Hamilton — on Washington's Proclamation of Neutrality of 1793. See also "Life and Works of John Adams," by Mr. Charles Francis Adams, index, Marbois, Vergennes. — ED.

[2] The volume of Travels in North America, in 1780–1–2, by the Marquis de Chastelleux, is rich in observations on the men and things of that period. The English translation of 1787 was republished in New York in 1827, with spicy notes. For instance, Mr. John ———— was "celebrated for duplicity on both sides of the water."— ED.

who so ordered the balancing interests of nations as to produce an irresistible motive in the European maritime powers to take our part. Hence the recognition of our independence by Spain and Holland, as well as France. Britain ought to have foreseen that it must have given joy to surrounding nations, tired and wearied out with the insolence and haughtiness of her domineering flag, — a flag which spread terror through the oceans of the terraqueous globe, — to behold the era when their forces should have arrived at such maturity and strength that a junction of national navies would produce an aggregate force adequate to the humiliation of Britain and her gallant and lofty navy. Nor could they resist the operation of this motive prompting them to assist in the cutting off of a member with which the growing aggrandizement and power of Britain were connected, as thus she would be disarmed of terror, and they should be at rest. If Britain doth not learn wisdom by these events, and disclaim the sovereignty of the ocean, the junction of national navies[1] will settle the point for her in less than half a century; so wonderfully does Divine Providence order the time and coïncidence of the public national motives, coöperating in effecting great public events and revolutions.

But the time would fail me to recount the wonder-working providence of God in the events of this war. Let these serve as a specimen, and lead us to hope that God will not forsake this people for whom he has done such marvellous things, — whereof we are glad, and rejoice this day, — having at length brought us to the dawn of peace. O Peace, thou welcome guest, all hail! Thou heavenly visitant, calm the tumult of nations, and wave thy balmy wing to perpetuity over this region of liberty! Let there be a tranquil period for the unmolested accomplishment

---

[1] See note 1 on p. 457, on the Armed Neutrality. — ED.

of the *Magnalia Dei* — the great events in God's moral government designed from eternal ages to be displayed in these ends of the earth.

And here I beg leave to congratulate my country upon the termination of this cruel and unnatural war, the cessation of hostilities, and the prospect of peace. May this great event excite and elevate our first, our highest acknowledgments to the Sovereign Monarch of universal nature, to the Supreme Disposer and Controller of all events! Let this, our pious, sincere, and devout gratitude, ascend in one general effusion of heartfelt praise and hallelujah, in one united cloud of incense, even the incense of universal joy and thanksgiving, to God, from the collective body of the United States.

And while we render our supreme honors to the Most High, the God of armies, let us recollect with affectionate honor the bold and brave sons of freedom who willingly offered themselves and bled in the defence of their country. Our fellow-citizens, the officers and soldiers of the patriot army, who, with the Manlys,[1] the Joneses, and other gallant commanders and brave seamen of the American navy, have heroically fought the war by sea and by land, merit of their once bleeding but now

---

[1] Captain John Manly, — " Jack Manly,"— of Marblehead, Massachusetts, under a naval commission from Washington, October 24, 1775, hoisted the first American flag on board the schooner *Lee*. To him the first British flag was struck; and, on the 28th of November, 1775, he brought into Gloucester the first prize taken in behalf of the entire country, the English ship *Nancy*, from London for Boston, freighted with military supplies, which were taken by land to Cambridge, to the joy of Washington, and which were of immense value to the besieging army at that moment of absolute want. This was one of the wonderful interpositions in our favor so remarkable in our whole history. They christened one piece " The Congress." Captain Manly, eminent in naval annals, died in Boston, 1793, aged fifty-nine. — Sabine's Fisheries of the American Seas, 200, 203; Babson's History of Gloucester, 397. — ED.

triumphant country laurels, crowns, rewards, and the highest honors. Never was the profession of arms used with more glory, or in a better cause, since the days of Joshua the son of Nun. O Washington! how do I love thy name! How have I often adored and blessed thy God for creating and forming thee the great ornament of human kind! Upheld and protected by the Omnipotent, by the Lord of hosts, thou hast been sustained and carried through one of the most arduous and most important wars in all history. The world and posterity will with admiration contemplate thy deliberate, cool, and stable judgment, thy virtues, thy valor, and heroic achievements, as far surpassing those of a Cyrus, whom the world loved and adored. The sound of thy fame shall go out into all the earth, and extend to distant ages. Thou hast convinced the world of the beauty of virtue; for in thee this beauty shines with distinguished lustre. Those who would not recognize any beauty in virtue in the world beside, will yet reverence it in thee. There is a glory in thy disinterested benevolence which the greatest characters would purchase, if possible, at the expense of worlds, and which may excite indeed their emulation, but cannot be felt by the venal great, who think everything, even virtue and true glory, may be bought and sold, and trace our every action to motives terminating in self, —

> "Find virtue local, all relation scorn;
> See all in self, and but for self be born." [a]

But thou, O Washington! forgottest thyself when thou lovedst thy bleeding country. Not all the gold of Ophir, nor a world filled with rubies and diamonds, could effect or purchase the sublime and noble feelings of thine heart in that single self-moved act when thou renouncedst the

[a] Dunciad, b. 4, p. 480.

rewards of generalship, and heroically tookest upon thyself the dangerous as well as arduous office of our generalissimo, and this at a solemn moment, when thou didst deliberately cast the die for the dubious, the very dubious alternative of a gibbet or a triumphal arch. But, beloved, enshielded, and blessed by the great Melchisedec, — the King of righteousness as well as peace, — thou hast triumphed gloriously. Such has been thy military wisdom in the struggles of this arduous conflict, — such the noble rectitude, amiableness, and mansuetude of thy character, — something is there so singularly glorious and venerable thrown by Heaven about thee, — that not only does thy country love thee, but our very enemies stop the madness of their fire in full volley, stop the illiberality of their slander at thy name, as if rebuked from Heaven with a "Touch not mine anointed, and do my hero no harm!" Thy fame is of sweeter perfume than Arabian spices in the gardens of Persia. A Baron de Steuben [1] shall waft its fragrance to the monarch of Prussia; a Marquis de Lafayette shall waft it to a far greater monarch, and diffuse thy renown throughout Europe; [a] listening angels shall catch the odor, waft it to heaven, and perfume the universe.

And, now that our warfare is ended, do thou, O man of God, greatly beloved of the Most High, permit a humble

---

[a] The author does not doubt but that the capital events in the mediatorial kingdom on earth into which angels desire to look, especially those which respect the Protestant Zion, are subjects of extensive attention in heaven, and that characters of real and eminent merit in the cause of liberty and virtue are echoed and contemplated with great honor in the celestial realms.

[1] Counties and towns in New York, Indiana, and Ohio, perpetuate the name of this brave and noble-hearted general, a volunteer in the cause of freedom in America. He remained in this country, and died at Steubenville, New York, November 28, 1798, aged sixty-four. There is an admirable outline of his life in Lossing's Field Book of the Revolution, ii., 342, and an adequate tribute to his worth and services may be found in his Life, by Friedrich Kapp, 1859, pp. 735. — ED.

minister of the blessed Jesus — who, though at a distance, has vigilantly accompanied thee through every stage of thy military progress, has watched thine every movement and danger with a heartfelt anxiety and solicitude, and, with the most sincere and earnest wishes for thy safety and success, has not ceased day nor night to pray for thee, and to commend thee and thy army to God — condescend to permit him to express his most cordial congratulations, and to share in the triumphs of thy bosom, on this great and joyous occasion. We thank the Lord of Hosts that has given his servant to see his desire upon his enemies, and peace on Israel. And when thou shalt now at length retire from the fatigues of nine laborious campaigns to the tranquil enjoyment, to the sweetness and serenity of domestic life, may you never meet the fate of that ornament of arms and of humanity, the great Belisarius, but may a crown of universal love and gratitude, of universal admiration, and of the universal reverence and honor of thy saved country, rest and flourish upon the head of its veteran general and glorious defender, until, by the divine Jesus whom thou hast loved and adored, and of whose holy religion thou art not ashamed, thou shalt be translated from a world of war to a world of peace, liberty, and eternal triumph!

The time would fail me to commemorate the merits of the other capital characters of the army. To do this, and to pay the tribute of fraternal honor and respect to our glorious allied army, will belong to the future Homers, Livys, and Tassos of our country; for none but Americans can write the American war. They will celebrate the names of a Washington and a Rochambeau, a Greene and a Lafayette, a Lincoln and a Chastelleux, a Gates and a Viomenil, a Putnam and a Duke de Lauzun, a Morgan, and other heroes, who rushed to arms and offered themselves voluntarily for the defence of liberty. They will take up a lamentation and drop a tear upon the graves of those mighty ones — those beauties of Israel — who have fallen in battle from the day of Lexington to the victory of Yorktown. And while they commemorate those who have lived through singular sufferings, — as those honorable personages, a Lovel, a Laurens, and a Gadsden, — the names of the illustrious martyr-generals, Warren, Mercer, Montgomery, De Kalb, Wooster, Thomas, with a Polaski, and others, will be recorded as heroically falling in these wars of the Lord. But I may not enlarge, save only that we drop a tear, or rather showers of tears, upon the graves of those other brave officers and soldiers that fell in battle, or otherwise perished in the war. "O that my head were waters, and my eyes a fountain of tears," that I might weep the thousands of our brethren that have perished in prison-ships, — in one of which, the *Jersey*, then lying at New York, perished above eleven thousand the last three years, — while others have been barbarously exiled to the East Indies for life. Come, mourn with me, all ye tender parents and friends, the fate of your dear — dear — But these scenes are too tender and distressing. Can we ever love Britain again? Can the tender, affectionate fathers and mothers, brothers and sisters, — can the numerous bemoaning friends and relatives, and, perhaps, the espoused bosoms of the tender sex, — can they, I say, ever forget the cruel mockings, scourgings, starvations, deaths, assassinations of their dearest offspring and connections in British captivity? Can they forget the numerous thousands of their captivated countrymen instantly consigned to destruction, to dungeons, prisons, places of variolous infection and certain death? Will they be soothed by telling them this is the fate of war? As well may inquisitorial cruelties be soothed by alleging they are salutary

corrections, and necessary for the good of the church.
Our enemies took occasion from this fate of war to reek
their vengeance, and to lash us with a severity too unmerciful ever to be forgotten. Can we forget the conflagra-
tions of Charlestown, Norfolk, Esopus, Fairfield, and other
American towns, laid in ashes by a Tryon and other incendiaries? [1] Were these the kindnesses American brethren
received from the hands of Britons and their more cruel
associates the Indians and loyalists? Can we forget the
barbarous tragedy of Colonel Haine, or the murder of
Captain Huddy, in violation of the most sacred laws of
war and of national honor? Blush, O Britain, for the
stain of your national glory! Can we ever forget with
what cruel and malicious delight they tortured, entowered,
and insulted an American plenipotentiary, — the illustrious Laurens, — although by the laws of honor and nations
the person of an ambassador is sacred? Can we ever
forget the cruel and infamous treatment of the Honorable
Mr. Gadsden? O Gadsden,[2] how I reverence thy piety,
thy firmness in captivity, thine intrepid and uncorrupted
patriotism, thine enlightened politics, thy unremitted fervor and zeal in the cause of liberty! But how painful is
it to recount the even less than ten-thousandth part of the
series of distresses, the complicated woe and misery, that
make up the system of sufferings which we have been
called to endure in the pangs and throes of the parturition
of empire, in " effecting our glorious revolution, in rescu-

[1] " Twelve temples, or houses of public worship, were burnt and demolished by the British, from Boston to Hudson's River, besides those burned
beyond."— Note to the second edition, 1785. — ED.

[2] For an account of the murder of Huddy by Tory refugees, of Lord
Rawdon's infamy in the execution of Colonel Hayne, and of Governor
Tryon's cruelty to the venerable Gadsden, see Lossing's Field Book of the
Revolution, ii., 366, 774, 768. — ED.

ing millions from the hand of oppression, and in laying the foundation of a great empire." [a]

The patriot army merits our commemoration, and so do the great characters in the patriotic Assemblies and Congress.   Let America never forget what they owe to those first intrepid defenders of her rights, the Honorable Mr. Samuel Adams, and the Hon. James Otis, Esq. ; add to these the Hon. Dr. John Winthrop, Hon. James Bowdoin, Esq., who, with others, were the marked objects of ministerial vengeance, who early stepped forth and heroically withstood tyranny, and alarmed their country with its danger, while venal sycophants were lulling us to rest and hushing us into silence.   His Excellency Mr. President Randolph merits our grateful commemoration, and so do the governors Rutledge, Ward, Livingston, Hopkins, Nash, Clinton, the Hon. Messrs. Wythe, Dyer, Sherman, Pendleton, Henry, Ellery, the Lees, President Huntington, Lynch, Witherspoon, Wolcott, Gov. Paca, Gov. Hall, Law, Marchant, President McKean, Ellsworth, Vandyke, Jefferson — Jefferson, who poured the soul of the continent into the monumental act of Independence.   These, and other worthy personages of this and the other states, will be celebrated in history among the cardinal patriots of this revolution.   All the ages of man will not obliterate the meritorious name of His Excellency Governor Hancock, as President of Congress at a most critical era, nor the meritorious names of that illustrious band of heroes and compatriots, those sensible and intrepid worthies who, with him, resolutely and nobly dared, in the face of every danger, to sign the glorious act of Independence.   May their names live, be preserved, and transmitted to posterity with deserved reputation and honor, through all American

[a] General Washington's address to the army, in general orders, April 19, 1783, on the cessation of hostilities.

ages![a] Those great civilians and ambassadors, the illustrious Franklin, Adams, Jay, and Laurens, have approved themselves equal to the highest negotiations in the courts of nations, been faithful to their country's liberties, and, by their great and eminent services, have justly merited to have their names sent forward to immortality in history with renown and unsullied glory.

Great and extensive will be the happy effects of this warfare, in which we have been called in Providence to fight out not the liberties of America only, but the liberties of the world itself. The spirited and successful stand which we have made against tyranny will prove the salvation of England and Ireland, and, by teaching all sovereigns the danger of irritating and trifling with the affections and loyalty of their subjects, introduce clemency, moderation, and justice into public government at large through Europe. Already have we learned Ireland and other nations the road to liberty, the way to a redress of grievances, by

---

[a] JOHN HANCOCK.

NEW HAMPSHIRE. — Josiah Bartlett, William Whipple, Matthew Thornton.

MASSACHUSETTS BAY. — Samuel Adams, John Adams, Robert Treat Paine, Elbridge Gerry.

RHODE ISLAND. — Stephen Hopkins, William Ellery.

CONNECTICUT. — Roger Sherman, Samuel Huntington, William Williams, Oliver Wolcott.

NEW YORK. — William Floyd, Philip Livingston, Francis Lewis, Lewis Morris.

NEW JERSEY. — Richard Stockton, John Witherspoon, Francis Hopkinson, John Hart, Abraham Clark.

PENNSYLVANIA. — Robert Morris, Benjamin Rush, Benjamin Franklin, John Morton, George Clymer, James Smith, George Taylor, James Wilson, George Ross.

DELAWARE. — Cæsar Rodney, George Read.

MARYLAND. — Samuel Chace, William Paca, Thomas Stone, Charles Carroll (of Carrollton).

VIRGINIA. — George Wythe, Richard Henry Lee, Thomas Jefferson, Benjamin Harrison, Thomas Nelson, Jr., Francis Lightfoot Lee, Carter Braxton.

NORTH CAROLINA. — William Hooper, Joseph Hewes, John Penn.

SOUTH CAROLINA. — Edward Rutledge, Thomas Heyward, Jr., Thomas Lynch, Jr., Arthur Middleton.

GEORGIA. — Button Gwinnett, Lyman Hall, George Walton.

open, systematical measures, Committees of Correspondence,[1] and military discipline of an armed people. Ireland has become gloriously independent of England.[2] Nor will the spirit rest till Scotland becomes independent also. It would be happier for the three kingdoms to subsist with parliaments and national councils independent of one another, although confederated under one monarch. The union of 1707 has produced the loss and dismemberment of America.[3] It is just possible that within this age some ill-fated counsellor of another connection might have arisen and prompted Majesty and Parliament to sanguinary measures against America; but it is more than probable that their enforcement would have been deferred, or procrastinated a century hence, or to a period when our accumulated population would have dictated wiser, milder measures to the British court; and so America, by a gentle, fraternal connection, would have remained cemented[4] to

[1] See pp. 44, 191, 199. — ED.

[2] January 1, 1800, ended that independence, and was the date of the legislative union between England and Ireland. — ED.

[3] The intensity of Dr. Stiles's detestation of the two Scotchmen, Bute and Murray, — which led him to say that the " union" of Scotland and England in 1707 " has produced the loss and dismemberment of America," probably because, by that union, the Scotch statesmen, hated for their arbitrary principles, were eligible to the English councils, — affords an amusing parallel to Dr. Johnson's inveterate prejudice against the Scotch. In his dictionary the Doctor defines oats as " a grain which in England is generally given to horses, but in Scotland supports the people." Bute was believed to be, by his personal influence, the evil genius of George III. and of England, and was profoundly hated there as well as in America; and the jurist Murray — Lord Mansfield — upheld the worst measures against America. Yet both were exemplary in private life. See pp. 69, 70, 86, 162, 168, 301, 343. — ED.

[4] The pathos with which Dr. Stiles speaks of " the painful and distressing separation and dismemberment" from the mother country, and his vehement denunciation of the " demon" Bute, do not exaggerate the loyal temper of our fathers. They would have then been content with

Britain for distant ages. But a Rehoboam counsellor stepped in, *et actum est de republica* — the Ten Tribes are lost.[1] Had it not been for the insidious and haughty counsels of a Bute and a Mansfield, imbued with principles incompatible with liberty, with the unwieldy faction of their despotic connections in the empire, America and Ireland had remained united with Britain to this day. Chagrined and mortified by the defeat and dishonor brought upon them by Butean counsels and dominion, as well as with their own curtailed and unequal weight in Parliament, Scotland, emulous of the glory of Ireland,

half the rights which the present British American Provinces enjoy. But the blindness of Governor Hutchinson to the character of his countrymen, and the consequent false impressions he gave to the British cabinet, the miserable weakness of Gage and Howe at Boston, and the madness of the king in forcing the colonies to union, show the providential government of God, and that his time for this great epoch in the history of human society was now come. — ED.

[1] To the second edition, 1785, the author here made this prophetic note: "And very soon will Bengal and the East Indies be lost and delivered from the cruelty and injustice of British government there. This will speedily be the fruit of Great Britain's departing from the commercial to the governmental idea concerning the East. The conflagrating and plundering qualities of a Clive, and the absurd haughtiness of the subsequent dominion, will at length rouse the spirit of those populous parts of the oriental empires, having learned the use of artillery and the European modes of war, to make one vigorous exertion and shake off this foreign yoke. It is not within the compass of human probability — it is absurd and absolutely impossible — that fifteen millions of people should long continue subjugated to the government of five or six million at the distance of half the circumference of the globe. This event may be accelerated by the necessary tripartite division of the navy in the oriental and Atlantic oceans. The union of European nations cannot fail of taking advantage of the future comparative weakness of British strength arising from this division. Too soon, alas! may Britain, with both wings lopped off, the East Indies and America, exhibit the spectacle among nations described by the Franklinean emblem of Magna Britannia with her colonies reduced. One cannot refrain from tears at contemplating the fate of nations, the rise and fall of empires."— ED.

will wish for and obtain a dissolution of the union, and resume a separate sovereignty. It must be the lenity, the wisdom, the gentle and pacific measures of an Augustan age that can conserve the remnant of the British empire from this tripartite division.

Nor will the British isles alone be relieved into liberty, but more extensive still will be the peaceable fruits of our righteous conflict. The question of the *mare liberum* and the *mare clausum*, heretofore discussed by the ablest civilians of tHe last century, will no more require the learned labors of a Milton, a Selden, a Grotius. This war has decided, not by the *jus maritimum* of Rhodes, Oleron, or Britain, but on the principles of commercial utility and public right, that the navigation of the Atlantic Ocean shall be free; and so probably will be that of all the oceans of the terraqueous globe. All the European powers will henceforth, from national and commercial interests, naturally become a united and combined guaranty for the free navigation of the Atlantic and free commerce with America. Interest will establish a free access of all nations to our shores, and for us to all nations. The armed neutrality[1] will disarm even war itself of hostilities against

---

[1] The authorship of this confederacy, which destroyed Britain's long-established sovereignty of the ocean, and greatly contributed to the ultimate independence of the United States of America, is attributed to several persons. 1. Mr. William Lee, of Virginia, a merchant in London, and some time agent of Congress at Vienna and Berlin during the war of the Revolution, wrote, December 10, 1780, to Governor Lee, of Maryland: "I feel no little pleasure in communicating to you the completion, so far, of this confederacy, as *the first traces were laid by myself two years ago; and if Congress had now in Europe ministers properly authorized to negotiate with the powers it would not be difficult to obtain a general acknowledgment from them of the independence of America, which was *my ultimate object in forming the outlines of this scheme!* "— See letter in National Intelligencer, August 23, 1859. 2. Mr. John Adams — diary, December 21, 1782 — heard the King of Sweden named as "the first inventor and suggester

trade — will form a new chapter in the laws of nations, and preserve a free commerce among powers at war. Fighting armies will decide the fate of empires by the sword, without interrupting the civil, social, and commercial intercourse of subjects. The want of anything to take will prove a natural abolition of privateering, when the property shall be covered with neutral protection. Even the navies will, within a century, become useless. A generous and truly liberal system of national connection, in the spirit of the plan conceived and nearly executed by the great Henry IV. of France,[a] will almost annihilate war itself.

We shall have a communication with all nations in

---

a Sully's Memoirs.1

of the plan." 3. On the evidence of "documents in my possession," says Mr. George Sumner, in his oration, Boston, July 4th, 1859, "I here render the honor" of the real authorship of the armed neutrality to Florida Banca, the minister of Spain. The official documents are in Anderson's Commerce, vi. 362–375, 406, edit. 1790. The universal terror from British privateers was the proximate cause of the league, and England's distress the opportunity. — ED.

1 Bohn's ed. of Sully, 1856, ii. p. 235; iv., Book xxx. This political scheme for a general council of the Christian powers of Europe was formed by Elizabeth of England and Henry IV. of France. The Edict of Nantes was intended as a part of the grand design. A senate, of about sixty-six commissioners, or plenipotentiaries, to be rechosen every three years, from all the governments of the Christian republic, was to be in permanent session, "to deliberate on any affairs which might occur, to discuss the different interests, pacify the quarrels, clear up and determine all the civil, political, and religious affairs of Europe, whether within itself or with its neighbors." The scheme bore a strong resemblance to the American "confederation," and was formed in part on the model of the ancient Amphictyons of Greece, an institution referred to by the framers of our own government. See the "Federalist." The total exemption of private property from capture on the high seas, as recently proposed by the United States government to European powers, would go far to realize the splendid prediction of the text, and, indeed, render "the navies useless," except for the noble missions of humanity, of science, and of national courtesies. — ED.

commerce, manners, and science, beyond anything heretofore known in the world.   Manufacturers and artisans, and
men of every description, may perhaps come and settle
among us.   They will be few indeed in comparison with
the annual thousands of our natural increase, and will be
incorporated with the prevailing hereditary complexion
of the first settlers; — we shall not be assimilated to them,
but they to us, especially in the second and third generations.[1]   This fermentation and communion of nations will
doubtless produce something very new, singular, and glorious.   Upon the conquest of Alexander the Great, statu-
ary, painting, architecture, philosophy, and the fine arts
were transplanted in perfection from Athens to Tarsus,
from Greece to Syria, where they immediately flourished
in even greater perfection than in the parent state.   Not
in Greece herself are there to be found specimens of a
sublimer or more magnificent architecture, even in the

[1] Dr. Cotton Mather says that in 1696, in all New England, there were
one hundred thousand souls.   Dr. Franklin thought that, of the one
million English souls in North America in 1751, not eighty thousand
"had been brought over sea."   Dr. Stiles, in 1760, estimated the inhabitants of New England at half a million; and Mr. Savage, in the Preface
of his Genealogical Dictionary, supposes that nineteen-twentieths of the
people of the New England colonies in 1775 were descendants of those
here in 1692, and that probably seven-eighths of them were offspring of
the first settlers, and originating from England proper.   He adds: "A
more homogeneous stock cannot be seen, I think, in any so extensive
region, at any time since that when the Ark of Noah discharged its pas-
sengers on Mount Ararat, except in the few centuries elapsing before the
confusion of Babel."   In an elaborate paper read before the American
Statistical Association, in March, 1859, by the President, Edward Jarvis,
M. D., it appears, as the result of long and minute calculation, based upon
the best available data, that the total persons of New England origin
living in the United States, in 1850, including the natives and those born
abroad since 1790, was 4,021,192, and that nearly or quite one-third of
the native white population have New England blood in their veins.   This
confirms Mr. Bancroft's estimate. — ED.

Grecian style, than in the ruins of Baalbec and Palmyra. So all the arts may be transplanted from Europe and Asia, and flourish in America with an augmented lustre, not to mention the augment of the sciences from American inventions and discoveries, of which there have been as capital ones here,[a] the last half century, as in all Europe.[2]

---

[a] AMERICAN INVENTIONS. — 1730, Reflecting Quadrant [commonly called Hadley's], by Mr. Thos. Godfry, at Philadelphia; 1731, Mercurial Inoculation, by Dr. Muirson; 1750, Electrical Pointed Rods, by Dr. Franklin; [1755, Terrestrial Comets, by President Clap;] 1762, Sand-Iron, by Dr. Jared Elliot; 1769, Quantity of Matter in Comets, by Professor Winthrop; [1776, Submarine Navigation by the power of the Screw, by Mr. Bushnel.][1]

[1] The parts within [ ] were added in the second edition, 1785. — ED.

[2] "Credat qui vult!" exclaimed a listener, when, with his masterly survey of the elements of empire and their potential future, the wise man in the pulpit opened his grand and comprehensive. vision of "The United States elevated to Glory and Honor," and of the national mission of goodwill to men; yet some, even of that generation, live to contrast the epoch of the nation's beginning — its three millions of inhabitants, scattered along the Atlantic border — with our present recognized position as "the greatest maritime nation on the face of the earth." The country was for many years embarrassed with the war debt, less in amount than our present annual national expenditure. Populous inland states, cities, and commerce, before whose statistics the national figures of 1783 dwindle to fractions, now press fast towards the Pacific, through whose "golden gate" floats a commerce exceeding the grand total when Washington became President, and whose senators are in the capitol.

> "Westward the course of empire takes its way."

Indeed, there were then living, sons of America, Fitch, in manhood, and Fulton, in youth, the inventors of steam navigation, whose genius was to span oceans, and unite continents as with a bridge, and make highways of rivers; and now Ericsson has revolutionized the marine of the world. Whitney, then a youth, was to create, by his cotton-gin, the chief staple of southern agriculture, and the principal even of England's manufactures; Bowditch, then in boyhood, was to rank with the great mathematicians and astronomers. The elder Edwards, the intellectual chief of his age, who "ranks with the brightest luminaries of the Christian church, not excluding any country or any age since the apostolic," and "as much the boast of America as his great countryman, Franklin;" Webster, the great lexicog-

The rough, sonorous diction of the English language may here take its Athenian polish, and receive its attic urbanity, as it will probably become the vernacular tongue of more numerous millions than ever yet spake one language on earth. It may continue for ages to be the prevailing and general language of North America.[1] The

rapher, who has no rival but Worcester, another of New England's sons; Irving, then *in arms*, preëminent in modern literature; and, in later times, Allibone, of equal rank in critical bibliography; Prescott, Sparks, Bancroft, Hildreth, Motley, in history; Bryant, Whittier, and Longfellow, in poetry; Copley, West, Stuart, Trumbull, Allston, Cole, Church, and Hosmer, among the masters in modern art; Mann and Barnard, in education; Lyndhurst, twice Lord Chancellor of England, Marshall, Jay, Parsons, Story, and Kent, in jurisprudence; Morse and Jackson, whose electric wire, "beating with the pulse of humanity," unites cities, kingdoms, and continents, annihilating time and space; Jackson, Wells, Morton, whose splendid discovery of anæsthetics is recognized by the world as one of the greatest boons given by any age to suffering humanity; Agassiz, the chief naturalist of the age, abiding with us; Draper, the accomplished delegate of American science at the British Association at Oxford; and Jarvis, the eminent statistician, representing his country with distinguished honor in the International Statistical Congress at London in 1860; — these, and many others, have already placed the United States in the front rank in science, letters, and art. — ED.

[1] The reader will be glad to compare the profound views presented by Dr. Stiles with the observations of a late able writer, who thinks that "the physical character of our own territory is such as to encourage the hope that our speech, which, if not absolutely homogeneous, is now employed by twenty-five millions of men in one unbroken mass, with a uniformity of which there is perhaps no other example, will escape that division which has shattered some languages of the Old World into fragments, like those of the confusion of Babel. The geography of the United States presents few localities suited to human habitation that are at the same time inaccessible to modern improved modes of communication. The carriage-road, the railway, the telegraph, the mails, the newspaper, penetrate to every secluded nook, address themselves to every free inhabitant, and speak everywhere one and the same dialect. Why or how external physical causes, as climate and modes of life, should affect pronunciation, we cannot say; but it is evident that material influences of some sort are producing a change on our bodily constitution, and

intercommunion of the United States with all the world
in travels, trade, and politics, and the infusion of letters
into our infancy, will probably preserve us from the provincial dialects, risen into inexterminable habit before the
invention of printing. The Greek never became the language of the Alexandrian, nor the Turkish of the Ottoman conquests, nor yet the Latin of the Roman Empire. The Saracenic conquests have already lost the pure
and elegant Arabic of the Koreish tribe, or the family of
Ishmael, in the corrupted dialects of Egypt, Syria, Persia,
and Indostan. Different from these, the English language
will grow up with the present American population into
great purity and elegance, unmutilated by the foreign dialects of foreign conquests. And in this connection I may
observe with pleasure how God, in his providence, has
ordered that, at the Reformation, the English translation
of the Bible should be made with very great accuracy
— with greater accuracy, it is presumed, than any other
translation. This is said, allowing that some texts admit
of correction. I have compared it throughout with the
originals, Hebrew, Greek, and Syriac, and beg leave to
judge and testify it to be a very excellent translation.[1]

we are just acquiring a distinct national character. That the delicate
organs of articulation should participate in such tendencies is altogether natural; and the operation of the causes which gave rise to
them is palpable even in our handwriting, which, if not uniform with
itself, is generally, nevertheless, so much unlike common English script
as to be readily distinguished from it." — Geo. P. Marsh, Lecture xxx.,
The English Language in America. — ED.

[1] The following decided language from one of our most distinguished
scholars and philologists embodies, it may be presumed, the opinion of
the great body of competent Greek and Hebrew scholars, and would
probably be affirmed by the American and British Bible Societies as the
result of their observation. The revision of 1611 is, and seems likely to
remain, in its strength and beauty, the standard. "I do not hesitate,"
says Mr. Marsh, "to avow my conviction, that if any body of scholars of

Nor do I believe a better is ever to be expected in this imperfect state. It sustained a revision of numerous translators, from Tyndal to the last review by the bishops and other learned divines in the time of James I., one hundred and eighty years ago, and has never been altered since.[a] It may have been designed by Providence for the future perusal of more millions of the human race than ever were able to read one book, and for their use to the millennial ages.

This great American Revolution, this recent political phenomenon of a new sovereignty arising among the sovereign powers of the earth, will be attended to and contemplated by all nations. Navigation will carry the American flag around the globe itself, and display the thirteen stripes and new constellation at Bengal and Canton,[1] on the Indus and Ganges, on the Whang-ho and the

---

[a] Vid. Lewis's Hist. Transl. Bib.

competent Greek and Hebrew learning were now (1860) to undertake, not a revision of the existing version, but a new translation, founded on the principle of employing the correct phraseology of the day, it would be found much less intelligible to the mass of English-speaking people than the standard version at this moment is;" and that to "hope of finding within the compass of the English language a clearer, a more appropriate, or a more forcible diction than that of the standard version, is to betray an ignorance of the capabilities of our native speech with which it would be in vain to reason;" and "that as there is no present necessity for a revision, so is there no possibility of executing a revision in any way that would be, or ought to be, satisfactory to even one Protestant sect, still less to the whole body of English-speaking Protestants." — Lectures on the English Language, Lecture xxviii., by Geo. P. Marsh. — ED.

[1] To the second edition, 1785, the author added this note: "Since the first edition, in 1783, this voyage has been happily performed, for the first time, in about fourteen months, by the *Empress of China*, a ship of three hundred and sixty tons, John Green, Esq., of Boston, commander. She sailed from New York Feb. 22, 1784, arrived at Canton, in China, Aug. 30, departed thence Dec. 27, on her return, and arrived safe at New York, May 11, 1785, with the loss of but one man in the whole voyage. And Aug. 9,

Yang-tse-kiang, and with commerce will import the wisdom and literature of the East. That prophecy of Daniel is now literally fulfilling — יְשֹׁטְטוּ רַבִּים וְתִרְבֶּה הַדָּעַת — there shall be a universal travelling to and fro, and knowledge shall be increased. This knowledge will be brought home and treasured up in America, and, being here digested and carried to the highest perfection, may reblaze back from America to Europe, Asia, and Africa, and illumine the world with truth and liberty.

That great civilian Dr. John Adams, the learned and illustrious American ambassador, observes thus:[a] "But the great designs of Providence must be accomplished; — great indeed! The progress of society will be accelerated by centuries by this Revolution. The Emperor of Germany is adopting, as fast as he can, American ideas of toleration and religious liberty; and it will become the fashionable system of Europe very soon.[1] Light spreads

---

[a] Lett. Dec. 18, 1781.

1785, the ship *Pallas*, Capt. John O'Donnel, arrived at Baltimore from China. She left Macao, in Canton, the 20th of January preceding. This was the second East India ship from China to America. The same month of Aug., 1785, a Swedish ship arrived also at Baltimore from Calcutta, in the East Indies. This is the third East India ship which arrived in America in the year 1785."— ED.

[1] Maria Theresa of Austria thought the cause of George III., against the colonies, to be "the cause of all sovereigns," and had "a high esteem for his Majesty's principles of government." She died November 29, 1780, and was succeeded by her son, Joseph II., then in his fortieth year. He used his despotic power with a wisdom and singularity that startled Europe. He ordered a new translation of the Bible to be made in the German tongue, established a free press, the equality of all Christian denominations, abolished the priestly censorship of books, which had been so rigorous "that on subjects of religion, morality, and government, a valuable and a prohibited publication were almost synonymous terms," founded public libraries, established educational institutions, abolished feudal slavery, and labored to educate and elevate his people. So precipitate and radical were his innovations, so fatal were they to superstition

from the day-spring in the west; and may it shine more and more until the perfect day." So spreading may be the spirit for the restoration and recovery of long-lost national rights, that even the Cortes of Spain may reëxist,

and mental and moral darkness, that Pius VI., old and feeble, made a winter journey, in February, 1782, to Vienna, to remonstrate against them, but in vain. At the accession of Joseph II. the United States government was seeking European alliances. Their history and principles became familiar to the statesmen and leading minds of Europe. Our minister, John Adams, published at Leyden, in April, 1781, his eloquent "Memorial" of their claim to respect and consideration, and in February, 1782, he wrote to his government that it had been translated and "inserted in almost every gazette in Europe;" that the King of Sweden had quoted its "very words" in his public answer and reproach to George III.; that Joseph II. had desired an interview with its author, and, "what is more remarkable, has adopted the sentiment of it concerning religious liberty into a code of laws for his dominions, — the greatest effort in favor of humanity, next to the American Revolution, which has been produced in the eighteenth century."

The Revolution raised Ireland to the position of a kingdom, and the contagion of its republican principles was felt throughout Europe. The French nobles, Lafayette, Rochambeau, D'Estaing, Lausun, and others, conveyed to their own country the popular sympathies and principles for which they had fought in America, and thus gave an impulse to the Revolution in France.

Historians and philosophers regard the American Revolution as the great epoch in the modern history of human society — of the world; as " commencing a new series of human history, a new system of political relations, which must involve in its combinations all the countries of the earth."

Washington stands out to the world as the grandest object of contemplation, the Father of the Republic to which is confided the great problem of popular government, of the broadest Christian freedom, and towards which the genius of liberty ever looks with hope, yet with solicitude; for whose prosperity the nations pray, as for one whose calamity will be the despair of humanity, and the triumph only of him who would destroy the image of God in man. How exalted the trust, how momentous the conduct of the American citizen! — Coxe's "House of Austria," Bohn's ed., chap. cxxiv.; "Life and Works of John Adams," 1852, vii., 404, 525, 527; Miller's Philosophy of History, ed. 1854, 145–147, 178, 181, 185, 186. — Ed.

and resume their ancient splendor, authority, and control of royalty.[a] The same principles of wisdom and enlightened politics may establish rectitude in public government throughout the world.

The most ample religious liberty will also probably obtain among all nations. Benevolence and religious lenity are increasing among the nations. The reformed in France, who were formerly oppressed with heavy persecution, at present enjoy a good degree of religious liberty, though by silent indulgence only. A reëstablishment of the Edict of Nantes would honor the Grand Monarch by doing public justice to a large body of his best and most loyal subjects. The Emperor of Germany last year published an imperial decree granting liberty for the free and unmolested exercise of the Protestant religion within the Austrian territories and dominions.[b] The Inquisition

a So jealous were the Cortes of their liberties, that the states of Arragon in particular, after sundry previous stipulations, exacted a coronation oath of the king, which was pronounced by the Justitia Arragonensis (who represented the person of the supreme power in the state), a power which they asserted to be superior to kings, in these words: *Nos qui valemos tanto comme vos, y podemos mas que vos, vos elegimos Rey : con estas y estas conditiones, intra vos y nos, un que manda mas que vos.* " We who are as powerful as you, and have more authority than you, elect you king; with the stipulated conditions, between you and us there is one (viz., the judiciary) higher in command than you." See a learned tract, De jure magistratuum in subdito et officio subditorum erga magistratus: printed at Lyons, 1576, full of jural and political erudition, and, for that age, full of liberty.

b The order of Jesuits, suppressed in rapid succession by the European princes, 1765, was finally abolished, 1773, by the sensible and sagacious Ganganelli, who bid fairer to reünite the Protestants, had it been possible, than any pontiff since the secession from Leo X. Nor can the order be revived, nor the suppression of religious houses in Spain and Austria, nor Austrian liberty, be prevented by the bigoted, austere Braschi, the present reigning pontiff.[1]

1 July 21–23, 1773, Ganganelli, Clement XIV., " established by the Divine Providence, *over kingdoms and nations,* in order to pluck up, destroy, disperse, dissipate, plant, or nourish, as may best conduce to the right cultivation of the" papal hierarchy, in his *bull* of that date, said: "After a mature deliberation, we do, out of our certain knowledge, and *the fulness of our apostolical power,* suppress and abolish the said company, . . .

has been, in effect, this year suppressed in Spain, where the king, by an edict of 3d of November, 1782, proclaimed liberty for inhabitants of all religions; and, by a happily conceived plan for literary reformation, the aurora of science will speedily blaze into meridian splendor in that kingdom. An emulation for liberty and science is enkindled among the nations, and will doubtless produce something very liberal and glorious in this age of science, this period of the empire of reason.[1]

The United States will embosom all the religious sects or denominations in Christendom. Here they may all enjoy their whole respective systems of worship and church government complete. Of these, next to the Presbyterians, the Church of England will hold a distinguished and principal figure. They will soon furnish themselves with a bishop in Virginia and Maryland, and perhaps another

so that the name of the company shall be, and is, forever extinguished and suppressed. . . . These our letters shall be *forever and to all eternity* valid, permanent, and efficacious, . . . observed by all and every whom they do or may concern, *now or hereafter*, in any manner whatever." The reason given was that the Jesuits were an *intolerable political and moral curse*. They had six hundred and sixty-nine colleges, one hundred and ninety-six seminaries, two hundred and twenty-three missions, twenty-two thousand seven hundred and eighty-two members, scattered over the world. August 17, 1814, another infallible Pope, Pius VII., abrogated the brief of his infallible predecessor, and reëstablished the order for *political purposes;* and it now infests our own country. The "fathers," leagued with the Pope's "venerable brothers, the archbishops, bishops," priests, etc., and "liberal Protestants" ! aid and comfort these priestly enemies to civil and religious liberty by money, pupils, and approbation. The policy of the Papal church is to keep the people in *perpetual infancy*, the sole basis of its own existence, and of despotism, its natural result and ally. See p. 416. — ED.

[1] In the second edition, 1785, the author appends this note: " Justly may we anticipate great alterations in society, and very beneficent improvements in the state of mankind, 'from the progressive refinement of manners, the growing liberality of sentiment, and, above all, the PURE AND BENIGN LIGHT OF REVELATION.' — General Washington."— ED.

to the northward, to ordain their clergy, give confirmation, superintend and govern their churches, — the main body of which will be in Virginia and Maryland, — besides a diaspora or interspersion in all the other states. The *Unitas Fratrum* for above thirty years past have had Moravian bishops in America; and I think they have three at present, though not of local or diocesan jurisdiction, their pastorate being the whole unity throughout the world. In this there ever was a distinction between the Bohemian episcopacy and that of the eastern and western churches; for, in a body of two thousand ancient Bohemian churches, they seldom had above two or three bishops. The Baptists, the Friends, the Lutherans, the Romanists, are all considerable bodies in all their dispersions through the states. The Dutch and Gallic and German Reformed or Calvinistic churches among us I consider as Presbyterian, differing from us in nothing of moment save in language. There is a considerable body of these in the states of New York, Jersey, Pennsylvania, and at Ebenezer, in Georgia. There is a Greek Church, brought from Smyrna; but I think it falls below these states. There are Westleians, Mennonists, and others, all which make a very inconsiderable amount in comparison with those who will give the religious complexion to America, which for the southern parts will be Episcopal, the northern, Presbyterian. All religious denominations will be independent of one another, as much as the Greek and Armenian patriarchates in the East; and having, on account of religion, no superiority as to secular powers and civil immunities, they will cohabit together in harmony, and, I hope, with a most generous catholicism and benevolence.[1] The example of

---

[1] Of the seven or eight denominations named by Dr. Stiles, some hardly survive, while others, as the Methodist and Baptist, have become numerous. *Twenty-one* religious denominations are enumerated in the census of the

a friendly cohabitation of all sects in America, proving that men may be good members of civil society and yet differ in religion, — this precedent, I say, which has already been intently studied and contemplated for fifteen years past by France, Holland, and Germany, may have already had an effect in introducing moderation, lenity, and justice among European states. And who can tell how extensive a blessing this American Joseph may become to the whole human race, although once despised by his brethren, exiled, and sold into Egypt? How applicable that in Genesis xlix. 22, 26 : "Joseph is a fruitful bough, even a fruitful bough by a well ; whose branches run over the wall. The archers have sorely grieved him, and shot at him, and hated him. But his bow abode in strength ; the arms of his hands were made strong by the arms of the mighty God of Jacob. The blessings of thy father have prevailed above the blessings of my progenitors, unto the utmost bound of the everlasting hill ; they shall be on the head of Joseph, and on the crown of the head of him that was separated from his brethren."

Little would civilians have thought ages ago that the world should ever look to America for models of govern-

---

United States for 1850, of which, counting the Methodist, Baptist, Presbyterian, Congregational, and Dutch Reformed, who are named in the order of their numerical ratio, as of the Congregational type, there were 29,607 churches ; and of all others, including Episcopal, Roman Catholic, Christian, and Friends, 8045 churches, — an aggregate of 37,652 churches, — showing the ratio of the former to the whole as about 4 to 5. The total of church accommodations was 14,270,139, of which 10,664,656 were of the Congregational type as above, and 3,605,483 of the others, — showing the ratio of the former to the whole as about 3 to 4, or 74.6 per cent. of the whole. The Methodists had 13,338 churches ; Baptists, 9360 ; Congregationalists, 1706 ; Episcopalians, 1461 ; Roman Catholics, 1227 ; Lutherans, 1221. They are unequally distributed over the Union, and the relation of denominational to moral, educational, and social statistics offers a most inviting and instructive inquiry. — ED.

ment and polity; little did they think of finding this most
perfect polity among the poor outcasts, the contemptible
people of New England, and particularly in the long despised civil polity of Connecticut,[1] — a polity conceived
by the sagacity and wisdom of a Winthrop, a Ludlow,
Haynes, Hopkins, Hooker, and the other first settlers of
Hartford, in 1636. And while Europe and Asia may
hereafter learn that the most liberal principles of law
and civil polity are to be found on this side the Atlantic,
they may also find the true religion here depurated from
the rust and corruption of ages, and learn from us to reform and restore the church to its primitive purity. It
will be long before the ecclesiastical pride of the splendid
European hierarchies can submit to learn wisdom from
those whom they have been inured to look upon with
sovereign contempt. But candid and liberal disquisition
will, sooner or later, have a great effect. Removed from
the embarrassments of corrupt systems, and the dignities
and blinding opulence connected with them, the unfet-
tered mind can think with a noble enlargement, and, with
an unbounded freedom, go wherever the light of truth
directs. Here will be no bloody tribunals, no cardinal's
inquisitors-general, to bend the human mind, forcibly to
control the understanding, and put out the light of reason,
the candle of the Lord, in man, — to force an innocent
Galileo to renounce truths demonstrable as the light of
day. Religion may here receive its last, most liberal,
and impartial examination. Religious liberty is peculiarly

[1] "In a 'Conspectus of a Perfect Polity,' the author has given the outlines of the constitution of a commonwealth, agreeing, in its great principles, with those of the constitution of the United States and of the individual states. But he maintained that a Christian state ought expressly
to acknowledge and embosom in its civil constitution the public avowal of
the 'being of a God,' and 'the avowal of Christianity.'" — Kingsley's
Life of Stiles. — ED.

friendly to fair and generous disquisition. Here Deism will have its full chance; nor need libertines more to complain of being overcome by any weapons but the gentle, the powerful ones of argument and truth. Revelation will be found to stand the test to the ten thousandth examination.

There are three coetaneous events to take place, whose futurition is certain from prophecy, — the annihilation of the pontificate,[1] the reässembling of the Jews, and the fulness of the Gentiles. That liberal and candid disquisition of Christianity which will most assuredly take place in America, will prepare Europe for the first event, with which the other will be connected, when, especially on the return of the Twelve Tribes to the Holy Land, there will burst forth a degree of evidence hitherto unperceived, and of efficacy to convert a world. More than three quarters of mankind yet remain heathen. Heaven put a stop to the propagation of Christianity when the church became corrupted with the adoration of numerous deities and images, because this would have been only exchanging an old for a new idolatry. Nor is Christendom now larger than it was nine centuries ago. The promising prospects of the *Propaganda fide* at Rome[2] are come to nothing; and it may be of the divine destiny that all other attempts for gospelizing the nations of the earth shall prove fruitless, until the present Christendom itself be recovered to the primitive purity and simplicity; at which time, instead of the Babel confusion of contra-

[1] By the conquest of Canada in 1759-60, God then and there ordained that America should be a free, and, to this end, a Protestant, nation. It would be a notable, a practical celebration of this era of American liberty if the final conflict of the same great principles should distinguish the years 1859-60 in the Old World's progress. Centuries mark the onward life of nations. — ED.

[2] See p. 466, notes b and 1. — ED.

dicting missionaries, all will harmoniously concur in speaking one language, one holy faith, one apostolic religion, to an uncontroverted world. At this period, and in effecting this great event, we have reason to think that the United States may be of no small influence and consideration. It was of the Lord to send Joseph into Egypt, to save much people, and to show forth his praise. It is of the Lord that "a woman clothed with the sun, and the moon under her feet," and upon "her head a crown of twelve stars," [a] should "flee into the wilderness, where she hath a place prepared of God," [b] and where she might be the repository of wisdom, and "keep the commandments of God, and have the testimony of Jesus." It may have been of the Lord that Christianity is to be found in such greater purity in this church exiled into the wildernesses of America, and that its purest body should be evidently advancing forward, by an augmented natural increase and spiritual edification, into a singular superiority, with the ultimate subserviency to the glory of God in converting the world.

When we look forward and see this country increased to forty or fifty millions,[1] while we see all the religious sects increased into respectable bodies, we shall doubtless find the united body of the Congregational, consociated, and Presbyterian churches making an equal figure with any two of them ; or, to say the least, to be of such magnitude as to number that it will be to no purpose for other sects to meditate their eversion. This, indeed, is enterprised, but it will end in a Sisyphean labor. There is the greatest prospect that we shall become thirty out of forty millions.[2] And while the avenues to civil improve-

---

ment and public honors will here be equally open to all sects, so it will be no dishonor hereafter to be a Presbyterian, or of the religious denomination which will probably ever make the most distinguished figure in this great republic. And hereafter, when the world shall behold us a respectable part of Christendom, they may be induced by curiosity with calmness and candor to examine whether something of Christianity may not really be found among us. And while we have to lament our Laodiceanism, deficient morals, and incidental errors, yet the collective system of evangelical doctrines, the instituted ordinances, and the true ecclesiastical polity, may be found here in a great degree of purity. Europeans, and some among us, have habituated themselves to a most contemptible idea of the New England churches — conceiving us to be only a colluvies of error, fanaticism, irregularity, and confusion.[a]

---

[a] Peters's History of Connecticut.[1]

[1] This celebrated work, by the famous Rev. S. A. Peters, LL.D., contains curious observations on the wonders of nature, art, and "fanaticism," in New England, the truth of which could be established only by the author's high reputation for veracity and godly simplicity. He describes a "chasm" in the Connecticut River, where "water is consolidated, without frost, by pressure, by swiftness, between the pinching, sturdy rocks, to such a degree of induration that no iron crow can be forced into it; . . . steady as time, and harder than marble, the stream passes irresistible, if not swift as lightning; one of the greatest phenomenons in nature. . . No living creature was ever known to pass through this narrow, except an Indian woman. . . . . How feeble is man, and how great that Almighty who formed the . . . . irresistible power and strength of waters!" In Windham the frogs "filled a road forty yards wide, for four miles in length, and were for several hours passing through the town, unusually clamorous. . . . . The event was fatal to several women. . . . I verily believe," Mr. Peters says, "an army under the Duke of Marlborough would, under like circumstances, have acted no better than they did." He is hopeless, "for the Church of England has lost the opportunity of civilizing, christianizing, and moderating the burning zeal of the dissenters in New England, who were honest in their religion, merely by the sinful

They have taken this idea in part from our brethren in
Britain, who have viewed us very much also in the same
light to this day. This, on the contrary, is the truth, that,
allowing for offences unavoidable, for imperfections and
controversies incident to the churches in their most
regular state, our churches are as completely reformed,
and as well modelled according to the Scripture plan, as
can be expected till the millennium. Particularly these
essential things may be found among them upon examination : that the churches, or particular congregations, are
regularly formed, and duly uphold public worship every
Lord's day, and this ordinarily in a very decent, solemn
manner; that the preaching of the word, baptism, and the
Lord's supper, are regularly and duly administered by the
pastors; that the pastors are orderly, and regularly set
apart to the ministry by the laying on of the hands of
the presbytery, or of those who have regularly derived
office power, in lineal succession, from the apostles and

omission of not sending a bishop to that country, who would have effected greater things among them than an army of fifty thousand men."
But the now mild and desponding Peters was, in 1774, a terrible son of
Mars, a bloody-minded leader of the " Church of England " militant, rejoicing in the prospect of " hanging work " among the uncivilized " dissenters." See his letter on page 195 of this volume. In the second edition
of his " History," " printed for the author," London, 1782, Mr. Peters
confidingly says: " Whatever other historical requisite it may want, it
must, I think, be allowed to possess originality and truth." Its claim to
originality has never been questioned, and the work has placed the learned
and reverend author among the celebrities of the " Church of England "
of that period. He heartily detested " preaching."

Mr. Kingsley says that " on examining the more prominent statements
of Peters, not one has been found which is not either false, or so deformed
by exaggerations and perversions as to be essentially erroneous. To
prove a truth upon the leading portions of his history would be, it is believed, an impossible task."— Hist. Disc. at New Haven, 1838, 83–90.
The Rev. Dr. Bacon calls it " that most unscrupulous and malicious of
lying narratives."— ED.

Jesus Christ. We have no classical or synodical tribunals, yet we have ecclesiastical councils ; and our church discipline, although not sufficiently attended to, is such that persons of evident scandal and immorality, and vicious ministers (of which, God be thanked! there have been but few, very few indeed), cannot live long in our churches. With all our humbling imperfections, I know of no amendment necessary, as to our general system of church polity. Nothing of moment, unless it be grace, — no doctrine, no ordinance or institution of the primitive churches, — but may be found in general reception and observance among us. If we are condemned for having no tribunals or judicatories out of the church, — which, however, is not true, — let it be remembered that neither Christ nor his apostles ever instituted any; and that in this respect we are just in the same state, with regard to ecclesiastical polity, as the one hundred and fifty churches of the apostolic age,[a] and particularly the seven churches of Asia in the time of St. John.

The invalidity of our ordinations is objected against us, and so of consequence the invalidity of all our official administrations. And, now that we are upon the matter, give me leave to exhibit a true though summary state of it, as the result of a very full, laborious, and thorough inquiry. It was the mistaken opinion of some of our first ministers in New England (than whom there never was a more learned collection, for they embosomed all the theological and ecclesiastical erudition of all ages), — it was, I say, their opinion, that the power of ordination of all church officers was in the church, by their elders. They well knew, from ecclesiastical and Scripture antiquity, that the power of election was there ; and they judged ordina-

a It has been computed that the churches of the apostolic age did not exceed one hundred and fifty or two hundred congregations in the whole world.

tion the lesser act; but their great reason was,[1] that the church might not be controlled by any exterior authority, whether Episcopal or Presbyterial, and so no more be harassed by bishops' courts, or any other similar tribunal. Our fathers held to an eldership, for they saw it in all antiquity, as well as the Bible; and it was their judgment that elders should be ordained by elders of the same church. The most of the first forty churches had ruling elders; a few had not.[2] These few created an early difficulty, on which our fathers early made a mistaken decision, that where there were no elders in the church, ordination might be done by the laying on of hands of delegated brethren. The introduction of ministers already ordained into the pastoral charge of a particular church was at first done by the lay brethren; and this was, from the beginning, improperly called ordination, how often soever repeated. A repetition of ordinations or baptisms does not nullify the first regular administrations. All the first New England ministers were ordained before. Thus Mr. Wilson was first ordained by a bishop in England; then, 1630, by Governor Winthrop and others, he was ordained teacher in Boston; he then ordained an elder; and upon the accession of Mr. Cotton, 1633, he was, by this elder and Governor Winthrop, again, a third time, ordained, and constituted pastor. So the learned and courtly Mr. Davenport was ordained by a bishop, then by the brethren, pastor of the church in New Haven, in 1639; and, 1688, was again ordained pastor of the first church in Boston by Elder Penn. Mr. Hooker was ordained a presbyter by a bishop in Eng-

1 See pp. x.–xv. — ED.

2 On the subject of ecclesiastical polity, see the admirable " Vindication of the Government of the New England Churches," by John Wise, A.M., fourth edition, Boston, 1860, published by the Congregational Board, with Rev. Dr. Clark's " Historical Introductory Note."— ED.

land, and then again by the brethren at Newtown, 1633, who removed with his church to Hartford. Mr. Bulkley, of Concord, and Mr. Noyes, of Newbury, and others, expressly adhered to their former ordinations in England by the bishops, though not as bishops, but as presbyters.[1] But in general the induction of the ministers of the first churches was performed by lay brethren, and this was called ordination, but should be considered, what in reality it was, only induction, or instalment of those who were vested with official power. These, as I said, were all ordained before by the bishops in England. Nor have I ever found with certainty more than one instance of lay ordination of a person never before ordained, the last century (and there are few but what I have examined), and this was done by the advice and under the inspection of ministers ordained by the bishops in England, one of whom prayed at the solemnity of the consecration, and all gave their approbation and right-hand of fellowship, which, in my opinion, amounts to their performing the ordination themselves, they being present and assisting in the transaction. This was at Woburn, 1642. I believe there were two or three more similar ordinations of unordained candidates before the ministers saw and corrected their error, which indeed was almost the only error of moment which the ministers went into the last century.[2]

Immediately upon publishing the Cambridge platform, 1648, our brethren in England remonstrated against allow-

[1] In a long note, " Winthrop's entries in a manuscript diary," August 27, October 25, 1630, November 22, 1632, October 10, 11, 1633, " 2m. 6d. 1637," April 24, 1639, are quoted to " evince that the ministers relied upon their ordinations in England." As the diary is now in print (see p. 491, note 2) the note is not reprinted. — ED.

[2] An elaborate and valuable series of papers on the Ecclesiastical Antiquities of New England was published by the Rev. Samuel Sewall in the American Quarterly Register, 1838-1842. — ED.

ing lay ordination. They alleged that we had no example in Scripture of lay ordination; that the sacerdotal gift, or office power, was conferred and given by the laying on of the hands of the presbytery,[a] and that we had examples of presbyterian ordination in Scripture; and not only that it was safest to proceed in this way, but that it was the only scriptural ground. These arguments convinced our fathers, and they immediately set about to remedy the practice which had hitherto, providentially, wrought no mischief, as the body of the pastors had been ordained by bishops. It instantly became a custom for some of the ordained ministers present to lay on hands in ordinations; it being for some time judged necessary that the delegated brethren should join, in token of subjection of the church to the pastoral care of the minister. But at length it became a custom, so early as before 1660, that, at the desire of the church, the ordaining ministers performed the whole—both conferred office power on the pastor elect by the laying on of hands, and committed the church to his pastoral charge, which, with the joint fellowship of the pastors and churches, finished the ordination. Thus ordinations were recovered into their right state and order the last century, and before lay ordinations had wrought any evil. Thus office power, by Scripture presbyters, continued to be transfused through the clergy. I have reason and even assurance to believe that there was no candidate ordained in New England before 1746[1] but whose ordination may be traced to the bishops in England. I have found no instance to the contrary, although I have searched and examined all the ordinations of the first half-century here, and most of them for the first hundred years.

a 1 Tim. iv. 14.

1 The author, in the second edition, 1785, adds a note, " The Ordination among the Separates began this year." — ED.

And as to the wild and enthusiastic period between 1740 and 1750, though it gave birth to perhaps thirty little Separate congregations, yet some have dissolved, others become regular, and the ten or a dozen now remaining are more and more convinced of the duty of seeking ordination from among the standing ministers.[1]   And it is remarkable that Mr. Thomas Dennison, now living, assisted, laid on hands, and gave the charge at the first ordination in 1746, and at the three succeeding ordinations among the Separates in New England, from whence all the ordinations in the churches of that description have proceeded.   And although in the first, but not in the others, he acted as a brother delegated by the church, and in the others as an elder of another church, yet it is remarkable, I say, that he himself had been ordained, in 1743, by one whose ordination I have traced to the Mathers and other Boston ministers, and through them up to the Bishop of Chester, and other bishops in England.   It is probable the few Separate churches remaining will in time become regular by seeking ordinations among the pastors of the standing churches where the ordinations are indubitable.

For, as I have said, the ordination of our clergy is regular and scriptural, and may be traced in the line of presbyters up to the apostolic age ; and so in general may the ordinations in this line through the whole Christian world, especially in the great divisions of Lutherans, Calvinists, and Church of England.   So wonderfully has Christ preserved the sacerdotal or presbyterian order in the church, that the succession in this line is without a doubt.   The

---

[1] Prince's " Christian History," Gillie's " Historical Collections," Tracy's " History of the Great Awakening," Dr. Clark's " History of the Congregational Churches in Massachusetts," chap. xiii., are among the many works on that memorable period.   See article Whitefield, George, in Allen's Biographical Dictionary. — ED.

first ninety-four ministers who came over and settled New
England, Long Island, and the Jerseys, before 1669, and
chiefly before 1640 — these, I say, were all educated[1] in
the English universities, and were ordained in England;
some of whom — as Hooker, Davenport, Chauncy, Lee,
Bulkley, Noyes, Norton — were men of universal reading
in theological literature, and were profoundly versed in the
writings of the Greek and Latin churches, in the councils
and historians, the fathers, the writers of the middle ages,
and the reformers, especially those miracles of human and
divine learning, Chauncy and Lee. Of these ninety-four,
one or two only were ordained by the Puritans, as the
fourteen[2] who came over after the ejection of 1662 were
ordained by the bishops, or more probably by the Presbyterians in the protectorate: all the rest by the bishops.
All these were ordained presbyters by the bishops in England; particularly the Rev. Mr. Richard Mather was ordained a presbyter by Dr. Morton, Bishop of Chester, 1618.[a]
The bishops did not intend to communicate ordaining
powers, but they really intended to convey all the power
of a Scripture presbyter, and by the Scripture we find this
power conferred by the laying on of the hands of the presbytery; which demonstrates that presbyters, as such, were
endued with the power of ordination.[b] If the succession
in the line of bishops might have been interrupted at the
Reformation, yet not so in the line of presbyters. Office
power has unquestionably been preserved in England,
among presbyters, not only to the times of its subjugation
to Rome by Austin the monk, but ages before, even to
Lucius, according to venerable Bede. And indeed we
have it more directly to the apostolic age, without going

a Life of Dr. Increase Mather.   b 1 Tim. iv. 14.

1 See pp. xiii.-xv. — ED.
2 Their names are given in Mather's "Magnalia," Book III. fol. 4. — ED.

through Rome, for Bishop Jewel asserts truly that the ancient churches of England were of Greek, that, is oriental, derivation. We have in this manner a historical evidence and assurance that the New England ordinations in particular may be traced back to the holy apostles.

There is not an instance, in the apostolic age, of bishops, priests, and deacons being stated officers of more than a single congregation. I risk this historic assertion with the examination of the whole learned world, although I well know that, like the evidences of revelation, it has been examined a thousand times with different judgments. Every congregation regularly and fully organized had them, as appears from Dionysius the Areopagite and St. Ignatius. The succession of bishops, who were only the first presbyters, as well as of the other elders, was preserved by ordinations performed by presbyters in or out of a church. And though ordinations were usually performed by three or more, yet if only one presbyter laid on hands it was valid. Titus, a single elder, was left thus to ordain elders in Crete. The church of Alexandria, founded by St. Mark, retained presbyterian ordination exclusive for three hundred years, as appears from Eutychius, the patriarch there in the ninth century, who wrote the originals of that church in Arabic, from which I have translated the following extract, viz. :

" The ninth year of Claudius Cæsar, while Mark the evangelist resided at Alexandria, Hananias being converted to Christianity, Mark baptized him, and constituted or ordained him chief father at Alexandria, and he became the first patriarch of Alexandria. Mark the evangelist likewise constituted and ordained twelve (Cashisha[a]) presbyters, with Hananias, who should abide with the patriarch, so that when there should be a vacancy in the patriarchate, they should elect one of the twelve presbyters, upon whose head the other

[a] The title Cashies is given to the Coptic clergy to this day.

eleven should impose their hands, bless him, and create him patriarch; and then elect some eminent person, and constitute him a presbyter with themselves, in the room of him who was made a patriarch, so that there should always be twelve. Nor did this institution concerning the presbyters cease at Alexandria, that they should create the patriarchs out of the twelve presbyters, until the times of Alexander, patriarch at Alexandria, who was of the number of the three hundred and eighteen" (at the Council of Nice, A. D. 325). "For he forbade the presbyters afterwards to create a patriarch, and decreed that, upon the death of a patriarch, the bishops should assemble and ordain a patriarch. And he farther decreed that, on a vacancy in the patriarchate, they should elect, either from the twelve presbyters, or from any other country, some eminent person, and create him patriarch. And thus evanished the ancient institution by which the patriarch had been created by the presbyters, and there succeeded in its place his decree concerning the creation of the patriarchs by the bishops. Thus, from Hananias to the time of Demetrius, who was the eleventh patriarch at Alexandria, there was no bishop in the provinces of Egypt; nor did any patriarchs before him constitute bishops. But he, being made patriarch, constituted three bishops. And he was the first Alexandrian patriarch who made bishops. Upon the death of Demetrius, Heraclas became patriarch, and constituted twenty bishops." [a]

Thus, in this most valuable piece or relic of ecclesiastical antiquity, we have preserved and transmitted to us a specimen and exemplar of a truly primitive and apostolic church. And herein we have a full proof that, while there were fifteen hundred pastors or Cashisha, yet there were no bishops in Egypt, in the posterior appropriate sense of the Latin and Greek churches, until the fourth century, although the Christians had by that time become so numerous in Egypt that, in the most severe and memorable persecution under Maximianus, the predecessor of Constantine the Great, one hundred thousand Christians were put to death there, and seven hundred thousand were sold

---

[a] Eutychij origines eccl. Alexand.

for slaves; a barbarity which satiated and glutted the malice of persecution, and wrought a conviction in the whole Roman Empire of the impossibility of subduing Christianity.

Correspondent to this idea of a church and its officers was the form particularly of the church of Ephesus, and the seven churches of Asia, in the apostolic age, and the churches of New England, wherein, at their primitive institutions, were originally two or more elders, besides the pastors and teachers, *i. e.*, four presbyters; although, having generally, though not universally, dropped the ruling elders, they now more nearly resemble the church of Philippi, in having at present only bishops and deacons. It might, however, be well to resume the eldership, as in the days of our ancestors.

Agreeable to this primitive idea of a church was the church of Ireland, planted and formed by that great light of Christendom, St. Patrick, who — as Titus travelled Crete, and ordained elders in every city — himself travelled Ireland, converted it to Christianity, and constituted three hundred and fifty-five churches, and in each ordained a set of elders, with a bishop at their head,[a] as did Mark in Alexandria; — agreeable to that of the Irish poet in the psalter of Cashet, which, doubtless, while it retains the historical sentiments, loses its beauty in translation:

> "The blesséd Patrick, with his priestly hands,
> The rite of consecration did confer
> Upon the most religious of his clergy,
> Three hundred and fifty-five in number.
> He likewise, for the service of the church,
> As many sacred structures did erect,
> And presbyters ordained three thousand."[1]

[a] Nonnius, speaking of St. Patrick, says: "Ecclesias 355 fundavit, episcopos ordinavit eodem numero, presbyteros autem usque ad tria millia ordinavit."— See Nonnius and Keating.

[1] See Neander's Church History, Torrey's trans., Bohn's ed. 1858, iii. 172–177. — ED.

[He began the conversion of Ireland about A. D. 432, and labored in it until his death, about A. D. 490, ætat. 122. His ecclesiastical laws and canons continued there four hundred years after his death, until after the Danish invasion. Although St. Patrick was born in Wales, yet he was educated and ordained in Gaul, and borrowed from thence the model of his churches; which shows that the Gallican churches, before their subjugation to Rome, as well as the Church of England in the time of the bishops and monks of Glastenbury, were similar in their ecclesiastical polity to the churches in Egypt before the Council of Nice, to those of Ireland in Patrick's day, to the present Waldensian *reliquiae*, or remnant of the ancient Gallic churches, and to the Calvinistic churches of the Reformation.][1] If the whole Christian world were to revert back to this original and truly primitive model, how far more simple, uniform, and beautiful, and even glorious, would the church universal appear, than under the mutilated, artificial forms of the pontifical or patriarchal constitutions of the middle and present ages; and how far more agreeable to the ecclesiastical polity instituted and delivered by the holy apostles. May this be exhibited and displayed in the American churches. Of this, it gives me joy to believe, there is the greatest prospect. The initial revival of this primeval institution is indeed already so well established here, where the Presbyterians hold so great a proportion in the American Republic, that there can be but little doubt but that in the ordinary course of events our increasing and growing interest, without any interference with the other sects, will at length ascend to such a magnitude, and become so great and respectable a part of Christendom, as to command the attention, con-

---

1 The lines in brackets were added in the edition of 1785. — ED.

templation, and fraternal love of our brethren and fellow-Christians of the church universal, and even of the world itself. And when the set time to favor Zion shall come in God's good and holy providence, while Christendom may no longer disdain to adopt a reformation from us, the then newly gospelized heathen may light up their candle at America. In this country, out of sight of mitres and the purple, and removed from systems of corruption confirmed for ages and supported by the spiritual janizaries of an ecclesiastical hierarchy, aided and armed by the secular power, religion may be examined with the noble Berean freedom, the freedom of American-born minds. And revelation, both as to the true evangelical doctrines and church polity, may be settled here[1] before they shall have undergone a thorough discussion, and been weighed with a calm and unprejudiced candor elsewhere. Great things are to be effected in the world before the millennium, which I do not expect to commence under seven or eight hundred years hence; and perhaps the liberal and candid disquisitions in America are to be rendered extensively subservient to some of the most glorious designs of Providence, and particularly in the propagation and diffusion of religion through the earth, in filling the whole earth with the knowledge of the glory of the Lord. A time will come when six hundred millions of the human race shall be ready to drop their idolatry and all false religion, when Christianity shall triumph over superstition, as well as Deism, and Gentilism, and Mohammedanism. They will then search all Christendom for the best model,

---

[1] Compare with this the remarkable words of John Robinson, the pastor of the Pilgrim Fathers, who said to them, on their embarkation at Delfthaven, in 1620: "Brethren, I am fully persuaded, I am very confident, that the Lord has more truth yet to break forth out of his holy Word." He probably had special reference to ecclesiastical polity. — ED.

the purest exemplification of the Christian church, with
the fewest human mixtures. And when God in his providence shall convert the world, should the newly Christian-
ized nations assume our form of religion, should American
missionaries be blessed to succeed in the work of Christianizing the heathen, — in which the Romanists and foreign Protestants have very much failed, — it would be an
unexpected wonder, and a great honor to the United
States. And thus the American Republic, by illuminating
the world with truth and liberty, would be exalted and
made high among the nations, in praise, and in name, and
in honor. I doubt not this is the honor reserved for us ;
I had almost said, in the spirit of prophecy, the zeal of the
Lord of Hosts will accomplish this.[1]

> " So the dread seer in Patmos' waste who trod,
>   Led by the visions of the guiding God,
>   Saw the dim vault of heaven its folds unbend,
>   And gates, and spires, and streets, and domes descend
>   Far down the skies. With suns and rainbows crowned,
>   The new-formed city lights the world around." [a]

a Vision of Columb. b. 2.[2]

[1] How gloriously this prophecy of America's mission to the world is
already being accomplished, appears, in part, in the noble history and
statistics of the Missionary, Bible, and Tract Societies of the United
States in their operations over the round world ; — missionaries not only
of the Christian home and civilization, but coädjutors in the fields of
science and philosophy. To them ethnology, philology, history, geography, commerce, are willing and continual debtors, as well as aids.
Perhaps the conquest of Canada may be adopted as the epoch of modern
missionary enterprise, when the door was wide opened to its benevolent
designs among the aborigines, — see Wheelock's narratives, — and from
that expanding, till it shall illumine the world with the gospel of Christian liberty. The natural political influence of American institutions
abroad hardly admits of statistical statement, as it is not the result of
organized associations. — ED.

[2] Dr. Stiles must have quoted these lines from the MS. of Mr. Barlow's
poem, which was not published till 1787. It was dedicated to the unhappy

Having shown wherein consists the prosperity of a state, and what reason we have to anticipate the glory of the American empire, I proceed to show,

II. That her system of dominion must receive its finishing from religion; or, that from the diffusion of virtue among the people of any community would arise their greatest secular happiness; all which will terminate in this conclusion: that holiness ought to be the end of all civil government — "that thou mayest be an holy people unto the Lord thy God."

On the subject of religion we might be concise and transient, if indeed a subject of the highest moment ought to be treated with brevity.

It is readily granted that a state may be very prosperous and flourishing without Christianity; — witness the Egyptian, Assyrian, Roman, and Chinese empires. But if there be a true religion, one would think that it might be at least some additional glory. We must become a holy people in reality, in order to exhibit the experiment, never yet fully made in this unhallowed part of the universe, whether such a people would be the happiest on earth. It would greatly conduce to this if Moses and Aaron, if the magistracy and priesthood, should coöperate and walk together in union and harmony. The political effort of the present day, through most of the United States, is to disunite, divide, and separate them,[1] through fear lest the United

Louis XVI., and was republished in Paris. This distinguished statesman's career illustrates the broad and deep influence of the American Revolution on European politics. He regarded the cross not as the emblem of Christianity, but of its corruptions by Popery. He died December 22, 1812, aged fifty-eight. Allen's Biog. Dict. has a full notice of him, with authorities. Where are his large collections, intended for a History of the United States? — ED.

[1] The *external* separation of church and state, now complete, leaves a nobler vantage-ground to the Christian Teacher in his duty to his coun-

States, like the five viceroyships of New Spain, should be entangled and oppressed with the spiritual domination of European and Asiatic hierarchies. As if, by the title of minister or pastor, we might not as well be reminded of the ministers of Holland and Geneva, or the mild and peaceable pastors of the primitive church, as of the domineering prelates and other haughty, intriguing dignitaries of the Romish church. Hence Aaron is spurned at a distance, and the Levites are beheld with shy contempt, as a useless, burdensome, dangerous tribe ; and, in some of the states, for the only sin of being priests of the Most High God, they are inhibited all civil offices, and, to a great degree, disfranchised of their civil immunities and rights of citizenship.[1] I thank my God for this ordering of his holy providence, — for I wish the clergy never to be vested with civil power, — while I am considering the spirit and disposition of the public towards the Church of God, indicated by such events. A general spirit reigns against the most liberal and generous establishments in religion ; against the civil magistrates encouraging or having anything more to do about religion than to keep the civil

try; and as Christian morals and principles are the true foundation of a free Christian commonwealth, how momentous is his responsibility to God and man for fidelity in " declaring all the counsel of God ! " The zeal, firmness, and integrity of the pulpit in " preaching the gospel," from the time of Mayhew to Stiles, was of vital importance to the triumph of our national freedom. But Christianity is perpetual, and for daily use. Most legislation involves or relates to public morals, questions *in foro conscientiæ*, and here Christianity has sovereign jurisdiction, which can be violated only by the sufferance of that teacher who, whether from timidity, weakness, or open treachery, is false to his Master, unworthy of his great commission, and sure of the contempt of men. Mayhew and Stiles are examples, for all time, of Christian manhood in the pulpit. " Politics and the Pulpit " is the title of an " essay " on the true relations of the pulpit, published by the American Tract Society. — ED.

[1] See p. 69, note 1, *et seq.* — ED.

peace among contending sects : as if this was all that is to be done for religion by the friends of Jesus. And hence, in designating to the magistracy and offices of government, it begins to be a growing idea that it is mighty indifferent, forsooth, not only whether a man be of this or the other religious sect, but whether he be of any religion at all; and that truly deists, and men of indifferentism to all religion, are the most suitable persons for civil office, and most proper to hold the reins of government; and that, to prevent partiality in governors, and emulation among the sects, it is wise to consign government over into the hands of those who, Gallio-like, have no religion at all.[1] This is Machiavellian wisdom and policy; and hence examples are frequently adduced of men distinguished truly for deism, perhaps libidinous morals, and every vice, yet of great abilities, it is said, — great civilians, lawyers, physicians, warriors, governors, patriots, politicians, — while as great or greater and more numerous characters, in the same departments, — a Thuanus, a Grotius, a Paul of Venice, a Sir Henry Wotton, a Sir Peter King, a Selden, a Newton, a Boyle, those miracles of wisdom and friends to religion and virtue, — are passed by with transient coolness and neglect. I wish we had not to fear that a neglect of religion was coming to be the road to preferment. It was not so here in our fathers' days.

Shall the Most High send down truth into this world from the world of light and truth, and shall the rulers of this world be afraid of it? Shall there be no intrepid Daniels, — great in magistracy, great in religion? How great was that holy man, that learned and pious civilian, when he shone in the supreme triumvirate at the head of an empire of one hundred and twenty provinces — venerable for political wisdom, venerable for religion!

1 See p. 69, *et seq.* — ED.

If men, not merely nominally Christians, but of real religion and sincere piety, joined with abilities, were advanced and called up to office in every civil department, how would it countenance and recommend virtue! But, alas! is there not too much Laodiceanism in this land? Is not Jesus in danger of being wounded in the house of his friends? Nay, have we gone already such lengths in declension that, if even the Holy Redeemer himself and his apostles were to reäppear among us, while unknown to be such, and importune the public government and magistracy of these states to become nursing fathers to the church, is it not to be feared that some of the states, through timidity and fearfulness of touching religion, would excuse themselves, and dismiss the holy messengers, the heavenly visitants, with coldness and neglect, though importuning the spouse with an "Open to me, my beloved, my sister, my dove"?

But after the present period of deism and skeptical indifferentism in religion, of timidity and irresolution in the cause of the great Emmanuel, perhaps there may arise a succession of civil magistrates who will not be ashamed of the cross of Christ, nor of patronizing his holy religion with a generous catholicism and expanded benevolence towards all of every denomination who love our Lord Jesus Christ in sincerity and truth, — patronizing it, I repeat, not with the insidious views of a Hutchinsonian[1] policy, but from a rational and firm belief and love of evangelical truth. Zion's friends will rejoice in Zion's welfare, and the religious as well as civil patriot will shine in the faces of the future Moseses and Joshuas of this land. So shone

---

[1] The theological world was some time disturbed by the speculative school founded by John Hutchinson, 1674-1737, who taught that all knowledge is contained in the Scriptures, and that every Hebrew root has a spiritual as well as an obvious sense. — Allibone; Gorton. — ED.

it in the first governor, Winthrop, and so shineth it in a
Washington. Yea, I glory in believing and knowing that
there are many now in the public magistracy of this and
the other states who feel with that illustrious and most
excellent governor, upon whom rested much of the spirit
of Samuel and David, and of Jehoshaphat, Hezekiah, and
Josiah — I mean Nehemiah the Tirshata, who, with Moses,
esteemed the reproaches of Christ greater riches than the
treasures of Egypt; who was of so pious, so noble, so patriotic a spirit, such a lover of his country and the true
religion, that he preferred the very dust of Zion to the
gardens of Persia, and the broken walls of Jerusalem to
the palaces of Shushan.

Whenever religion is erected on the ruins of civil government, and when civil government is built on the ruins
of religion, both are so far essentially wrong. The church
has never been of any political detriment here, for it never
has been vested with any civil or secular power in New
England, although it is certain that civil dominion was
but the second motive, religion the primary one, with our
ancestors in coming hither and settling this land.[1] It was
not so much their design to establish religion for the
benefit of the state, as civil government for the benefit of
religion, and as subservient and even necessary towards
the peaceable enjoyment and unmolested exercise of religion — of that religion for which they fled to these ends
of the earth. An institution is not made for the laws, but
the laws for the institution. I am narrating a historical
fact, not giving a position or principle which by shrewd
politicians may be abused to justify spiritual tyranny, and
to support the claims of the pontificate over all the civil
states, kingdoms, and empires in Christendom.

The American Nehemiah, the opulent[2] and pious Gov-

---

[1] See pp. xii., xv.-xix. — ED.

[2] This gentleman's name is made familiar by his History, first published

ernor Winthrop I., and the other first magistrates of the
several New England republics, were men of singular
wisdom and exemplary piety.   And, God be thanked! the
senatorial assembly of this happiest of all the United
States still embosoms so many Phinehases and Zorobabels,
so many religious patriots, the friends of Jesus and his
holy religion; and that the Messiah's cause is here accompanied with civil government and the priesthood; — allusively the two olive trees upon the right of the candlestick
(the churches) and upon the left; the two golden branches
which through the two golden pipes, Moses and Aaron,
empty the golden oil out of themselves,[a] and diffuse their
salutary influence of order and happiness through the
community.

a Zech. iv. 11.

in 1790, at Hartford, under the care of Mr. Webster, and two later editions,
ably edited by Mr. Savage.   Another work from his pen, the "Short
Story" of the Antinomian troubles, has been treated with editorial severity, under the supposition that it was written by another hand, Rev.
Thomas Welde.   Some of his manuscripts are yet unpublished.   Dr.
Stiles's impression of Winthrop's "opulence" is corrected by his own letters
in Mr. Savage's "appendix," which show that "one great motive" to his
migrating to New England was the care of his family; that he had lived
for some years in an unsettled condition; as early as 1623 he wrote to his
son, "I wish oft God would open a way to settle me in Ireland;" that
he was embarrassed by debt, and finally sold his land for about £1500;
"you must sell it speedily, for much debt will lie upon us,"—letter August
14, 1630, — which left him enough to win a new home in the New World.
Here, too, he had pecuniary difficulties, which certainly leave no "blemish" upon his memory, and of which his own account may be read in the
History, vol. i., 474–477.

It would be safe, in point of time, to attribute the favorite portrait of
Winthrop (see p. 154) to Ruben's pencil, but not to Vandyke's, for he probably did not set foot in England till after Winthrop's departure, in March,
1629.   Those artists sought for commissions from the court and nobility.

Eliot's and Allen's Dictionaries have good notices of Winthrop.   See
an article by Mr. R. C. Winthrop, in Bridgman's "King's Chapel Memorials," 1853, pp. 309–315; "Historical Magazine," 1857, p. 321; 1858, pp.
22, 170, 224; also this volume, pp. xi., xxiii., notes. — Ed.

As to nominal Christianity, I have no doubt but that it will be upheld for ages in these states.   Through the liberty enjoyed here, all religious sects will grow up into large and respectable bodies.   But the Congregational and Presbyterian denomination, however hitherto despised, will, by the blessing of Heaven, continue to hold the greatest figure in America, and, notwithstanding all the fruitless labors and exertions to proselyte us to other communions, become more numerous[1] than the whole collective body of our fellow-Protestants in Europe.   The whole proselytism of New England in particular, for sixty or seventy years past, has not exceeded eight or ten thousand, while our augment in that term, by natural increase, has been half a million.   The future difference in our favor will be far greater, even admitting a tenfold increase of proselytism.   We anticipate with pleasure the growth and multiplication of our churches.   God grant that we may not, like the seven churches of Asia, have a name to live, while we are dead.   Happy will it be for us should we become a holy people, zealous of good works; for it is undoubtedly the will of Heaven, and especially after the recent salvations of the Most High, that we should be a holy people unto the Lord our God.

It is greatly to be wished that these principles of our common Christianity might be found in general reception among all the churches of these states :

The Trinity in unity, in the one undivided essence of the Great Jehovah.

The sacred Scriptures are of divine inspiration.

In the immense universe, two little systems of intelligences, or orders of being, have lapsed, and that unhappily we have the dishonor of being one of them.

The second person of the coëternal Trinity, having as-

[1] See pp. 440, 468, notes. — ED.

sumed human nature, made a real atonement for sin, and
by his vicarious obedience and sufferings exhibited that
righteousness and vicarious merit by which alone we are
forgiven and justified.

The Holy Ghost is equally a divine person with the
Father and the Son, sharing with them divine, supreme,
equal, and undivided honors.

True virtue consists in a conformity of heart and life to
the divine law, which is as obligatory upon Christians as if
eternal life was suspended on perfect obedience.

The eternal principle of holiness essentially consists in
divine love, a disinterested affection for moral excellency,
a delight in the beauty and glory of the divine character,
that is, the supreme love of God. And connected with
and issuing from this is a joyful acquiescence in his will,
a rejoicing in his sovereignty and universal dominion.

While salvation and pardon are of free grace, the retri-
butions of eternity will be according to our works.

Whenever I find these principles, with others connected
with them, and the real belief of them evinced by an
amiable life, there I judge the essentials of Christianity to
be found, and thither my charity and benevolence extend
with equal ardor and sincerity, be the religious denomination as it may. Of these, the doctrines of the divinity of
the Lord Jesus, and his real vicarious atonement, are the
most important — the Jachin and Boaz, the pillar-truths of
the gospel, the *articuli stantis et cadentis ecclesiæ.*

This was the system of theology brought over from the
other side of the flood by our pious forefathers, now with
God. The more this is realized in a state, the more will
its felicity be advanced; for, certainly, the morals of
Christianity are excellent. It enjoins obedience to magistracy, justice, harmony, and benevolence among fellow-
citizens; and, what is more, it points out immortality to

man. Politicians, indeed, usually consider religion only as
it may affect and subserve civil purposes, and hence it is
mighty indifferent to them what the state of religion be,
provided they can ride in the whirlwind and direct the
storm. Nothing is more common than to see them in
every country making use of sects, for their own ends,
whom they in their hearts despise and ridicule with supreme contempt. Not so the Christian patriot, who from
his heart wishes the advancement of Christianity much
less for the civil good than for the eternal welfare of
immortal souls. We err much if we think the only or
chief end of civil government is secular happiness. Shall
immortals, illuminated by revelation, entertain such an
opinion? God forbid! Let us model civil society with the
adoption of divine institutions so as shall best subserve
the training up and disciplining innumerable millions for
the more glorious society of the church of the first-born.
Animated with the sublime ideas which Christianity in-
fuses into a people, we shall be led to consider the true
religion as the highest glory of a civil polity. The Christian institution so excelled in glory, that the Mosaic lost all
its glory. So the most perfect secular polity, though very
excellent, would lose all its glory when compared with a
kingdom wherein dwelleth righteousness, a community
wherein the religion of the divine Jesus reigns in vigor
and perfection.

Let us institute a comparison of religions in three different polities, which will sufficiently represent the state
of the whole world. And may that spirit which justly
springs from such a comparison animate all, whether in
humble life or in the most elevated stations among mankind. We may consider three contiguous empires, of the
same civil polity, all alike as to the social virtues, laws of
justice, benevolence, and the morals of civil society, — for

I mean to institute a very liberal and candid comparison. On the one of these shall be established the idolatry of the Bonzas, as a specimen of all the idolatrous religions; deism shall cover the second; and, of the unidolatrous religions, I will select for the third, not the Mohammedan, not the Jewish, but the Christian, in its purest apostolic form.

As to the first, the species of idolatry is indifferent, whether ancient or modern, that of the Druids or Zoroaster, of the Bramins or Romanists, or, lastly, that of the great Lama of Potola, which is the most extensive as well as most splendid religion on earth, being the religion of one-third of the human race. Let us select the last; it has for its basis, in common with all other idolatrous systems, adoration and worship, of some kind or other, to a hierarchy of celestial spirits, as our intercessors and protectors under the supreme God. These have been in all ages the Mahuzzim of Daniel, who predicts the apostasy of the church to the worship of Mahuzzim departed souls, invisible spirits, as intercessors with God. This is the real basis of all idolatry, ancient and modern. These were the Baalim and the heroes. And it is just indifferent whether we sacrifice and pray to Hercules or St. Paul, to the thirty thousand gods of Athens or the saints of the calendar, as advocates with the Father of the universe. Now, let the inhabitants of an empire be resolved into religious assemblies and convocations for the sacrificial worship of these inferior divinities, with a splendid ceremonial and priesthood: who does not see, in these enlightened realms, that all this is religious delusion, a transfer of worship to the creature from the Creator?—who may well say, "Who hath required this at your hands?" If it be said that supreme worship is not rendered to the saints of the pontifical canonization, so neither was it by the Ten Tribes, all of whom but eight thousand kissed the calves and worshipped the

numerous Baalim, heroes, or demi-gods. Dr. Middleton
has shown that the specifical worship, with a change of
names only, is paid at Rome to the modern canonized
saints, as to the deified heroes of the ancient Romans and
Greeks. The last effort of the philosophers against Christianity was in the time of Julian ; and they subordinated
the whole system of ethnical worship to the worship of
the Supreme Being, asserting that as Christians acknowledged the ministry of angels, so they held with the ministry of genii that of deceased and departed spirits, who
must be supposed to retain a peculiar affection for their
families, cities, and kingdoms on earth, especially for those
who should have referred themselves to their protection,
and intercession with the Deus O. M. the Supreme God.
Thus they defended themselves upon the very same reasoning as that upon which the Christian idolatry is defended. We are directed to ask the prayers of our fellow-
Christians on earth, and, by parity, why should we not ask
their prayers in heaven, where they must be supposed to
have far greater influence ? And if we are directed to
treat one another, and especially great benefactors of our
country, with public respect while here, why not, by parity,
continue this respect and the symbols of honor to them in
heaven ? What a beautiful gradation is there, it is said,
in the ethnical and Christian worship, or ascription of
gratitude to inferior and powerful intercessors ! And how
does it tend to keep alive our minds, and impress them
with glorious ideas of that grand, august, and beautiful
system of agency and subordinate administrations in the
great government of the One Great Supreme ! How
beautiful the subordinate mediation of angels and saints,
under the all-comprehensive mediation of the blessed
Jesus, through whom all worship, adoration, and homage
is to ascend to the Sovereign of the universe ! Let us be

assured that the Romanists think themselves to have great reason for the adoration of the superior powers.

Adjacent to this an empire of the same excellent constitution shall be overspread with deism exclusively. And to give the idea the most candid extent, perhaps beyond the desires of a Tyndal, or even of a Shaftesbury, — the amiable Confucius of deism, — not to mention the smaller and more desultory geniuses of a Hume or a Voltaire, — neither of whom had any more taste or judgment in religion or moral reasoning than Cicero in poetry or Cibber for the drama, — I say, to give the fairest idea of perfect deism, let the people of this empire be resolved into occasional, but not too frequent, worshipping assemblies, for worshipping the God of nature under the direction of the illuminated brethren, or of some right worshipful brother ; and also to thank God for his goodness in this life, and for a certain prospect' of a blessed immortality, if there should be any; when, perhaps, some noble minds, spirits of elevated and sublime genius, of bold, refined, and independent sentiment, might descant upon the common principles of social virtue and benevolence. I have certainly done justice to deism, although we hear nothing of pardoning mercy, because truly we need none, — such being the excellency and dignity of man, who, as Phocelides saith, is the image of God, that he well answers the end of existence, merits reward, and must hereafter be happy under the all-comprehending, the most benevolent administration of the universal Father. How pure and sublime is natural religion !

Christianity shall be the establishment of the third territorial empire. And to preclude the sectarian prejudications from disturbing the clearness and calmness of the mental perception, let any one overspread it with the Bible Christianity according to his own idea. I, for myself might overspread the whole with the Congregational churches, being not simply satisfied, but sure, from a thorough perlustration of all ecclesiastical history, that they are nearly apostolical as to doctrine and polity. And let this justice further be done, that religion shall reign in the hearts and lives of the people at large; and that it be the great and harmonious endeavor of the ruling characters and influential personages through the state, both by example and precept, to support such a reign of virtue and holiness. All that is valuable and truly excellent in the other empires is embraced; and, in addition, we have discoveries, and offers, and assurances, great in the confession of all men, if true, and glorious beyond description, — infinitely momentous indeed, and infinitely surpassing what is to be found in all the mythologies or moral systems around the globe. But I do not enlarge.

Ten thousand myriads of ages hence, in which of these three would the civilian, the patriot, the man of religion wish to have been found? — in which to have acted his part? — for most certainly they are not indifferent — and, in advancing its glory, to have exerted the talents and activity with which the Author of Nature had blessed him?

Which of these governments is it probable would most contribute to the secular welfare, and be attended with the greatest dignity, and even the greatest worldy splendor? But, above all, which most subservient to eternity and its momentous concerns? In which, as a school of institution and discipline, should we enjoy the happiest advantages for immortality? Which of these empires would be the favorite of Jesus? Or is he indeed an unconcerned spectator of human affairs? If not, why should we doubt or hesitate to give the preference to the Christian Republic? If revelation be not true, it does us no

hurt; we are as safe and as well off as others, having all
their moral virtue. But if revelation be true, it is true exclusively, and therefore to be attended to at peril. This is no
proof; but it is a reason for exciting our attention to its
evidence, both in miracles and prophecy, as well as in a certain internal beauty and glory opened by Heaven upon a
benighted world. Peradventure, with other happy millions,
we may be also blessed to perceive it to be not a cun-
ningly devised fable, as was conceived by that impious pontiff who could exclaim, *Eheu! quantum lucrifecit nobis
hæc fabula Christi?* but the wisdom and power of God, to
have issued from the fountain of unerring wisdom and
consummate benevolence; — which will be the case, the
happy fact, the moment we perceive the evidence of the
one single fact of the resurrection of .Christ, after his
undoubted crucifixion, — a fact testified by eye-witnesses,
and supported by evidence preserved in memoirs which
have come down to us with greater authenticity than Jus-
tin or Tacitus, — evidence, I say, overlooked indeed, but
never overthrown, and which at once will support the
whole glorious superstructure of Christianity.

But I need pardon that I should institute this comparison in a Christian assembly, and in a country where we
seem to be in no danger of idolatry, and where, God be
thanked! deists are very thinly sown; although, like
another set of men among us of illaudable and invidious
description, they magnify themselves into legions.

I have supposed all religions equal as to virtue, and that
civil virtue is the only end of civil society; but I must
resume both these mistakes. Vices and every species
of wickedness are found, more or less, to enter into the
essence of all religions except that of 'divine revelation. If
Christians are wicked, and even should they surpass the
Gentiles in vice, their religion never taught them so. But

the very institution of the festivals of the ancient gods and goddesses directly taught the most impure obscenities and libidinous revellings. And this is continued to this day in the East Indies. An Indian Bramin, Arunasalem, a Pandarums, or priest of Tarmaburam, was converted to Christianity in 1765,[a] upon which the college of Pandarum sent him a letter to reclaim him. Too long, says he in his reply, — too long have I been a witness to public lewdness in the sacrifices and worship of your pagodas or temples. My conscience told me these institutions could not come from a pure and holy God. O my God! how do I lament that I have been twenty-eight years thine enemy! No ablution, no sacrifice of Lingam, can wash away sin and purify the soul; the blood, sufferings, and sacrifice of Jesus Nadar, the Redeemer, alone cleanse from all sin.[1]

This, with a survey of the state of man in all ages, may show us that ethnic morals do not merit the high encomiums, the rapturous eulogies, which some have given them. Nor are deistical morals very promising. A world, a universe full of Rochesters and Chesterfields — what would it be ? — characters which may blaze their moment in an earthly court, but can never shine in the court above.

Modern deists, — but why do I say modern ? for the very fraternity is but of yesterday, — the deists have more lately improved and adopted suicide and fate into their system, holding it in common with the Bramins of Asia and the Aulic chieftains in Africa. We might trace the matter of suicide through a tract of ages, from Calenus, the Indian philosopher, who from the funeral pile laughed at Alexander the Great, to that sublime genius, that deis-

[a] Born 1737.

[1] The author's note of two pages, on the Religion of India, is omitted. — ED.

tical madman, who lately "stole away" out of life with
his wife and four children at once, — "closing the eyes
of six persons out of perfect humanity and the most en-
dearing fondness and friendship." [a]

Sir William Temple, Sale, and other learned deists, fond
of depreciating Christian virtue by comparisons, have ex-
tolled and celebrated the Mohammedan, Chinese, and
other oriental morals, as far superior to the Christian.
But the learned historiographer, Principal Robertson, asserts, with historic verity, that upon the comparison of
Europe, in particular, in its Gentile and Christian ages,
her morality will appear to have been greatly improved
and meliorated, and that the ethnic morals fell far below
the Christian.   While we have to confess and lament the
vice rampant in Christendom, we have reason to believe
that the more Christianity prevails in a country, civil society will be more advanced, ferocious manners will give
way to the more mild, liberal, just, and amiable manners of
the gospel.

Be it granted that in all countries are to be found men
of integrity, honor, benevolence, and excellent morals,
even where vice has a prevalent reign to the greatest ex-
cesses of a general licentiousness; yet, supposing a community, a kingdom, a world, overspread with such characters, with the finest morals of a Socrates or a Confucius,
what would be the moral state of such a country in comparison with one overspread with the reign of the Christian morals? — I mean in perfection.

How much soever we may admire the morals of Plato
or Epictetus, they are not to be compared with those
taught by Moses and the divine Jesus.   Nor are we to
conceive that civil virtue is the only end of civil govern-

a William Beadle, who, professing himself a deist, on the eleventh of December, 1782, cut the throats of his wife and four children, and then pistoled himself.

ment. As the end of God's government is his declarative glory in the holiness and happiness of the universe, so all civil government ought to subserve the same end. The most essential interests of rational beings are neglected when their secular welfare only is consulted. If, therefore, we defend and plead for Christianity from its secular and civil utility only, and leave it here, we dishonor religion by robbing it of half, nay, its greatest glories. It serves a higher purpose; for, although it subserves the civil welfare infinitely beyond the morals of deism and idolatry, yet it also provides for the interests of eternity, which no other religion does. It opens to us the most grand and sublime discoveries concerning God, reconciliation with him, and the reünion of this lapsed world with the immense universe. Discoveries momentous and interesting beyond conception! — without which we are left to perfect incertitude, if not totally in the dark, with respect to eternity and its vast concerns.

Should we have recourse to the goodness of God, yet of all beings angels would think that man should be the last to reason from the benevolence and goodness of the Universal Parent to the impossibility of his offspring being involved in future ill, when from thence we might equally reason against the existence of present ill. If some distant seraph, who never knew or heard of ill, should reason thus, it would be no marvel, perhaps; but that we, with all our sins and sufferings about us, should go into such reasonings, is the height of folly, the absurdity of absurdities. And why should that Infinite Goodness preserve the numerous millions that die in finished though half-punished vice, that did not preserve the lives of those upon whom the tower of Siloam fell — who did not avert the desolations of Lisbon, Naples, Herculaneum,

and Palermo ?   Cast thine eyes thither, O man, remember
the battle, and do no more.[a]

If, instead of reasoning from the works and word of
God, and thus ascending upwards into Deity, we

> " Take the high priori road,
> And reason downward, till we doubt of God";[b] —

if, by inductive reasonings from the perfections of God
to what can and what cannot be, we should, among other
things, boldly conclude a Trinity and the Incarnation of the
eternal Word absurd nullities, and yet it should appear in
another state that a crucified Jesus sits at the right hand of
the Majesty on high, —how would these mighty sensible
characters, these fine geniuses, these sublime, these foolish
reasoners, be disappointed !   May I be forgiven a very
earnest solicitude here, having myself passed through the
cloudy, darksome valley of skepticism, and stood on the
precipice, from whence I was in danger of taking a juve-
nile leap into the irrecoverable depths of deism ; for so
rare are the Forbeses and the Jenningses, the instances of
emancipated real infidels, that *nulla vestigia retrorsum*[c]
may be inscribed on the temple of deism.   Knowing these
dangers, I pity from my heart, and almost bleed at every
pore, for those who are caught in the vortex, and are captivated with the wily, satirical, delusory, and deficient reasonings of deism.   Elevated with the pride of mental
enlargement, of a supposed untrammeled understanding,
they ascend aloft above the clouds of prejudices into the
Pisgah heights, from whence they fancy that they see all
religions the same — that is, equally nothing but priestcraft and artificial error; whereupon they compliment themselves as endowed with a superiority of discernment in
morals, with high sensibility, sentimental and liberal ideas,

a Job xli. 8.   b Pope.   c No return from hence.

and charm themselves with other fine self-applied diction, which in truth only clothes the tedium, the weariness of half-discussed, unfinished inquiries; or perhaps the hope that at worst the want of certain knowledge may pass with God, if there is any, as a sufficient excuse for some of the doubtful levities of life.

But errors in judgment, it is said, will be of no account with God. In ten thousand matters they may not. We may trifle on many things, but on the things that respect eternity, the things of religion, it is too solemn, too danger- ous to trifle. Although most religions are false and ridic- ulous, there may however be one which we must renounce or trifle with at our peril. For if revelation be true, as most assuredly it is, it is in Jesus only that we have eternal life. Infidels, and those excessively benevolent Christians who consider all religions alike and equally ridiculous, do well in their calmer moments to ponder those words of the eternal Judge: "Whosoever shall deny me before men, him will I also deny before my Father which is in heaven."[a] Where then will a Judas and a Beadle appear? Step forth, thou Herbert, the father of deism! Come hither, ye Bolingbrokes, Tindals, Collinses, Humes, Voltaires, with all your shining abilities, and that disappointed group of self-opinionated deniers of the Lord "that bought them," with that cloud of deluded followers who "would not that I should reign over them," — evanish from my presence, with all the light of your boasted wis- dom, into the blackness of darkness, for ever and ever! On what principles can the despised, the amiable Jesus with- hold or recede from so awful a sentence, so tremendous a denunciation?

How infinitely happier they who, believing the record

---

[a] Matt. x. 33; John iii. 36.

which God giveth of his Son, have received him, and are
become the sons of God! Is it nothing — is it a small
thing to be initiated into the glorious idea of God and the
Trinity revealed in the Scriptures? — to contemplate the
hierarchy and government of the universe, and the high
dignity of that most illustrious Personage who is our Inter-
cessor, Advocate, and Sovereign? Shall this light come
into the world, and we neglect it? And shall it be said
that these views do not animate a sublimer virtue than the
motives taken from civil society? Shall the consideration
of being citizens of a little secular kingdom or community
be equally animating with those taken from our being
citizens of the august monarchical republic of the universe?
But I must desist, with only observing that the United
States are under peculiar obligations to become a holy
people unto the Lord our God, on account of the late
eminent deliverance, salvation, peace, and glory with which
he hath now crowned our new sovereignty.[a]

I have thus finished the two heads upon which I at first
proposed to discourse. And I shall not further trespass
upon the patience of this very honorable auditory by an
application, but close with the addresses usual upon this
anniversary solemnity.

To GOVERNOR TRUMBULL:

I beg leave in the first place, with the greatest honor,
the most profound and dutiful respect, to address myself
to his Excellency the Governor of this State.

May it please your Excellency: We account ourselves
happy, most illustrious sire, that, by the free election and
annual voice of the citizens, God hath for so many years
past called you up to the supreme magistracy in this commonwealth. And while we rejoice that this state em-

a Deut. iv. 34.

bosoms numerous characters equal to the highest offices of government, yet should this day's election fall again upon him who, according to the interpretation of his name, [a] Jehovah hath given us, it would diffuse a joy through the United States. And should you now resign the chair, you would enjoy the reflection that you had been carried through a scene of the most distinguished usefulness, and lived to see the end of the war, and establishment of American liberty and independence.

It is observable that, by a particular turn of genius and a peculiar discipline in early life, God often prepares great characters for that future usefulness and eminence for which they are designed in the world. This was conspicuous in the instances of Joseph, Moses, and Daniel, — neither of whom in youth thought that they were training up for the eminent spheres of action in which they afterwards moved.

Endowed with a singular strength of the mental powers, with a vivid and clear perception, with a penetrating and comprehensive judgment, embellished with the acquisition of academical, theological, and political erudition, your Excellency became qualified for a very singular variety of usefulness in life. Instituted in the sciences, the Hebrew literature, and theology, you were not only prepared for the sanctuary, but, being expert in all questions touching the law of your God, you became qualified to judge how we, the ministers of the gospel under your government, ought to behave ourselves in the house of God, while it has pleased God to call you up to other services in civil life. Thus the great Melchisedec was priest of the Most High God, and king of Salem. So Moses, though of the tribe of Levi, and learned in all the wisdom of Egypt, was called of God to be king in Jeshurum.

a Jonathan, Jehovah-natan.

An early entrance into civil improvement, and fifty years'[a] service in our country, with an uncommon activity and dispatch in business, had familiarized the whole rota of duty in every office and department antecedent and preparatory to the great glory of your Excellency's life, the last 'eight years' administration at the head of this commonwealth, — an administration which has rendered you the *Pater Patriæ*, the father of your country, and our *dulce decus atque tutamen.*

We adore the God of our fathers, the God and Father of the spirits of all flesh, that he hath raised you up for such a time as this,[b] and that he hath put into your breast a wisdom which I cannot describe without adulation, a patriotism and intrepid resolution, a noble and independent spirit, an unconquerable love of liberty, religion, and our country, and that grace by which you have been carried through the arduous labors of a high office with a dignity and glory never before acquired by an American governor. Our enemies revere the names of Trumbull and Washington. In honoring the state and councils of Connecticut, you, illustrious sire, have honored yourself to all the confederate sister states, to the Congress, to the Gallic empire, to Europe, and to the world, to the present and distant ages. And, should you now lay down your office and retire from public life, we trust that you may take this people to record, in the language in which that holy patriot, the pious Samuel, addressed Israel, and say unto us:[c] "I am old and gray-headed, and I have walked before you from my childhood unto this day. Behold, here I am ; witness against me before the Lord : whose ox have I taken ? or whose ass have I taken ? or whom have

---

[a] 1733, elected representative; 1740, elected into the council; 1766, elected deputy-governor; 1769, elected governor.

[b] Esth. iv. 14.   [c] 1 Sam. xii. 2.

I defrauded? whom have I oppressed? or of whose hand have I received any bribe, to blind mine eyes therewith? and I will restore it you. And they said, Thou hast not defrauded nor oppressed us, neither hast thou taken aught of any man's hand. And he said unto them, The Lord is witness against you, and his anointed is witness this day, that ye have not found aught in my hand. And they answered, He is witness."

May you receive a reward from the Supreme Governor of the universe, which will be a reward of grace. For, although your Excellency might adopt the words of that illustrious governor, Nehemiah, and say, "Think upon me, my God, for good, according to all that I have done for this people," [a] yet your ultimate hope for immortality will be founded in a more glorious merit than that achieved by mortals in the most illustrious scenes of public usefulness. May the momentary remnant of your days be crowned with a placid tranquillity; and, when you shall have finished your work on earth, may you be received to the rewards of the just, and shine in the general assembly of the first-born through eternal ages. Amen.[1]

To the Lieutenant Governor and Council:

With great respect would I next address myself to his Honor Lieutenant-Governor Griswold,[2] and the rest of the honorable Councillors of this State.

May it please your Honor, and the other Members of the Honorable Council: That senatorial order must be truly

[a] Neh. v. 19.

[1] He died August 17, 1785, aged seventy-four. We add Washington's tribute: "*A long and well-spent life in the service of his country places Governor Trumbull among the first of patriots.*" Mr. I. W. Stuart's "Life" of the Governor, 1859, 1 vol. 8vo, pp. 700. — Ed.

[2] Matthew Griswold, afterwards governor, died 1790, aged eighty-three. — Ed.

important which stands upon the general voice and election of the public at large, because it must comprehend men of such public and conspicuous merit as to be known among all our tribes — men of approved patriotism and wisdom, as well as popularity. We esteem it our happiness that our governors and our nobles proceed from ourselves. When we consider the trifling and inferior characters of the most of the venal counsellors in the late royal governments, when compared with the solid wisdom of the council of this state, we may be convinced that a Legislature standing upon a free election of the people to be governed, bids fair to ensure more wisdom and incorruptibility than if in the appointment of the most august sovereigns in the world.

We glory in it that this state has at all times furnished gentlemen, in the appointment of the people, of abilities equal to every department and branch of dominion, whether legislative or executive. It is particularly happy that men impressed with the feelings of the people, of great knowledge in laws and jurisprudence, in the civil polity especially of this state, have hitherto been and still are found at the council-board, in the military departments, and in the highest judiciary tribunals of this commonwealth.

This state has ever preserved a grave, sensible, and weighty council, in a pretty delicate situation indeed, but of great prudence and influential wisdom. It is this council which combines and consolidates the whole commonwealth.

The general anniversary election dictates annually the general sense of the community. And while a rotation to a considerable degree, though not by constitution, yet by usage, and the mutability of the human passions, and in the course of events, does in effect take place, we have been happy, however, and I hope always shall be, in the retention of a number of ancient and venerable councillors to transmit the wisdom and experience of their predecessors, and to give a steady and immutable complexion to the succession in the General Assembly, especially as to the capital matters of law, liberty, and government.

We glory in you, gentlemen, as our crown of rejoicing. We securely confide our liberties and safety, the civil, religious, and literary welfare of this republic, to your superintendence. We pray God that in all your momentous deliberations and resolutions you may be guided by the wisdom from above — by the mighty Counsellor, the Prince of Peace. Amen.

To THE HOUSE OF REPRESENTATIVES:

It is my duty, in the next place, to pay the tribute of public honor to the respectable and numerous body of the lower House of Assembly, the second branch in the honorable Legislature and sovereignty of this state.

Mr. Speaker,[1] *and Gentlemen of the House of Representatives:* Your House is already formed standing on the free, local elections of a free people. From the character of your constituents we doubt not you bring with you the love of liberty, justice, and public right. Assembled from all our tribes to consult the public good, so far as this is left to your judgment, you will act with well-informed wisdom and integrity; while, so far as you know the minds of your constituents, may we not presume that you will hold it your duty to act and represent their judgments, be your own as they may? You have matters of high moment to attend to, and some of a very insidious nature. Besides

---

[1] In the second edition, 1785, the author adds this note: "The Hon. Col. William Williams, Member of Congress at the Declaration of Independence."— ED.

matters of *internal government*, a liquidation of the expenditures of the war, *finance, revenue, funds*, are some of the subjects before this Assembly. It is not impossible but you may perceive some hovering genius, something of an anti-American spirit, flitting about, and at times alighting upon some within the walls of the Senate. Will you not hunt it down, and send it to the shades? May you all be inspired with a real, hearty, and uncorrupted patriotism and firmness in the cause of liberty and independence. Let an independent liberality of sentiment, and reverence for right and equity, reign in this branch of the Senate, that the world may see that the administration of the united branches combined in the sovereignty of this state is conducted with a certain plain but noble dignity and majesty.

This Assembly, at every session for eight years past, has been full of the most anxious and weighty concerns for our bleeding country. But this House is no more called to raise armies, or, amidst the most complicated distresses, to devise means for their support. What a load, what a burden and weighty care has devolved upon this House through the war! But these conflicts are at an end, and you will be now called to the arts of peace, and to promote the welfare and aggrandizement of our country.

And while this honorable House is attending to the secular concerns of civil government, may we not humbly wish that you would not repudiate the idea of being nursing fathers to our spiritual Israel, the church of God within this state? Give us, gentlemen, the decided assurance that you are friends of the churches, and that you are the friends of the pastors, who have certainly in this trying warfare approved themselves the friends of liberty and government.[1] Your predecessors, one hundred years ago,

1 See p. 437, and note. — ED.

accounted this among their principal honors. They were solicitous to promote religion and learning, and to give suitable encouragement to both.

And, in this connection, will it be forgiven me if I humbly recommend Yale College to the smiles of government? Through the good hand of our God upon us, we may truly say, in the language of the sons of the prophets to Elisha, "Behold, now, the place where we dwell is too strait for us." [a]   May we not humbly ask of the public that they would be pleased to build us another house, or the necessary edifices for the reception and accommodation of the youth, but about one-third of the students being provided for in the present college edifice?   Was I not so nearly connected with it, I might say with truth, what has often been told me by others, that there is not a state upon the continent but would account such a seat of learning, in whose hands soever it might be, as an illustrious ornament to their community.

A trust may be well executed when the end of the trust is answered, although there may have intervened some mismanagements.   Small bodies as well as great, not even congresses and assemblies, — and, may I not add, not even this honorable assembly excepted, — are not only frequently aspersed and censured, but have sometimes erred; so, perhaps, have the governors of the college : when, however, upon a candid inquiry, it may be found that in money concerns they have managed with an unexampled frugality, even to parsimony, that never was there more done to purpose with so small means in a literary institution, and that the college is at present in a pretty flourishing state.   At my accession, in 1778, the number of matriculated undergraduates in the four classes was one hundred and nineteen, and this current year they have

[a] 2 Kings vi. 1.

been two hundred and fifty-one.[a]   And in point of schol-
arship and literature, I hope we do not fall very far behind
the other sister colleges in America.

How happy, were its foundations and emoluments adequate to the civil and religious purposes of this institution!
An enlargement of the public library, a complete apparatus
for experimental philosophy, premiums for stimulating
genius in every branch of literature, endowments of professorships, especially those of philosophy, law, and medi-
cine, would be of inconceivable benefit in the liberal
education of youth.   These things I doubt not will be
effected in time, but the *literati* wish to see them accomplished in the present day.

The college has often, since its foundation,[b] experienced

---

[a] There are ten colleges in the United States, from New England to Virginia
inclusive, besides two intended ones in the Carolinas. The numbers of undergraduates in the most considerable are estimated as follows:

Harvard College, ...	founded	1636,	. .	150 undergraduates.
William and Mary College, .	"	1698,	. .	100	"
Jersey College, ...	"	1746,	. .	60	"
Philadelphia College, . . .	"	1755,	. .	30	"
Dartmouth College,[1] . . .	"	1769,	. .	80	"

[b] A. D. 1700.[2]

[1] The catalogues show —

At Yale, . .	1859 .	. .	6,810	graduates and	641	students.		
Harvard, .	1860 .	. .	7,110	"	"	860	"	
Brown, . .	1860 .	. .	2,043	"	"	232	"	
Dartmouth,	1858 .	. .	3,068	"	"	368	"	in 1860.
Williams, .	1859 .	. .	1,995	"	"	236	"	in 1860.
Bowdoin, .	1858 .	. .	1,284	"				
Amherst, .	1857 .	. .	1,237	"	"	242	"	

See p. 437, note 1. — ED.

[2] The earliest entry on the Colonial Records in regard to the establishment of a college bears date " At a General Court, held at Guilford, June
28, 1652," when they passed a vote of " thanks to Mr. Goodyear for his
kind proffer to the setting forward such a work." Stephen Goodyear
was Deputy Governor of New Haven colony, and to him seems to belong
the honorable distinction of making the first offer to endow " a college at
New Haven."— Barber's History of New Haven, 1831, p. 20, and Hoad-
ly's New Haven Colonial Records, 1858, pp. 141, 370, note. — ED.

the liberality and smiles of the General Assembly, for which it is always ready to return and repeat its thanks and gratitude. Some unhappy differences of sentiment, together with the war, have interrupted the stream of public munificence. But is there no balm in Gilead to heal the wound? Is there no way to accommodate and adjust matters so as to conciliate the friendship of the state towards its university?

The states of Holland, in the midst of their expensive wars in the cause of liberty, founded and endowed the University of Leyden. Should this state be pleased to endow two or three professorships, and appoint a board of civilians to elect the professors, in concurrence with the present corporation, and see that the moneys granted by the state were applied to the use to which they were appropriated by the General Assembly — might this not give satisfaction?

But I trespass upon your patience. All the great interests of this state, whether as a separate sovereignty or in its connection with the United States, are entrusted to you: a very weighty trust. You have a thousand pious prayers going up for you daily at the throne of grace. You have all the patriots saying, Be strong, O Zorobabels! You have all the ministers inculcating obedience to you. And may you, above all, have the influential guidance of unerring Wisdom, to render you acceptable to the multitude of your brethren, to make you eminent blessings in your day, and reward you with immortality and glory in the world to come. Amen.

To the Ministers:

And I now turn myself to the pastors of the churches.

Reverend and Beloved Brethren: I have not assumed upon me to dictate to the civil magistracy, nor do I dictate

to the sacerdotal order, albeit I might speak to the most
of my brethren present as being such a one in years as
Paul the aged. Condescend, however, holy brethren, to
receive a humble address from one who loves the order
with a sincere and fervent affection, although παντῶν τῶν
ἁγιων ἐλαχίστο ἐλαχιστότερος.

Permit me, then, to say, that, while we do not fail to
inculcate obedience to the magistracy and laws, and
recommend to our people the election of a pious magistracy, our principal work is not secular, but spiritual and
divine. Let us with the greatest assiduity devote ourselves to our Lord's work, as ambassadors of the Prince
of Peace. Let us preach the divinity and unsearchable
riches of Christ, and salvation by his atonement, that
theological system which places the whole of redemption
upon free grace — a grace free as to us, though merited by
the holy Redeemer. Let us search the Scriptures for the
real evangelical verity, and inquire not so much for new
theories in divinity as what truths were known and
realized in faith and life by the primitive Christians of the
apostolic age and the three first centuries; and believe
that no other system, no other doctrines, are essentially
necessary to carry men to heaven in these ages than those
which enabled the myriads of holy martyrs to seal the
testimony of Jesus with their blood.

There is but one true system of theology, and this has
been equally known in all the Christian ages. For although great improvements and discoveries are daily making in philosophy and natural science, yet there have been
no new discoveries in divinity since the apostolic age; — I
do not mean merely no new revelation, but of the innumerable latent truths concealed in the Bible, — and there
are infinitely greater treasures hidden there than in nature,
— none have been perceived in later ages but what have

been as clearly discerned by the contemplative theologians of all ages. The sentiments are the same, though clothed in different diction. Philosophy, as I said, is improving; nor has the progress of civil society yet reached its summit; but divinity, I apprehend, has been long at a stand, having ages ago come to the highest perfection intended us at present by Heaven, which did not design any further improvement in it from the sealing of the vision till the second coming of Christ. In the millennium these hidden treasures will be brought forth. But, for the preceding period, divinity will be and remain at a stand, except perhaps that towards the close of it the prophecies will disclose themselves.

Religion has had and will have different fashions, even where it is still essentially the same. Previous to the tenth century the writings of St. Augustine gave an extensive complexion to theology; afterwards, Lombard's collection of sentences or opinions of evangelical divines; but he was shoved into neglect by Aquinas, who reigned umpire till the Reformation. Luther followed Augustine, and Calvin Aquinas. The real theology of Melancthon, Calvin, Archbishop Cranmer, and Owen, was one and the same.

We despise the fathers and the pious and learned divines of the middle ages; pious posterity will do the same by us, and twirl over our most favorite authors with the same ignorant pity and neglect. Happy they if their favorite authors contain the same blessed truths!

I rejoice that God has hitherto preserved a learned and evangelical ministry in these churches. The theology in general reception comprehends all the excellent things of our common Christianity. And if some favorite *hurekas*, some fancied discoveries, should be burnt up in the day of the Lord, yet there will be left as great an abundance of precious stones, of the tried and pure gold of truth, as in

any part of the world. Indeed, we have gotten all the
light of Christendom, and we need no more. We have
enough ; we are wealthy in sacred knowledge. We may
spend long lives in making ourselves masters of that vast
treasure of sacred wisdom which holy men of great light
have attained. May I comprehend with all saints the
height and depth of this knowledge! May my God
possess me of this treasure, and I am content. All this
knowledge, to the greatest extent of the human limit, has
been gotten and acquired over and over again and again.
Like other science, to every generation it seems new,
while it is only possessing the knowledge similar to our
predecessors'.

Moreover, charity, union, and benevolence are peculiarly
ornamental in the ministerial order. Let us cherish these
amiable graces in ourselves and others. Let us be faithful. And the nearer we come to the solemn moment
when we must render our account to God the Judge, the
more may we be quickened and animated in the ministry;
and think no labor, no assiduity too great, nothing too
much to be done for the salvation of precious and immortal souls; nothing too much for the cause and kingdom of
Him who hath loved us to the death. May you, holy
brethren, " be strong in the grace which is in our Lord
Jesus Christ." May the work, the pleasure of the Lord,
prosper in your hands. May you be honored of Jesus to
turn many to righteousness. And when the Chief Shepherd shall appear, may you receive a crown of glory which
fadeth not away. Amen.

To the Assembly at Large:

And now, my fellow-citizens of this independent republic, my fellow-Christians of every order and denomination
in this assembly, and all you that fear God and hear me
this day, give audience.

The Most High planted our fathers, a small handful, in this Jeshimon, and lo! we, their posterity, have arisen up to three millions of people.[a] Our ears have heard, and our fathers have told us, the marvellous things God did for them; but our eyes have seen far more marvellous things done for us, whereof we are glad and rejoice this day. Should our ancestors look down from the high abodes of Paradise into this assembly, and attend to the things which we have been this day commemorating, methinks they might catch a sensation of joy at beholding the reign, the triumph, of liberty on earth. Hitherto has " our bow abode in strength, and our arms been made strong by the hands of the mighty God of Jacob." And while, amidst the festivity of this Anniversary Election, we congratulate one another and our country upon the cessation of hostilities, and that, having fought the good fight, our warfare is ended, let us not fail to look through providence up to the God of providence, and give glory to God the Lord of Hosts, the God of our fathers, whom " let us serve with a perfect heart and a willing mind." Let us cultivate and cherish the virtues of the divine as well as civil life, bearing in mind that we are all hastening to that period wherein all the glories of this world will be swallowed up and lost in the glories of immortality. Be it our great ambition, our incessant endeavor, to act our parts worthily on the stage of life, as looking for and hastening to the coming of our Lord Jesus Christ. May we be prepared for the solemnities of a far more august assembly than the most splendid assembly on earth. We are ardently pursuing this world's riches, honors, powers, pleasures; let us possess them, and then know that they are nothing, nothing, nothing. They serve a temporary gratification, evanish,

a Deut. x. 22.1

1 See p. 211, note 1. — ED.

and are no more. But we cannot be dissuaded from the pursuit. Death, however, kindly ends it. Let us think that we have two worlds to live for, proportion our attention to their respective interests, and we shall be happy forever. We shall then be prepared to shine in the assembly of the just, at the right hand of the Sovereign of Life. How glorious to bear a part in the triumphs of virtue, the triumphs of the Redeemer, in the last day of the great and general assembly of the universe! How glorious to make a part of that infinitely honored and dignified body which, clothed with the Redeemer's righteousness and walking in white robes, shall be led by the Messiah through the shining ranks of archangels, seraphims, and the innumerable hosts of the whole assembled universe, up to the throne of God; and, being presented to and received by the triune Jehovah, shall be seated with Jesus in his throne at the summit of the universe, to the conspicuous view and for the eternal contemplation of the whole intellectual world, as an everlasting monument of sovereign grace! "to the intent that now unto the principalities and powers in the heavenly places might be known by the church the manifold wisdom of God, according to the eternal purpose which he purposed in Christ Jesus our Lord:"[a] to whom be glory in the church through the never-ending succession of eternal ages. AMEN.

a Eph. iii. 10, 11.

INDEX.

530INDEX.

The reverse of the title pages was unavoidably omitted in the Index.

DATE DUE
